An Evolutionary Theory of Economic Change

RICHARD R. NELSON AND SIDNEY G. WINTER

AN EVOLUTIONARY THEORY OF ECONOMIC CHANGE

THE BELKNAP PRESS OF HARVARD UNIVERSITY PRESS
CAMBRIDGE, MASSACHUSETTS, AND LONDON, ENGLAND   1982

LIBRARY OF CONGRESS CATALOGING IN PUBLICATION DATA

Nelson, Richard R.
    An evolutionary theory of economic change.

    Bibliography: p.
    Includes index.
    1. Economics.   2. Economic development.
3. Organizational change.   I. Winter, Sidney G.
II. Title.   III. Title: Economic change.
HB71.N44   338.9′001   81-13455
ISBN 0-674-27227-7   AACR 2

To

KATHERINE   GEORGIE

MARGO   JEFF

LAURA   KIT

Preface

WE BEGAN THIS BOOK over a decade ago. Our discussions of the promise and problems of evolutionary modeling of economic change date back years before that. For both of us, this book represents the culmination of work that began with our dissertations.

Our initial orientations were different. For Nelson, the starting point was a concern with the processes of long-run economic development. Early on, that concern became focused on technological change as the key driving force and on the role of policy as an influence on the strength and direction of that force. For Winter, the early focus was on the strengths and limitations of the evolutionary arguments that had been put forward as support for standard views of firm behavior. This soon broadened to include the general methodological issues of "theory and realism" in economics, the contributions of other disciplines to the understanding of firm behavior, and reconsideration of the evolutionary viewpoint as a possible framework for a more realistic economic theory of firm and industry behavior. From the earliest days of our acquaintance, the existence of significant overlaps and interrelations between these areas of research interest was apparent. Nelson's studies of the detailed processes of technological change led him to appreciate the uncertain, groping, disorderly, and error-ridden character of those processes— and the difficulty of doing justice to that reality within the orthodox theoretical scheme. In Winter's case, a study of the determinants of firm spending on research and development formed the empirical arena in which it first became apparent that much of firm behavior could be more readily understood as a reflection of general habits and strategic orientations coming from the firm's past than as the result of a detailed survey of the remote twigs of the decision tree extending into the future.

It was not, however, until the collaboration that led to this book was well underway that we realized that its purpose and promise were well defined by two relationships between our areas of interest. First, among the many obstacles to understanding the role of technological change in economic life, an important subset arise from the intellectual constraints associated with the treatment of firm and industry behavior that is now standard in economic theory. Second, among the many benefits that may derive from a theoretical approach that reconciles economic analysis with the realities of firm decision making, the most important relate to improved understanding of technological change and the dynamics of the competitive process.

Our cooperative intellectual endeavor commenced when we were both at the RAND Corporation in Santa Monica in the 1960s. Many people at that remarkably stimulating and intellectually diversified place influenced our thinking. Burton Klein deserves special mention. He conveyed to us a body of truth that has been recognized many times in the history of ideas, but that somehow always stands in need of rediscovery, reinterpretation, and persuasive illustration. Creative intelligence, in the realm of technology as elsewhere, is autonomous and erratic, compulsive and whimsical. It does not lie placidly within the prescriptive and descriptive constraints imposed by outsiders to the creative process, be they theorists, planners, teachers, or critics. To progress with the task of understanding where creative thought is likely to lead the world, it is therefore helpful to recognize first of all that the task can never be completed. Our evolutionary theory of economic change is in this spirit; it is not an interpretation of economic reality as a reflection of supposedly constant "given data," but a scheme that may help an observer who is sufficiently knowledgeable regarding the facts of the present to see a little further through the mist that obscures the future.

We committed ourselves to writing this book after Nelson had moved on to Yale and Winter to Michigan. For a few years the problems of long-distance coauthorship imposed significant costs in terms of the rate of progress of the collaborative effort, but there were also some benefits in the form of opportunities to test ideas in forums provided by two different universities. (Of course, the airlines and the telephone company derived substantial benefits from the arrangement, too.) With Winter's move to Yale in 1976, the communication costs fell and we began to take more seriously the idea of pulling the work together in the form of a book. Major efforts in that direction were made in 1978 and 1979. As our families, colleagues, and editors are well aware, the "almost done" phase of the project lasted almost three years.

In this protracted process of research and writing, we received support and assistance in a variety of forms and from a variety of sources. We will attempt here to acknowledge the main elements of our indebtedness under several major headings, but are uncomfortably aware that some of the lists are far from complete.

Our greatest intellectual debts are to Joseph Schumpeter and Herbert Simon. Schumpeter pointed out the right problem—how to understand economic change—and his vision encompassed many of the important elements of the answer. Simon provided a number of specific insights into human and organizational behavior that are reflected in our theoretical models; but, most important, his work encouraged us in the view that there is much more to be said on the problem of rational behavior in the world of reality than can be adequately stated in the language of orthodox economic theory.

Financial support for our work came from several sources. A major grant from the National Science Foundation, through its Division of Social Sciences, provided important momentum at an early stage. Some of the most recent research that is reported in this book was also supported by the NSF, under a grant from the Division of Policy Research and Analysis. The Sloan Foundation, through a grant to the Applied Microeconomics Workshop at Yale, was a major source of support for our research during the interval between the NSF grants. In addition, we received financial and other support from the Institute of Public Policy Studies at Michigan and the Institution for Social and Policy Studies at Yale. The directors of these organizations during the period in question—J. Patrick Crecine and Jack Walker at IPPS, Charles E. Lindblom at ISPS—deserve special thanks for their encouragement and for their skill at the tricky business of promoting intellectual contact among the social science disciplines.

In our efforts to develop computer simulation models as one type of formal evolutionary theory, we have depended heavily on the contributions of a series of skilled programmers and research assistants. We had the good fortune to attract to this role individuals who became intellectually engaged in the substance of our undertaking, and who contributed, along with their technical expertise, suggestions and criticisms regarding the underlying economics. The first of these was Herbert Schuette; his contributions to much of the work reported in Chapter 9 led to his inclusion as a coauthor of the principal previous publication of that work. We would like to acknowledge those contributions again here. Stephen Horner and Richard Parsons did most of the original programming for our simulation model of

Schumpeterian competition, and contributed a number of helpful suggestions to its formulation. Larry Spancake helped us transfer that model to the Yale computer. Abraham Goldstein and Peter Reiss followed in his footsteps as keepers of the beast at Yale, feeding it and training it in response to our requests and assisting in much of the analysis that helped us understand its behavior.

Many scholars have listened to our presentations, read our drafts and articles, and provided advice, encouragement, and criticisms. In Yale seminars and conversations, we have learned particularly from Susan Rose Ackerman, Donald Brown, Robert Evenson, Lee Friedman, Eric Hanushek, John Kimberly, Richard Levin, Richard Murnane, Guy Orcutt, Sharon Oster, Joe Peck, John Quigley, and Martin Shubik. During Winter's years at Michigan, he received similar benefits from interactions with Robert Axelrod, Michael Cohen, Paul Courant, J. Patrick Crecine, John Cross, Everett Rogers, Daniel Rubinfeld, Peter Steiner, Jack Walker, and Kenneth Warner. A great many friends and colleagues elsewhere have also given us the benefit of their reactions and suggestions on one occasion or another. We wish to thank particularly Richard Day, Peter Diamond, Avinash Dixit, Christopher Freeman, Michael Hannan, Jack Hirshleifer, James March, Keith Pavitt, Almarin Phillips, Michael Porter, Roy Radner, Nathan Rosenberg, Steve Salop, A. Michael Spence, David Teece, and Oliver Williamson.

As our research progressed, we reported on it in articles published in *The Economic Journal, The Quarterly Journal of Economics, Economic Inquiry, Research Policy, The Bell Journal of Economics,* and *The American Economic Review.* We thank the editorial boards of these journals for permission to use parts of our earlier articles in chapters of this book; specific citations are provided in the chapters involved. We are similarly indebted to North-Holland Publishing Co. for permission to use previously published material in Chapter 12.

Three individuals—Richard Levin, Richard Lipsey, and B. Curtis Eaton—did us the great favor of reading large portions of our draft manuscript and making detailed comments. We are greatly indebted to them, and wish to take especial care to exonerate them from responsibility for the final result. Many other people provided useful comments on portions of the manuscript; we particularly want to thank Katherine Nelson and Georgie Winter.

The preparation of the last typed version of the manuscript was a process haunted by the ghost of deadlines passed. Under those trying circumstances, we were fortunate to have the benefit of the outstanding typing skills of Margie Cooke.

In its final phase, our project benefited substantially from our decision to commit the book to Harvard University Press. General editor Michael Aronson provided suggestions and encouragement. Our copy editor, Maria Kawecki, did what she could to improve our prose. She did so with great tact, and with remarkable insight into what it was that we had been trying to say. Whatever errors and infelicities of expression remain constitute a minute fraction of those originally present, and that fraction may well be largely attributable to the stubbornness of the authors rather than to any lack of diligence on the part of the copy editor.

Each chapter of the book has its own history, and almost every one of those histories is complex. The informed reader may discern that a few chapters seem to be predominantly Nelson, while a few others are predominantly Winter. But in most chapters our individual contributions are thoroughly intermingled, and every chapter has been shaped by the hands of both authors. We share responsibility for the work as a whole. Together, we wish to absolve all of our friends and critics from responsibility for the product, while again expressing our gratitude for their interest. Such absolution is more than a ritual in the case of this book, for there certainly are some among those acknowledged above who consider our effort to be largely misguided.

Our collaboration has not been a separate, self-contained segment of our lives. Rather, it has been a way of life for ourselves and our families. Our children, young when we began, grew up with "the book." In the early days, the book provided the occasion for visits between New Haven and Ann Arbor. In recent years, the book has been a background theme of summer vacations on Cape Cod—or perhaps, on some occasions, it was the vacation that was in the background. We have established a virtual tradition of celebratory dinners marking the "completion" (to some stage) of the book. Our families have shared all this with us; we know that they share a sense of fulfillment, relief, and even amazement that it is done. To them we dedicate the book.

Contents

I

OVERVIEW AND MOTIVATION

1

Introduction

IN THIS VOLUME we develop an evolutionary theory of the capabilities and behavior of business firms operating in a market environment, and construct and analyze a number of models consistent with that theory. We propose that the broad perspective provided by an evolutionary theory is useful in analyzing a wide range of phenomena associated with economic change stemming either from shifts in product demand or factor supply conditions, or from innovation on the part of firms. The specific models we build focus in turn on different aspects of economic change—the response of firms and the industry to changed market conditions, economic growth, and competition through innovation. We draw out the normative as well as the positive implications of an evolutionary theory.

The first premise of our undertaking should be noncontroversial: it is simply that economic change is important and interesting. Among the major intellectual tasks of the field of economic history, for example, certainly none is more worthy of attention than that of understanding the great complex of cumulative change in technology and economic organization that has transformed the human situation in the course of the past few centuries. Among policy issues regarding the world economy today, none present a more critical mix of promise and danger than those that reflect the wide disparities in present levels of economic development and the strains that afflict societies struggling to catch up. In the advanced economies, meanwhile, successful modernization has brought forth new concerns about the long-term ecological viability of advanced industrial society and renewed questions about the relation between material success and more fundamental human values. Among the focal concerns of theoretical economics in recent years have been the roles of information, the formation of expectations by economic actors, detailed analysis of markets functioning given the presence of various "imperfections," and new versions of old questions about the efficiency of market systems. Much of this work seeks to comprehend, in stylized theoretical settings, the unfolding of economic events over time. Thus, any significant advance in understanding of the processes of economic change would cast new light on a range of intellectually challenging questions that are of great social consequence.

We expect, however, that many of our economist colleagues will be reluctant to accept the second premise of our work—that a major reconstruction of the theoretical foundations of our discipline is a precondition for significant growth in our understanding of economic change. The broad theory that we develop in this book, and the specific models, incorporate basic assumptions that are at variance with those of the prevailing orthodox theory of firm and industry behavior. The firms in our evolutionary theory will be treated as motivated by profit and engaged in search for ways to improve their profits, but their actions will not be assumed to be profit maximizing over well-defined and exogenously given choice sets. Our theory emphasizes the tendency for the most profitable firms to drive the less profitable ones out of business; however, we do not focus our analysis on hypothetical states of "industry equilibrium," in which all the unprofitable firms no longer are in the industry and the profitable ones are at their desired size. Relatedly, the modeling approach that we employ does not use the familiar maximization calculus to derive equations characterizing the behavior of firms. Rather, our firms are modeled as simply having, at any given time, certain capabilities and decision rules. Over time these capabilities and rules are modified as a result of both deliberate problem-solving efforts and random events. And over time, the economic analogue of natural selection operates as the market determines which firms are profitable and which are unprofitable, and tends to winnow out the latter.

A number of our fellow economists do share with us a sense of general malaise afflicting contemporary microeconomic theory.[1] It is

---

1. It is noteworthy that since 1970 several of the presidential addresses given annually before the American Economic Association have lamented the state of economic theory. Leontief's address (1971) is explicitly concerned with the inability of microeconomic theory to come to grips with empirical realities. Tobin's address (1972), and Solow's (1980), are focused on macroeconomics, but are substantially concerned also

widely sensed that the discipline has not yet located a path that will lead to a coherent and sustained advance beyond the intellectual territory claimed by modern general equilibrium theory. The discovery of such a path will, it is believed, require a theoretical accommodation with one or more of the major aspects of economic reality that are repressed in general equilibrium theory. Much of the most interesting theoretical work of the past two decades may be interpreted as exploratory probing guided by a variety of different guesses as to which of the possible accommodations are the most important ones to make. Considerable attention has been given to imperfections of information and of competition, to transaction costs, indivisibilities, and increasing returns, and to some of the relations among these. It has been recognized that general equilibrium theory's austere description of the institutions of capitalism becomes woefully inadequate as soon as any of these accommodations to reality are made—and, on the other hand, that the actual institutional devices employed in real market systems constitute a complex and challenging object for theoretical study. The fruits of these exploratory efforts include a good deal of work that is intellectually impressive when taken on its own terms, much that is directly useful in understanding certain portions of economic reality, and some that seems likely to be of lasting value regardless of the future course that economics may take. But the great majority of these exploratory probes have carried along (or at least intended to carry along) almost all of the basic conceptual structure that orthodoxy provides for the interpretation of economic behavior.

We regard that structure as excess baggage that will seriously encumber theoretical progress in the long run, however much its familiarity and advanced state of development may facilitate such progress in the short run. Here, obviously, our appraisal of the situation is more radical than anything that can be associated with the "general malaise" referred to above. What we offer in this book is,

---

with the adequacy of the theoretical foundations that orthodox microeconomics provides for macroeconomics. Similar themes have been sounded in addresses to other professional organizations; see, for example, Hahn (1970), Phelps Brown (1972) and Worswick (1972). The sense of malaise is also reflected in a number of the review articles in the *Journal of Economic Literature*. Shubik (1970), Cyert and Hedrick (1972), Morgenstern (1972), Preston (1975), Leibenstein (1979), Marris and Mueller (1980), and Williamson (1982) all complain explicitly about the inability of the prevailing theory to come to grips with uncertainty, or bounded rationality, or the presence of large corporations, or institutional complexity, or the dynamics of actual adjustment processes. We do not aim in this footnote, or in the book as a whole, to identify all the souls that are kindred at least in their surface diagnosis of the problem, if not in their deeper diagnoses or prescriptions. We know that in this respect we are part of a crowd.

we believe, a plausible promise that fundamental reconstruction along the lines we advocate would set the stage for a major advance in understanding of economic change—and, at the same time, make it possible to consolidate and preserve most of the discipline's significant achievements to date. To make full delivery on such a promise is not a task for two authors, or for a single book.

1. THE TERMS OF THE DISCUSSION: "ORTHODOX" AND "EVOLUTIONARY"

We have above made the first of many references to something called "orthodox" economic theory. Throughout this book, we distinguish our own stance on various issues from the "orthodox" position. Some such usage is inevitable in any work that, like the present one, argues the need for a major shift of theoretical perspective on a wide range of issues. However, there may be some who would deny that any "orthodoxy" exists in economics, apart from a widely shared commitment to the norms and values of scientific inquiry in general. Others would agree that an orthodoxy exists in the descriptive sense that there are obvious commonalities of intellectual perspective and scientific approach that unite large numbers of economists. But they would strenuously deny there is an orthodox position providing a narrow set of criteria that are conventionally used as a cheap and simple test for whether an expressed point of view on certain economic questions is worthy of respect; or, if there is such an orthodoxy, that it is in any way enforced. Our own thought and experience leave us thoroughly persuaded that an orthodoxy exists in this last sense, and that it is quite widely enforced. We do concede that contemporary orthodoxy is flexible and ever-changing, and that its limits are not easily defined. It therefore seems important to attempt, if not an actual definition, at least a clarification of our use of the term.

We should note, first of all, that the orthodoxy referred to represents a modern formalization and interpretation of the broader tradition of Western economic thought whose line of intellectual descent can be traced from Smith and Ricardo through Mill, Marshall, and Walras. Further, it is a *theoretical* orthodoxy, concerned directly with the methods of economic analysis and only indirectly with any specific questions of substance. It is centered in microeconomics, although its influence is pervasive in the discipline.

To characterize the actual content of contemporary orthodoxy is a substantial undertaking, with which we will concern ourselves recurringly in this book. Here we address the question of how one might check our claims that particular views and approaches are "orthodox"—or, alternatively, the question of how we would defend ourselves against a claim that we are attacking a straw man or an obsolete, primitive form of economic theory. The first recourse should be to the leading textbooks used in the relatively standardized undergraduate courses in intermediate microeconomics. These texts and courses expound the theoretical foundations of the discipline at a simplified level. They are generally viewed as providing important background for understanding applied work in economics—often, in fact, as providing *essential* background for applied work done at a respectable intellectual level. The best of the texts are notably insistent on the scientific value of abstract concepts and formal theorizing, and offer few apologies for the strong simplifications and stark abstractions they employ. Neither do they devote much space to caveats concerning the theory's predictive reliability in various circumstances. In these respects and others, they prefigure the treatment of the same issues in advanced texts and courses in theory. Indeed, it often appears that doctoral-level courses in economic theory are distinguished from intermediate-level courses primarily by the mathematical tools employed, at least so far as the core topics are concerned.

There is, admittedly, a degree of caricature involved when texts aimed at college sophomores and juniors are nominated to represent modern economic theory. Many of the strong simplifying assumptions commonly employed—perfect information, two commodities, static equilibrium, and so on—are emphasized in such texts for reasons having to do with the perceived limitations of the students, and not because the discipline has nothing better to offer. And if the conclusions of the analysis are sometimes put forward without due emphasis on the qualifications to which they are subject, it is not necessarily because the importance of those qualifications is not recognized by the author. It is more likely because the students are seen as deserving a reward for their struggles with the logic of the argument, and as positively demanding clear-cut answers to put in the exam book. In many respects, orthodoxy is more subtle and flexible than the image of it presented in the intermediate texts.

There are, however, some very important respects in which the portrait is drawn true. First of all, the logical structure of the intermediate texts underlies much of the informal discussion of economic events and policies engaged in by economists and others with substantial economics background. This is particularly the case with views concerning the efficiency properties of market systems: there seems to be a remarkable tendency for discussion of this question to throw off the encumbrances of advanced learning and revert to a more primitive and vigorous form. In this sense, the conclusions of intermediate analysis seem much more indicative of "where the discipline stands" than do appraisals that are theoretically more sophisticated, but also more difficult and less familiar to nontheorists. Second, the strong simplifying assumptions of the intermediate texts often have close analogues in advanced work, right out to the theoretical frontiers. It is a caricature to associate orthodoxy with the analysis of static equilibria, but it is no caricature to remark that continued reliance on equilibrium analysis, even in its more flexible forms, still leaves the discipline largely blind to phenomena associated with historical change. Similarly, defenders of orthodoxy may justifiably disdain to reply to criticisms of perfect-information assumptions, but they have something at risk if the criticism focuses instead on the assumption that all possible contingencies can be foreseen and their consequences weighed. Thus, although it is not literally appropriate to stigmatize orthodoxy as concerned only with hypothetical situations of perfect information and static equilibrium, the prevalence of analogous restrictions in advanced work lends a metaphorical validity to the complaint.

Last, there is one key assumption in the structure of orthodox thought that does not get significantly relaxed or qualified as one passes from intermediate to advanced theory; on the contrary, it becomes stronger to support a greater weight. This is the assumption that economic actors are rational in the sense that they optimize. In elementary instruction or in popular exposition, this assumption of economic rationality may be presented as a conceptual expedient justified by the realistic observation that people have objectives which they pursue with a certain amount of consistency, skill, and forethought. At the intermediate level, the assumption takes on a stark appearance that strains credulity, but then intermediate theory is pretty stark overall. In advanced forms of orthodoxy, while recognition of informational and other "imperfections" softens the general theoretical picture regarding what the actor knows, no such compromise with reality affects the treatment of economic rationality. As theoretical representations of the problems faced by economic actors increase in realistic complexity and recognition of uncertainty regarding values of the variables, there is a matching increase in the feats of anticipation and calculation and in the clarity of the stakes imputed to those actors. Never is such a theoretical actor confused about the situation or distracted by petty concerns; never is he trapped in a systematically erroneous view of the problem; never is a plain old mistake made. It is a central tenet of orthodoxy that this is the *only* sound way to proceed; recognition of greater complexity in the problem *obligates* the theorist to impute a subtler rationality to the actors. Thus, with regard to rationality assumptions, to allow orthodox theory to be championed by its elementary and intermediate versions is to waive a set of objections that become particularly telling at the advanced level.

The foregoing discussion should make clear the sources of a problem that will arise repeatedly in the analysis that follows. Theoretical orthodoxy is manifested at a variety of levels, and displays a variable mix of strengths and shortcomings. Some of the shortcomings of elementary versions are corrected in advanced treatments; others are merely papered over. Sometimes a deficiency undergoes mutation to a new but analogous form, and some deep problems get exacerbated as the theory gets "better." We attempt to cope with this complex situation by modifying our references to orthodoxy with clarifying phrases—"textbook" or "simple" orthodoxy versus "advanced" or "recent developments," and so forth. We also distinguish between "formal" orthodoxy, displayed in logically structured theorizing, and the "appreciative" version which is more intuitive and modified by judgment and common sense. (This distinction is discussed further in the following chapter.) These devices are not entirely adequate to the task, but it does not seem reasonable to interrupt our discussion repeatedly for the sake of clarifying and documenting each criticism of orthodoxy. We hope that we have here provided an adequate guide, at least for those familiar with economic theory, to the way in which such detailed indictments might be developed.

Our use of the term "evolutionary theory" to describe our alternative to orthodoxy also requires some discussion. It is above all a signal that we have borrowed basic ideas from biology, thus exercising an option to which economists are entitled in perpetuity by virtue of the stimulus our predecessor Malthus provided to Darwin's thinking. We have already referred to one borrowed idea that is central in our scheme—the idea of economic "natural selection." Market environments provide a definition of success for business firms, and that definition is very closely related to their ability to survive and grow. Patterns of differential survival and growth in a population of firms can produce change in economic aggregates characterizing that population, even if the corresponding characteristics of individual firms are constant. Supporting our analytical emphasis on this sort of evolution by natural selection is a view of "organizational genetics"—the processes by which traits of organizations, including those traits underlying the ability to produce output and make profits, are transmitted through time. We think of organizations as being typically much better at the tasks of self-maintenance in a constant environment than they are at major change, and much better at changing in the direction of "more of the same" than they are at any other kind of change. This appraisal of organizational functioning as relatively rigid obviously enhances interest in the question of how much aggregate change can be brought about by selection forces alone.

The broader connotations of "evolutionary" include a concern with processes of long-term and progressive change. The regularities observable in present reality are interpreted not as a solution to a static problem, but as the result that understandable dynamic processes have produced from known or plausibly conjectured conditions in the past—and also as features of the stage from which a quite different future will emerge by those same dynamic processes. In this sense, all of the natural sciences are today evolutionary in fundamental respects. Perhaps the most dramatic illustration of this point is the increasing acceptance of the cosmological theory of the Big Bang, a conception that regards all of known reality as the continuously evolving consequence of one great antecedent event. At a less cosmic level, science has come to see the continents as shifting with sporadic violence beneath our feet, the changing behavior of the Sun as a possible factor in human history, and the world's climate as threatened with major and perhaps irreversible change as a consequence of industrialization. Against this intellectual background, much of contemporary economic theory appears faintly anachronistic, its harmonious equilibria a reminder of an age that was at least more optimistic, if not actually more tranquil. It is as if economics has never really transcended the experiences of its childhood, when Newtonian physics was the only science worth imitating and celestial mechanics its most notable achievement.[2]

There are other connotations that have at most a qualified relevance to our own evolutionary approach. For example, there is the idea of gradual development, often invoked by an opposition between "evolutionary" and "revolutionary." Although we stress the importance of certain elements of continuity in the economic process, we do not deny (nor does contemporary biology deny) that change is sometimes very rapid. Also, some people who are particularly alert to teleological fallacies in the interpretation of biological evolution seem to insist on a sharp distinction between explanations that feature the processes of "blind" evolution and those that feature "deliberate" goal-seeking. Whatever the merit of this distinction in

---

2. In his *Dynamic Economics* (1977) Burton Klein discusses at some length this failure of economics to recognize the profound changes in the view of "what science is" that have occurred in the natural sciences, principally physics. His perceptions of the problems with contemporary orthodox economics are consonant with ours in many respects.

the context of the theory of biological evolution, it is unhelpful and distracting in the context of our theory of the business firm. It is neither difficult nor implausible to develop models of firm behavior that interweave "blind" and "deliberate" processes. Indeed, in human problem solving itself, both elements are involved and difficult to disentangle. Relatedly, our theory is unabashedly Lamarckian: it contemplates both the "inheritance" of acquired characteristics and the timely appearance of variation under the stimulus of adversity.

We emphatically disavow any intention to pursue biological analogies for their own sake, or even for the sake of progress toward an abstract, higher-level evolutionary theory that would incorporate a range of existing theories. We are pleased to exploit any idea from biology that seems helpful in the understanding of economic problems, but we are equally prepared to pass over anything that seems awkward, or to modify accepted biological theories radically in the interest of getting better *economic* theory (witness our espousal of Lamarckianism). We also make no effort to base our theory on a view of human nature as the product of biological evolution, although we consider recent work in that direction to be a promising departure from the traditional conception of Economic Man.

2. Evolutionary Modeling

It is not an easy matter to state precisely what orthodox theory entails. Our evolutionary theory, as we shall develop it in this volume, is similarly flexible and will take on diverse forms depending on the purpose of the particular inquiry. There is, nevertheless, a characteristic modeling style associated with each theory, a style that is defined by the features that diverse models have in common. The principal purpose of this section is to describe the general style of evolutionary modeling. Before proceeding to that task, we briefly set forth an analogous characterization of orthodox modeling, for the sake of the contrast provided.

The Structure of Orthodox Models

There are some readily identifiable building blocks and analytic tools employed in virtually all models within contemporary orthodox theory of the behavior of firms and industries.[3] These same struc-

---

3. We are concerned here only with *describing* in general terms the structure of orthodox models; in the next two chapters we discuss the adequacy of of orthodox modeling of economic change and offer a critique of the basic orthodox concepts.

tures are visible in models spanning a very diverse set of specific inquiries. While our discussion of the orthodox art form will be quite general, it might be useful for the reader to keep in mind the central and best-known example of orthodox modeling of firm and industry behavior: the standard textbook model of the determination of firm and industry inputs and outputs, and prices.

In orthodox theory, firms are viewed as operating according to a set of decision rules that determine what they do as a function of external (market) and internal (such as available capital stock) conditions. The theory contains a sharp answer to the question "Why are the rules the way they are?"—an answer that also yields predictions about the scope or characteristics of the rules. The rules reflect *maximizing* behavior on the part of firms. This is one structural pillar of orthodox models.

A maximization model of firm behavior usually contains three separable components. First, there is a specification of what it is the firms in the industry are seeking to maximize—usually profit or present value, but in some cases the objective is something different or more complex. Second, there is a specification of a set of things that the firms know how to do. Where the focus is on production in a traditional sense, these things might be specified as activities or techniques, assumptions made about the characteristics of activities and their mixability and about the properties of the "production set" thus determined. But in models concerned with other questions, the set of things a firm knows how to do might comprise advertising policies or financial asset portfolios. The third component of a maximizing model is the presumption that a firm's action can be viewed as the result of choice of the action that maximizes the degree to which its objective is achieved, given its set of known alternative actions, market constraints, and perhaps other internal constraints (like the available quantities of factors that are fixed in the short run). In some models, the representation of maximizing behavior takes into account information imperfections, costs, and constraints.

The maximization approach permits the deduction of a decision rule or set of rules employed by a firm—a rule or rules that specify a firm's actions as a function of market conditions, given its capabilities and objectives. It attempts a theoretical *explanation* of firm decision rules in the sense that it traces their origin and accounts for their characteristics by reference to these underlying considerations, together with the maximization procedure. The decision rules themselves are the operational part of the theory. In some cases a maximization model generates predictions about the form of the decision rules. For example, if the production set is strictly convex and firms treat prices as parameters, the "output supply rule" relating production to product price is continuous and a price increase never decreases the output supplied. More generally, the maximization hypothesis leads analysts to try to figure out why a firm is doing something, or what it would do differently under different conditions, on the basis of an assessment of its objectives and its choice set.

The other major structural pillar of orthodox models is the concept of *equilibrium*. This is an extremely powerful and flexible concept; a full equilibrium in an orthodox model may be an equilibrium in two or three distinguishable senses relating to a number of different components or variables within the model's overall structure. The role and result of all these equilibrium conditions is to generate within the logic of the model conclusions about economic behavior itself—as distinguished from the conclusions about the *rules* of behavior that are generated by the maximization analysis. In the most basic example, the supply and demand curves in a market are simply aggregations of behavioral rules of individual sellers and buyers, which for each actor describe the transaction quantity that would be most desirable at each possible value of the market price. The *actual* value of the price—and hence the actual behavior of the actors—is determined by the supply-demand equilibrium condition, which picks out the specific price for which the aggregate desired purchase quantity precisely equals the aggregate quantity sellers wish to sell. Although the details may be different and much more complex, the spirit of equilibrium analysis in economics is almost always the same as in this basic example: to impose an equilibrium condition is to add an equation to the mathematical system characterizing the model and thus to provide for the determination, within the model, of the value of another variable.

Formal models embodying the central orthodox concepts of maximization and equilibrium have been built with a variety of mathematical tools. Indeed, the range and rate of change of the set of mathematical devices employed to explore an essentially constant set of theoretical concepts is such as to make one suspect that the key mechanisms in the process involve the levels of mathematical sophistication attained by researchers and their audiences, and not any deep affinities between the mathematical tools and the subject matter. Calculus techniques are, however, increasingly central in the intermediate and advanced pedagogy of the subject, and they have long been an important research tool. They do seem to provide a natural and efficient way of expressing some of the key ideas of orthodoxy, particularly those relating to maximizing behavior. Given some ancillary assumptions about the shape and smoothness of the frontiers of the choice set and other constraints, maximizing choices can be deduced by setting the appropriate derivatives equal to zero.

Lagrangian multipliers associated with the constraints have a natural connection to theoretical understanding of pricing. Equilibrium of the set of firms in question implies that the equations characterizing their maximizing behavior must be simultaneously satisfied. These mathematical ideas seem to fit the subject matter extremely well; undoubtedly, that is at least partly because they have significantly influenced the development of thinking about the subject matter.

The Structure of Evolutionary Models

The decision rules employed by firms form a basic operational concept of our proposed evolutionary theory as well as contemporary orthodoxy. However, we reject the notion of maximizing behavior as an explanation of why decision rules are what they are; indeed, we dispense with all three components of the maximization model—the global objective function, the well-defined choice set, and the maximizing choice rationalization of firms' actions. And we see "decision rules" as very close conceptual relatives of production "techniques," whereas orthodoxy sees these things as very different.

Our general term for all regular and predictable behavioral patterns of firms is "routine." We use this term to include characteristics of firms that range from well-specified technical routines for producing things, through procedures for hiring and firing, ordering new inventory, or stepping up production of items in high demand, to policies regarding investment, research and development (R&D), or advertising, and business strategies about product diversification and overseas investment. In our evolutionary theory, these routines play the role that genes play in biological evolutionary theory. They are a persistent feature of the organism and determine its possible behavior (though *actual* behavior is determined also by the environment); they are heritable in the sense that tomorrow's organisms generated from today's (for example, by building a new plant) have many of the same characteristics, and they are selectable in the sense that organisms with certain routines may do better than others, and, if so, their relative importance in the population (industry) is augmented over time.

Undoubtedly, there is a great deal of business behavior that is not, within the ordinary meaning of the term, "routine." Equally clearly, much of the business decision making that is of the highest importance, both from the point of view of the individual firm and from that of society, is nonroutine. High-level business executives do not, in the modern world, spend humdrum days at the office applying the same solutions to the same problems that they were dealing with five years before. We do not intend to imply any denial of these

propositions in building our theory of business behavior on the notion of routine. For the purposes of economic theorizing, the key
point is somewhat different. It is that most of what is *regular and predictable* about business behavior is plausibly subsumed under the
heading "routine," especially if we understand that term to include
the relatively constant dispositions and strategic heuristics that
shape the approach of a firm to the nonroutine problems it faces. The
fact that not all business behavior follows regular and predictable
patterns is accommodated in evolutionary theory by recognizing that
there are stochastic elements both in the determination of decisions
and of decision outcomes. From the point of view of a participant in
business decision making, these stochastic elements may reflect the
result of tumultuous meetings or of confrontations with complex
problems under crisis conditions; but from the viewpoint of an external observer seeking to understand the dynamics of the larger
system, the significant point about these phenomena is that they are
hard to predict. Conversely, if they were *not* hard to predict, the observer would be inclined to interpret the tumult and the sense of
crisis as some sort of organizational ritual—a part of the routine.

Our use of several different terms for different types of routines is
meant to convey our appreciation that, for some purposes, it is important to distinguish between a production technique whose operation is tightly constrained by machinery or chemistry and procedures
for choosing what technique to employ at a certain time, and also
between a relatively low-order procedure or decision rule (for example, the way a new order is handled or an inventory decline recognized and responded to) and a higher-order decision rule or policy
(for example, a rule to switch from use of oil to natural gas as fuel
when the relative price ratio hits a certain level, or the custom of
keeping advertising expenditures roughly in proportion to sales).
But, as the use of the common term "routine" indicates, we believe
that these distinctions are subtle and continuous, not clear and
sharp. Orthodox theory makes a sharp distinction between the
choice set and choosing—between what is involved in operating a
particular technique and what is involved in deciding what technique to use. In our evolutionary theory we see strong similarities in
these. In mixing up batches of raw materials, decisions have to be
made as to whether the composition and temperature are right or
not, and, if not, what to do. If there is a rationale for orthodoxy's policy of denying theoretical recognition to this element of choice in
firm behavior by including it in the description of technique, it presumably has to do with the fact that the choices are made in a routinized manner, and perhaps also that they are not an important source
of variability in the firm's profits. But empirical studies of pricing

behavior, inventory management, and even advertising policies reveal a similar "by-the-rule" character of firm decision making in these arenas. In some cases, though not in all, routinization holds sway in particular decision-making arenas because the important action is elsewhere—perhaps in finance, R&D policy, or coping with regulation.[4] Thus, orthodoxy's unwillingness to give parallel treatment to the similar forms of routinized behavior involved in "doing" and "choosing" remains a puzzle and will be a recurring theme in this book.

In any case, evolutionary modeling highlights the similarities among different sorts of routines. At any time, a firm's routines define a list of functions that determine (perhaps stochastically) what a firm does as a function of various external variables (principally market conditions) and internal state variables (for example, the firm's prevailing stock of machinery, or the average profit rate it has earned in recent periods). Among the functions thus defined might be one that relates inputs required to output produced (reflecting the firm's technique), one that relates the output produced by a firm to market conditions (the supply curve of orthodox theory), and one that relates variable input proportions to their prices and other variables. But whereas in orthodox theory the available techniques are a constant datum, and decision rules are assumed to be the consequence of maximization, in evolutionary theory they are treated as simply reflecting at any moment of time the historically given routines governing the actions of a business firm.

Although the routines that govern behavior at any particular time are, at that time, given data, the characteristics of prevailing routines may be understood by reference to the evolutionary process that has molded them. For the purposes of analyzing that process, we find it convenient to distinguish among three classes of routines.

One of these relates to what a firm does at any time, given its prevailing stock of plant, equipment, and other factors of production that are not readily augmented in the short run. (In effect here we are defining the basic unit "period" in our evolutionary modeling, as a counterpart to Marshall's "short run.") These routines that govern short-run behavior may be called "operating characteristics."

A second set of routines determine the period-by-period augmentation or diminution of the firm's capital stock (those factors of pro-

---

4. A major theme of R. A. Gordon's classic study of corporate decision making (Gordon, 1945) is that many of the decisions with which economic theory is concerned (such as price and output determination) are made by routinized procedures, while corporate executives actually spend their time on matters of greater importance— which also happen to be matters that resist orthodox modeling.

duction that are fixed in the short run). The extent to which actual investment behavior follows predictable patterns probably varies a good deal from one situation to another. In some cases the decision making surrounding the question of whether to build a new plant may not be much different in kind from the decision making regarding whether or not to continue to run a particular machine that has been operating roughly, or to stop it and call in the maintenance crew. In other cases, the new plant decision may be more like a decision to undertake a major R&D program on a recently opened technological frontier, a problem without real precedent that is dealt with through improvised procedures. Which of the two patterns obtains probably depends importantly on the size of the investment project relative to the existing activity of the firm. As suggested above, this spectrum of realistic possibilities corresponds in evolutionary theory to a range of differing roles for stochastic elements in the representation of investment decision making. In the particular models we shall develop later in this volume, the investment rule used by firms will be keyed to the firm's profitability, and perhaps to other variables. Thus, profitable firms will grow and unprofitable ones will contract, and the operating characteristics of the more profitable firms therefore will account for a growing share of the industry's activity.

The selection mechanism here clearly is analogous to the natural selection of genotypes with differential net reproduction rates in biological evolutionary theory. And, as in biological theory, in our economic evolutionary theory the sensitivity of a firm's growth rate to prosperity or adversity is itself a reflection of its "genes."

Finally, we view firms as possessing routines which operate to modify over time various aspects of their operating characteristics. In a sense, the model firms of evolutionary theory can be thought of as possessing market analysis departments, operations research shops, and research and development laboratories. Or there may be none of these organizational devices built into a firm, but at least from time to time some people within the firm may engage in scrutiny of what the firm is doing and why it is doing it, with the thought of revision or even radical change. We propose that these processes, like other ones, are "rule guided." That is, we assume a hierarchy of decision rules with higher-order procedures (for example, scrutiny of the currently employed production technique, or the undertaking of a study of a range of possible modifications in advertising policy) which act occasionally to modify lower-order ones (the techniques used to make a particular part, or the procedure determining the mix of raw materials employed, or current decision rules regarding advertising expenditure). And there may even be procedures of a still higher order, such as occasional deliberations regarding the adequacy of present research and development policy, or of the methodological soundness of the marketing studies being used to guide advertising policy.[5]

These routine-guided, routine-changing processes are modeled as "searches" in the following sense. There will be a characterization of a population of routine modifications or new routines that can be found by search. A firm's search policy will be characterized as determining the probability distribution of what will be found through search, as a function of the number of variables—for example, a firm's R&D spending, which in turn may be a function of its size. Firms will be regarded as having certain criteria by which to evaluate proposed changes in routines: in virtually all our models the criterion will be anticipated profit. The particular model we shall employ for search will depend on the question we are probing.

Our concept of search obviously is the counterpart of that of mutation in biological evolutionary theory. And our treatment of search as partly determined by the routines of the firm parallels the treatment in biological theory of mutation as being determined in part by the genetic makeup of the organism.

As in orthodoxy, the characterization of individual firms in evolutionary theory is primarily a step toward analyzing the behavior of industries or other large-scale units of economic organization. The models in this book are of "industries"—that is, situations in which a number of broadly similar firms interact with one another in a market context characterized by product demand and input supply curves. In modeling these situations we often find it convenient to assume that "temporary equilibrium" is achieved—to abstract from such short-run dynamic processes as those that establish a single price in the market in a single period. However, we emphatically do not assume that our model industries are in long-run equilibrium, or focus undue attention upon the characteristics of long-run equilibria.

The core concern of evolutionary theory is with the dynamic process by which firm behavior patterns and market outcomes are jointly determined over time. The typical logic of these evolutionary processes is as follows. At each point of time, the current operating characteristics of firms, and the magnitudes of their capital stocks and other state variables, determine input and output levels. Together with market supply and demand conditions that are ex-

---

5. This image of a hierarchical structure of rules, with higher-level rules governing the modification of lower-level ones, is essentially that presented by Cyert and March (1963, ch. 6).

ogenous to the firms in question, these firm decisions determine market prices of inputs and outputs.[6] The profitability of each individual firm is thus determined. Profitability operates, through firm investment rules, as one major determinant of rates of expansion and contraction of individual firms. With firm sizes thus altered, the same operating characteristics would yield different input and output levels, hence different prices and profitability signals, and so on. By this selection process, clearly, aggregate input and output and price levels for the industry would undergo dynamic change even if individual firm operating characteristics were constant. But operating characteristics, too, are subject to change, through the workings of the search rules of firms. Search and selection are simultaneous, interacting aspects of the evolutionary process: the same prices that provide selection feedback also influence the directions of search. Through the joint action of search and selection, the firms evolve over time, with the condition of the industry in each period bearing the seeds of its condition in the following period.

Just as some orthodox ideas seem to find their most natural mathematical expression in the calculus, the foregoing verbal account of economic evolution seems to translate naturally into a description of a Markov process—though one in a rather complicated state space. The key idea is in the final sentence of the preceding paragraph: the condition of the industry in each time period bears the seeds of its condition in the following period. It is precisely in the characterization of the transition from one period to the next that the main theoretical commitments of evolutionary theory have direct application. However, those commitments include the idea that the process is not deterministic; search outcomes, in particular, are partly stochastic. Thus, what the industry condition of a particular period really *determines* is the probability distribution of its condition in the following period. If we add the important proviso that the condition of the industry in periods prior to period t has no influence on the transition probabilities between t and $t + 1$, we have assumed precisely that the variation over time of the industry's condition—or "state"—is a Markov process.

Of course, a vast array of particular models can be constructed within the broad limits of the theoretical schema just defined. Each particular model defines a particular Markov process, which may be analyzed with the aid of the mathematical propositions relating to Markov processes in general. For such analysis to reach conclusions of economic interest, however, there must be a lot of specific eco-

---

6. Alternatively, firm decisions and market prices may be jointly determined in each time period.

nomic content in the model. General theorems about Markov processes are not themselves of economic interest; they are just tools that are useful in attempting to extract the conclusions that have been introduced into the model through its specific assumptions. For example, it may be possible to show that the industry approaches a "long-run equilibrium," which may be either a static condition or a probability distribution of the industry state that applies (approximately) to all dates in the remote future. And if an approach to such an equilibrium is in fact implied in the model's assumptions, it will ordinarily be possible to describe some properties of such an equilibrium—for example, to describe the operating characteristics of firms that survive.

An important determinant of the success of efforts to extract such conclusions is the complexity of the model. This brings us to an important point regarding the scope of evolutionary theory and, more particularly, of the class of Markov models of industry evolution. At an abstract level, this modeling schema has enormous generality. We may think of a "firm state" as comprising descriptions of the firm's physical state (plant and equipment), information state (contents of file drawers and human memories), operating characteristics, investment rules (affecting transitions of physical state), recording rules (affecting transitions of information states), and search rules (affecting transitions of operating characteristics, recording rules, and search rules). All of these descriptions could in principle be highly detailed. We can think of an "industry state" description as involving the list of all firm state descriptions, for all firms in being and also for potential or deceased firms, together with a list of environmental variables that may be determined as given functions of time and/or as functions of the firm states. The transition rules for this complex industry state description are largely implicit in the description itself. Operating characteristics map physical and information states into current actions. Current actions and the date determine the environmental variables. Firm by firm, the current firm state and values of environmental variables are mapped into a new firm state by application of investment, recording, and search rules. And the process continues.

There is nothing wrong with the foregoing as an abstract conceptualization. However, the point of a modeling effort is not just to describe a system, but to describe it in such a way that its behavior may in some degree be understood. It is for this reason that the models that appear later in this book are very simple examples within the abstract scheme just described. Like most of our orthodox colleagues, we distinguish sharply between the power and generality of the theoretical ideas we employ and the much more limited results that our specific modeling efforts have yielded thus far.

3. Plan of the Volume

In the following chapter, we examine and diagnose some key deficiencies of orthodox theory. Our own response to those deficiencies is placed against the backdrop provided by past criticisms of orthodoxy and by the broader tradition of economic thought.

At the end of Part I, we offer an option. Most readers, we hope, will be interested in our attempt to offer a plausible cure for certain deep-seated inadequacies of economic theory. These inadequacies involve, of course, the flagrant distortion of reality represented by economists' basic assumptions about individual and organizational capabilities and behavior. Part II sets forth this attempt. It contains no formal models itself, but rather develops the image of individual and organizational functioning that underlies and guides the subsequent modeling. We first scrutinize with some care the conceptual foundations of orthodoxy's treatment of these topics. We then set forth an alternative view focused on sequences of coordinated behavior—individual skills and organizational routines. Among other things, this analysis makes clear that there is no sharp line separating the performance of actions from the choosing of actions. Most important, Chapter 5 seeks to establish that the formal models that appear later in the volume are well founded in a realistic account of organizational capabilities and behavior generally, and of the sources of continuity therein in particular. The assumptions of the formal models seek to capture some of the main tendencies that emerge from the detailed mechanisms described in Part II.

Some readers will be interested above all in the style of formal theorizing that characterizes evolutionary theory, in the answers that evolutionary models give to standard analytical questions, and in the new lines of attack developed for the more recalcitrant problems of economic analysis. We suggest that these readers skip Part II and proceed to Part III, in which we deal with two of the central questions explored in the positive theory of firm and industry behavior: the characteristics of industry equilibrium and the response of firms and the entire industry to changed market conditions. By exploring these traditional questions with the concepts and tools of evolutionary theory, we develop the basis for comparisons with orthodoxy both in terms of methods and of results. It becomes clear that a number of familiar theoretical conclusions can survive a shift to new foundations—but new interpretations and caveats surround them.

Part IV is concerned with developing and exploring several evolutionary models of long-run economic growth. It will be argued that the treatment of innovation within an evolutionary model provides a far better basis for modeling economic growth fueled by technical advance than does the neoclassical model amended by the introduction of variables that represent technical advance. In particular, we shall develop the point that an evolutionary theory of growth offers a framework that is far more capable of integrating micro and macro aspects of technical advance than is the more orthodox, formal approach.

In Part V, we turn to a problem that has resisted effective attack with conventional theoretical tools: analysis of the processes of competition through innovation described by Joseph Schumpeter (1934, 1950). We develop models capable of exploring and identifying strands of the rich web of relationships between market structure and innovation that such processes involve. One of the aspects explored will be the line of causation that connects successful innovation to firm growth to change in market structure. But we shall consider, as well, the more traditionally conceived Schumpeterian "tradeoffs" and some of the associated policy issues.

The analysis reverts to a less formal style in Part VI, where we discuss normative economics from the perspective provided by the evolutionary view of positive economics. Many of the traditional questions of normative theory will be dismissed as too artificial to be helpful surrogates for real issues, others will receive somewhat different answers, and a number of policy questions that are not brought into view with orthodox lenses will be observed and considered. In particular, the issue of the strengths and weaknesses of free enterprise as a means of organizing supply will be seen in a light quite different from that provided by contemporary welfare economics theory.

A final chapter reviews the progress made and points to the much larger agenda of tasks not yet undertaken.

2

The Need for an Evolutionary Theory

IT IS INCUMBENT upon those who propose a major shift of theoretical orientation to point out in some detail the deficiencies of the prevailing theory or the advantages of the prevailing alternative—or preferably both. Our case for the advantages of an evolutionary theory is presented throughout this volume in the course of our development and illustrative application of the theory itself. In this chapter we introduce our critique of orthodoxy and attempt to place it in the context of other work that has broken with the orthodox tradition.

There are numerous respects in which orthodox theory seems to us erroneous or inadequate. Accordingly, a critique might plausibly be initiated from any of a number of different perspectives. One possible emphasis would be methodological, since highly disputable questions of scientific methodology are raised by the defensive devices that shield orthodoxy from the facts of individual and organizational behavior. A survey of some of the more salient of those facts would provide an alternative perspective. Yet another might emphasize a critical appraisal of the sort of evidence that is typically put forward in *support* of the orthodox explanatory scheme. All of these approaches will be taken at one point or another in this book. But it seems appropriate to begin with an examination of orthodoxy's difficulties in the analysis of various facets of economic change—the same important theoretical tasks with which our evolutionary alternative is principally concerned.

1. THE AWKWARD TREATMENT OF ECONOMIC CHANGE BY ORTHODOX THEORY

Much of economic analysis is concerned with predicting, explaining, evaluating, or prescribing change. Presumably, then, the adequacy of a theory of firm and industry behavior should be assessed in good part in terms of the light it sheds on such phenomena as the response of firms and the industry as a whole to exogenous change in market conditions, or how it illuminates the sources and consequences of innovation. We are not the first to point out that orthodox theory tends to deal in an *ad hoc* way with the first problem, and ignores or deals mechanically with the second.

The theory of firm and industry behavior put forth in contemporary textbooks and certain advanced treatises certainly appears to address the first problem directly; indeed, this is what positive theory seems to be mostly about. Formal orthodox theory purports to explain the determination of equilibrium prices, inputs, and outputs under various underlying product demand and factor supply conditions. In the context of partial equilibrium industry analysis, for example, the heart of the theoretical exercise involves the derivation of output supply functions (firm and industry output as a function of factor and product prices), functions relating input proportions of firms to relative factor prices (presuming movements along isoquants), and so on. But, despite appearances to the contrary, the theory does not directly address the question: What happens if the demand for the product of the industry increases, or if the price of a particular factor of production rises? That is, it does not address the question unless one assumes both that behavioral adjustments are instantaneous and that these changes in market conditions and the resulting equilibrium prices are perfectly forecast in advance by everybody. More realistically, firms must be understood as making time-consuming responses to changed market conditions they had not anticipated on the basis of incomplete information as to how the market will settle down.[1]

On this plausible interpretation, firm behavior in the immediate aftermath of a change in market conditions cannot be understood as "maximizing," in the simple sense of that term embraced by the theory in question, and the industry must be understood as being

---

1. In his *Foundations* (1947) Samuelson clearly articulates the "out of equilibrium" character of actual firm and industry responses to shocks. Since that time the profession has grown somewhat casual about the problem, in the context of partial equilibrium analysis. See, for example, the treatment of dynamics, introduced almost as an afterthought, in Henderson and Quandt (1980, pp. 159–169).

out of equilibrium at least for a time after the shock. Absent the perfect-foresight assumption or something very close, one must admit that changes in market conditions may come as a surprise to at least some firms in the industry. Once the unanticipated change comes, firms' prevailing policies, keyed to incorrect expectations, are not profit maximizing in the actual regime. Explicit models that recognize the problem tend to incorporate the assumption that, faced with a shock that makes old policies suboptimal, firms adapt to the changed conditions by changing their policies in an appropriate direction.[2] Seldom do these models assume that the changes are made instantly or once and for all. Positing adaptive (rather than maximizing) responses to unforeseen shocks is partially an implicit or explicit concession to the existence of some adjustment costs or "friction" in economic adjustment; friction, however, is a phenomenon that is not generally considered in the textbook accounts of optimizing behavior.

Some recent papers have recognized explicitly the adjustment cost/friction phenomenon, and have attempted to deal with it by treating the time path of response to an unforeseen shock as optimal, given adjustment costs.[3] But such an approach founders if it is admitted that the response of firms in the industry to the initial set of disequilibrium prices will likely change those prices in ways that cannot be foreseen in advance, unless one goes back to the initial perfect-forecasting assumption. Indeed, it is a rather delicate and complicated theoretical matter even to define an optimum adjustment strategy in a context where there are many firms, unless some very stringent assumptions are made.

Thus, contrary to the apparent impressions of many economists, the operative theory (if one can call it that) of firm and industry response to changed market conditions is not derivable from the textbook formalism about profit maximizing and equilibrium constellations. Rather, the theory actually applied in the interpretation of real economic events is one that posits adaptive change (specified in any of several plausible ways) and typically involves two key pre-

---

2. In particular, notions of adaptive behavior have often been the implicit or explicit rationale for the use of distributed lags in applied econometrics. For discussions emphasizing that this sort of statistical specification is incompatible with strict orthodox theoretical principles, see Griliches (1967) and Nerlove (1972).

3. Formal analysis of the effects of various forms of economic friction has been undertaken in a number of advanced theoretical papers dealing with investment behavior and market functioning. See, for example, Gould (1968), Lucas (1967b), Treadway (1970), and a number of the papers in the volume by Phelps et al. (1970). For an empirical approach that emphasizes continuing optimal adjustment to changing market conditions, see Nadiri and Rosen (1973).

sumptions. One of these is that the *direction* of adaptive response is the same as the direction of the change in profit maximization constellations. The second is that the adaptive processes ultimately *converge* to the new equilibrium constellation.

At best this theory is an *ad hoc* mix of maximizing and adaptive models of behavior, and is not at all consistent with orthodoxy's rhetorical emphasis on the unique validity of the maximizing approach. At worst, there are some serious analytic stumbling points along the road. If decisions are taken at discrete time intervals, adaptive adjustment in "the right direction" may overshoot the goal—the well-known cobweb problem. Even in the absence of discreteness, differences in the presumed nature of adaptive response (for example, whether output increases or price increases in response to excess demand) can affect the stability conditions. Adaptive models may or may not generate time paths that converge to equilibrium. And whether they do or do not in a particular case, if the adaptive behavior model is accepted as characterizing how firms respond to unanticipated events, it should be recognized that its account of the process is not the formal model expounded in most textbooks and treatises. Verbal descriptions of adjustment, especially in elementary texts, do carry an adaptive flavor. This sort of discrepancy is not uncommon in theoretical discussion.

In general equilibrium theory, the same basic problem appears in another form. The objectives of the analysis are, of course, less pragmatic and applied, and more concerned with the functioning of highly idealized systems. F. H. Hahn (1970), in his presidential address to the Econometric Society, surveyed the accomplishments of the mathematical theory of general equilibrium, and called attention to the fact that economists had made little progress in modeling plausible processes of disequilibrium adjustment that converge to general competitive equilibrium. He noted that the institutional assumptions on which most of the extant stability theorems depend (Walrasian tâtonnement) are plainly artificial, while models slightly closer to reality fail to yield the desired result in realistic cases. He concluded that, absent understanding of dynamic adjustment processes out of equilibrium, "the study of equilibrium alone is of no help in positive economics. Yet it is no exaggeration to say that the technically best work in the last twenty years has been precisely that. It is good to have it, but perhaps the time has now come to see whether it can serve in an analysis of how economies behave. The most intellectually exciting question on our subject remains: Is it true that the pursuit of private interests produces not chaos but coherence, and if so, how is it done?" (Hahn, 1970, pp. 11–12).

In spite of Hahn's suggestion that "the time has now come," the years that have passed since he wrote have yielded no significant progress on the problems he identified. The reason is simply that thoroughgoing commitment to maximization and equilibrium analysis puts fundamental obstacles in the way of any realistic modeling of economic adjustment. Either the commitment to maximization is qualified in the attempt to explain how equilibrium arises from disequilibrium, or else the theoretical possibility of disequilibrium behavior is dispatched by some extreme affront to realism. Applied work has tended to take the former path, and more abstract theoretical work the latter.

Much the same strains have distorted orthodox attempts to analyze innovation and technical change. To begin with, it is noteworthy that such analyses constitute a specialized literature, ignored not only in most of the theory textbooks, but also in the rest of the research literature. This segregation certainly does not reflect any corresponding isolation of technical change and innovation from other phenomena of economic reality. Rather, it is implicit testimony that the orthodox theoretical engines operate more smoothly in (hypothetical) environments from which these change phenomena are absent. The task of coping with the complications they introduce has been faced up to only when the particular characteristics of a specific subject matter have plainly left no other choice open—and sometimes not even then.

Technical advance is now acknowledged by economists to be a central force behind a wide variety of economic phenomena: productivity growth, competition among firms in industries like electronics and pharmaceuticals, patterns of international trade in manufactured goods, and many more. But recognition of its importance in these contexts long predated the attempts to represent its role in formal modeling. Such attempts have often reflected a grudging recognition that the data would continue to rebuff any theoretical structure from which technical advance is excluded. And the resulting models have typically grafted variables relating to technical advance onto orthodox theory in ways that aim to preserve as much as possible of the standard theoretical structure. In our view, these responses have been inadequate.

This intellectual syndrome surely marks the post–World War II theorizing about long-run economic growth. Empirical studies in the 1950s established that the historical growth of gross national product (GNP) per worker in the United States could not be accounted for by increases in complementary inputs per worker: there was a large unexplained residual. When models appeared that "predicted" the appearance of such a residual as a result of something called "technical advance," they preserved most other aspects of orthodox static theory. In particular, they maintained the basic assumptions that the firms in the economy maximize profit faultlessly and that the system as a whole is in (moving) equilibrium.[4]

It is, however, an institutional fact of life that in the Western market economies—the economies that growth theory purports to model—much technical advance results from profit-oriented investment on the part of business firms. The profits from successful innovation are *dis*equilibrium phenomena, at least by the standard of equilibrium proposed in the models in question. They stem largely from the lead over competitors that innovation affords. And it is also a fact of life that the success of innovation is very hard to predict in any detail: different decision makers and firms make different bets even while under the same broad economic influences, and *ex post* some prove right and others wrong. Given these facts, the retention in growth theory of a static conception of profit maximization tended to hinder understanding of economic growth rather than facilitate it. Paradoxically, it had this effect because it underemphasized and obscured the part that the pursuit of profit plays in the growth process. For the sake of a formal adherence to the orthodox canon, growth theory abstracted from the uncertainty, the transient gains and losses, the uneven, groping character of technical advance, and the diversity of firm characteristics and strategies—that is, from the key features of the capitalist dynamic.

In principle, these features could have been much better accommodated in a more sophisticated theory embodying subtler applications of orthodox theoretical principles. Indeed, the fact that such a theory does not exist today must be attributed largely to the difficulty of constructing it rather than to a failure to appreciate the desirability of doing so. But while the difficulties imposed by the complexity of the subject matter are certainly substantial, it is important to note that orthodox theorists operate under additional severe constraints that are self-imposed. When properly invoked (by orthodox standards), the notions of maximization and equilibrium that are required to model uncertainty, diversity, and change are delicate and intricate intellectual devices. Extremely stringent criteria of consistency must be satisfied in models properly built around these notions—so stringent that their effect is to make situations that have been simplified and stylized to the point of absurdity blossom into challenging puzzles.[5] There is no gainsaying the intellectual achieve-

---

4. We discuss these issues in considerable detail in Part IV.

5. The general theoretical approach identified with the term "rational expectations" is supremely orthodox in the sense that the consistency requirements associated with a rational expectations equilibrium are supremely stringent. What is note-

ment represented by the solution of such puzzles, but the achievement would be more interesting if only there were some reason to
think that reality actually displays the consistency that the orthodox
theorist struggles so valiantly to represent.

It is not surprising that growth theorists generally chose to rely
upon simple conceptions of maximization and equilibrium, rather
than attempting to carry the weight of the combined difficulties
(inevitable and self-imposed) that the phenomena of growth present
to orthodox theorizing. What is significant is that there was so little
willingness to compromise further, that maximization and equilibrium retained the honored place in the theory while the key substantive phenomena were ejected.

A different response to the same problem has dominated the literature concerned with the nature of competition in industries marked
by high rates of innovation. Schumpeter's basic contributions have
been widely invoked by economists in their verbal accounts of
behavior in these industries, but have received only a few attempts
at formalization. Economic theorists, working with ideas of profit
maximization and equilibrium, have known in their bones that it
would be extremely difficult to build a model of Schumpeterian competition out of such components. As a result, until recently at least,
economists whose motivation is to describe and explain economic
phenomena as they see them, rather than to test or calibrate a particular body of theory against data, have had to work with verbal theoretical statements for which there is no established formal counterpart. Sometimes, in obeisance to the canons of acceptable economic
argument associated with prevailing formal theory, these economists
point to profit-seeking behavior and call it profit maximization, and
to tendencies of dynamic competition to wipe out quasi-rents generated by past innovative success and call this equilibrium. However, it should be recognized that these conceptions of profit maximization and equilibrium are a far cry from those of contemporary
formal theory, whether at textbook or advanced levels. Moreover, the
intellectual coherence and power of thinking about Schumpeterian
competition have been quite low, as one would expect in the absence
of a well-articulated theoretical structure to guide and connect research.

There have been a number of attempts in recent years to model
Schumpeterian competition. Most of these have employed the ortho-

---

worthy about this approach, aside from its indifference to descriptive accuracy at the
individual actor level, is that its total dedication to the consistency aesthetic often
forces the use of the most extreme simplifying assumptions in the statement of the
model.

dox building blocks of maximization and equilibrium. Several have been quite ingenious. They have managed to call attention to certain phenomena that might obtain in the real world of Schumpeterian competition, and to provide at least pieces of plausible explanation for these. However, invariably they have two limitations. First, the requirement that the model adhere rigorously to the concepts of maximization and equilibrium has forced the theorists to greatly simplify and stylize the processes of R&D, industrial structure, the institutional environment, and so forth. Second, the simplifying assumptions employed obscure what seems to us to be essential aspects of Schumpeterian competition—the diversity of firm characteristics and experience and the cumulative interaction of that diversity with industry structure.

2. DIAGNOSIS AND PRESCRIPTION

Many of our criticisms of orthodox analysis are familiar enough, at least within the individual theoretical contexts to which they refer. Less familiar, and more controversial, is our suggestion that the difficulties of such analysis are largely a reflection of fundamental limitations arising from orthodoxy's canonical assumptions of profit maximization and equilibrium. If this suggestion is correct, the problems are not fully inherent in the subject matter, but on the other hand there is no reason to think that orthodox theorizing will ultimately overcome them. They will persist, though perhaps in altered form, until theoretical tools of quite different design are directed at them.

In economic theory, as in other spheres, novel designs are never innovative in all respects; they borrow heavily from what has gone before. This is certainly the case with our own proposal. Following is a concise statement of our key differences with orthodoxy—and also of the main points of agreement.

First, we believe it is a powerful theoretical hypothesis that economic actors—particularly business firms—have objectives that they pursue. Profit is an important one of these objectives. Indeed, in the specific models we present in this volume, profit is the only business objective explicitly recognized. And this assumed objective operates in our models of business behavior in the standard way—that is, as a criterion for choice among contemplated alternative courses of action. If this much were all that "profit maximization" implied, our models would be models of profit-maximizing behavior.

The profit maximization assumption of formal orthodox theory is, however, much stronger than the view with which we have expressed agreement. It involves very definite commitments on the nature of the alternatives compared and the comparison process. We explore these commitments in detail in Chapter 3. Here we make the point concisely and a bit too starkly: the orthodox assumption is that there is a global, faultless, once-and-for-all optimization over a given choice set comprising all objectively available alternatives.[6] This clearly conflicts with, for example, an assumption that the firm operates at all times with a status quo policy, the profitability of which it inexactly compares, from time to time, with individual alternatives that present themselves by processes not entirely under its control—changing policies when the comparison favors the presented alternative over the current status quo. This latter assumption is more in the spirit of evolutionary theory: it is an assumption of "profit seeking" or "profit-motivated striving," but certainly not of profit maximization.

In a sufficiently calm and repetitive decision context, the distinction between striving for profit and profit maximization may be of little moment, but in a context of substantial change it matters a great deal. Strict adherence to optimization notions either requires or strongly encourages the disregard of essential features of change—the prevalence of Knightian uncertainty (Knight, 1921), the diversities of viewpoint, the difficulties of the decision process itself, the importance of highly sequential "groping" and of diffuse alertness for acquiring relevant information, the value of problem-solving heuristics, the likely scale and scope of actions recognized *ex post* as mistaken, and so forth. Many years ago Schumpeter remarked: "While in the accustomed circular flow every individual can act promptly and rationally because he is sure of his ground and is supported by the conduct, as adjusted to the circular flow, of all other individuals, who in turn expect the accustomed activity from him, he cannot simply do this when he is confronted by a new task . . . Carrying out a new plan and acting according to a customary

---

6. Although this characterization is stark, it is not erroneous. Some orthodox theoretical models appear superficially to fall outside its scope—for example, models of optimal search and other models of sequential decision making appear not to involve a once-and-for-all optimization. But close scrutiny discloses that what is modeled is indeed a once-and-for-all choice of an optimal *strategy* of response to the unfolding situation; indeed, the fact that this reduction to once-and-for-all choice is made possible is the essence of the analytical power of the notion of a strategy. This means that the actors in sophisticated orthodox models, like those in simpler ones, are conceived of as incapable of response to truly unanticipated information. Either they are essentially right about the problem from the start, or they can only deal with an unanticipated environment by responding, "Does not compute."

one are things as different as making a road and walking along it"
(Schumpeter, 1934, pp. 79, 85). In a similar vein, Baumol more recently said: "In all these [maximizing models] automaton maximizers the businessmen are and automaton maximizers they remain.
And this shows why our body of theory, as it has developed, offers
us no promise of being able to deal effectively with the description
and analysis of the entrepreneurial function. For maximization and
minimization have constituted the foundation of our theory, as a result of this very fact the theory is deprived of the ability to provide an
analysis of entrepreneurship" (Baumol, 1968, p. 68). Change, in
short, presents distinctive problems that automaton maximizers are
ill-equipped to solve, and that theories incorporating automaton
maximizers are ill-equipped to analyze.

We are similarly in partial accord with orthodoxy (with similarly
important qualifications) on concepts of competition and equilibrium. Competitive stimuli and pressures are, we agree, an important
part of the environment for the decision making that goes on in each
of the firms in an industry. Competitive forces not only shape voluntary business decisions—they help to set involuntary, survival-
related constraints on business decisions. And it is certainly useful,
in attempting to understand the overall tendencies of a model constellation of competitive forces, to ask where the whole dynamic
process is likely to wind up—that is, to look for a stable equilibrium
configuration in which those particular forces would no longer be
producing change.

Again, orthodoxy goes much further. In the most typical formulation, notions of competition and equilibrium are employed in
tandem at an early stage of the modeling logic, and produce a drastic
narrowing of the range of possibilities contemplated. Such models
do not explicate the competitive struggle itself, but only the structure
of relations among the efficient survivors. Obviously, they cannot
address such questions as the duration of the struggle or the durabil-
ity of the mistakes made in the course of it.

This theoretical neglect of competitive *process* constitutes a sort of
logical incompleteness, noted in the discussion of the preceding section. It is only in equilibrium that the model of optimizing behavior
by many individual actors really works. Disequilibrium behavior is
not fully specified (unless it is by *ad hoc* assumptions). But this
means that there is no well-defined dynamic process of which the
"equilibrium" is a stationary point: consistency relations, and not
zero rates of change, define equilibrium. The question of how equilibrium comes about cannot be posed in fully orthodox theoretical
terms (without *ad hoc* assumptions), and thus necessarily cannot be
answered.

We propose, in short, that orthodoxy's basic intuitions about economic reality are potentially much more helpful in understanding economic change than are the modern formalizations of those intuitions. While purpose and cogitation are fruitful assumptions to make in modeling the behavior of firms, strict profit maximization is not. Similarly, although it is legitimate and fruitful to model the processes by which actions taken by individual firms impinge on the others and in turn cause them to modify their actions, it is not fruitful to view that process as being always at or near equilibrium.

Why does the orthodox approach ultimately prove to be so crippling? It is because of the combined force of two shortcomings, neither of which would be fatal in itself. The first is the oft-noted lack of descriptive realism in the characterization of behavior and events. By adhering tenaciously to its extreme abstractions, orthodoxy forces economics into increasing isolation from sources of information and insight that could be of great value to it—from management theory and practice, psychology, organization theory, and business history, for example. The severe abstractions and the isolation they entail might be a justifiable cost if they adequately performed their function of facilitating analysis of complex systems. But it is only at the textbook level that the abstractions truly have a simplifying effect. This is orthodoxy's second critical shortcoming: in advanced theoretical work, and in many applied contexts, its apparatus is cumbersome. Faced with the facts of uncertainty and change, it attributes great explanatory force to elaborate hypothetical structures of preference and subjective probability. In gross disregard of Occam's Razor, it multiplies these entities far beyond the empirical necessities imposed by any reasonable prospect of endowing them with operational content.

If the foundations were empirically secure, the attention lavished on the ornate logical superstructure would be understandable. If the superstructure were austere and of immediate practical use, expedient commitments to shaky foundations might be justified. Increasingly, orthodoxy builds a rococo logical palace on loose empirical sand.

3. Allies and Antecedents of Evolutionary Theory

In intellectual evolution, as in other sorts, the accidents and incidents along the way play an important role in the transformation of relatively simple and amorphous beginnings into the complex structures of later times. Thus, while traits of economic theory today betray both its classical origins and its present scientific utility, it would be a mistake to suppose that these considerations, either separately or in combination, fully account for the form that this theory takes today. Adam Smith might have had other and more robust intellectual descendants than contemporary orthodoxy—and more adequate interpretations.

A distinctive feature of intellectual evolution is that successive generations of the contending "species" often leave to posterity their own interpretations of the evolutionary struggle itself—though without, of course, the benefit of full foresight as to its future course. The choices and accidents, the refinements and extensions that molded present orthodoxy have been discussed and disputed both as they occurred and retrospectively. Many of the theoretical issues with which we are concerned in this volume have a long, complex, and sometimes tedious history in the literature of the discipline. They are treated in the work of economists now considered in the "mainstream," but more particularly in the writings of others now classified primarily as critics and heretics. There are broad themes around which the individual issues may be organized—the nature and behavior of the firm and of market processes and structures, the character of capitalist social institutions more generally, and a range of questions concerning methodology, philosophy, and value. These themes interweave, however, and the historical dimension of the pattern contributes further complexity.

In the preceding section we have laid out our central agreements and disagreements with contemporary orthodoxy; here we do the same for a number of the critics and for earlier mainstream authors. This survey is, necessarily, neither exhaustive nor detailed, but it should suffice to suggest the main patterns of contrast, complementarity, and intellectual indebtedness that define the place of our work in the literature.

Managerialism and Behavioralism

We begin by considering two heterodox approaches to analysis of the business firm that have been developed in recent decades and that are marked by a comparatively strong commitment to some type of formal theorizing.

"Managerialist" thinking diagnoses the problem of orthodox theory as a failure to represent correctly the motives that directly operate on business decisions. Contrary to the tenets of orthodoxy, the objectives pursued by firms include more than merely profits. Baumol (1959), who proposed to replace profits with another simple objective—revenue (subject to a profit rate constraint)—and Williamson (1964), who proposed a more general model of managerial utility maximization, are two important examples of the class. Some authors have paid particular attention to the processes and means by which stockholders or the capital market as an institution imperfectly constrains the pursuit of managerial objectives. Under this heading one can place Marris (1964), Williamson (1970), Jensen and Meckling (1976), and Grossman and Hart (1980). As the last two examples illustrate, and as we further argue in Chapter 3, the gap between managerialist and orthodox analysis is sometimes small.

In our view, these proposals yield useful insights into questions of managerial behavior and performance that obviously cannot be addressed within the strict orthodox framework (since in that framework management is just another input). However, the particular problems with traditional theory that we have discussed above, and to which our analytic proposals are addressed, are not stressed by the "managerial motivation" theorists. Baumol, Williamson (in this guise), and other creators of managerial models generally have assumed that managers maximize whatever it is they seek to achieve, with full cognizance of all possible actions they might take and the consequences of choosing any. Our central concern is with the maximization postulate as a characterization of how managers make decisions given their objectives. And that concern is relevant whether the objective is profit or something different or more general.

Distinct from the managerialist view, but consistent with many elements of it, is the "behavioralist" position. Behavioralists, taking their lead from the work of Herbert Simon (1955a, 1959, 1965), stress some or all of the following elements. Man's rationality is "bounded": real-life decision problems are too complex to comprehend and therefore firms cannot maximize over the set of all conceivable alternatives. Relatively simple decision rules and procedures are used to guide action; because of the bounded rationality problem, these rules and procedures cannot be too complicated and cannot be characterized as "optimal" in the sense that they reflect the results of global calculation taking into account information and decision costs; however, they may be quite satisfactory for the purposes of the firm given the problems the firm faces. Firms satisfice; a firm is unlikely to possess a well-articulated global objective function in part because individuals have not thought through all of their utility tradeoffs and in part because firms are coalitions of decision makers with different interests that are unlikely to be fully accommodated in an intrafirm social welfare function.[7]

We accept and absorb into our analysis many of the ideas of the

---

7. The basic reference is, of course, Cyert and March (1963).

behavioral theorists. Our basic critique of orthodoxy is connected with the bounded rationality problem. We base our modeling on the proposition that in the short and medium run the behavior of firms can be explained in terms of relatively simple decision rules and procedures. Much more than the behavioralists, however, our concern has been with economic change. Therefore, we have put much more stress than they on processes that link changes in firm decision rules and procedures (including productive techniques) to a changing economic environment.

We are in sympathy with the behavioralist position that firms should not be viewed as having stable, finely graded yardsticks for the comparison of alternatives, and in some of our models we have included a variant of the "satisficing" idea put forth by Simon (1955a, 1959), and Cyert and March (1963). Leibenstein (1966) has made use of a similar idea, calling it "inert areas." However, in other models we have employed the profit yardstick in a relatively conventional way. We remain pragmatic about this issue. Finally, we follow the behavioralists in regarding computer simulation as a legitimate approach to the formal representation of theoretical schemes that, for one reason or another, do not lend themselves to analytical treatment. There are, however, some differences of philosophy and emphasis that distinguish our uses of simulation techniques from those illustrated in, for example, the work of Cyert and March.

We diverge from the behavioral theorists in our interest in building an explicit theory of industry behavior, as contrasted with individual firm behavior. This means on the one hand that our characterizations of individual firms are much simpler and more stylized than those employed by the behavioral theorists, and on the other hand that our models contain a considerable amount of apparatus linking together the behavior of collections of firms. Perhaps in the future it will become possible to build and comprehend models of industry evolution that are based on detailed and realistic models of individual firm behavior. If so, our work will at that point reconverge with the behavioralist tradition.

Analysts of Firm Organization and Strategy

A considerable literature has developed on the relationships linking the growth and profitability of a firm to its organizational structure, capabilities, and behavior. Several different but largely complementary strands are involved. Penrose (1959) provided the elements of an analysis linking firm growth, structure, and the nature of the management function. Though she was apparently unaware of Coase's (1937) transaction cost approach to the nature of the firm, her analysis is largely consistent with it. More recently, Williamson in a number of works has woven the transaction cost theme together with other conceptual strands in a series of highly insightful analyses of firm scope, organizational structure, and related policy issues (1970, 1975, 1979, 1981).

A line of work centered in the Harvard Business School has explored a concept of business strategy in its relation to the organization of the firm; Chandler's (1962, 1977) historical analysis from this point of view has been particularly influential. The strategy concept involved in this tradition is distinctive. Implicitly, at least, it involves acceptance of the basic premise of bounded rationality—that the economic world is far too complicated for a firm to understand perfectly; therefore the attempts of firms to do well must be understood as being conditioned by their subjective models or interpretations of economic reality. These interpretations tend to be associated with strategies that firms consciously devise to guide their actions. Such strategies differ from firm to firm, in part because of different interpretations of economic opportunities and constraints and in part because different firms are good at different things. In turn, the capabilities of a firm are embedded in its organizational structure, which is better adapted to certain strategies than to others. Thus, strategies at any time are constrained by organization. But also a significant change in a firm's strategy is likely to call for a significant change in its organizational structure.[8]

As should be obvious by now, we have considerable sympathy for these lines of analysis. Our treatment of firm behavior, in Part II, draws on the work of Williamson and others, as well as on that of the behavioralists. In some of our models, the higher-order decision rules or policies with which we endow our firms may metaphorically be interpreted as their strategies. In these models firms have different strategies, and a central analytic concern is the viability or profitability of firms with different strategies. And although in the models described in this book we do not permit firms to change their strategies, such changes are quite admissible within the logic of our theory. Indeed, within an evolutionary theory, change in strategy or policy can be treated in exactly the same way as change in technique.

We also are strongly sympathetic with the proposition that firm

---

8. Caves and Porter (1977) and Caves (1980) offer interpretations of the business strategy literature and establish the relevance and usefulness of its concepts in the context of industrial organization economics. The gap between the concerns of that literature and those of orthodox microeconomic theory has been narrowed by the theoretical contributions of several economists, particularly Spence (1979, 1981; see also Porter and Spence, 1982).

organization is an important variable for analysis in its own right. There are strong connections both between a firm's strategy and its appropriate organizational structure, and between the techniques commanded by a firm and its organization. Largely in the interests of establishing an understandable linkage between individual firm behavior and industry behavior, our formal models in this book suppress considerations of internal structure and organizational change. But in principle, an evolutionary theory can treat organizational innovation just as it treats technical innovation. The problems of business strategy, like the issues explored by the behavioralists, clearly call for a rich and detailed modeling of individual organizations; the long-run challenge is to discover modeling techniques and analytical methods that will make a rich treatment of the individual firm compatible with tractability in the analysis of larger systems.

One feature that distinguishes our analysis from most of the work under the present heading is the explicitness of our rejection of the orthodox view of firms as optimizing actors—a view that tends to be presumed in the strategy literature. To our eyes, the situation here parallels that noted above in our discussion of Schumpeterian competition. The sort of "maximizing" imputed to firms in these informal analyses is so remote from the concept employed in orthodox formal models as to make its invocation plainly ritualistic. And indulgence in the ritual merely tends to postpone the day when formal theory might actually have substantial and fruitful application in these areas.

Views of the Activist Firm

Several prominent critics have focused their attention on the passive nature of the firms depicted by orthodox theory. They have proposed that in the most dynamic industries firms try to modify the demand for their products and engage in the development of new technologies, rather than merely reacting to market conditions by choosing the most appropriate technology for those conditions. Economists like J. M. Clark (1955), Galbraith (1967), and, of course, Schumpeter have stressed that typical market structures are not perfectly competitive and that firms employ advertising and research and development as central competitive weapons. A corollary to this emphasis has been a tendency to downplay the importance of price competition, particularly of the idealized form represented by standard competitive models, and to view large firms and relatively concentrated market structures as the typical case in the "interesting" part of the economy, if not in the economy as a whole. These perspectives converge in an assessment of the large corporation as a critical feature of the institutional dynamics of modern capitalism, as a relatively autonomous chooser of society's means and to some extent of its effective ends, and as the stimulus for the development of new social institutions for its control and accommodation.

Of this bundle of concerns, it is really only the role of the large firm in technological change that we address seriously in this book. Even in that arena, our formal models are restricted, in the interests of simplicity, to the case of "disembodied" process innovation in an industry in which firms produce a homogeneous product. We do not analyze advertising or, indeed, do anything about reforming consumer theory: the theory implicit in our models is orthodox. And we touch only briefly on the implications of our theory for the complex institutional design problems in which the role of the large corporation is central. All of these limitations and lacunae simply reflect our inability to address all the important problems at once, and are not intrinsic features of the evolutionary approach. They remain, at the end of the book, on the long agenda of important unfinished business.

Where our proposals for theoretical revision diverge from those of the most prominent critics of the sort just mentioned is in our concern with developing a formal theoretical structure with analytical power. Many of those economists who have criticized economic theory because of its static nature seem to be content with stressing that valid point and positing some generalities about Schumpeterian competition at a verbal level, but appear to have no particular interest in developing a formal theory of Schumpeterian competition. We are centrally concerned with the development of formal theory.

Schumpeter

The influence of Joseph Schumpeter is so pervasive in our work that it requires particular mention here. Indeed, the term "neo-Schumpeterian" would be as appropriate a designation for our entire approach as "evolutionary." More precisely, it could reasonably be said that we are evolutionary theorists *for the sake* of being neo-Schumpeterians—that is, because evolutionary ideas provide a workable approach to the problem of elaborating and formalizing the Schumpeterian view of capitalism as an engine of progressive change. Although Schumpeter had some harsh words for loose invocations of evolutionary ideas in the analysis of economic development (1934, pp. 57–58), we believe that he would have accepted our evolutionary models as an appropriate vehicle for the explication of his ideas.

There are, of course, numerous points of varying importance on which our perspectives and conclusions differ from those of Schumpeter. Their number, and the fact that many of them are subtle, make it impractical to attempt a survey here. It does seem appropriate to remark on the extent to which the influence of the Schumpeterian vision has been limited over the years for want of adequate development (particularly *formal* theoretical development) of constitutive or complementary ideas. For example, Schumpeter's credentials as a theorist of bounded rationality could hardly be more incisively established than in the following passage from *The Theory of Economic Development:*

The assumption that conduct is prompt and rational is in all cases a fiction. But it proves to be sufficiently near to reality, if things have time to hammer logic into men. Where this has happened, and within the limits in which it has happened, one may rest content with this fiction and build theories upon it . . . Outside of these limits our fiction loses its closeness to reality. To cling to it there also, as the traditional theory does, is to hide an essential thing and to ignore a fact which, in contrast with other deviations of our assumptions from reality, is theoretically important and the source of the explanation of phenomena which would not exist without it. (Schumpeter, 1934, p. 80)

Because Simon and others have taught us much about what behavior is like when it is *not* "prompt and rational," we are in much better a position to challenge the "traditional theory" from this point of view than was Schumpeter himself. On this issue and others, our position on the shoulders of the giant gives us a somewhat different perspective.

We are not alone in this regard. While the mainstream of economic analysis of technical change has repressed the bounded rationality problem, many scholars of technical change have recognized it, if sometimes implicitly. Our formal theoretical view is consonant, we believe, with the writings on technical change of such economic historians as Rosenberg (1969, 1974, 1976) and David (1974), industrial organization economists like Peck (1962) and Phillips (1971), scholars of contemporary industrial technical change and of public policy issues like Mansfield (1968, 1971, 1977), Pavitt (1971), Freeman (1974), and Klein (1967, 1977). With few exceptions these scholars have not tried to formalize their implicit theory about what is going on. Gunnar Eliasson's work (1977) is an exception, as is Carl Futia's (1980), and our theoretical structure has much in common with theirs in being both formal and explicitly evolutionary.

Frank Knight and the Modern Austrians

Schumpeter stressed innovation as deviation from routine behavior, and argued that innovation continually upsets equilibrium. Other scholars also have stressed the importance of breaking from routine, but have placed less emphasis on innovation—at least if that term connotes major novelty. Both Knight (1921) and Hayek (1945) have argued that the economic world is continually throwing up new situations that constitute opportunities to make a profit if the situation can be comprehended and seized appropriately. Perhaps a freeze destroys the citrus crop in Florida, or a new fad about Pandas develops, or an oil field is discovered under Cape Cod. What profitable business opportunities are thereby opened up, or foreclosed? Hayek has stressed that the hard economic problem is to respond appropriately to such changes. Knight argued that a key characteristic of such changes is that it is impossible to calculate the right thing to do; what is appropriate and what is not will be revealed only by events.

In recent years, Kirzner (1979) has drawn on and developed these ideas, articulating what he has called a (neo-) Austrian approach to analysis of market behavior. He has argued that the focus of theoretical attention ought to be on market processes, rather than on equilibrium conditions. We certainly are in accord. Littlechild and Owen (1980) have explored the neo-Austrian approach mathematically. We apply evolutionary theory to analyze the effect of autonomous changes in market conditions, as well as change induced by endogenous innovation. Our theory is a theory about market processes.

Evolutionary Theorists

The general idea that market competition is analogous to biological competition and that business firms must pass a survival test imposed by the market has been part of economic thought for a long time. Systematic development of the idea is, however, much rarer in the literature. For the most part, it has been briefly invoked for broad rhetorical purposes or as an auxiliary defense for the assumption of profit maximization. We briefly survey its use in the latter connection in Chapter 6.

Among the contributions that have taken the evolutionary point of view more seriously, Alchian's 1950 article "Uncertainty, Evolution and Economic Theory" stands out as a direct intellectual antecedent of the present work. In that article, Alchian noted the difficulties in extending standard microeconomic theory to the case of uncertainty, and particularly emphasized the importance of examining the role of uncertainty from the *ex post* viewpoint, when some actions are seen to be successful and others mistaken. He proposed that evolutionary mechanisms would tend to bring about responses to changed market conditions on the part of populations of firms that were in accord with the predictions of orthodox theory. And he suggested that such a line of argument might provide a sounder guide and rationale for the use of the standard tools of economic analysis—but did not emphasize that quite different tools might turn out to be appropriate if such a shift of foundations were to occur.

Alchian offered only a few sketchy suggestions for specific models reflecting his approach. Winter (1964) investigated some differential equation models of selection processes as part of a general examination of the economic natural selection argument. The models served to stress in particular the distinction (and relationship) between a behavioral routine or rule and a particular action: what matters to survival is the actions taken in environments that occur repeatedly, not those taken very infrequently or those that exist only as the potential response a rule would yield to environmental states that never occur. Farrell (1970) explored a simple evolutionary model of speculative behavior with a quite different mathematical tool—the theory of branching processes. Dunn (1971) presented a view of economic and social development similar in many ways to ours. However, he did not develop his analysis formally.

In her 1952 critique of the use of biological analogies in economics, Penrose raised, among other questions, the problem of whether there exists an economic counterpart of genetic inheritance. To some extent, this problem had been anticipated by Alchian (1950, pp. 215–216), who emphasized the "reproduction" via imitation of rules of behavior. Winter (1971) made the connection to the work of the behavioralists, proposing that the observed role of simple decision rules as immediate determinants of behavior, and operation of the satisficing principle in the search process for new rules, provided the required genetic mechanism.

There has recently developed a flurry of intellectual exchange activity across the interdisciplinary frontiers where biology meets economics, other social sciences, and law. Evolutionary theorists in biology have directly borrowed concepts from modern formal economic theory (later we shall remark upon some of the awkwardness that is introduced to biological theory by taking the maximization and equilibrium notions too seriously). In turn, a number of economists have participated in the interdisciplinary literature on sociobiology that has burgeoned since the publication of E. O. Wilson's book (1975).[9] Hirshleifer (1977a), in particular, has emphasized both the unifying and synthesizing value of sociobiological ideas in the social sciences and the range of specific insights that sociobiology and economics can draw from each other. The sociobiological literature, or that part of it which applies evolutionary theory to human social behavior, links analysis of biological selection mechanisms to a long-standing tradition of study of sociocultural evolution. Campbell (1969) provided an excellent survey of that broad field and argued for the merits of a variation and cultural selection-retention theory of sociocultural evolution. Our own work may be viewed as a specialized branch of such a theory, as may the work of economists and lawyers exploring the evolution of the common law and the efforts of organization theorists who have taken the evolutionary tack.[10] Indeed, a great web of intellectual connections links all the work cited in this paragraph (and much more): the shared ideas relate sometimes to specific substance, often to analytical concepts and formalisms, and always to a common evolutionary philosophy.

Classical, Marxian, and Neoclassical Antecedents

Although our theoretical views are clearly at odds with much of present orthodoxy, they are quite consonant with the tradition of microeconomic theorizing as it existed from the time of Adam Smith up until around World War II. What today's orthodoxy represents is, above all, a particular (and not inevitable) refinement and elaboration of the core ideas from that broader tradition relating to market functioning and self-interested behavior. The price paid for the refinement has been a considerable narrowing of focus and a tendency to segregate from the main corpus of theory the questions and phenomena for which the refined theory is ill-suited.

The title of Book I of *The Wealth of Nations* is "Of the causes of improvement in the productive powers of labor and of the order according to which its produce is naturally distributed among the different ranks of the people." The book commences with a discussion of what today would be called the sources and consequences of technical advance. John Stuart Mill, like Smith, provides a rich historical discussion of the evolution of both productive techniques and eco-

---

9. See, for example, Becker (1976) and the exchange that followed among Hirshleifer (1977b), Tullock (1977), and Becker (1977).

10. On the evolution of the common law, see Cooter and Kornhauser (1980) and references cited therein. The evolutionary, ecological approach to organizational analysis is set forth in Hannan and Freeman (1977); see also Kaufman (1975).

nomic institutions to set the context for the narrower economic analysis, and his economic theory is to a considerable extent dynamic, not static.

Much of Marxian economic theory is evolutionary. Many of the recent attempts to formalize Marx, both by economists sympathetic to Marx and by those of more orthodox leanings, have, we think, been tightly bound by the analytical tools of contemporary orthodoxy. As a result, they have failed to do justice to his ideas about the laws of economic change. Some of our own ideas are quite compatible with those of Marx, in that we stress both that capitalist organization of production defines a dynamic evolutionary system and that the distribution of firm sizes and profits also must be understood in terms of an evolutionary system. However, while in some of our models the share of labor and capital is endogenous, we have not followed Marx and his contemporary sympathizers to the extent of focusing our analysis on the determinants of the profits-wages split. Nor does the play of political power have much of a role in the formal evolutionary models developed in this book, although in our discussion of normative economics from an evolutionary viewpoint, we do present some initial outlines of an endogenous theory of the evolution of government policies. Where a Marxian would most likely fault our discussion is in our failure to employ the ideas of contradictions and of class in our positive evolutionary modeling and our normative analysis. We have not found these concepts particularly useful.

Marshall is now generally regarded as a precursor or source of today's formal neoclassical economics. So he was, in the sense that he introduced to economics a portion of its present technical apparatus and stressed in particular that market analysis must consider both the supply and the demand side. But it is explicit in the *Principles* that his real interest was in economic dynamics:

The Mecca of economics lies in economic biology rather than economic mechanics. But biological conceptions are more complex than those in mechanics; a volume on foundations must therefore give a relatively large place to mechanical analogies; and frequent use is made of the term equilibrium, which suggests something of a statical analogy. This fact, combined with the predominant attention paid in the present volume to the normal conditions of life in the modern age, has suggested the notion that its central idea is "statical" rather than "dynamical." In fact it is concerned throughout with the forces that cause movement; and its key note is that of dynamics rather than statics. (Marshall, 1948, p. xiv)

Also, it is widely recognized that Marshall's writings reveal a somewhat agonized effort to balance the demands of rigorous theorizing with those of descriptive accuracy in the analysis of an evolving system (see Koopmans [1957], and Samuelson [1967]). A striking example of the effect of these tensions is Marshall's imperfectly drawn distinction between statical increasing returns to scale and what we would today call induced scale-augmenting technical change. Contemporary commentary on this tends to rebuke Marshall for his affront to the logic of purely static analysis; the fact that he quite correctly emphasized the role of (informational) increasing returns as an economic mechanism of irreversible change receives less attention. On this question and many others, our evolutionary theory is closer to the original Marshallian doctrine than is contemporary orthodoxy.

Similarly, although Pigou (1957; parts first published as *Wealth and Welfare*, 1912) is widely regarded as the source of contemporary welfare economics, he followed his teacher Marshall in attempting to analyze an economic world in continuing flux. Indeed, for Pigou economic change and the slowness of economic institutions in responding effectively to change were prime reasons for the problems recounted in his *Economics of Welfare*. This is the position we ourselves shall adopt in our treatment of the normative issues illuminated by an evolutionary theory.

Thus, while we break with contemporary orthodoxy on a number of issues that have concerned other critics before us, it is also true that our theory is compatible with, or even a natural extension of, a line of economic thought that goes back through Marshall to the classics. This appraisal raises two related questions. First, why did economic theory take the "wrong road"? Second, why have contemporary critics of orthodoxy had so little success in getting the error corrected? These and some wider questions about the intellectual forces operating in the development of the discipline are examined in the following section.

4. THE NATURE OF FRUITFUL THEORIZING IN ECONOMICS

The answer to the first question can be located in Marshall's own ambivalence. It has already been suggested that there was a strong tension in Marshall between having a theory that captured what he saw as the key structural aspects of the economic system and of economic processes, and having an abstract theory that was analytically tractable and logically complete. Given the mathematical tools at his disposal, he could not reconcile these two objectives. He recognized the great importance of the latter to the progress of economics as a science. That the discipline responded to his leadership in formal theory construction rather than to his richer insights into economic reality probably reflects what the pursuit of "science" was thought to entail.

More generally, a reading of the economic literature and reflection upon the role of economic theory in economic analysis suggest that theory is used in two distinguishable ways. These two modes are sufficiently different so that one may reasonably think of two different kinds of theory as being involved. When economists are doing or teaching theory *per se* or reporting the results of empirical work designed to test a particular aspect of theory, the theoretical style is stark, logical, formalized. In contrast, when economists are undertaking applied work that is of interest for policy reasons or are explaining, to an audience interested in that question *per se*, why certain economic events happened, theoretical ideas tend to be used less formally and more as a means of organizing analysis. These two different styles of theorizing we shall call *formal* and *appreciative*. Although they are quite different, both kinds of theorizing are necessary for economic understanding to progress satisfactorily, and there are strong if subtle connections between them.

The adherents of a broad theoretical structure share a way of looking at phenomena, a framework of appreciation. A theory defines the economic variables and the relationships that are important to understand, gives a language for discussing these, and provides a mode of acceptable explanation. Implicitly, therefore, a theory classifies some phenomena as peripheral, unimportant, and theoretically uninteresting; also it implicitly characterizes certain ways of talking about economic phenomena and certain kinds of explanations as ill-informed and unsophisticated.

In its role of providing a framework for appreciation, a theory is a tool of inquiry, and in skillful applied research that tool is used flexibly, bent to fit the problem, and complemented by any other tools that happen to be available and that appear to be useful. The focus is on the endeavor in which the theoretical tools are applied. In contrast, when economists or other scientists are pursuing the formal development of a theory, or undertaking empirical work as a specific check on theory, the focus is on improving or extending or corroborating the tool itself: they are exploring possible logical connections that have not been seen before, seeking implications of certain sets of assumptions, developing abstract parables that display possible causal mechanisms for particular phenomena, and trying to understand at an intuitive level the implications that seem to flow from deductive theorizing. In these activities, as contrasted with use of a theory as a framework of appreciation, the premium is on analytical tractability and power.

Formal and appreciative theory are linked in a number of ways.

Formal theory is an important source of the ideas invoked in appreciative theory. The formal theoretical enterprise extends and sharpens the tools used by the more empirically or policy-oriented members of the discipline. But in a well-working scientific discipline, the flow of influence is not only from formal to appreciative theorizing, but in the reverse direction as well. Phenomena identified in applied work that resist analysis with familiar models, and rather casual if perceptive explanations for these, become the grist for the formal theoretical mill. Formal theoretical structures are augmented so that the previously uninterpretable phenomena now have an interpretation. Somewhat informal explanations in the style of appreciative theory are abstracted, sharpened, and made more rigorous. These linkages also can be seen as constraints. In particular, if certain mathematical limitations prohibit formal theorizing from proceeding fruitfully in certain directions, appreciative theory tends to respond to the blockage too, and to be pulled where formal theory does proceed fruitfully.

Marshall clearly recognized the distinction between these two different forms of theorizing and the desirability of close connections. So, albeit implicitly, has the economics profession at large. What probably was a binding constraint in Marshall's time on the range of analytically tractable styles of formal theorizing has played an extremely powerful role in determining how formal theory in economics has evolved, and has thereby shaped appreciative theory as well. But since Marshall's time, that constraint has been considerably relaxed. A wider range of mathematical knowledge has become available, including in particular the modern mathematical theory of stochastic processes. The stock of mathematical competence in the discipline is vastly larger than it was. The advent of the computer has made available the computer program as a type of formal theoretical statement, and simulation as a technique of theoretical exploration. These developments now make possible what Marshall obviously wanted but could not reasonably attempt with the mathematical tools he had then—the development of a formal evolutionary theory.

Our answer to the first question—why theory evolved along the lines it did—provides the basis for our answer to the second question—why the contemporary heterodox tradition in economics has had so little impact on thinking within the profession. In the appendix to *The New Industrial State,* Galbraith (1967) proposes his own answer to the question: the hostile reaction to heterodox ideas should be attributed to parochialism and (intellectual) vested interests. There certainly are parochialism and vested interests in the sense that the profession as a whole has an enormous stake in a coherent theoretical structure, that the prevailing structure provides a powerful if particular way of looking at things, and that it is hard to shift focus. But one could argue as well that the failure of the heterodox tradition to influence the profession stems from its lack of appreciation of the importance and nature of theory in economics. Heterodox critics also tend not to understand the varied and extremely flexible nature of prevailing theory.

Indeed, a major reason for heterodoxy's lack of influence is that many complaints or proposals can be accommodated by slight changes of meaning, treated and accommodated as special case models, or absorbed by broadening the theory somewhat, all with very few ripples. The fact that prevailing theory itself defines what are reasonable and sophisticated objections to prevailing theory and what distinguishes appropriate from inappropriate proposals for amendment or reform is another defense. It is employed primarily when the complaint seems uninteresting and unimportant, but tends to be used also in cases where the complaint is potentially important but not easily treated by marginal modifications of the theory. Thus, proposals that firms are interested in objectives other than profits are readily absorbed in special models and held at the periphery of orthodoxy. More general complaints that the theory of the firm does not adequately recognize the market-shaping activities of large corporations are absorbed into appreciative theory but not formal modeling, and the tension between appreciative and formal theory is ignored. But the proposal that such firms are governed by shifting coalitions and that therefore their objectives are not readily expressed in maximizing language is dismissed as ill-informed or atheoretical at the level of appreciative theory as well as formal theory.

If the contemporary critics of orthodox theory can be accused of not appreciating the importance of a coherent theoretical structure and of underestimating the resiliency and absorptive capacity of prevailing orthodox theory, the defenders of orthodoxy can be accused of trying to deny the importance of phenomena with which orthodox theory deals inadequately and at the same time overestimating the potential ability of models within the orthodox framework somehow to encompass these phenomena. Perhaps economists should be less pessimistic about the prospects of developing a broad-gauge economic theory that encompasses much of what contemporary orthodoxy does but is not subject to its basic difficulties.

ORGANIZATION-THEORETIC FOUNDATIONS OF ECONOMIC EVOLUTIONARY THEORY

3

The Foundations of Contemporary Orthodoxy

SYSTEMATIC UNDERSTANDING of the events that take place within individual business firms never has been a high-priority objective on most economists' research agendas. Rather, attention has been focused on the behavior of larger systems—industries, sectors, the national or global economy. To facilitate the task of addressing important questions about these larger systems, the individual organization has been treated in highly stylized terms that are dictated almost entirely by the functional role of the organization in the analysis at hand at the moment. Thus, the theoretical firm is not merely a "black box"—it is a black box whose input and output channels may be modified by assumption at the convenience of the investigator. Without apology, the individual economist may, in a series of inquiries, treat "firms" as choosers from very different sets of possible actions—for example, productive input combinations, price policies, and securities issues. That there are real organizations that actually do all these things more or less simultaneously is a fact that recedes into the background until it virtually disappears from view.

Our approach in this book is in many ways similar. The emphasis is on the analysis of the larger systems, not on the individual actors. And because the theoretical treatment of the latter is essentially instrumental to the investigation of other matters, that treatment is flexible and opportunistic in the traditional style. For the sake of logical precision in the analysis of a particular question about a larger system, we make strong simplifying assumptions in building a model addressed to that question; then, upon taking up a different question, we may make quite different assumptions about the same matters. The justification for this apparently inconsistent approach is strictly pragmatic. It simply is not possible to keep any substantial number of the causal links of reality in sharp logical focus simultaneously. We can make such sharpness compatible with adequate scope only by attending to different parts separately and with different foci. The temporary narrowings of our field of vision are a price we must pay, given our unwillingness to abandon entirely the quest for logical precision.

It is our strongly held belief, however, that modeling at an industry- or an economy-wide level ought to be guided and constrained by a plausible theory of firm capabilities and behavior that is consistent with the microcosmic evidence. We argue in the present chapter that orthodox theory is inadequate in this respect, and in the following two chapters develop the view of events at the individual firm level that underlies our evolutionary theory. Although many of the considerations brought to light in this discussion will receive no explicit attention later in the book, we regard our specific modeling efforts as summarizing the main implications of our view of the micro level. They do so in a variety of different ways, each of which is appropriate to the task of understanding some particular class of events at a more aggregative level. We hope at least to persuade the reader that *if* the underlying realities correspond reasonably closely to the image here set forth, then the models presented in later chapters are useful ones to develop and explore.

Our first task is to get the issues out in the open. To this end, we undertake in the present chapter a critical survey of the conceptual foundations of orthodox economic theory. We identified in the first chapter a number of basic differences in underlying assumptions between orthodox theory and our proposed evolutionary one. Here it is useful to highlight the differences in presumptions made about the nature of the "know-how" possessed by business firms. Orthodox theory treats "knowing how to do" and "knowing how to choose" as very different things; we treat them as very similar. Orthodoxy assumes that somehow "knowledge of how to do" forms a clear set of possibilities bounded by sharp constraints, and that "knowledge of how to choose" somehow is sufficient so that choosing is done optimally; our position is that the range of things a firm can do at any time is always somewhat uncertain prior to the effort to exercise that capability, and that capabilities to make good choices in a particular situation may also be of uncertain effectiveness. The issues here involve the internal structure of the productive organization: What is really involved when an organization is "capable" of something? How does an organization remember its capabilities? What is involved in "choosing" to do one thing rather than another? What kinds of capabilities are involved in choosing?

In Chapter 1 we also described the three basic building blocks of orthodox models of the firm: objectives, a set of things a firm knows how to do, and optimizing choice given those objectives and capabilities and other internal and external constraints. As the above questions suggest, our principal concern in this chapter will be with the latter two building blocks—in particular with the conceptions of human capabilities and behavior that seem to underlie them. We will set the stage in our discussion by considering a topic that has received more discussion in the economic literature: the sense in which business firms might be regarded as having objectives, and the question of where these objectives come from.

1. THE OBJECTIVES OF BUSINESS FIRMS

In the simplest orthodox model of business firms the objective is simply profit, or market value, and the more the better. But many scholars have qualified or questioned this simple specification. There have been efforts to shore up the standard formulation by detailing the linkage between owner interests and management actions. Objectives other than profit value have been proposed by some authors, while others have questioned whether firms have consistent objectives at all, in the sense of choice criteria representable by a scalar-valued function. The criticisms range from the highly heretical (such as Cyert and March on organizational goals) to the obviously orthodox (such as the recent literature on "stockholder unanimity"). Because of the scope and thoroughness of existing discussions in the literature, it is both impossible and unnecessary to review all the issues here; we attempt only to identify the major themes. There are, however, some aspects of orthodoxy's treatment of the motivational sources of firm behavior that relate importantly to our concerns with the modeling of capabilities and that have received only limited attention in the literature. To these we will devote more attention.

The amount of effort that has been devoted to the problem of the objectives of the business firm can be regarded as indicative of the severity of the intellectual strain produced by two opposed considerations. On one side is the institutional fact of the large business organization—the sheer number of individuals involved, the diversity of their roles and the complexity of their relationships, the relative permanence of the organization and its concerns compared to the typical terms for which individuals serve as employees, stockholders, or even as chief executive officers. On the other side is the individualist utilitarian philosophy underlying neoclassical economic theory, together with such specific manifestations thereof as the optimality theorems of modern welfare economics. In this philosophical framework, economic organization in its entirety is appraised for its effectiveness in satisfying the wants of individuals. *A fortiori*, the business firm is viewed as *in some sense* an instrumentality of individuals, rather than as an autonomous entity. If the business firm in question is Miller's Mill, there is no real problem in accommodating this need of the normative framework by assuming that the operations of the mill directly reflect the interests of Miller. If it is General Mills, a similar linkage between the actions of the firm and the interests of its owners remains "natural" for orthodox normative theory, but is of doubtful credibility for descriptive purposes. The strain becomes severe.

A variety of developments in contemporary orthodoxy are responsive, in one way or another, to the need to replace the "Miller's Mill" approach with something more plausible. All seem to involve heavy reliance on the categories and conclusions of *market* analysis to shore up the theory of the firm. In the general equilibrium theory and portfolio theory branches of the discussion, maximization of the market value of the firm is unambiguously the objective of the firm. The reason is that in the austere environment of complete and perfectly competitive markets, there is no alternative desideratum left against which the value of the firm might be traded off.

In another line of argument, with a slightly more plausible institutional façade, the "market" for the control of the firm is the one whose effective functioning keeps the firm in line. It is to the external discipline provided by the takeover raider, rather than the internal discipline imposed by Miller, that society looks for the effective functioning of the mill.[1] There have also been some tentative moves toward a view that is distinctive at once for its intellectual boldness and for its faithfulness to the individualist tradition—the view that the firm *is* a market, a particular pattern of voluntary exchange relations, and not a unitary actor at all. Whereas before it seemed that the mill was essentially one of the economic roles of Miller, now it is seen to be essentially an organized market in the nexus wheat, flour, grinding services, labor time, and so forth. In this perspective, relations between superior and subordinate within an organization appear indistinguishable from market-mediated relationships: "Telling an employee to type this letter rather than to file that document is like

---

1. For a discussion of this argument, see Williamson (1970, ch. 6). A recent formal treatment is O. A. Hart (1977), whose conclusions are for the most part negative with respect to the efficacy of the takeover discipline.

my telling a grocer to sell me this brand of tuna rather than that brand of bread" (Alchian and Demsetz, 1972, p. 777).

More radical suggestions for resolving the basic tensions in the theory of the firm have been put forward by a number of authors. These alternative approaches are distinguished, and marked as unorthodox, by a greater concern for "descriptive realism" in the treatment of the objectives of the large business firm and by a corresponding willingness to sacrifice contact with the normative branch of contemporary orthodoxy. One major camp, briefly discussed in Chapter 2, is that of the managerialists—those who argue that orthodox theory errs primarily by identifying the firm's interests with those of a constituency that is frequently quite passive (stockholders) rather than those of an obviously and necessarily active constituency (managers). Although managerialists have not fully agreed on an answer to the follow-on question—What, then, are the interests of the manager?—there is substantial consensus that some measure of the size or growth of the firm provides at least a partial *operational* answer to this question, and corresponds to one major area of possible divergence between the interests of stockholders and managers.[2] It has not escaped notice, however, that the pursuit of firm size as a long-run objective entails concern for profitability in the short run. Because of this linkage, and because managerialist analysis is typically conducted with analytical tools made familiar by orthodoxy, managerialism is in some ways a rather mild heresy. Perhaps it will be reassimilated to the main faith in some future ecumenical movement. It may come to be regarded as a refinement of rather than an alternative to the orthodox theory—a refinement that may become well established in certain rather narrow application areas, such as models of managerial consumption-on-the-job and certain problems of corporate finance.

Another heterodox approach, less sharply delineated than the managerialist school, denies that firm behavior can be interpreted as pursuit of the interest of a single dominant constituency. Rather, it sees behavior as the consequence of a bargaining process structured by shifting patterns of coalition formation. This view was put forward, in particular, by Cyert and March (1963). For them the "goals" or "objectives" of the firm cannot be characterized by an objective function of a grand optimization that imposes a coherent structure on all the firm's actions. In their view, the question of the firm's objective, in that sense, can never be resolved because it would involve too much time-consuming bargaining over too many hypothetical

---

2. See Marris (1964) and Baumol (1962), among others. Heal and Silberston (1972) present a simple analysis of alternative growth objectives.

choices. Rather, the firm persists in a state of "quasi-resolution of conflict," and the firm's goals may be conceived as akin to the terms of a treaty among the participants, according to which they will jointly seek to deal with their common environment. As in the case of treaties among nations, a shift in that environment may render the treaty obsolete, in which case a period of renewed negotiation or overt conflict may ensue.[3]

Even if shared interests and effective bargaining among top managers suffice to produce agreement on high-level objectives, divergent interests regarding implementation may still be a major factor in the concrete behavior of the firm. Objectives like profit, market share, or growth do not serve to guide action in the absence of specific understanding as to how they are to be achieved. Unless this understanding is obvious, shared by all those who are involved in decision making, even the deepest commitments to a common ultimate objective will not serve to focus attention and coordinate action. To serve this purpose, objectives must be articulated in such a way that they are relevant to the decisions at hand. The person responsible for deciding whether or not to repair a machine is afforded little help by his acquiescence in a general profit goal for the firm; he must have an objective defined in terms of the predictable consequences of his own actions. Put another way, objectives to guide action must be proximate, and specialized to the decisions in question. This suggests, on the one hand, that *choice* of operational objectives is an important arena of managerial *decision*. On the other hand, it prompts recognition of the abundant opportunities for conflict that inhere in the task of dividing operational responsibilities among middle managers, and in the elaboration of systems of control and incentive that are required to align the actions of low-level employees with high-level objectives.

In fact, the discussion in Cyert and March about quasi-resolution of conflict and the literature on divergence of interests between stockholders and managers represent only a small segment of a seriously neglected problem: the shaping role of intraorganizational conflict. Williamson, in his analysis of "opportunism" in the employment relation, has traced the outlines of a more substantial piece (1975, ch. 4). Doeringer and Piore (1971) have called the attention of economists to the role of internal labor markets in partially reconciling worker and manager interests. Economists have yet to concern

---

3. Although the business press frequently reports the internal policy struggles of large firms in a manner that clearly involves informal use of a coalition model, there is little scholarly literature in economics that takes this perspective. The proposals of March (1962) and Cyert and March (1963) have been largely ignored.

themselves with such things as managerial career systems and their possible implications for the time horizons affecting managerial choice, or for the willingness to cut losses when an undertaking or policy commitment is threatening to fail.

These considerations lead us to concur fully with Cyert and March on one major point: possession of a complete, clearly defined objective function is not a necessary condition for business operation in the real world; all that is required is a procedure for determining the action to be taken. While criteria for choosing form an important part of many such procedures, the criteria need not be derived from some global objective function. And it seems to us, as it did to them, that this proposition has an important corollary: the imputation of such an objective function to the firm is not a *sine qua non* of effective theory construction. Presumably, if the firms in the world can get along without being entirely clear about their goals, so can the firms in a theoretical model. The concern that orthodoxy has lavished on the question of objectives is a reflection of the logical imperatives of its own normative structure—and also, as we have suggested, of its aspiration to reach broad normative conclusions on the efficacy of market mechanisms. To discard that normative baggage is to greatly expand the available options for dealing with motivational issues in the theory of the firm.

Most of these options seem to fall under one or the other of two broad theoretical strategies. The first would restore, at the level of the individual organization member or subunit, the assumption of definite objectives that has been discarded at the level of the firm as a whole. It would then seek to understand the behavior of the firm as a whole in terms of the divergent interests of various constituencies and the specific procedures by which those interests interact to produce the actions of the firm as such. Some orthodox theorists, willing to grant the implausibility of treating large firms as unitary actors, might well concur with behavioralists on the general appropriateness of this reductionist strategy. They would differ sharply, of course, in the modeling of the procedures by which divergent interests interact: orthodoxy would favor some noncooperative game framework, while behavioralism would draw more heavily on insights from organization theory and studies of "bureaucratic politics."[4] In empirical application, both approaches suffer under limitations of access to data on the nature of constituent interests and on the structure of the internal political process—and also, when such

4. Allison's study of the Cuban missile crisis (Allison, 1971) includes a fascinating application of the "bureaucratic politics" approach to the explanation of a series of important decisions by the U.S. government.

access is possible, on the complexity of the phenomena and their relative remoteness from the crude and aggregative measures of overt firm behavior with which the economist typically wants to deal.

The second strategy is the one we adopt in our own modeling efforts, and in some ways lies closer to textbook orthodoxy. It seeks to capture with a few simple assumptions the most consistently operating and powerful motivational forces tending to shape the behavior of the firm as a whole. Recognizing that the real causal sources of firm actions do involve divergent interests and complex internal political processes, it nonetheless emphasizes the utility of a simple and tractable approximation that relates directly to the questions of interest, compared with a more elaborate and realistic treatment that risks inconclusiveness on those questions. However—and at this point we diverge from orthodoxy—this approach to business motivation does not warrant a great effort to assure that behavior is represented as being "perfectly prompt and rational." On the contrary, in view of the nature of the deliberate approximation to the complex underlying reality, it is more natural to represent large-scale motivational forces as a kind of persistent pressure on decisions, a pressure to which the response is sluggish, halting, and sometimes inconsistent. And it may be noted that this is the same view of dominant motivational forces to which one is led if one regards them not as the result of an intellectual quest for perfect consistency, but as the outcome of an imprecise and unsubtle evolutionary purging of motives that diverge excessively from survival requirements. For problems that demand a more refined and exact treatment of business objectives, the appropriate tack is not to polish up the rationality with which the model firm pursues its imputed simple objective of profit or growth, but rather to recall that firms as such do not actually *have* objectives—that is, to revert to strategy one.

Most economists would, we suspect, readily concede the inadequacy of the conceptualization of the firm as a rational actor when the task is to explain particular decisions by particular large firms. The concession only underscores the question of why, in general theory construction, the objective function approach is so deeply entrenched. There are many other ways to represent motivational influences in a theoretical model; our own models illustrate only a few of the possibilities. In particular—as our own models illustrate—the plausible assumption that making money (in some sense) is a dominant business motivation need not be represented as profit or present value or market value maximization. The choice of those specific representations is easily understood as a response to demands for definiteness, precision, and internal consistency. But the source of those demands is not to be found in the realities of business behavior. They are demands that economic theorists impose upon themselves, perhaps in the mistaken belief that the achievement of definiteness, precision, and internal consistency in the *theory* requires the imputation of the same traits to the subject matter.

2. Production Sets and Organizational Capabilities

Although, as indicated above, there has been extensive discussion in the economic literature about the motivational aspect of the theory of the firm, there has been startlingly little examination of the implicit theory of the capabilities of business firms that is employed as a key building block in orthodox theory.

The orthodox mode of formal representation of what an organization can do rests on the concept of a production set. The elements of the set are vectors of input and output quantities; to say that a vector is in the production set is to say that it corresponds to a productive transformation that the organization can accomplish. Or, as Debreu put it, "A given production y may be technically possible or technically impossible for the jth producer. The set Y of all production possible for the jth producer is called the production set" (Debreu, 1959, p. 38). Depending on the purpose of the inquiry, the fact that production processes take time may or may not receive explicit attention in the formal representation. Also, the basic formalism can, but need not, be elaborated to include detailed representation of the internal structure of the production process—for example, by including intermediate products in the list of commodities and by identifying production "activities" with particular stages in the production process.

The production set idea is very general, but traditionally, at least, the capabilities so described related to production of goods in the everyday sense of that term. A long tradition in economic writing suggests that "production" is the sort of thing that happens either on a farm (corn) or in an establishment in the metalworking branch of manufacturing (pins, widgets). In recent years, however, the range of capabilities to which economists have applied the production set idea has increased greatly. While it may be "obvious" that concepts introduced for corn and widget production are readily and appropriately transferable to furniture storage, haircuts, and vending machine services, it does seem that some anxiety might be justified concerning the extendability of the same apparatus to, for example, the services produced by attorneys, educators, psychiatrists, and parents. We shall attempt to articulate this anxiety later on. But for the most part in this volume we adhere to tradition: when we speak of production capabilities, we have manufacturing prominently in mind.

What determines a firm's production set? Why is it what it is? On the surface, at least, orthodoxy is relatively clear about this. It is a state of knowledge that the production set is supposed to characterize—not, for example, the ultimate limits imposed by physical law, or the limits imposed by the actual conditions of input availability. Arrow and Hahn are quite explicit: "The production possibility set is a description of the state of the firm's knowledge about the possibilities of transforming commodities" (1971, p. 53).

What is the nature of this knowledge? Here the orthodox position is less plain. Considering the weight that this conceptualization of productive knowledge must bear in the overall structure of economic theory, the literature contains surprisingly little discussion intended to motivate and defend the approach. However, the connotation clearly is of knowledge "of a way of doing something" or "technological knowledge." Technological knowledge often is identified with a "book of blueprints" or with the knowledge of engineers and scientists. The latter is at least consistent with the view that specific operational knowledge exists in the context of theoretical understanding, while the "blueprints" metaphor suggests that knowledge is unitized, organized in packages labeled "all you need to know about X." Implicit in both metaphors, and in other discussions, is the view that technological knowledge is both articulable and articulated: you can look it up. At least, you could if you had the appropriate training.

Consistent with the notion of a book with a finite number of blueprints, in some treatments the production set is viewed as being generated by a finite number of activities or techniques that a firm knows how to operate. In the formal statement of models of this kind, certain assumptions generally are made about the characteristics of these individual activities—fixed input coefficients, constant returns to scale, and independence of other activities. The firm's production set then is defined as the input-output combinations achievable with all possible levels and mixes of the activities known to the firm. In other treatments economists simply assert certain characteristics of the set—for example, that the frontier of the set is described by a Cobb–Douglas production function. From either perspective, one important feature of the production set concept as it is employed is that, using our terms, a producer either has a capability or he does not. He knows how to run an activity or he does not; he has the blueprints or he does not. There are no fuzzy edges to the set, in fact or in mind.

The identification of a firm's production set with a "state of knowledge" could be interpreted as inviting consideration of a range of further questions. Why is the state of knowledge what it is? How does it change over time? Is it the same for all firms at a given time? For the most part, orthodoxy has declined to examine these issues.

In the standard treatment, the production set is simply taken as given. Issues of its change over time are not considered. The question of whether different firms have different production sets is not treated in a uniform way in orthodox models, but neither is it much discussed. In general, it appears that the most natural assumption within the orthodox framework is that all firms' production sets are identical—the blueprint file is a matter of public information. To make the sets different is implicitly to postulate positive costs of information transfer from firm to firm—a plausible view. But to make them different and *immutable*, as orthodoxy does when it takes this path, is implicitly to postulate that such costs are indefinitely large—an assumption that is clearly not in the spirit of the usual orthodox treatment of information.

The specialized literature on technical change forms, of course, a major exception to the proposition that production sets are viewed as constant over time. There, the typical model views the technological knowledge underlying the production set as changing over time as a result of "technological progress." In turn, technological progress may be viewed as exogenous, or as the consequence of a costly activity called "research and development." In effect R&D expenditure is treated as if it were purchases of an infinitely durable, indivisible fixed input ("knowledge") whose presence enhances the productivity of other inputs. Such formulations typically assume a total separability of R&D from actual production, in the sense that the expansion of the production set could take place even if production itself did not. This, of course, is consistent with the interpretation, noted above, that technological knowledge is articulated knowledge. It is the sort of thing that can be recorded, stored at negligible cost, and referred to when needed. The small group of "learning by doing" models depart from this tradition, but they remain an unconnected and unexplored annex to orthodox doctrine about production capabilities.

To the extent that different firms do different R&D and to the extent that there exist secure patent rights, or industrial secrecy, models that assume endogenous technological advance logically ought to admit that firms almost surely will differ in terms of their production sets. Strangely enough, however, virtually no extant model makes such an admission.

Consideration of the production set concept, as it is employed, seems to us to raise three critical questions. If "technological knowl-edge" is what defines a firm's capabilities, where in the firm does that knowledge reside? What rationale can be given for the presump-tion that there is a sharp boundary line between what a firm can and cannot do? How does the knowledge possessed by one firm relate to that possessed by others, and to the "state of knowledge" in the soci-ety generally? We consider these questions in turn.

Where does the knowledge reside? As we have already noted, two metaphors dominate the meager discussions in orthodox literature that seek to explicate the basic idea of technological knowledge pos-sessed by a firm. One is the "symbolic records" metaphor—for ex-ample, the notion that the knowledge is stored in a blueprint file. The other is the "knowledge specialist" metaphor—for example, the idea that there is a "chief engineer" to whom the "entrepreneur" looks for a succinct account of the economically relevant aspects of the array of technical possibilities. Although both of these metaphors are suggestive of aspects of the real phenomenon of possession of capabilities by a firm, it seems clear that they are *merely* suggestive and fall far short of being an adequate account of the matter.

Engineering blueprints, and symbolic design records more gener-ally, do not contain an exhaustive account of the methods involved in the actual exercise of a productive capability. As a matter of fact, blueprints often are quite gross descriptions of what to do, and seldom define a detailed job breakdown, much less provide "how to do it" instructions at the job level. As a matter of logical principle, it seems clear that a symbolic record could not provide an exhaustive account of the methods required for its own interpretation; rather, the use of such records presumes the availability of intelligent inter-preters drawing on knowledge not contained in the records them-selves. And as a matter of economics, cost considerations clearly limit the extent to which organizations maintain records of their methods and activities, and the records actually maintained are much less complete than they logically might be.

Similarly, the "chief engineer" metaphor is not viable. It seems inescapable that, in the typical and significant cases, the "knowl-edge" possessed by a firm is not possessed by any single individual within the firm. In the case of a manufacturing establishment of some size and sophistication, it would certainly be unusual if any single individual knew how to perform each and every task in the entire process. This is true even if the "tasks" involved are produc-tive tasks in a narrow sense, and becomes more emphatically so if the tasks include control functions, maintenance, purchasing and mar-keting, and so on. Furthermore, the notion of a collection of describ-able "tasks" obviously falls far short of characterizing what the firm as a functioning entity "knows." What it "knows" includes the system of coordinating relations among the tasks—the relations that combine the tasks into a productive performance.

Thus, the possession of technical "knowledge" is an attribute of the firm as a whole, as an organized entity, and is not reducible to what any single individual knows, or even to any simple aggregation of the various competencies and capabilities of all the various individuals, equipment, and installations of the firm. This observation conforms to the accounts in orthodox textbooks, which rarely mention the "chief engineer" or any other approach to the issues considered here. The usual textbook treatment ascribes the ability effectively to combine inputs to the firm itself, as an actor, and characterizes that ability by the production set. But this approach goes implausibly far: it abstracts the possession of capability *entirely* from the inputs. It postulates a latent capacity to organize that, being totally disembodied from that which is organized, resides in nothing. It would have us believe that there is such a thing as an automobile firm that owns no plant, hires no workers, and produces no automobiles, yet retains the capability to produce automobiles and is ready to do so at the whim of the market.[5] To provide a plausible account of the relations between the capabilities of an organization and the capabilities of individual organization members, giving both the "reductionist" and the "holistic" viewpoints their due, is a major conceptual undertaking—and one that orthodoxy has not yet seriously attempted.

What real considerations could produce a sharp boundary between "technically possible" and "technically impossible" production activities? Certainly, there is no problem with saying that there are some things a firm can do and some it cannot. As an example of the former, we could point to something that the firm is actually doing, and for an example of the latter we could refer to some hypothetical process whose characteristics violate physical law. However, as we have noted, standard usage of the production set concept contemplates a set of intermediate size, a set including (in most cases) more than what is actually done, and (certainly) less than the full range of the physically possible. The boundary is the boundary of knowledge.

Whatever "knowledge" means in the organizational context, the

---

5. It is interesting that J. de V. Graaf, a thoughtful commentator on the interpretation of welfare economics, responded to this difficulty be rejecting the standard approach in favor of the view that "the ultimate repositories of technological knowledge in any society are the men comprising it." His attempt to reconstruct the theory on this basis was, we think, unconvincing, but the intellectual discomfort that motivated it was fully justified. See Graaf, *Theoretical Welfare Economics* (1957, p. 16).

state of knowledge is certainly subject to change. It is subject to change by deliberate choice, as when effort is exerted to discover the answer to a specific question, and it is subject to change by unchosen and unwelcome processes, as when an explosion or breakdown signals the infeasibility of an attempted course of action. It is subject to increase, as when production workers learn "by doing" to do their jobs more efficiently, and to decrease as workers forget the details of tasks they have not recently performed. It may be increased by means trivially cheap, such as a look at the Yellow Pages, or by expensive research and development, as in the design of a new computer system. It may be expanded by drawing on what others already know, as by reading reports or directly observing others' practice, or there may be an expansion of the limits of what is perceived to be physically possible. An attempt to improve it may be a matter of looking up the answer in a source known to contain the answer, or an extended search for a problem solution that may not exist.

Where, in all of these dimensions, are the discontinuities that could plausibly give rise to production sets with sharp boundaries? The production set approach seems to rest, albeit implicitly, on a claim that such discontinuities exist. Only on that assumption is it legitimate to consider the firm's position at the "knowledge margin" fixed while exploring the way changing conditions affect its adjustment at other margins. Only on that assumption does the logic of the firm's choice among known techniques, on which so much effort has been expended, relate to a real subject matter.

How does the knowledge possessed by one firm relate to that of others, and to the knowledge environment generally? As we have noted, the standard orthodox response to this question is simply to ignore it, and to take each firm's production set as "given." This position constitutes a powerful labor-saving device built into the structure of orthodox theory. In standard competitive models, it leaves market prices as the sole channel of causal influence linking the actions of different firms. It thus makes possible the decomposition of the problem of price and output determination into an optimization exercise at the firm level, with prices given, followed by an equilibrium analysis at the market level, with firm supply and demand schedules given. To recognize that nonprice information flows among firms are an important phenomenon is to forgo the intellectual economies afforded by this decomposable structure. But it is also to face reality.

The discussion above of the indefinite boundaries of a firm's knowledge touched briefly on some obvious ways in which firms can augment their own knowledge by reaching out into the environment—into their industry or into society more broadly. Information about the activities and methods of other firms can be obtained by a variety of means—by buying and studying their products; by hiring away their technically expert employees; by reading accounts of their activities in trade journals, reports of securities analysts, and their mandatory filings with government agencies; by hiring consultants who work with the other firms of the industry as well; by reading copies of their patents or the publications of their research scientists; by overt purchase or exchange; or by covert schemes of industrial espionage. None of these methods are so cheap and effective as to make it plausible to assume that anything known to one firm is known to all. None are so expensive or ineffective as to justify an assumption that each individual firm is an island of technological knowledge, complete unto itself. And all of these methods are actually used.

Similarly, the firm can reach out through its R&D activity and otherwise, to the knowledge resources of the society at large. Its research scientists can read the publications of academic and government scientists, as well as those of other industrial researchers. It can learn from its suppliers and its customers. Performing R&D under government contract may provide an opportunity to learn things useful in its market-oriented activities. Acquisition of or merger with another firm can bring whole packages of capability under unified control. And again, these options vary widely in cost and effectiveness, and none are neglected.

Presumably there is no room for dispute concerning the existence of these phenomena, and little room for disputing their importance. Yet in orthodox economic modeling, they are either absent entirely, or, in discussions that admit technological change, treated in an awkward and inhibited fashion. We argued in Chapter 1 that the source of the inhibition is largely to be found in the orthodox commitments to optimization and equilibrium, but perhaps it derives also from an understandable reluctance to confront the complexities of a dynamically evolving, imperfectly defined state of knowledge that changes in response to the behavior of actors throughout the society. Our own efforts in this direction are set forth in Parts IV and V.

3. BEHAVIOR AS MAXIMIZING CHOICE

Given capabilities and objectives, the orthodox explanation of behavior—what firms do, given constraints—runs in terms of maximizing choice. The postulate that firm behavior results from maximizing choice leads the theorist to analyze an optimizing decision rule for the firm, a rule that maps from market conditions and other variables external to the firm to the feasible action that scores highest on the firm's objective function. Both of the terms "maximizing" and "choice" warrant some scrutiny.

Simple textbook treatments generally presume that the actions taken by firms are truly *maximizing* in the sense that, given the circumstances, there are no better actions. However, we stressed earlier that recent sophisticated versions of the theory back off from that presumption. Lags between decision and effective action are recognized, along with the possibility that predictions of what the market will be are not perfect: maximization becomes maximization of expectation. That all potentially available information may not be fully exploited at decision time also is recognized. Maximization must be understood as recognizing information costs as well as other costs.

It is not clear whether the new most complex models of decision making with limited and costly information are intended to capture, as well, the fact of limited information-processing capacity, or the possibility that firms may be wrong in their understanding of the decision problems they face. Some economists seem to believe that models of maximizing behavior under limited information do adequately capture these more general implications of bounded rationality.

We think this is a misconception, and a serious one. In orthodox decision theory, the capacity to *process* information is invariably treated as costless and unlimited in amount; as Marschak and Radner explain, economic man is a perfect mathematician (Marschak and Radner, 1972, p. 315). Among other and more consequential implications, this says that the actors represented in economic theory already know all the theorems ("mere" logical truths) about their behavior that theorists struggle to prove. This affront to realism is not innocuous. It opens the door to full reliance on the notion of a fully preplanned behavior, even in contexts where the level of complexity involved is such as to overwhelm the aggregate capacity of Earth's computers. At the same time, it shuts the door on the study of devices that individuals and organizations actually employ to cope with their severe information-processing constraints—devices that often have a key influence on the actions taken. And it suppresses the role of the firm's own internal organization as a determinant of the effective level of uncertainty to which the firm's actions are subject.

Perhaps the most extensive evidence on this point comes not from the realm of economic activity, but from the history of intelligence failures in international relations. A consistent theme in retrospective studies is that failure occurs not because the intelligence system failed to acquire warning signals but because it failed to process, relate, and interpret those signals into a message relevant to available choices.[6] Difficult conceptual issues are involved in judging the extent to which such failures may be explained by "mistakes," "derelictions of duty," or "irrational behavior." But nothing could be more plainly relevant to their explanation than the fact that intelligence analysts and decision makers have only a limited amount of time each day, limited communication channels to connect their systems, and limited assistance in the task of organizing, analyzing, and *thinking about* the available information. Sometimes, highly "obvious" and emphatic signals get lost in the noise as a result of these limitations. We see no reason to think that economic decision making is any different in this regard.

There is similarly a fundamental difference between a situation in which a decision maker is uncertain about the state of X and a situation in which the decision maker has not given any thought to whether X matters or not, between a situation in which a prethought event judged of low probability occurs and a situation in which something occurs that never has been thought about, between judging an action unlikely to succeed and never thinking about an action. The latter situations in each pair are not adequately modeled in terms of low probabilities. Rather, they are not in the decision maker's considerations at all. To treat them calls for a theory of attention, not a theory that assumes that everthing always is attended to but that some things are given little weight (for objective reasons).

In short, the most complex models of maximizing choice do not come to grips with the problem of bounded rationality. Only metaphorically can a "limited information" model be regarded as a model of decision with limited cognitive capacities. It is inadequate in many contexts because it does not explain or predict how a decision maker actually will behave: the metaphor is then nearly devoid of content. In fact, in most formal theorizing, the simple unsophisticated version of maximization is employed, perhaps augmented by partial recognition of limits on predictive capacities. The firm is visualized as truly optimizing its choices, given constraints and uncertainty.

We now turn our attention to the presumption that behavior is the result of *choice*. Contemporary appreciative theory is comfortably vague about what "choice" means, and the vagueness signals a problem with the concept. Sometimes "choice" refers to a process involving deliberation. But sometimes choice is understood to be involved in the following of a preassigned decision rule without deliberation, the decision rule itself in this usage presumed to be the result of ancestral deliberation. And in some of the more careful de-

---

6. In particular, this is a major theme in Roberta Wohlstetter's excellent study of the Pearl Harbor attack (Wohlstetter, 1962).

fenses of the theoretical use of optimization assumptions, there even is an admission that the firms may *never* go through any explicit calculating deliberation.

It seems useful to distinguish between processes for taking action that do involve a considerable amount of deliberation, and processes that involve more or less mechanical following of a decision rule. One might question whether the latter processes involve much real choosing using the everyday sense of that term. But, more important, if one knew that a certain class of action was the result of individuals following a prescribed decision rule, this would seem to be an interesting fact in itself, regardless of the provenance of the rule. Such information might lead the analyst to study, and perhaps model, the decision rule being employed. Indeed, if it is not assumed that the decision rule is truly a maximizing one, or one that is maximizing within the particular model of the firm being employed by an economist, this would seem the only way to proceed. The analyst might go on to analyze why the decision rule is what it is, the analysis involving some theory of decision rule creation and change. And, from this perspective, it would be interesting to go on to analyze the adequacy of prevailing decision rules and rule-change processes in terms of how well they enable the firm to cope with the circumstances it faces. That is, the decision rules employed by a firm ought to be regarded as an important part of its overall capabilities, in the same sense as the production activities in its production set. In our reading, this is not the perspective that orthodox theory takes regarding, for example, the pricing policies or advertising policies of firms.

As we shall elaborate in the next two chapters, a considerable portion of what is treated as "choice" in traditional theory indeed largely involves following prescribed decision rules. But this is not to deny that in many cases there is a certain—perhaps considerable —amount of deliberation involved. Again, if this is known, it is useful information. It is not useful as evidence in support of a theory that presumes that firms truly maximize something; the difficulty with this theory is the fact that, even if firms explicitly *try* to maximize, they cannot *truly* maximize. Rather, it is useful because it calls attention to the processes of deliberation. An analyst aiming to explain or predict action that is known to have come from processes involving considerable deliberation might want to exploit known aspects of deliberation processes in organizations. It is useful to list several of these.[7]

---

7. For a series of case studies that bring out a number of the points made in the following paragraphs, see March and Olsen (1976).

First, deliberative choice reflects a lack of complete preplanning adequate to the state of affairs. One deliberates about a choice because one has not thought through in advance what one would do under such circumstances, or, if such predeliberation has gone on, because for some reason the particular context has made the preplanning incomplete or inadequate for the present purposes. Deliberation signals problems or opportunities of the present status quo that were at least partly unanticipated.

Second, deliberative choice is contingent: its outcome depends on the special circumstances of the situation in which choices are made. In general, it is particular unanticipated problems or opportunities that trigger deliberation, and the deliberation is focused at least initially on these. But deliberative choice is likely to be influenced also by a broader set of particular circumstances.

Third, deliberative choice is fragmented. The temporal aspect of its fragmentation has already been noted, but in large organizations it is likely to be fragmented as well along lines of organizational authority and responsibility. A variety of differing information bases and organizational interests impinge on different aspects of the same interrelated decision problem. Commitments to a course of action may be made in one group or set of meetings, while crucial information on the risks or costs of that action resides, untapped, in another. The timing or compatibility of intendedly complementary actions may be deficient because responsibility is divided along functional or input-category lines, and within each such area of responsibility there are competing concerns that pull attention and effort away from the joint task. Warnings of unfavorable developments may suffer delay or distortion in communication to higher authority, because they may seem to reflect adversely on the performance of those charged with responsibility in the area in which the problems arise. These and similar categories of difficulties are the classic manifestations of the fragmentation of choice in large organizations, described by organization theorists from a variety of disciplinary perspectives. Theorists of *optimal* organization have made some progress in modeling informational fragmentation, less progress in modeling intraorganizational conflict, negligible progress in representing the realities of personal power and reputation—and have done nothing that departs from the basic assumption of the choice monad: the simultaneous confrontation of all constraints.

Finally, the occasions of choice are often opportunities for the clarification and elaboration of goals. Questions of "what we are trying to accomplish here" often come in for active consideration, not in the mode of logical deduction from premises accepted in the past, but rather in a mode that recognizes the specifics of the choice situation as posing issues of general direction, balance, and tradeoff that had not hitherto been confronted. Since issues of this kind are raised and partially resolved in a sequential, contingent process of choice, there is a sense in which the objectives of an organization are a "path-dependent" historical phenomenon. Even if the underlying motivational picture is constant and starkly drawn—such as "We are in business to make money"—the delineation of objectives in terms sufficiently precise to inform choice is ordinarily deferred to an actual choice situation.

All of these facets indicate that deliberation is a form of economic activity in its own right, constrained by the scarcity of inputs and by the existing state of the "technology" of deliberation. Although the new sophisticated interpretation of maximizing behavior recognizes information costs, it remains committed to a sharp distinction between having and operating an activity or capability, and choosing an action. This fact accounts for some strikingly paradoxical features of orthodoxy's perspective on economic organization and economic change. An improvement in information-processing techniques that is linked to a metal-shaping device—for example, a numerically controlled machine tool—clearly falls under the "technological change" rubric and is quite typical of the sort of thing economists have in mind when they seek to measure technological change. By contrast, an information-processing improvement that is linked to a deliberative process—such as an econometric model of the firm's output market, or a linear programming procedure to help decide which factories should ship to which warehouses—is theoretically invisible to orthodoxy because it is part of the choice process. Similarly, orthodoxy seems incapable of recognizing that different firms may have different ways of making choices. These differences in the processes of deliberating ought to be a central part of the explanation of why firms make different choices.

Similarly, there is a process of implementation that follows real choice and is also a form of economic behavior in its own right, shaped by input scarcity and the state of implementation technology. For example, the choice of a price policy or pricing rule does not actually suffice to get the proper prices into the catalogs, onto the goods, and into the billing system. Sometimes, implementation costs may constitute a major factor in the choice of the price policy itself. The exercise of an organizational capability is involved in implementing a newly decided pricing policy for goods, just as much as in producing them. Similarly, specific capabilities are exercised in the actual carrying out of market transactions, in the processes of internal control, in record keeping, and so on. That these aspects of business behavior go virtually unnoticed in theoretical economics is certainly not attributable to inhibitions about broadening the scope of the production concept: applications of that concept made in the analysis of health, education, and child rearing testify to the weakness of those inhibitions. Neither, certainly, is it the case that the issues involved are so trivial as to make explicit attention by managers or theorists unnecessary—consider, for example, the complexities of the problem of preventing embezzlement by computer. Rather, the reason the production-like aspects of implementation remain virtually hidden from orthodox eyes is that implementation, like deliberation, is so intimately related to choice—and choice is simply something done optimally.

The above discussion suggests that ability to deliberate and implement are elements of a firm's capabilities, just as is its command over a particular technical production process. But if this is so, the sharp separation in orthodox theory between capabilities and choosing becomes suspect. The processes of economic choice, like technical capabilities in a narrower sense, can undergo technological progress or regress. And the questions we have raised about the knowledge that underlies capabilities are as relevant to capabilities for choosing as they are to capabilities for producing. In particular, the proposition that the limits of a firm's capabilities are not sharply defined is relevant to both. A firm may be uncertain of its judgmental and deliberative competence in a given area of activity just as it may be uncertain about its technical competence, and a variety of ways of improving its capabilities are open to it.

4

Skills

THE PRECEDING CHAPTER explored the triad of ideas that underlie orthodox explanations of why firms do what they do—objectives, choice sets, behavior as maximizing choice. This chapter begins the task of developing the basic postulates about behavior in evolutionary theory. Although our theory is concerned with the behavior of business firms and other organizations, we find it useful to begin the analysis with a discussion of some aspects of individual behavior. An obvious reason for doing so is that the behavior of an organization is, in a limited but important sense, reducible to the behavior of the individuals who are members of that organization. Regularities of individual behavior must therefore be expected to have consequences, if not counterparts, at the organizational level. More directly relevant to our development here is the value of individual behavior as a *metaphor* for organizational behavior: the idea that "individuals are complex organizations too" has considerable power. And the indirect approach to organizational behavior, by way of this metaphor, has the advantage that the discussion can be based to a large extent on the empirical data of everyday observation and introspection.

Because our real concern is with organizations, we make no attempt to be balanced and comprehensive in our discussion of individual behavior. Rather, we highlight those aspects of the subject that provide, in our view, the most helpful introduction and truest guide to phenomena at the organizational level. Even in the pursuit of that objective, we depart somewhat from a balanced appraisal in the direction of attempting to compensate for the biases of the orthodox treatment of the subject. Our attention is drawn to example situations that tend to reveal the inadequacies of orthodox conceptual categories at the same time as they illustrate the relevance of the categories we propose. We neglect the areas where the orthodox view is informative and fruitful; were we to consider those areas in detail, we would argue that the evolutionary scheme subsumes the orthodox one and delineates its proper uses.

Specifically, the focus of this chapter is on the skilled behavior of individuals. We propose that individual skills are the analogue of organizational routines, and that an understanding of the role that routinization plays in organizational functioning is therefore obtainable by considering the role of skills in individual functioning. We do not, of course, suggest that the concept of skill is the *unique* key to individual behavior, but it is a very important key. Routinization is relatively more important as a feature of organizational behavior than skill is as a feature of individual behavior, but it is still less than the whole story. In both realms, close examination of the nature of skillful/routinized behavior brings to light the shortcomings of optimization notions as an approach to understanding the basis of the effective functioning of an individual/organization in an environment.

By a "skill" we mean a capability for a smooth sequence of coordinated behavior that is ordinarily effective relative to its objectives, given the context in which it normally occurs. Thus, the ability to serve a tennis ball well is a skill, as is the ability to engage in competent carpentry, drive a car, operate a computer, set up and solve a linear programming model, or judge which job candidate to hire. The first few of these skills might be regarded by orthodox theory as capabilities in a choice set; the last few are intimately involved with the act of choosing. We emphasize that these skills have many characteristics in common, regardless of whether we think of them as capabilities or choice behavior.

In the first place skills are programmatic, in that they involve a sequence of steps with each successive step triggered by and following closely on the completion of the preceding one. Second, the knowledge that underlies a skillful performance is in large measure tacit knowledge, in the sense that the performer is not fully aware of the details of the performance and finds it difficult or impossible to articulate a full account of those details. Third, the exercise of a skill often involves the making of numerous "choices"—but to a considerable extent the options are selected automatically and without awareness that a choice is being made.

These three aspects of skilled behavior are closely interrelated. If, for example, it were *not* the case that behavior options are selected "automatically" in the course of the exercise of a skill, then the performance as a whole would not have the quality of being a connected, unitary "program." And the difficulty of articulating the basis for such automatic choices forms an important part of the total problem of explaining how the performance is accomplished. Nevertheless, the three aspects are conceptually distinguishable, have been emphasized in different degrees by different authors in the past, and play somewhat different roles in our own account of individual and organizational behavior. We therefore discuss them separately.

1. SKILLS AS PROGRAMS

A variety of terms have been used in the literature of social science to denote a smooth sequence of behavior that functions, in some sense, as an effective unit. "Skill" is obviously one such; there is, in particular, a substantial psychological literature relating to skills and skill learning. The terms "plan," "script," "habit," "routine," and "program" have also been used to name either the same concept or a very closely related one. But there are obvious differences in connotation among these terms, and exploration of these various connotations can be informative.

To think of skills as programs is to evoke the image of a computer program. Clearly, the development of the modern electronic computer and its associated software has had an important and widely diffused influence on theoretical thinking about the phenomena that concern us here.[1] Computer programs that simulate complex, patterned behaviors have been developed over a wide range of human and organizational activity. These efforts have shown, above all, that the logical processes of a digital computer can mimic very "skillful" and "intelligent" behaviors, at least in the sense of providing a sufficient account of numerous observable aspects of such behavior. Here, however, we will not review specific examples of this sort of research, but will consider only the broad parallels between skills and (computer) programs.

The following features of computer programs are analogous to, and instructive regarding, corresponding features of human skills. First, a program functions as a unit, and its execution is ordinarily a

---

1. For discussions of the influence of cybernetic theory and computer modeling on psychology, see Miller, Galanter, and Pribam (1960, ch. 3) and Newell and Simon (1972, historical addendum, esp. pp. 878–882).

highly complex performance relative to the actions required to initiate the performance. Second, although loops and "go to" statements and conditional branching statements complicate the picture, the basic organization scheme of a program is serial. There is a beginning and an end (or at least there is supposed to be an end). Also, resumption following an unplanned interruption of program execution is often problematic, and it is easier to start over from the beginning than it is to complete the partial performance. Third, considering that it is performed by an automaton, it is clear that the execution of a computer program is literally "automatic." Finally, the speed and accuracy with which an appropriately programmed computer accomplishes its task are often considered impressive. One standard of "impressiveness" may be human performance on the same task, but perhaps a more useful standard from the point of view of the informativeness of the analogy would be the performance that could be achieved using the computer but not the program—that is, by directly commanding each individual step.

The points about skills implied in the above statements about programs are largely self-evident, but some brief elaboration may be useful. As regards "functioning as a unit," it may be noted that, for both programs and skills, there are recognizable "units" at various levels of organization. Larger units are organized complexes of smaller ones, in which the latter may nevertheless retain some individuality. Thus, for even a moderately proficient touch-typist, the typing of words like "the," "and," "here," "in," and "as" is executable at a stroke, while "sincerely yours" is both a unit and a two-unit complex. Probably very few typists have fingers for which "antidisestablishmentarianism" is a familiar rhythm; nevertheless, a skilled typist will break that word into familiar units and thereby execute it much more quickly than a novice can. Typing skill also serves to illustrate the point about serial organization—essentially, that the order in which component units of a skill are executed is a significant fact about the structure of the skill itself. A typist who can rattle off "through" without a thought is likely to have to slow down and pay attention to type "hguorht," or even "ughthro."

Skilled human performance is automatic in the sense that most of the details are executed without conscious volition. Indeed, a welcome precursor of success in an effort to acquire a new skill is the diminishing need to attend to the details. And it is a familiar fact that attempting to attend to the details often has a disruptive effect: in many competitive situations in athletics, the arts, and other spheres, success depends importantly on the ability of the performer to "stay loose" and "not clutch"—that is, to resist the pressures that might cause destructive attention to intrude into the details of the performance.[2] It is not uncommon for a performer who is particularly noted for this ability to be compared, approvingly, to a computer or other machine.

Although "impressiveness" is obviously a matter of degree and relative to expectation, only the most phlegmatic can escape being impressed, at some point, by a skillful performance. Indeed, "world class" performances in a variety of intellectual, artistic, and athletic pursuits often fall in the range of the "awesome" rather than that of the merely impressive. In such cases, of course, one is led to speculate about the role that the basic mental and physical equipment of the performer plays in high skill. For this reason, it is perhaps more relevant to our concerns to consider the reaction of the novice to the moderately skilled tennis player, skier, pianist, or solver of differential equations. At least for an observer unjaded by exposure to superstars, performances made possible by a few years of lessons and regular practice are often highly impressive—and depressing, because illustrative of a goal that seems unattainable. This gap between a skilled performer and a novice with the same "basic equipment" is the analogue of the difference between having the computer and also the right program for the task, and having the computer only.

2. Skills and Tacit Knowing

The late scientist-philosopher Michael Polanyi wrote extensively of the central place in the general scheme of human knowledge occupied by knowledge that cannot be articulated—tacit knowledge. On the simple observation "We know more than we can tell," Polanyi built an entire philosophical system (Polanyi, 1967, p. 4). Though the full import of "tacit knowing" in Polanyi's philosophy can only be hinted at by examples of what would ordinarily be called "skills," such examples do provide familiar and compelling illustrations of phenomena of broad significance. In fact, in Polanyi's *Personal Knowledge* (1962), the discussion of skills (ch. 4) plays a role analogous to our own discussion here. It provides a useful perspective on other realms of knowledge—in his case, that of scientific knowledge; in ours, that of organizational capability.

To be able to do something, and at the same time be unable to explain how it is done, is more than a logical possibility—it is a common situation. Polanyi offers a good example early in his discus-

---

2. Of course, the skilled performer must also avoid the opposite error of being too relaxed and "losing his concentration." But the concentration required is on the objective of the performance at each moment, not on the details of the procedure.

sion of skills: "I shall take as my clue for this investigation the well-known fact *that the aim of a skillful performance is achieved by the observance of a set of rules which are not known as such to the person following them.* For example, the decisive factor by which the swimmer keeps himself afloat is the manner by which he regulates his respiration; he keeps his bouyancy at an increased level by refraining from emptying his lungs when breathing out and by inflating them more than usual when breathing in; yet this is not generally known to swimmers" (Polanyi, 1962, p. 49).

The difficulty of explaining the basis of a skilled performance comes to the fore in the teaching or learning of skills. Polanyi's swimming example suggests that in some cases the difficulty may arise from the fact that the "instructor" is quite unaware of the key principles, and that he actually serves less to instruct than to detect and reward randomly occurring improvements in performance. In other cases, the instructor may be able, or at least be subjectively confident that he is able, to explain the matter in detail. But the detailed instruction offered typically consists of a list of subskills to be executed in sequence, and the instructions neither convey the ability to perform the subskills with requisite efficiency nor assure the smooth integration of those subskills into the main skill. This point is emphasized by Miller, Galanter, and Pribam, commenting on a description of how to land an airplane: "When skillfully elaborated and executed it will serve to get pilot and craft safely back to earth. It is a short paragraph and could be memorized in a few minutes, but it is doubtful whether the person who memorized it could land a plane, even under ideal weather conditions. In fact, it seems likely that someone could learn all the individual acts that are required in order to execute the Plan, and still be unable to land successfully. The separate motions, the separate parts of the Plan, must be fused together to form a skilled performance. Given the description of what he is supposed to do, the student still faces the major task of learning how to do it" (Miller, Galanter, and Pribam, 1960, pp. 82–83).

Instruction in a skill typically consists in large part of the imposition of a discipline of practice, a portion of which is supervised by the instructor. Verbal instruction is included, but is predominantly in the form of critique of practice. Illustration by the instructor and (attempted) imitation by the learner is often employed as an alternative mode to verbal instruction and critique. As Miller et al. indicate, verbal instruction by itself—the information in the "how-to-do-it" book—provides only a starting point at best for the acquisition of the skill. Possession of such a book—the articulable portion of the knowledge involved—may be indicative of ambition to learn, but it certainly does not certify possession of the skill.

The limitations of verbal instruction are even more apparent when the learner is attempting to reacquire a skill that has become rusty. Only in extreme cases does the how-to-do-it book prove useful in the reacquisition of a rusty skill. The remnant of the skill itself, lying latent in the brain, is typically more helpful as a restarting point than any collection of more words could be. What is needed is renewed practice and constructive criticism, not the beginner's handbook.

These propositions do not relate only to psychomotor skills. With minor modification, they extend to the realm of specific cognitive skills such as facility in mathematical manipulation of a particular type, the ability to solve the theoretical exercises characteristic of a certain area and method of scientific inquiry, or the ability to generate good solutions to complex production scheduling problems. The manipulation of equations in elementary algebra will serve as an example. Clearly, the axioms of the real number system together with a relatively short list of problem-solving heuristics (like "isolate the unknown") do constitute, in a sense, an articulated account of the skill involved. Equally clearly, the skilled manipulator in action has little or no conscious awareness of this articulated characterization of his activity. He does not think "distributive law—rearrange terms—factor out X" and so on, but simply "perceives" productive transformations of the expression and carries them out, often making several transformations at once in the course of rewriting the expression. There is, in Polanyi's terms, only "subsidiary awareness" of the rules being employed, whereas there is "focal awareness" of the expression manipulated.

It seems clear that the "tacitness" of a skill, or rather of the knowledge underlying a skill, is a matter of degree. Words are probably a more effective vehicle for communicating the skills of elementary algebra than for those of carpentry, and more effective for carpentry than for gymnastic stunts. Also, a trait that distinguishes a good instructor is the ability to discover introspectively, and then articulate for the student, much of the knowledge that ordinarily remains tacit. The same knowledge, apparently, is more tacit for some people than for others. Incentives, too, clearly matter: when circumstances place a great premium on effective articulation, remarkable things can sometimes be accomplished. For example, it has been established in occasional emergency situations that it is not impossible to convey by radioed verbal commands enough information on how to fly a small plane so that a person who lacks a pilot's skills can bring the plane in for a landing.[3]

---

3. This observation runs somewhat contrary to the statement of Miller, Galanter, and Pribam quoted above. But it is clear that a pilot who entirely lacks tacit knowledge of how to land is a pilot with whom one would prefer not to ride.

As we observed previously, a variety of terms have been used in the social science literature to refer to concepts closely related to "skill." It is interesting and somewhat curious that the array of terms employed in this connection includes several whose connotations are to a degree *adverse* to tacitness. The above passage from Miller, Galanter, and Pribam is indicative of the fact that their notion of a "Plan" is intimately related to the usual idea of a skill, and also to the idea that words may not suffice to communicate a plan. Yet the word itself, in ordinary usage, usually refers to something that is articulable and capable of being represented symbolically. A similar observation holds for "program," a term favored by March and Simon, among others.

Schank and Abelson employ the term "script" to refer to "a structure that describes appropriate sequences of events in a particular context, . . . a predetermined, stereotyped sequence of actions that defines a well-known situation" (Schank and Abelson, 1977, p. 41). As with "plan," the connotations of "script" clearly favor the notion that the knowledge involved can be articulated. Nevertheless, scripts turn out to resemble skills rather closely, as the reference to "stereotyped sequence" suggests. To the extent that there is a distinction, the key to it lies in the fact that Schank and Abelson are concerned above all with the process by which natural language is understood. This concern entails a focus upon the successful use of language: the inquiry relates to how this is accomplished in human beings and how it might be accomplished by a computer. A vast realm of tacit knowledge is nevertheless implied by the computer programs that Schank and Abelson devise to represent the processes of understanding. They are well aware of, but do not focus upon, the fact that these programs imply a great deal of information processing that is not part of the conscious activity of a human being who is trying to understand. Indeed, were it *not* the case that the inferential processes they attempt to model are imperfectly accessible to conscious thought, the modeling task would be trivial and unworthy of the attention they bestow upon it. Thus, it seems that their approach to understanding of language does parallel Polanyi's characterization of skill as involving "the observance of a set of rules which are not known as such to the person following them."

In an important sense, the researcher who is attempting to build a computer model of human psychological processes is in a position analogous to that of a student attempting to learn a skill from an instructor. Both are betting that language can serve to communicate useful guidance to the underlying structure and details of a complex performance: the student seeks such guidance from his instructor and the researcher seeks it from his subject or, introspectively, from himself. Both would like to know how the thing is really done, the student for the sake of being able to do it and the researcher for the sake of being able to explain how it is done. Both are aware that, to the extent they experience difficulty in achieving their goals, language is an imperfect tool for conveying the information they need. Language can communicate a framework, but a great deal of filling-in remains to be done after the resources of language are exhausted; much of the filling-in involves laborious trial-and-error search. Perhaps both the student and the researcher tend to suffer from ambivalence regarding the limitations of language. Both hope that words will smooth their individual paths to achievement; both know that there is no distinction in the achievement if the path is too smooth.

For many reasons, it is important to try to identify the determinants of the "degree of tacitness"—that is, the considerations that make tacit knowledge a more important part of the picture in some cases than in others. As a preliminary step in this direction, we will consider here the sources from which the limits on the articulation of knowledge derive. Such limits seem to arise in three distinguishable ways.

There is, first of all, a limit imposed by the feasible time rate of information transfer through symbolic communication, which may be well below the rate necessary or appropriate in the actual performance. In the case of serving a tennis ball or performing a gymnastic stunt, the law of gravity imposes a tight constraint on the rate at which critical portions of the maneuver are performed. Thus, although step-by-step description is possible, and pretrial instruction and posttrial criticism are both helpful, it is not realistic to offer detailed instruction *during* an attempt. And although the learner can attempt to store pretrial instruction in memory and consciously retrieve it as the action is performed, the effectiveness of this tactic is severely limited by the speed and simultaneity of the information processing required. Ultimately, therefore, the learner has to work out the details of the coordination problem for himself. His knowledge of those details remains tacit, is recollected without conscious awareness, and is probably no more susceptible to articulation than his instructor's corresponding knowledge was.

Time-rate considerations also figure, though in a somewhat different way, in learning touch typing or piano playing. In these cases, it is at least possible to enhance the role of articulation and of conscious awareness by slowing the time rate of the performance, and this fact is commonly exploited in learning. Nevertheless, the details of an *accomplished* performance are tacit: it is not the case that one can learn to perform the task on the "slow" setting and then simply push the "fast" button to produce an expert performance.

A second consideration that limits the articulation of the knowledge underlying a skill is the limited *causal depth* of the knowledge. Polanyi's swimming example illustrates the point that possession of a skill does not require theoretical understanding of the basis of the skill. In fact, it seems quite clear for all psychomotor skills that the actual mode of storage of the knowledge in the nervous system makes no use of the terms in which physicists, physiologists, and psychologists would describe the skilled performance. Yet this does not imply that an attempt to *articulate* the basis of the skill would not benefit from the availability of this terminology. Perhaps some novice swimmers would be helped by Polanyi's brief explanation of the body's buoyancy. More generally, we may note that a skilled performance takes place in a context defined by the values of a wide range of variables relevant to the performance; these may include aspects of the performer's physical state, as well as conditions of air pressure and lighting, gravitational forces, and so forth. The performer need not be aware of the existence of all of these variables, let alone of their relevance to the performance. This means that the performer simply relies upon these variables being in acceptable ranges, and is in no position to describe what it is that he relies upon. Should the values of some of the variables change so that the constraints are violated, the limited causal depth of the knowledge involved will impede or prevent effective adjustment to the change.

The third aspect of the limitation of articulation is the *coherence* aspect—that of the whole versus the parts. Efforts to articulate "complete" knowledge of something by exhaustive attention to details and thorough discussion of preconditions succeed only in producing an incoherent message. This difficulty is probably rooted to a substantial extent in the related facts of the linear character of language-based communication, the serial character of the "central processor" of the human brain, and the relatively limited capacity of human short-term memory. Given these facts, the possibilities of articulating both the details and the coherent patterns they form— the relationships among the details—are necessarily limited. At a given point in a text, a passage is encountered in a context established by nearby passages; to convey the fact that it is also meaningfully connected to other parts of the text requires more words, and places demands on the reader's memory. Similarly, it is difficult to form coherent three-dimensional mental images from exposures to a number of two-dimensional cross-sections of an object. To cope with these limitations of human powers of articulation and symbolic information processing, a variety of aids are employed that present information about patterns and structures directly to the eyes—aids such as photographs, diagrams, graphs, flowcharts, and holograms. There is a rapidly advancing technology of such aids.

In short, much operational knowledge remains tacit because it cannot be articulated fast enough, because it is impossible to articulate all that is necessary to a successful performance, and because language cannot simultaneously serve to describe relationships and characterize the things related. This observation provides us with at least a starting point for assessing the relative significance of tacit knowledge in different situations. The knowledge contained in the how-to-do-it book and its various supplements and analogues tends to be more adequate when the pace of the required performance is slow and pace variations are tolerable, where a standardized, controlled context for the performance is somehow assured, and where the performance as a whole is truly reducible to a set of simple parts that relate to one another only in very simple ways. To the extent that these conditions do not hold, the role of tacit knowledge in the performance may be expected to be large.

Finally, it should be emphasized that costs matter. Whether a particular bit of knowledge is *in principle* articulable or necessarily tacit is not the relevant question in most behavioral situations. Rather, the question is whether the costs associated with the obstacles to articulation are sufficiently high so that the knowledge *in fact* remains tacit.

3. SKILLS AND CHOICES

While the exercise of a skill involves the selection of behavior options, the selection process is highly automatic. This raises the question of whether it is at all appropriate to discuss this process in terms of "choice." In the terminology of the previous chapter, the sort of choice that takes place in the process of exercising a skill is choice without deliberation. To the extent that the conceptual baggage carried by the term "choice" includes a lot of things that are associated with deliberation, it may be quite misleading when applied to the automatic choices involved in skills. As we noted, orthodox theoretical discussion is inconsistent and ambiguous on whether choice involves deliberation, but it is quite clear in maintaining that there is a sharp distinction between capability and choice behavior. The two issues are obviously related: the choice among behavior options that takes place in the exercise of a skill typically involves no deliberation *and* it is a constituent of the capability that the skill represents. These issues are deep and important ones.

From one point of view, *all* of the coordinated sequential behavior involved in the exercise of a skill is chosen behavior. A large range of available alternative behaviors is continually being rejected in favor of the behavior sequence called for in the program. When a driver makes the small adjustments of the steering wheel required to keep his car on an approximately straight path down the road, he "chooses" not to let the car drift off the road, and also "chooses" not to turn the wheel abruptly and throw the car into a skid. When he decelerates as he catches up to a car in front of him, he "chooses" not to maintain his speed and crash into the rear of that car.

However, any experienced driver can attest on the basis of introspection that these and many other micro-units of driving skill are normally selected and performed entirely without attention or awareness. The conscious mind may be devoted to looking for a street sign, planning the day's activity, or carrying on a conversation while these "choices" are being made. That this phenomenon of programmed choice is of the essence of driving skill becomes apparent when the contrasting case of the student driver is considered: it is the novice who really *chooses* not to drive off the edge of the road—if "really choosing" means "paying attention to what is desired and deliberately acting to accomplish what is desired." The skilled driver does not (deliberately) choose to keep the vehicle on the road, but merely accomplishes this result incidental to a choice to exercise his driving skill for the purpose of getting from one place to another.

In general, choice plays a larger role in the selection of large units of behavior than of small ones. The action of directing the car onto the northbound on-ramp of a freeway is more likely to involve choice than the multitude of shallow turns involved in negotiating a straight stretch of road. But this generalization must be qualified very significantly by reference to the *frequency* with which the unit of behavior occurs. For example, if the turn onto the northbound on-ramp is part of the regular commuting trip to work, it may have a degree of automaticity approaching that involved in the microskills of control of the car. Such automaticity reflects, of course, the fact that the turn onto the ramp is but a component in the macroskill "driving to work"; it is accomplished in a "programmed" way in its normal place in that larger sequence of behavior.

The picture is further complicated by the fact that particular units of behavior, of whatever scale, are not assigned permanently and uniquely to the categories "chosen" and "automatic." Rather, circumstances affecting the immediate goals and attention allocation of the performer are an important determinant of whether a particular unit is run off automatically, or as a result of deliberate choice. A driver's selection of the speed of his vehicle may be a choice made in response to posted limits, with conscious reflection on the probabilities of speed traps and on the costs and benefits of alternative times of arrival at his destination. But speed is also subject to automatic adjustment in response to traffic density, driving conditions, and other influences. The driver may choose to pay attention to his speed—that is, he may choose to choose his speed—but he may also let speed selection occur automatically, just as he keeps the car on the road automatically. An important possibility, especially for a driver who has recently had a speeding ticket, is that he may choose to *try* to choose his speed *and fail:* his automatic responses may take over in spite of his intentions. Similarly, to revert to our previous example, a driver may find himself going up the on-ramp "on the way to work" when it is actually Saturday morning and he had intended to go to the hardware store.

There are corresponding points to be made about the relation of a skilled performance to its preconditions. We noted above that such a performance takes place in a context set by the values of a large number of variables; the effectiveness of the performance depends on those variables being in appropriate ranges. The performer typically relies, without conscious thought, on the constraints being satisfied. In some cases, and certainly when the existence of the constraints is unknown to the performer, there may be no practical alternative to such unconsidered reliance. In other cases, the performer may have occasion to worry about possible difficulties and perhaps be led to consider adjustments in the performance, or to forgo it altogether. For example, a driver normally relies on the effective functioning of the braking system, but worries about brake failure may sometimes receive conscious attention and there may then be a choice between normal reliance and doing something about the possible problem. As in the case of selection of behavior options, contingencies of intention and attention will determine where, in the enormous range of preconditions that might conceivably fail, occasional worries rise to consciousness.

We may now take stock of the relations of skills and choice. The picture is complex, but in general it seems to contrast sharply with the emphasis that orthodoxy gives to choice in the explanation of behavior, and also with its insistence on a strict conceptual distinction between capability and choice. Skills are deep channels in which behavior normally runs smoothly and effectively. It is far from the case that behavior must take a unique course, but the reconciliation of smoothness and effectiveness with the availability of numerous options is accomplished by making option selection largely automatic. Skillful acts of selection from the available options are constituents of the main skill itself: they are "choices" embedded in a capability.[4] Deliberate choice plays a narrowly circumscribed role,

---

4. March and Simon (1958, pp. 26, 141–142) and Schank and Abelson (1977, pp. 42–57) are explicit on the point that the entities they respectively call "programs" and

limited under normal circumstances to the selection of the large-scale behavior sequence to be initiated. This suppression of choice is certainly associated with, and is probably a *condition* for, the smoothness and effectiveness that skilled behavior confers. On the other hand, it is possible for choice to intrude into the skilled performance. Option selections that are normally automatic may be made deliberately, or behavior may be diverted entirely from the deep channels of skill. The modification of skilled performance by deliberate choice greatly expands the potential diversity, flexibility, and adaptability of behavior—but always at an opportunity cost in terms of forgone uses of conscious attention, and usually at the cost of introducing some hesitation and awkwardness into an otherwise smooth flow of behavior.

Thus, there is in a sense a tradeoff between capability and deliberate choice, a tradeoff imposed ultimately by the fact that rationality is bounded. The advantages of skill are attained by suppressing deliberate choice, confining behavior to well-defined channels, and reducing option selection to just another part of the program. There are attendant risks that the thing done well may be the wrong thing, or that unnoticed contextual abnormalities may be rendering the performance ineffective or irrelevant. There are, on the other hand, advantages to being open-minded, deliberate, and wary in the choice of actions at all levels of detail—but there are attendant risks of being tardy, poorly coordinated, and unskillful in action itself.

4. THE USES OF SKILL NAMES

Skills, like computer programs, govern performances that are complex relative to the actions that are required to initiate them. The manifold coordinated details of the performance seem to take care of themselves once the decision to exercise the skill is made and a few initial steps are taken. This differential in complexity between initiation and the full performance is mirrored in the use of language to describe and discuss skills. It is, as we have emphasized, difficult or impossible to use language to characterize the "inner workings" of a skill, but words serve quite well in thinking and communicating about skills considered as units of purposive behavior. We make effective use of skill names and skill-related verbs in planning and

---

"scripts" do not determine *unique* sequences of behavior, but rather are complex entities involving numerous options, dependencies on environmental cues, and embedded "choices."

problem solving, and rarely reflect on the extreme complexity of the actual behaviors that these symbols represent.

If we are planning a trip from New Haven to Boston, and going by car is one of the transportation options, we consider that option with very little regard to the "overwhelming" magnitude of the information-processing task involved in driving the car—ordinarily, it suffices to assure ourselves that at least one of the potential occupants of the vehicle knows how to drive. If we are remodeling the kitchen, we may plan to hire the services of a plumber, a carpenter, and an electrician, and we care that we hire "good ones" and do not pay too much—but we do not concern ourselves with the detailed structure of these complex skills and their relationship to the particular problems posed by the kitchen plan. If we are bothered by a vision problem it is helpful to know the meaning of "ophthalmologist" and "optician," but the relevant meaning is the "what for" meaning, not the "how to" meaning that is known to the possessors of these skills.

Of course, planning and problem solving are skills in their own right. There are detailed behavioral programs for planning specific sorts of activities, and more loosely defined problem-solving skills of broader applicability. In the exercise of these cognitive skills, an important role is played by language and, in particular, by the names of other skills that may or may not be possessed by the planner or problem solver. This observation leads to an important distinction regarding the scope of the capabilities possessed by an individual —namely, the distinction between "knowing how to do X" and "knowing how to get X accomplished." Given an appropriate environment, and the resources and skills required for implementation of plans in that environment, an effective planner can get a lot of things accomplished that he does not personally know how to do. One does not need to be an ophthalmologist or an optician to get new glasses prescribed and made. However, even in this simple case the problem of getting the desired result accomplished may be quite difficult for a planner who does not have command of the relevant vocabulary of skill names.[5] In cases where the required vocabulary is larger and more esoteric, the planning difficulties associated with the lack of that vocabulary are correspondingly greater.

Thus, the planning vocabulary of an individual is an important determinant of the range of things that the individual can get accom-

---

5. At least in the opinion of many ophthalmologists, public understanding of the distinction between "ophthalmologist" and "optometrist" is sufficiently shaky so that many individuals with vision problems (as opposed to "needs for new glasses") do not receive appropriate care.

plished. That there exist people in the economy who could perform a task that one cannot perform oneself is of little help unless one knows how to locate such a person for the purpose of arranging a transaction, and such a quest is difficult to pursue effectively unless one knows or can discover the name of the skill or capability one is seeking. But vocabulary is clearly only one variable among many that affect the ability to get things accomplished, and the vocabulary variable interacts subtly with the others. We have noted that all skills are context-dependent in various ways, but the effectiveness of planning and implementation skills is particularly dependent upon detailed features of the *social* context.

For one thing, the "right" vocabulary is itself socially defined. The word that it is really important to know may be the heading under which the required capability is listed in the Yellow Pages. Or the key feature of the social context may be an organization of which the individual is a member, and the vocabulary the individual needs to command may be the specialized planning vocabulary of that organization. In a great many situations—such as getting a car repaired —the effectiveness of planning and implementation by an individual who will not ultimately do the thing himself is considerably enhanced by possession of some level of the required skill, as a complement to knowledge of the skill name. The extent to which this is the case depends on social arrangements affecting such things as the degree of standardization of services performed, the costs of verifying performance, certification arrangements, interpersonal trust, and the definition and enforcement of contractual obligations. If the service performed is of a standardized type, if the requisite quality of performance is sharply defined and easily verified, and if the performer is clearly and effectively liable for the consequences of deficiencies in his performance, a simple market purchase of the service is likely to be a satisfactory means of implementation for a planner who knows only the name of the service he needs to buy. Where these conditions are absent and the planner is not protected by certification and trust from the possible incompetence or opportunism of the performer, he may have to concern himself with the details of the performance in an effort to assure that he gets what he needs at a reasonable price. To be useful, such concern needs to be guided by normative standards for the details—by knowledge of *how* the thing should be done.

Obviously, it would be nice if social arrangements involving standardization, certification, and so forth could be further elaborated so as to sharpen and assure the meanings of skill names. This would promote efficiency through the division of labor, by relieving planner-purchasers of the need to concern themselves with the details of the skilled performances they obtain from others. Unfortunately, skills really are complex, and there are intrinsic limits to the extent to which effective planning can be conducted by manipulating a limited vocabulary of symbols representing these complex entities, limits that are particularly stringent when the planning relates to novel circumstances. We now turn to an examination of the sources of these intrinsic limits.

5. Ambiguity of Scope

Performance of a complex skill involves, we have remarked, the integration of a number of more elementary units of action. Often, these more elementary units constitute subskills that are optional components of the main skill, selected in response to cues in the performer's environment. Thus, the integration required is not just a matter of the relation of the subskills to one another, but also of their relation to information arising from the environment. Further, the same observations apply to the subskills: they involve integration of still more elementary units, or "subsubskills," and the integration may again involve relations with the environment as well as within the units. Continuing this descent through the hierarchical structure of the main skill, one comes ultimately to a domain of neurological and physiological considerations for which the "subskill" terminology is not really appropriate—but reducibility to still more elementary units of action remains possible.

Because skills are such complex, structured entities, and also because of the considerations that limit the articulation of the knowledge applied in a skillful performance, there is inevitably some ambiguity regarding the scope of a skill. This ambiguity has two aspects. There is, first of all, what may be termed *operational* ambiguity. It involves predictive uncertainty as to what a particular individual who possesses "the skill" can actually accomplish in an attempt to exercise that skill under particular circumstances. The second aspect is the *semantic* ambiguity of the skill name, the uncertainty regarding the denotation of the term. Operational ambiguity is obviously one source of semantic ambiguity: to be uncertain about whether a particular electrician, functioning as an electrician, will be able to bring about a desired result under particular circumstances is to be a bit vague about what it means to be an electrician. What is more important, semantic ambiguity arises in discussions that abstract from the particular possessor of the skill and the particular circumstances of its exercise. Uncertainty about what an electrician is arises in large part from the diversity of electricians and the diversity of tasks and circumstances involved in the exercise of the skills of an electrician.

Both sorts of ambiguity are subject to reduction by deliberate effort to that end. By considering the past performances of a particular possessor of the skill, and the characteristics of the particular circumstances in question in relation to those that surrounded the past performances, it may be possible to sharpen predictions concerning the specific instance. By extending the discussion to subskills, particular tasks, and quality differentials among possessors of the skill, some of the ambiguity that surrounds the generic skill name can be eliminated. However, neither of these sorts of clarification is costless, and neither can be totally effective. Both require detailed knowledge of the skill in terms of the mix of subskills involved, the preconditions of effective performance, and so forth. To the extent that this sort of knowledge is tacit, only a person who possesses the skill himself is likely to be in a position to reduce ambiguity by the methods described. To the extent that there are preconditions for effective performance that are simply unknown, or that the tacit knowledge underlying actual performance cannot be brought to bear on the more abstract tasks of assessment and prediction, some part of the ambiguity is simply irremediable.

To amplify these points somewhat, consider again the example of the ability to drive a car. This skill is not just the ability to make the vehicle follow a desired course with acceptable accuracy, but also the ability to use a wide range of cues in the environment—other vehicles, traffic signs and lights, and so on—as the basis for determining the details of the course itself. The integration and coordination involved in the skilled performance as a whole is not merely of the sort represented in taking a curve smoothly through the coordination of pressure on the accelerator and turning of the wheel, but also the relatively automatic use of a large store of information as the basis for interpretive intermediation of sensory input and muscular response. In ordinary discussion about driving, we have little occasion to attend to the complexity of the skill and the implications of that complexity for the variability of specific driving performances across individuals and across situations. We treat the ability to drive as a dichotomous variable, assuming that the skill is possessed in satisfactory degree or not at all, and regard driver training as a process that transfers individuals from the "unskilled" category to the "skilled." This way of talking and thinking about driving skill is typically adequate and we have no need to belabor the complexities and distinctions of the matter. Occasionally, though, distinctions are confronted. If a teenage son or daughter is planning a trip with friends, we may concern ourselves with experience levels, attitudes toward taking chances, and specific experience with passing on two-lane roads. We may need someone to run an errand and have only a stick-shift car available, and confront the question of whether the assembled "drivers" include anyone who can shift gears. In such cases, we drop our habitual, implicit homogenization of driving skill and—with the aid of a good many additional words—articulate the distinctions that concern us regarding subskill mixes and so forth.

Sometimes, however, highly relevant distinctions escape conscious consideration or effective articulation. Adverse effects on performance may arise from causes that do not announce themselves. The ability to control a skid on an icy road will not come in for timely consideration if it is not expected that the roads will be icy. What is not identified cannot be considered, and what is not anticipated cannot be considered in advance. But even fully identifiable and anticipated causes of performance change can resist *effective* consideration because of the tacit basis of skill. Consider the American driver who, after the overnight flight to London, confronts for the first time the problem of driving on the left, in an unfamiliar vehicle with the steering wheel on the right. It may be clear enough, in advance of the trip, that the combination of jet lag, fatigue, and unfamiliar task environment is potentially capable of producing a degradation of driving performance. It may also be clear that "being careful"—which in this case means deliberately attempting to rely less on tacitly known skill—is likely to be at least partially effective as a compensating factor. But the problem of assessing the weight of these considerations, for the purpose of deciding whether the plan is acceptable or not, is intractable because of the tacit basis of driving skill. A full conscious override of habitual response is not possible, and if it were it would mean the abandonment, not the effective adaptation, of driving skill. The planner might reflect that the problem is surely not that serious; the muscular coordination aspect of controlling the vehicle will not require much attention. On the other hand, those muscular responses are tightly linked to visual cues, and the cues do not have their accustomed import. Habitual responses will be modified and the American driver will "get the hang of it" after a while, but it is hard to say how much experience will be needed or what risk levels might be involved in acquiring it. There is thus a significant degree of ambiguity about whether an American driver, driving for the first time "on the wrong side of the road," knows how to drive or not. The ambiguity is partly a matter of uncertainty concerning the fate of the individual driver, and partly a reflection of the fact that the phrase "knows how to drive" papers over many significant distinctions.

Of course, if the American driver never goes to England, he may never directly confront this particular illustration of the ambiguous scope of skills. If he goes with sufficient frequency, he may develop a driving-on-the-left subskill that is as much an integrated, tacitly known part of his overall driving skill as the ability to adjust to dense city traffic after coming off the ramp of a relatively uncrowded freeway. It is the differences between the environment in which a skill (and associated terminology) is developed and a relatively novel environment in which it is exercised that highlight its operational (and semantic) ambiguities. A fully static world would never pose the problem of using relatively concise language to consider the matching of complex skills with novel, complex task environments. The matches would all have been made, and could be counted on to work precisely as well in the future as they had in the past. But the real world is not static.

6. THE SKILLS OF THE BUSINESSMAN

Our primary purpose in this examination of individual skills has been to establish a useful starting point for the appraisal of the corresponding issues in the case of the large, complex organization. Much of the discussion of "theory and realism" in the economic theory of the firm has, however, been implicitly or explicitly concerned with the case of the single proprietorship. The question of whether or in what sense the business firm can be said to maximize profits has for the most part been treated in the literature as equivalent to a question about the decision-making skills of the proprietor.

The contributions of Machlup to the marginalist controversy of the forties, Friedman's methodological essay (Friedman, 1953), and Machlup's review of the issues in his presidential address of 1967 are the major papers that set forth the defense of the orthodox theory of the firm against critics who complained of its lack of realism. Although the scope and technical sophistication of orthodox theory have vastly increased during the more than three decades since the marginalist controversy, and although a number of contributions have been made to the discussions of the broader methodological issues involved, the main arguments in defense of doing economic theory in the orthodox style remain approximately where Friedman and Machlup left them. Or perhaps, indeed, there has been a retrogression—some contemporary theorists seem to operate on the basis of a methodological creed that is little more than a caricature of Friedman's sophisticated and carefully hedged position. We therefore confine our review to the classic statements.

In the course of making their methodological points about why it is not worthwhile for economists to think concretely and in detail about a realistic account of the sources of business behavior, Friedman and Machlup managed to say or imply a great deal about what such a realistic account would be like. Much of what they said can easily be translated into and summarized in the language that we have employed in this chapter. The following attempt at such a translation reveals a high degree of convergence between their perspective and ours.

An experienced businessman acting in the pursuit of pecuniary gain is an individual exercising a complex skill. As with any such skill, the pursuit of gain is based on tacit knowledge of relevant conditions and involves at most subsidiary awareness of many of the details of the procedures being followed. The economic theorist's abstract account of business decision making is not to be confused with the businessman's skills; it serves different purposes and those purposes place a high premium on articulation. Clear articulation of his methods may be valueless, or even counterproductive, for the businessman. It is therefore quite illegitimate to seek to appraise the validity of the theoretical account of business decisions by asking businessmen whether their procedures match the theoretical constructs. Such a method founders first on the general observation that the possibilities for articulating the basis of high skill are limited; second, even if this fact were somehow of minimal importance in the specific context of business decision, there would be no reason to expect that the language chosen by the businessman to articulate his skill would be the language of economic theory. There is, after all, no reason to expect a bicyclist to be able to explain in the language of physics how he remains upright, but this does not imply that he usually falls over.

That the foregoing is a plausible encapsulation of many of the Friedman–Machlup points may be corroborated by the following specific references. In the context of his famous analogy between the businessman and the expert billiard player, Friedman remarked as follows: "The billiard player, if asked how he decides where to hit the ball, may say that he 'just figures it out' but then also rubs a rabbit's foot just to make sure; and the businessman may well say that he prices at average cost, with of course some minor deviations when the market makes it necessary. The one statement is about as helpful as the other, and neither is a relevant test of the associated hypothesis" (Friedman, 1953, p. 22). Even more explicitly, Machlup wrote in 1946: "Businessmen do not always 'calculate' before they make decisions, and they do not always 'decide' before they act. For they think that they know their business well enough without having to make repeated calculations; and their actions are frequently routine. But routine is based on principles which were once considered and decided upon and have then been frequently applied with decreasing need for conscious choices. The feeling that calculations are not always necessary is usually based upon an ability to size up a situation without reducing its dimensions to definite numerical values" (Machlup, 1946, pp. 524–525). Since driving an automobile has been prominent among our own examples of the exercise of individual skill, we acknowledge Machlup's earlier treatment of the topic by quoting at some length from his well-known analogy between the theory of the maximizing firm and the "theory of overtaking":

What sort of considerations are behind the routine decision of the driver of an automobile to overtake a truck proceeding ahead of him at slower speed? What factors influence his decision? Assume that he is faced with the alternative of either slowing down and staying behind the truck or of passing it before a car which is approaching from the opposite direction will have reached the spot. As an experienced driver he somehow takes into account (a) the speed at which the truck is going, (b) the remaining distance between himself and the truck, (c) the speed at which he is proceeding, (d) the possible acceleration of his speed, (e) the distance between him and the car approaching from the opposite direction, (f) the speed at which that car is approaching, and probably also the condition of the road (concrete or dirt, wet or dry, straight or winding, level or uphill), the degree of visibility (light or dark, clear or foggy), and the condition of the tires and brakes of his car, and—let us hope—his own condition (fresh or tired, sober or alcoholized) permitting him to judge the enumerated factors. Clearly, the driver of the automobile will not "measure" the variables; he will not "calculate" the time needed for the vehicles to cover the estimated distances at the estimated rates of speed; and, of course, none of the "estimates" will be expressed in numerical values. Even so, without measurements, numerical estimates or calculations, he will in a routine way do the indicated "sizing-up" of the total situation. He will not break it down into its elements. Yet a "theory of overtaking" would have to include all these elements (and perhaps others besides) and would have to state how changes in any of the factors were likely to affect the decisions or actions of the driver. The "extreme difficulty of calculating," the fact that "it would be utterly impractical" to attempt to work out and ascertain the exact magnitudes of the variables which the theorist alleges to be significant, show merely that the *explanation* of an action must often include steps of reasoning which the acting individual himself does not *consciously* perform (because the action has become routine) and which perhaps he would never be *able* to perform in scientific exactness (because such exactness is not necessary in everyday life).

The businessman who equates marginal net revenue productivity and marginal factor cost when he decides how many to employ need not engage in higher mathematics, geometry, or clairvoyance. Ordinarily he would not even consult with his accountant or efficiency expert in order to arrive at his decision; he would not make any tests or formal calculations; he would simply rely on his sense or his "feel" of the situation. There is nothing very exact about this sort of estimate. On the basis of hundreds of previous experiences of a similar nature the businessman would "just know," in a vague and rough way, whether or not it would pay him to hire more men. (Machlup, 1946, pp. 534–535)

It appears that it might be difficult for a disinterested judge to distinguish between the Friedman–Machlup perspective on the realities of business decision making and our own. Some greater divergence will appear as we develop our own argument further, but the paradox that has arisen here will by no means be resolved by that development alone. On the same stylized fact—"business decision making is the exercise of a skill comparable to other skills, such as driving a car or playing billiards"—Friedman and Machlup built a defense for orthodox theory and we propose to build an alternative to that theory.

What is one to make of this? At a superficial level, the paradox is easily dealt with. The disagreement is not, indeed, about the stylized fact; it is about the arguments that link the fact to conclusions about the relative merits of its interpretation in orthodox or evolutionary theory. A full analysis and comparison of these linking arguments, as between orthodoxy and evolutionary theory, would be a major task. Much of this book is concerned with it, directly or indirectly. However, merely noting that the central problem is how to model skilled behavior opens the way for a substantial clarification of the issues. Orthodoxy treats the skillful behavior of the businessman as maximizing *choice*, and "choice" carries connotations of "deliberation." We, on the other hand, emphasize the *automaticity* of skillful behavior and the suppression of choice that this involves. In skillful behavior, behavioral options are selected, but they are not deliberately chosen. This observation directs attention to the processes by which skills are learned, the preconditions for the effective exercise of skill, and the possibilities for gross error through automatic selection of the wrong option.

To identify skillful behavior with *maximizing* choice is an even larger step from the realities of skill. Skills are attributed to individuals largely on the basis of comparisons with other individuals who are less skilled or unskilled. Formal orthodox theory, on the other hand, does not rate solutions as maximizing because they are better than some other observed solutions, but because they are the best feasible solutions. It thus premises a standard of performance that is independent of the characteristics of performers; the attribution "skilled driver" involves no such premise. This observation points us toward the deeper problems involving the definition of the feasible set. What are the possibilities that a skillful performance makes the best of? Are the tacit skills of the driver overtaking a truck such as to make no-passing zones unnecessary or counterproductive? Do they warrant the practice of giving American drivers licenses to drive in England without a driving test? Are we entitled to doubt—as Machlup seems momentarily to doubt—that the typical driver adequately assesses possible impairments of his own capacities?

Such questions have their parallels in the numerous policy issues that involve, in one way or another, the scope and quality of business decision making. To assess business decision making as (merely) skillful is to recognize the potential significance of a number of questions that orthodoxy tends to ignore. Are market conditions the same as they have been? Is the range of technological options the same? If conditions have changed, are businessmen aware of that? Even if conditions have not changed, have businessmen experimented enough with the available options? If the answers to such questions are in the negative, the observation that business decision making involves the exercise of skill is not entirely reassuring as to its likely quality. One may legitimately be concerned about problems analogous to the possibility that the American driver in England will seek to avoid the oncoming traffic by steering his car to the right.

5

Organizational Capabilities and Behavior

THIS CHAPTER PRESENTS an alternative to orthodoxy's view of organizational behavior as optimal choice from a sharply defined set of capabilities. Our view of organizational behavior has been molded by the contributions of a number of organization theorists and economists—March and Simon, Allison, Gouldner, Perrow, Doeringer and Piore, Williamson, Schumpeter, and others. What is distinctive about our treatment of organizations derives first of all from its place in our broader evolutionary framework; this accounts in particular for the attention we devote to the nature and sources of continuity in the behavioral patterns of an individual organization. Second, the analysis here builds upon that of the previous chapter and exploits the parallels between individual skills and organizational routines. Relatedly, the influence of Michael Polanyi (not usually counted as an organization theorist) is strong in this chapter, though less explicit than in the previous one.

Scope. There are a great many different sorts of organizations, and it is implausible that a given collection of concepts and propositions would apply uniformly, or even usefully, to all of them. The sorts of organizations we have in mind are, first of all, organizations that are engaged in the provision of goods and services for some outside clientele, and have at least vague criteria for doing well or poorly. The salient examples are business firms concerned with survival and profits, but much of our analysis is relevant, perhaps with minor modification, to other sorts of organizations.

Second, since "routine" is a key concept in our theoretical framework, the framework applies most naturally to organizations that are engaged in the provision of goods and services that are visibly "the same" over extended periods—manufacturing hand tools, teaching second graders, and so forth—and for which well-defined routines structure a large part of organizational functioning at any particular time. As we shall argue later on in this chapter the notion of routine can usefully be stretched to relate to a number of activities that would not ordinarily be described by that term. Nevertheless, organizations that are involved in the production or management of economic change as their *principal* function—organizations such as R&D laboratories and consulting firms—do not fit neatly into the routine operation mold.

Third, the discussion relates primarily to organizations that are "large and complex." The role of this restriction is simply to maintain the focus on phenomena that are distinctively organizational. The organizations we envisage are ones that face a substantial coordination problem, typically because they have many members, performing many distinct roles, who make complementary contributions to the production of a relatively small range of goods and services. In such organizations, most of the working interactions of a large number of the members are primarily with other members rather than with the organization's environment. Also, while the organizations we describe are of the sort that have a top management that is concerned with the general direction of the organization, the scale and complexity of the organization are presumed to make it impossible for that top management to direct or observe many of the details of the organization's functioning.[1]

Terminology. The importance of the concept of organizational routine in our discussion and the parallel with individual skill have already been noted. We use "routine" in a highly flexible way, much as "program" (or, indeed, "routine") is used in discussion of computer programming. It may refer to a repetitive pattern of activity in an entire organization, to an individual skill, or, as an adjective, to the smooth uneventful effectiveness of such an organizational or individual performance. The term "organization member" is also

---

1. Some parts of the discussion that follows are of clearest relevance at the "establishment" level—that is, at the level of an organizational unit that has a particular geographic location. Our analysis suggests that the memory of an organization that comprises many widely separated establishments may exist mainly in the establishments, or if not it is of quite a different sort than it is in a single establishment. Significant questions relating to economic policy are involved here—for example, the question of how much difference it is likely to make to the operations of a particular plant if it is transferred as a functioning unit from one very large corporation to another. We have not pursued these questions.

used flexibly: although in most cases we use it to mean an individual, it is sometimes convenient to think of an organizational subunit as a "member" of the larger organization. Such a perspective is called for, in particular, when the information exchanges by which coordination is achieved within the subunit are quite rapid and predominantly nonsymbolic, so that the coordinating processes resist articulation in a way that parallels the case of individual skills.

In our conceptualization, an organization member is by definition a unit that can accomplish something on its own. A production worker, for example, may be able to put together subassembly H without interacting with other members, provided that the necessary parts are at hand, the lights are on in the work area, and so forth. He might also be able to put together subassembly K, provided likewise that the parts are at hand, and the lights are on. A typical organization member has certain skills or routines. The set of skills or routines that a particular member could perform in some appropriate environment will be called the *repertoire* of that member. Although the activities of other working members affect the local working environment of a particular member, and thereby his feasible behaviors, it is to be understood that strictly concurrent action by other members is not a precondition for his performance. Thus, in the example of the assembly operation, the state of the parts bins mediates the relationship between the member doing the assembly and the member or members who keep the bins full, but there is no requirement for concurrent action or very short-term interaction.[2]

Plan. The method and structure of our discussion parallels that followed by Schumpeter in *The Theory of Economic Development* (1934). We begin by considering the analogue of Schumpeter's "circular flow" at the level of the individual organization. The situation portrayed is unchanging or cyclically repetitive; it is an unrealistically quiet and static condition. We then gradually introduce into the picture more of the processes of change, displaying some of the connections between planned change and unplanned change, and examine finally the role of routine in innovation.

The first section below considers routine as organizational memory; we provide here an answer to the question raised earlier as to where organizational capabilities reside. Section 2 discusses routine

---

2. For the purposes of a detailed analysis of organizational coordination, it might be helpful to admit to the roster of "organization members" any feature of the total situation that constitutes an identifiable unit with a distinctive role in the total performance—including machines, parts bins, and even tables or particular areas of the floor. A complex machine, for example, may embody what amounts to tacit knowledge: the machine gets the job done, but nobody can explain how it does it.

as truce; here we recognize the divergence of interests among organization members and provide the basis for a rationale that, nonetheless, organizations can be modeled without explicit attention to the fact that many participants are involved. (We do not intend to deny here that for some purposes it is important, for some essential, to recognize the conflict of interest contained in and reflected by organizational behavior.) In Section 3, we consider routine operation as the target of efforts directed to organizational control, to replication of existing routines, and to imitation of routines employed by other organizations. We pause in Section 4 to take explicit note of some of the parallels between organizational routines and individual skills. Section 5 examines the relationship of our concept of routine operation to orthodoxy's claim that firms optimize—and to the fact that at least some firms employ explicit optimization methods to make some sorts of decisions some of the time. The penultimate section explores the connections between routinized behavior and innovative behavior—and finds much less opposition between these two ideas than is commonly thought. The concluding section summarizes the message to be carried forward to the modeling efforts of Part III.

1. ROUTINE AS ORGANIZATIONAL MEMORY

It is easy enough to suggest that a plausible answer to the question "Where does the knowledge reside?" is "In the organization's memory." But where and what is the memory of an organization? We propose that the routinization of activity in an organization constitutes the most important form of storage of the organization's specific operational knowledge. Basically, we claim that organizations *remember* by *doing*—although there are some important qualifications and elaborations.

The idea that organizations "remember" a routine largely by exercising it is much like the idea than an individual remembers skills by exercising them. The point that remembering is achieved largely through exercise, and could not be assured totally through written records or other formal filing devices, does not deny that firms keep formal memories and that these formal memories play an important role. But there must be much more to organizational memory than formal records. Further, cost considerations make "doing" the dominant mode of information storage even in many cases where formal records could in principle be kept.

To see how exercise of a routine serves as parsimonious organizational memory, consider an organization in fully routine operation and ask what really needs to be remembered, given that such a state has been achieved. Under such a regime, the situations of individual members and of the organization as a whole contain no significant novelties: the situations confronted replicate ones that were confronted the previous day (or week, month, or year) and are handled in the same way. The scope of the activity that actually takes place in such a static condition and the operational knowledge involved are extremely restricted. Members perform only a minute fraction of the routines they have in repertoire. The lathe operator and the lathe turn out a few specific parts; there is an indeterminately larger number that they could (after appropriate setup and learning) produce. The operator's skills as truck driver and short-order cook are never drawn upon, and perhaps are unknown to other organization members. Routine operation of the organization as a whole certainly does not require that the lathe operator maintain his skill in cooking bacon and eggs, or in the machining of parts for products that were discontinued three years previously; neither does it require that other members remember that the lathe operator possesses or once possessed these skills. If the same state of routine operation is expected to continue indefinitely, there is no economic benefit to be anticipated from holding this sort of information in the organization's memory. (As an obvious corollary, if there is a positive cost to storing information, this sort of "irrelevant" information will tend *not* to be held in memory under the "equilibrium" condition of continuing routine operation.)

What is required for the organization to continue in routine operation is simply that all members continue to "know their jobs" as those jobs are defined by the routine. This means, first of all, that they retain in their repertoires all routines actually invoked in the given state of routine operation of the organization.

There is, however, much more to "knowing one's job" in an organization than merely having the appropriate routines in repertoire. There is also the matter of knowing what routines to perform and when to perform them. For the individual member, this entails the ability to receive and interpret a stream of incoming messages from other members and from the environment. Having received and interpreted a message, the member uses the information contained therein in the selection and performance of an appropriate routine from his own repertoire. (This may, of course, be merely a "relay message" routine, or even a "file and forget" routine.)

The class of things that count as "messages" in this characterization is large and diverse. There are, first of all, the obvious examples of written and oral communications that take overtly the form of directives to do this or that. Such directives involve the exercise of formal authority, a phenomenon that has been the focus of a great deal of organizational literature. Then there are the written and oral communications that do not take this form but that are responded to in much the same way. For example, descriptions of what is "needed," when directed to the member whose job it is to meet that need, often function as directives. Even a simple description of the situation, without explicit reference to a need, may function this way. Then there are all the hand signals, gestures, glances, whistles, bell ringing, and so on that can serve in lieu of oral and written communication for these same purposes. Another broad subclass of examples follows a pattern wherein the performance of a routine by one member produces an alteration in the local working environment of another, and the alteration simultaneously makes the performance of a particular routine feasible and carries the message that it should be performed. An assembly line is one example: the arrival of the partly assembled product at a particular station (as a consequence of the performances of other members) both makes possible the performance of the operation done at that station and indicates that the performance is now called for. The arrival of a draft of a letter or document on a secretary's desk makes possible its typing, and may also indicate that its typing is now called for. In still another large subclass, there are messages to which an individual member responds that do not, in any immediate sense, come from other human members. They may come from clocks and calendars—the start of the working day is an obvious example. They may come from meters, gauges, and display boards that convey information on the current state of machines or of other aspects of the working environment and the progress of activity. Or they may come from outside the organization, as when an order or invoice or application form arrives in the mail.[3]

The ability to receive these various sorts of messages involves the possession of certain sensory capacities, plus, let us say, an ordinary ability to understand the natural language of written and oral communication in the wider society of which the organization is a part. These are abilities that usually characterize an organization member quite apart from his role in the organization—that is, they are the sorts of things a new member typically brings to the organization.

---

3. The fact that there are such diverse sources and media for the messages to which organization members respond in carrying out their duties is suggestive of the problems of defining "authority" in a useful way. To confine attention to directives from superior to subordinate, or even to communications of all sorts from superior to subordinate, is to ignore most of the details of the coordinating information flow. On the other hand, it is hard to deny that the relations of superior and subordinate often have a lot to do with how the subordinate responds to, for example, messages from the clock.

What about the ability to interpret the messages—to make the link between a message and the performance that it calls for? It is just as necessary as knowing the job, but much more specific to the organization and the job. It is one thing to know how to tell time; it is another to know when to arrive at work, and what it is that you do at about 10 A.M. on the last working day of the month. It is one thing to see a partly assembled automobile in front of you on the line and another to see it as a call for the particular steps that are yours to perform. Even directives that appear to be in "plain English" often require interpretation in a manner that is quite specific to the organizational context. For example, they often omit reference to the typical locations of objects or individuals named in the directives; only someone who has been around the place long enough can easily supply the interpretation. But, in addition, the internal language of communication in an organization is never plain English: it is a dialect full of locally understood nouns standing for particular products, parts, customers, plant locations, and individuals and involving very localized meanings for "promptly, " "slower," "too hot," and so on.[4]

The activity of formulating and sending appropriate messages we regard as the performance of a routine by the organization member concerned. This view seems convenient because, as we have noted, there is an important range of cases in which message origination occurs incidentally in the performance of a routine that nominally is directed to other ends. For example, no distinct problem of message formulation arises if the message is conveyed by the partly finished product, passed along to the member who should deal with it next. The burden of the communication process in this case and many similar ones falls upon the receiver who (to know his job) must be able to discern the implications for his own action that are implicit in the changes in his immediate environment—changes that others, by merely doing *their* jobs, have produced. But there are, of course, many organizational roles whose performance does involve message formulation in a conventional sense. For organization members in such roles, there are additional requisites of knowing the job that parallel the ones involved in receiving and interpreting such messages. These include, again, the abilities to speak and write the natural language of the society to which the organization belongs, but also the important additional requirement of command of the organizational dialect. Such command is certainly not to be taken for

---

4. Kenneth Arrow, among others, has given particular emphasis to the internal dialect or "code" of an organization as a key source of the economies that formal organization provides and as an important cause of persistent differences among organizations. See Arrow (1974, pp. 53–59).

granted in a new organization member, but is imputed by assumption to members in an organization in a state of routine operation.

The overall picture of an organization in routine operation can now be drawn. A flow of messages comes into the organization from the external environment and from clocks and calendars. The organization members receiving these messages interpret them as calling for the performance of routines from their repertoires. These performances include ones that would be thought of as directly productive—such as unloading the truck that has arrived at the loading dock—and others of a clerical or information-processing nature—such as routing a customer's inquiry or order to the appropriate point in the organization. Either as an incidental consequence of other sorts of action or as deliberate acts of communication, the performance of routines by each organization member generates a stream of messages to others. These messages in turn are interpreted as calling for particular performances by their recipients, which generate other performances, messages, interpretations, and so on. At any given time, organization members are responding to messages originating from other members as well as from the environment; the above description of the process as starting with information input from external sources or timekeeping devices is merely an expositional convenience. There is, indeed, an internal equilibrium "circular flow" of information in an organization in routine operation, but it is a flow that is continuously primed by external message sources and timekeeping devices.

For such a system to accomplish something productive, such as building computers or carrying passengers between airports or teaching children to read and write, some highly specific conditions must be satisfied, different in each particular case. The specific features that account for the ability of a particular organization to accomplish particular things are reflected, first of all, in the character of the collection of individual members' repertoires. Airlines are the sorts of organizations that have pilots as members, while schools have teachers. The capabilities of a particular sort of organization are similarly associated with the possession of particular collections of specialized plant and equipment, and the repertoires of organization members include the ability to operate that plant and equipment. Finally, of course, the actual exercise of productive capability requires that there be something upon which to exercise it—some computer components to assemble, or passengers to carry, or children to teach. These are the considerations recognized in the "list of ingredients" level of discussion of productive capability, which is standard in economic analysis. There is also a "recipe" level of discussion, at which "technologies" are described in terms of the principles that underlie them and the character and sequencing of the subtasks that must be performed to get the desired result. This is the province of engineers and other technologists, and to some extent of designers and production managers.

But just as an individual member does not come to know his job merely by mastering the required routines in the repertoire, so an organization does not become capable of an actual productive performance merely by acquiring all the "ingredients," even if it also has the "recipe." What is central to a productive organizational performance is coordination; what is central to coordination is that individual members, knowing their jobs, correctly interpret and respond to the messages they receive. The interpretations that members give to messages are the mechanism that picks out, from a vast array of possibilities consistent with the roster of member repertoires, a collection of individual member performances that actually constitute a productive performance for the organization as a whole.[5] To the extent that the description above is valid, skills, organization, and "technology" are intimately intertwined in a functioning routine, and it is difficult to say exactly where one aspect ends and another begins. This is another way of arguing that "blueprints" are only a small part of what needs to be in an organizational memory in order that production proceed effectively. Furthermore, once the set of routines is in memory by virtue of use, blueprints may not be necessary save, perhaps, as a checkpoint to assess what might be wrong when the routine breaks down.

Given this picture, it is easy to see the relationship between routine operation and organizational memory—or, alternatively, to identify the routinization of activity as the "locus" of operational knowledge in an organization. Information is actually stored primarily in the memories of the members of the organization, in which reside all the knowledge, articulable and tacit, that constitutes their individual skills and routines, the generalized language competence and the specific command of the organizational dialect, and, above all, the associations that link the incoming messages to the specific performances that they call for. In the sense that the memories of individual members do store so much of the information required for the performance of organizational routines, there is substantial truth in the proposition that the knowledge an organization possesses is reducible to the knowledge of its individual members. This is the

---

5. We have passed over here the problem of what makes the organization member *willing* to respond appropriately to a message he receives and correctly interprets. This issue is addressed in the following section.

perspective that one is led to emphasize if one is committed to the view that "knowing" is something that only humans can do.

But the knowledge stored in human memories is meaningful and effective only in some context, and for knowledge exercised in an organizational role that context is an organizational context. It typically includes, first, a variety of forms of external memory—files, message boards, manuals, computer memories, magnetic tapes—that complement and support individual memories but that are maintained in large part as a routine organizational function. One might, therefore, want to say that they are part of organizational memory rather than an information storage activity of individual members. Second, the context includes the physical state of equipment and of the work environment generally. Performance of an organizational memory function is in part implicit in the simple fact that equipment and structures are relatively durable: they and the general state of the work environment do not undergo radical and discontinuous change. A fire or severe storm may break the continuity. The destruction caused by such an event is informational as well as physical, for there is a disruption of the accustomed interpretive context for the information possessed by human members. One might therefore be tempted to say that an organization "remembers" in part by keeping—and to the extent that it succeeds in keeping—its equipment, structures, and work environment in some degree of order and repair. Finally, and most important, the context of the information possessed by an individual member is established by the information possessed by all other members. Without the crane operator's ability to interpret the hand signal for "down a little more" and to lower the hook accordingly, the abilities to perceive the need for the signal and to generate it are meaningless. To view organizational memory as reducible to individual member memories is to overlook, or undervalue, the linking of those individual memories by shared experiences in the past, experiences that have established the extremely detailed and specific communication system that underlies routine performance.

What requires emphasis in the foregoing account is the power of the supposition that "the organization is in a state of routine operation" to limit the scope of the organizational memory function that needs to be performed. While each organization member must know his job, there is no need for anyone to know anyone *else's* job. Neither is there any need for anyone to be able to articulate or conceptualize the procedures employed by the organization as a whole. Some fraction of the necessary coordinating information may be communicated among members in explicit, articulated form, but there is heavy reliance on the communication implicit in performances that nominally serve other, directly productive purposes. There is no need for an exhaustive symbolic account of the organization's methods; in any case, because much of the knowledge involved is tacit knowledge held by individual members, such an account cannot exist. Yet the amount of information storage implicit in the successful continuation of the routinized performance of the organization as a whole may dwarf the capacity of an individual human memory. The complexity and scale of the productive process may far surpass what any "chief engineer," however skilled, could conceivably guide.[6]

It is by no means the case, however, that routinization entirely frees organizational memory and organizational performance from constraints imposed by human memory limitations. It is important here to distinguish between the memory requirements of a complex coordinated performance taking place at a given time and the requirements of a flexible performance in which the organization as a whole does quite different things at different times. The complexity of performance at a given time can be greater in a larger organization. With a larger number of members and thus a larger number of human memories among which the organizational memory function can be divided, greater complexity can be consistent with constant or declining demands on the memories of individual members. All members can, simultaneously, remember their jobs by doing them. The situation is quite different with respect to flexibility of organizational performance over time. Flexibility involves variation of the organizational performance in response to variation in the environment.[7] For the organization to respond routinely with a wide variety of specialized routine performances, each "customized" for a particular configuration of the environment, members must be able to retain in repertoire the specialized individual routines involved, and to recall the meaning of a set of messages sufficiently rich to differentiate all the required performances from one another. They must do so in spite of the long time intervals elapsing between the performances of at least some specialized routines and the receipts of some particular messages. (That there are such intervals is of course

---

6. We have already noted in Chapter 3 the limitations of the "chief engineer" and "book of blueprints" parables that occur in orthodox accounts of productive knowledge.

7. It might also involve response to variations in directives from top management, but presumably those variations reflect changes in the environment. In any case, the story would be much the same for arbitrary changes in directives.

implied by the supposition that the list of performances or messages to be distinguished is long.) Especially in the case of the tacit components of high skill, the phenomenon of memory loss or increasing rustiness over time is important. A skill that is only exercised briefly every year or two cannot be expressed with the smoothness and reliability of one consistently exercised five days a week. And unexpected lapses by individual members tend to have amplified disruptive effects on organizational performance, since by themselves they create further novelties in the organization's state—novelties with which existing routines and communication systems may be unprepared to deal.

These are the considerations that link routine operation with remembering by doing. It is not just that routinization reflects the achievement of coordination and the establishment of an organizational memory that sustains such coordination. It is that coordination is preserved, and organizational memory refreshed, by exercise —just as, and partly because, individual skills are maintained by being exercised. It may be possible to achieve flexibility by scheduling drills for the specific purpose of maintaining infrequently exercised capabilities, or even by having standby units that do nothing but drill for particular contingencies. But these are obviously costly ways of maintaining organizational memory, at least as compared with genuine "doing" that is directly productive. And, as is well known, the quality of the practice afforded by a drill is inevitably degraded by the fact that it is merely a drill.

2. ROUTINE AS TRUCE

Our discussion to this point has been concerned with the cognitive aspects of the performances of organization members—with the question of whether they know what to do and how to do it. We have ignored the motivational aspect—the question of whether they would actually choose to do what is "required" of them in the routine operation of the organization as a whole. Relatedly, the image of coordination that we have presented involves no mention of authority figures, backed by a system of incentives and sanctions, who cajole or coerce the required performances from other members. It is not, however, part of our intention to ignore the divergence of interests among organization members, or to assume implicitly that members are somehow fully committed to the smooth functioning of the organization. Here we fill in the part of the picture of routine operation that involves motivational considerations and intraorganizational conflict.[8]

First of all, our concept of routine operation should not be confused with performance according to the nominal standards of the organization. Neither should the proposition that members correctly interpret and appropriately respond to messages they receive be taken to imply that members do what they are told. Nominally, the workday in a particular organization may run from 9:00 to 5:00, but it may be the case (routinely) that very little activity that is productive from the organization's point of view gets done before 9:30 or after 4:45. Similarly, days or weeks may pass between the nominal deadlines for the completion of particular tasks and the typical dates at which they are actually completed. Repeated follow-up requests or orders may, quite routinely, be part of the system of messages that ultimately results in "timely" performance by other organization members. The priority system used by a particular member in allocating effort among tasks may make use, routinely, of the information contained in the overtones of panic or fury in the incoming messages. In short, routine operation is consistent with routinely occurring laxity, slippage, rule-breaking, defiance, and even sabotage. Such behaviors typically violate nominal standards and expectations in an organization, but they do not necessarily violate empirically based expectations or have consequences for output that are inconsistent with results being statistically stable and within the expected range. They may be expected, adapted to, and allowed for—even to the point where a sudden reversion to nominal standards by some organization members would be disruptive of the achieved state of coordination.

Although nominal standards of performance are not necessarily relevant, it is nevertheless true that some sort of stable accommodation between the requirements of organizational functioning and the motivations of all organization members is a necessary concomitant of routine operation. What signals the existence of an accommodation is not the conformity of behavior to standards of performance laid down by supervisors or codified in job descriptions, but that members are rarely surprised at each other's behavior and also that involuntary separations of members from the organization do not occur.

The usual mechanisms of internal control are, of course, a part of

---

8. In regard to the context of this section, we acknowledge a diffuse intellectual indebtedness to a large number of authors: Coase (1937), Simon (1951), March and Simon (1958), Doeringer and Piore (1971), Ross (1973), Williamson (1975, ch. 4), and Leibenstein (1976).

the context that helps define the *de facto* contracts that individual members make with the organization. Some of the clerks in the retail store might simply ignore the customers if the manager did not check up occasionally—but the manager does, routinely, check up occasionally, and this keeps the problem within limits. Some fraction of workers may in fact take every opportunity to shirk. This means that the "contracts" of these workers call for them to deliver an amount of work that is defined by the level of managerial supervision; a change in that level would mean a change in the *de facto* contract, but no such change occurs in the context of routine operation. Again, if banks did not have elaborate routinized systems of financial control, it is likely that more bank employees would exploit their positions to their own financial advantage, whether by dipping directly into the till or by approving doubtful loans to undertakings in which they have an interest. As it is, the operation of the control system is a major component of the routine tasks of many bank employees: every job is partially defined by the system's existence and illicit appropriation of bank funds is not (routinely) an important form of compensation.

The examples just given illustrate the way in which control of organization members is effected through mechanisms operating routinely as part of the jobs of other organization members, and serving primarily to threaten sanctions, including dismissal, for behavior that deviates from organizational requirements in specified prohibited directions and in excessive degree. Such rule-enforcement mechanisms play a crucial but limited role in making routine operation possible. On the one hand, they largely prevent or deter individual members from pursuing their own interests along lines that are so strongly antithetical to organizational requirements as to threaten the feasibility of any coordinated performance at all. In this sense, they are crucial in keeping the underlying conflicts among organization members from being expressed in highly disruptive forms.

Ordinarily, however, control systems of this type leave individual members with substantial areas of behavioral discretion, areas that embrace performances of widely differing appropriateness or value from the organizational perspective. Except for tasks involving very low levels of skill, performed under conditions favorable to close observation of several workers by a single supervisor, it is not practical to monitor and control behavior so closely that only organizationally appropriate behaviors are permitted. Within the substantial zone of discretion that exists in most cases, the conformity of individual member behavior to organizational requirements is motivated by considerations other than the routinized organizational mechanisms that "enforce the rules." A variety of other motivating considerations exist. In some cases it is possible to measure individual member "output" reasonably well; reward (or freedom from sanction) can then be conditioned on achievement of a satisfactory output level. In others, organizationally appropriate behavior may be as attractive to the individual member as any other behavior in the zone of discretion left by the rule-enforcement system. Or members may regard themselves as being in a long-term exchange relationship with the organization and may expect future rewards for effective behavior in the present. The importance and efficacy of these motivators and of others not mentioned may be expected to vary among tasks, among rule enforcement, output monitoring and promotion systems, and also, importantly, across member cultures and subcultures that inculcate differing attitudes toward the responsibilities and rewards of organizational membership.[9]

In routine operation, the combined effect of the rule-enforcement mechanism and other motivators is such as to leave members content to play their roles in the organizational routine—but "content" only in the sense that they are willing to continue to perform up to their usual standard, to the accompaniment of the usual amount of griping and squabbling. Conflict, both manifest and latent, persists, but manifest conflict follows largely predictable paths and stays within predictable bounds that are consistent with the ongoing routine. In short, routine operation involves a comprehensive truce in intraorganizational conflict. There is a truce between the supervisor and those supervised at every level in the organizational hierarchy: the usual amount of work gets done, reprimands and compliments are delivered with the usual frequency, and no demands are presented for major modifications in the terms of the relationship. There is similarly a truce in the struggle for advancement, power, and perquisites among high-level executives. Nobody is trying to steer the organizational ship into a sharp turn in the hope of throwing a rival overboard—or if someone is trying, he correctly expects to be thwarted.

When one considers routine operation as the basis of organizational memory, one is led to expect to find routines patterned in ways that reflect characteristics of the information storage problem that they solve. When one considers routine operation as involving a truce in intraorganizational conflict, one is led to expect routines to

---

9. The considerations just mentioned are among those involved in discussion of "internal" labor markets and the "dual labor market" theory. See Doeringer and Piore (1971) and Williamson (1975, ch. 4).

be patterned in ways that reflect features of the underlying problem of diverging individual member interests. The obvious example of such patterning is the existence of rule-enforcement mechanisms as an ongoing feature of organizational routine, even when serious breaches of the rules are infrequent and most of the sanctions that are nominally available are not applied.

But more subtle manifestations, specific to a particular organizational context, frequently exist. Like a truce among nations, the truce among organization members tends to give rise to a peculiar symbolic culture shared by the parties. A renewal of overt hostilities would be costly and would also involve a sharp rise in uncertainty about the future positions of the parties. Accordingly, the state of truce is ordinarily considered valuable, and a breach of its terms is not to be undertaken lightly. But the terms of a truce can never be fully explicit, and in the case of the intraorganizational truce are often not explicit at all. The terms become increasingly defined by a shared tradition arising out of the specific contingencies confronted and the responses of the parties to those contingencies. In the interpretive context of such a tradition, actions by individual members have connotations related to the terms of the truce. In particular, a contemplated action otherwise sensible both for the organization and for the member taking it may have to be rejected if it is likely to be interpreted as "provocative"—that is, as signaling a lessened commitment to the preservation of the truce and a corresponding willingness to risk overt conflict for the sake of modifying the routine in a manner favored by the member who initiates the change. On the defensive side, each member strives to protect his interests by standing prepared to deliver a firm rebuff not only to actions by others that clearly threaten those interests, but also to actions that might be quite innocuous were it not for their possible interpretation as probes of his alertness or determination to defend his rights under the truce.

The apparent fragility of the prevailing truce and the implied need for caution in undertaking anything that looks like a new initiative is thus reinforced by the defensive alertness (or alert defensiveness) of organization members seeking to assure that their interests continue to be recognized and preserved. The result may be that the routines of the organization as a whole are confined to extremely narrow channels by the dikes of vested interest. Adaptations that appear "obvious" and "easy" to an external observer may be foreclosed because they involve a perceived threat to internal political equilibrium.

Of course, organizations vary in the extent to which these mechanisms operate, as they do in other respects. But it seems safe to say that fear of breaking the truce is, in general, a powerful force tending to hold organizations on the path of relatively inflexible routine.

3. ROUTINE AS TARGET: CONTROL, REPLICATION, AND IMITATION

So far, we have emphasized that a state of routine operation in an organization is in many ways self-sustaining. Judging by the preceding sections, an organization might be expected to encounter difficulty in departing from its prevailing routines, but it should have no trouble in conforming to them. Although this generalization is more than half of the story and is a basic assumption of our evolutionary models, it is subject to important qualification. Just keeping an existing routine running smoothly can be difficult. When this is the case, the routine (in its smoothly functioning version) takes on the quality of a norm or target, and managers concern themselves with trying to deal with actual or threatened disruptions of the routine. That is, they try to keep the routine under control.

The preceding sections do suggest that there is typically going to be some difficulty encountered in deliberately creating a complex new routine where none existed before. Organization members have to learn the system of coordinating messages. They may have to add new skills to their individual repertoires, and they need to achieve a first reconciliation of their expectations regarding the distribution of costs and benefits in the situation. In such a context—for example, the initial operation of a new plant—the eventual achievement of a state of routine operation also serves as a target for managerial effort, much as it does in the context of control of an existing routine. Because there are important parallels between these "routine as target" situations, we discuss them together here. But there are also important differences, relating to the definiteness of the target presented and the adequacy of the available information as to how it may be attained. With regard to these dimensions of difference, there is a continuum of situations ranging from the edge of full routine—"getting this production line working well, like it was yesterday"—to the edge of major innovation—"opening a plant to build small computers similar to those just introduced by our rival, only better and cheaper." In the formal models of the following chapters, this continuum gets represented by distinct categories and sharp discontinuities. Here we admit that everything is a matter of degree—and examine some of the variables that distinguish the "degrees" of different cases.

Control

An organization is not a perpetual motion machine; it is an open system that survives through some form of exchange with its environment. Even its most durable machines and oldest hands undergo change with the passage of time and through the organizational process itself, and ultimately are replaced. On a much shorter time scale, current inputs of various kinds flow in, and outputs flow out. The organization's routine, considered as an abstract "way of doing things," is an order that can persist only if it is imposed on a continually changing set of specific resources. Some part of this task of imposing the routine's order on new resources is itself handled routinely; another part is dealt with by *ad hoc* problem-solving efforts. Either the routinized or the *ad hoc* part of the task may fail to be accomplished if the environment does not cooperate—for example, if it fails to yield, on the usual terms, the resources that are required.

A major part of the control problem is related, directly or indirectly, to the fact that productive inputs are heterogeneous. The firm itself creates distinctions among inputs in the course of "imposing the routine's order" upon them; it buys a standard type of machine in the market and bolts it to the floor in a particular location in the shop, and it hires a machinist and familiarizes him with the particular capabilities and layout of its equipment and the tasks that are typically performed. Further differentiation occurs incidental to the input's cumulative experience with the idiosyncratic environment of the firm; the machine suffers particular wear patterns and the machinist particular patterns of frustration with his supervisor. But of course the firm also confronts the fact that different units of the "same" input may have distinctive characteristics when they are offered to the firm for purchase, and that the entire distribution of characteristics displayed by different units offered concurrently may itself be changing over time. This prepurchase heterogeneity in the market complicates the problem of postpurchase modification, since the same treatment applied to different units will not necessarily produce the same result. Finally, because machines and workers may pass through the market again after a stay in a firm, the modifications resulting from experience in firms contribute to heterogeneity in the market.

The problem posed for the firm is somehow to acquire inputs with the particular characteristics required for the smooth functioning of its routines, in the face of the fact that such inputs may not be available on the market at all, or, if available, may not be readily distinguishable from other inputs whose characteristics make them less effective or positively dangerous. Since this problem cannot be solved totally and consistently, a corollary task is to limit the damage associated with imperfections in the solution to the primary problem.

The general tactics applied in dealing with these matters are much the same regardless of the class of inputs considered. A basic tactic is to *select* from the alternatives available from the supply side of the input market those particular inputs that are compatible with the routine. This process is complicated and imperfect if input characteristics are difficult and costly to ascertain, and is further complicated by tension with the cost-control problem, arising from the fact that the range of alternatives available is affected by the price offered. There is then an effort to *modify* acquired inputs so that they meet the requirements of the routine—to dilute, grind, trim, or sort the raw material to a uniform standard, to teach the clerk the filing system and the portion of the organizational dialect relevant to its use, to bolt down and adjust the new machine, or to instruct the new executive in the rudiments of the technology he is now managing. Of course, if too big a mistake has been made at the selecting stage, adequate modification may be impossible. The central damage-limiting tactic is to *monitor* the organizational process to detect the shirking or slow worker, the embezzler, the purchased component that fails too often, the paint that does not adhere, and so forth—and, having detected them, to reinvoke the "modify" tactic or to "select" anew from the market. Some of these problems are of course difficult to detect, particularly the ones that actively seek to avoid detection. As a last resort it may be possible to *adapt* the routine itself so that it either is more tolerant of heterogeneity or so that it can respond routinely to information on varying input characteristics with compensatory adjustments elsewhere. The latter presumes, of course, that available information permits a sorting of inputs into categories of adequate homogeneity.

The first three of these tactics are routinely pursued by various functional subunits within virtually all large organizations. The "selecting" function described is what purchasing and personnel departments do. Some "modifying" is also done by the personnel department and by trainers, supervisors, and co-workers, or, for non-human inputs, by engineers or production workers. "Monitoring" is done by line supervisors, but is also an aspect of financial control and of quality control. However, the fact that such routinized arrangements exist does not assure that they are comprehensive or fully efficacious. Some input selection problems arise too infrequently to be dealt with routinely: major purchases of durable equipment and recruitment of high-level executives cannot be entirely routine matters themselves and may be the occasion of major discontinuities in the functioning of the organization as a whole. And if the arrays of alternatives that input markets present to the firm change rapidly enough in adverse directions, existing routines for dealing with input heterogeneity are likely to be overwhelmed. Then the organization will either have to adapt its routines or see them go seriously out of control. Finally, the less that is known about what input characteristics are relevant and the more difficult it is to detect the relevant characteristics, the more likely it is that the only symptoms of adverse change in input characteristics will be inexplicable difficulties in carrying out the routine.

As the examples above indicate, the consequences of control lapses are diverse and variable. The plant may have to shut down for a few hours or days while the mess is straightened out. A bad batch may have to be thrown away. Perhaps the customers will get an inferior product; with luck they won't even notice, but there is the possibility of getting hit with a big product liability suit. Or perhaps the stockholders collectively will just be a bit poorer, to the tune of whatever the embezzler got away with.

The sorts of consequences that are of particular interest here are those that relate to organizational memory and the long-run continuity of routine. Control lapses may be the cause or effect of memory lapses. We have, for example, emphasized that the memories of individual organization members are a primary repository of the operational knowledge of the organization. Some part of the information thus stored may be readily replaced if the particular member storing it leaves the firm; the former employee may have been the only one who knew how to run a particular machine, but it may be easy to hire a replacement who knows how to run it. Or it may be that the knowledge of the employee who has departed is fully subsumed in the knowledge of his supervisor, who remains. But in some cases the memory of a single organization member may be the sole storage point of knowledge that is both idiosyncratic and of great importance to the organization. The knowledge may be tacit—say, an intuitive grasp of the priority structure of the competing demands on the employee's time that are signaled by incoming messages. It may be articulable but not written down—the first names, marital status, and preferred recreations of the important customers in the region, or the action that is called for when a particular machine starts to vibrate too much.

The loss of an employee with such important idiosyncratic knowledge poses a major threat to the continuity of routine—indeed, if the departure is unanticipated, continuity is necessarily broken. The new person hired to fill the role may eventually restore a semblance of the old routine, but only by picking up the knowledge more or less from scratch, guided by whatever clues his predecessor left lying about and by the indications provided by those in adjacent roles, within or outside the organization. However, those in adjacent positions may be taking the opportunity to attempt to redefine his organizational role in their own interest, so their advice is not fully trustworthy. For this reason, and because the new role occupant may himself be different in significant and durable ways from his predecessor, and also as the result of other contingencies affecting the role-learning process, it is highly unlikely that a near replica of the predecessor's role performance will result. In short, the organizational routine will mutate.

Mutations, of course, are not always deleterious. To put it another way, maintenance of prevailing routine is often an operational target, but it is not an ultimate objective. Modifications of routine that involve improvements in role performance are presumably welcome. However, in functioning complex systems with many highly differentiated and tightly interdependent parts, it is highly unlikely that undirected change in a single part will have beneficial effects on the system; this, of course, is the basis for the biological proposition that mutations tend to be deleterious on the average. An organization member trying to do a better job can presumably accomplish something more than "undirected change," but changes that seem like obvious improvements viewed from a particular role can easily have adverse effects elsewhere in the system. With the aid of a comprehensive understanding of the system as a whole, beneficial directed change in a part might reliably be accomplished. But since nobody in a complex organization actually has that sort of comprehensive understanding, it is clear *a fortiori* that a new employee does not have it.

It is not surprising, therefore, that the control processes of (surviving) organizations tend to resist mutations, even ones that present themselves as desirable innovations. For the particular mutagenic event of loss of a member with a unique knowledge store, the form of the resistance obviously depends on whether the departure is anticipated or not. On the assumption that it is not, control efforts will focus on the selection of a suitably malleable successor who will at least try to respond to the routinized demands placed on the role. The efforts of the veterans to instruct the recruit in the requirements of his role will be colored by their concern to achieve a new truce at least as favorable as the old one; as a result, those efforts will tend to disabuse that successor of "naïve" aspirations toward innovative change. When the departure is anticipated, on the other hand, the incumbent is likely to be enlisted in an effort to train one or more possible successors. How well this goes depends on, among other things, the degree to which the knowledge involved is tacit, the degree to which experience during the training period is representative of the full job, and—importantly—whether the incumbent really wants to succeed in imparting the knowledge to his successor.

Although the question of whether the organization can maintain continuity of routine is posed particularly clearly by the example of turnover in a key role, all organizational problems of "keeping things under control" pose that question in some degree. Time and environmental changes buffet the organization with potentially mutagenic events, against which its control systems struggle. In the long run, the most important threats to the maintenance of a successful routine may be the insidious ones, the changes that either escape the control system's notice entirely or else are susceptible to "symptomatic relief" that leaves adverse underlying trends uncorrected. If, for example, the organization fails to maintain an adequate general level of pay relative to alternatives in the market, it may happen that the quality and motivation of its personnel gradually decline, perhaps with adverse consequences for the quality of its product or service that develop a little too slowly to be detected and linked to the pay problem. Against the simpler and more visible problems, on the other hand, the routinized control system may be deployed so massively that it has the collateral effect of impeding adaptation when adaptation is actually necessary. The fact that organizations need to have routinized forms of resistance to unwanted change in routines thus becomes yet another reason why organizational behavior is so strongly channeled by prevailing routine.

Replication

The axiom of *additivity* is fundamental in orthodox production theory. It implies, among other things, that any feasible pattern of productive activity can be faultlessly replicated: an exact doubling of output per unit time is accomplished by an exact doubling of input. In concrete terms, the claim advanced in this proposition is captured by the image of a plant on a particular site producing a particular output mix in a particular way; on an identical site elsewhere, an identical plant is constructed and produces the identical output mix in the identical way. Or, as F. H. Hahn put it, "If two identical entrepreneurs set up two identical plants, with an identical labor force, to produce an identical commodity x, then the two together will produce twice the amount of x that could be produced by one alone" (Hahn, 1949, p. 135).

So stated, the proposition seems to have the compelling quality of the answer to a very elementary arithmetic problem. Presumably, the posit of identical entrepreneurs is supposed to entail an identity of productive technique, and the identical plants are not just identical in themselves, but situated in identical environments. After suitable amplification of this sort, the claim may be regarded as a simple tautology or perhaps as an assertion of the universal validity of physical law.

The question is whether the proposition says anything that is helpful in interpreting economic reality. For it to do so, the terms "identical entrepreneurs," "identical plants," and "identical labor force" must have empirical counterparts at least in the sense that they describe limiting cases that are often approached in real situations. In the context of orthodox thought, the idea that these connections to reality exist is supported by: (1) a habit of taking the idea of homogeneous input categories seriously, so that the "identical labor force" assumption is not blatantly contrafactual; (2) a propensity to think of individual entrepreneurs as the repositories of productive knowledge, so that positing "identical entrepreneurs" assumes identity of productive knowledge; and (3) a tendency to regard productive knowledge as articulable and free of idiosyncratic elements, so that the supposition of "identical entrepreneurs" does not relate to an exceedingly remote happenstance.

In our evolutionary models, we make the same assumption that perfect replication is possible, with a similar image in mind of a second plant identical to the first and employing identical routines.[10] However, our interpretation of the assumption is quite different from the orthodox one, and our commitment to it considerably less deep. A basic conceptual distinction is that we think of replication as being a costly, time-consuming process of copying an *existing* pattern of productive activity. Though in our modeling we abstract from the costs and make the simplest assumption about the time required, this is still a very different concept from the orthodox one, which is concerned entirely with the structure of *ex ante* possibilities. To put it another way, our assumption relates to what can be accomplished starting from the status quo of a functioning routine, whereas the long-run orthodox theory to which the additivity axiom relates has no notion of a status quo at all. Further, we regard the feasibility of close (let alone perfect) replication as being quite problematic—more problematic than the feasibility of continuation through time of the

---

10. We will limit our discussion of replication to the simple case of establishing the same routine in a plant identical to the original. Some of the same issues arise in almost any case of capacity expansion; a typical situation is that capacity is increased by a partial replication that relaxes the constraint imposed by a particular class of input services. However, partial replications involve some additional complications that we do not treat here.

existing routine, which is itself no foregone conclusion, as the above discussion points out. As an initial perspective on the problem, we would not recommend the Hahn tautology, but the following account from Polanyi: "The attempt to analyze scientifically the established industrial arts has everywhere led to similar results. Indeed, even in modern industries the indefinable knowledge is still an essential part of technology. I have myself watched in Hungary a new, imported machine for blowing electric lamp bulbs, the exact counterpart of which was operating successfully in Germany, failing for a whole year to produce a single flawless bulb" (Polanyi, 1964, p. 52).

The point emphasized by evolutionary theory is that a firm with an established routine possesses resources on which it can draw very helpfully in the difficult task of attempting to apply that routine on a larger scale. Because the creation of productive organizations is *not* a matter of implementing fully explicit blueprints by purchasing homogeneous inputs on anonymous markets, a firm that is already successful in a given activity is a particularly good candidate for being successful with new capacity of the same sort. The replication assumption in evolutionary models is intended primarily to reflect the advantages that favor the going concern attempting to do more of the same, as contrasted with the difficulties that it would encounter in doing something else or that others would encounter in trying to copy its success.

To understand the nature of these advantages, it is helpful first of all to consider the similarities between replication and control, and the deeper connections to the problem of organizational memory. In replicating an existing routine, the firm seeks to impose that routine's order on an entire new set of specific inputs. That task is a magnified version of one for which the firm already possesses routinized arrangements. For example, its existing personnel and training operations have the capability to "select and modify" the sorts of employees the routine requires. By diverting these existing capabilities at least in part to the tasks associated with the new facility, it can avoid difficulties that would be very likely to arise if the manning of that new facility were accomplished by an equally new and inexperienced personnel operation. The new plant will ultimately need its own personnel department (at least if "replication" is taken literally), but the new production system does not have to be hampered by the early mistakes of a new personnel department that may be learning to operate in a novel labor market environment. And a functioning production system that is effective enough to detect mistakes by the new personnel department can then help that department to learn its job.

More generally, the existing routine serves as a template for the new one. The use of the template makes possible a relatively precise copying of a functioning system that is far too large and complex to be comprehended by a single person. It is not necessary for there to be a central file that contains an articulate account of how the whole thing is done. Rather, for each organizational role that is a unique storage point for important and idiosyncratic organizational knowledge, it is necessary that the individual who will occupy that role in the new plant acquire the knowledge required for its performance. This may be accomplished by having that individual observe or be actively trained by the incumbent of that role in the old system, or by transferring the incumbent to the new system and leaving his trained successor in the old one. The collection of new role occupants thus created will make a coordinated, routinely functioning productive organization of the new facility, because the roles were coordinated in the old one—provided that the copying of the individual roles is accurate enough.

Of course, the process described will in general impose some costs in terms of the functioning of the old plant. It is unlikely that there will be enough slack resources available for training new personnel or for actually performing, temporarily, some functions in the new plant. For the replication story to make economic sense, the benefits obtained must exceed or be expected to exceed these costs. This issue is basically one of investment analysis. If the old plant is enjoying a *temporary* period of high prosperity, to be followed by normal or low profits, the opportunity costs of replication may indeed be excessive.[11] The knowledge transfer must make it possible to capture a flow of rents in the new plant that lasts long enough to compensate, in present value terms, the loss of rents in the old plant. The likelihood of this sort of pattern is obviously enhanced to the extent that a large knowledge transfer can be carried out with only small sacrifices in the old plant. Here it is relevant that the costs of a small number of anticipated departures or absences from key positions in the old plant are likely to be small, since such isolated gaps pose just the sort of problem that the control system routinely handles. On the other hand, the value of only a few people who know what they are doing may be enormous in providing the basic matrix of the routine in the new plant. That is, there are likely to be diminishing returns to experienced personnel, in terms of learning costs saved, in both plants. The transfer of a small number of experienced personnel from the

---

11. When long-run prospects are favorable but current profits are also high, it can happen that constructing a new plant *de novo* is preferable to replication involving current opportunity costs, even though replication is absolutely profitable and would be the preferred mode of expansion under less favorable conditions.

old, predominantly experienced plant to the new, predominantly inexperienced one saves a lot of learning costs in the latter and incurs only small ones in the former. Finally, because of imbalances arising from indivisibilities or for other reasons, there may be some resources in the old plant that are actually idle and can be costlessly applied to the replication effort or transferred to the new plant.

There are some potential obstacles to replication that may be difficult to overcome even at very high cost. Some employees at the old plant may be exercising complex skills with large tacit components, acquired through years of experience in the firm. Others may have skills of lesser complexity and tacitness, but be very poor at teaching those skills to someone else—doing and teaching are, after all, different. Some members may for various reasons be unwilling to cooperate in the process of transferring their segment of the memory contents to someone else; they may, for example, be unwilling to disclose how easy their job really is, or the extent of the shortcuts they take in doing it.[12] Finally, personal relationships may be an important factor, particularly in the structure and stability of the truce that the existing routine represents. The personnel department is not likely to be up to the challenge of locating a suitably matched *set* of new role occupants who can be relied upon to maintain the same sort of truce. For these reasons and more, the template provided by the existing routine may not yield a good copy. There will be some mutation of the routine as it is transferred to the new plant.

Of course, perfect replication is no more of an ultimate objective than perfect control. What matters is not that the plant be the same, but that it work with overall efficiency comparable to the old one.

Contraction

If an existing routine is a success, replication of that success is likely to be desired. In particular, in the models to follow, the organization in question is a business firm for which success is roughly measured by profits, and replication of productive routines is motivated by a desire to replicate the profit flows that those routines make possible. There are symmetric questions to be addressed if the existing routine is a failure—that is, unprofitable. But while the questions are at least roughly symmetric, the answers are not. Because of their obvious importance to our models of economic selection, we digress briefly to consider them.

---

12. The question of the incentives of organization members to disclose idiosyncratic information of importance to the organization's functioning is addressed by Williamson under the rubric "information impactedness" (Williamson, 1975, ch. 4).

One important asymmetry between replication and contraction is that while the former is typically an *optional* response to success, the latter is typically a *mandatory* response to failure. As usual, the situation is clearest in the case of business firms, though there are analogous problems in other sorts of organizations. If the revenues derived from the sale of the routine's outputs fail to cover the costs of the routine's inputs, then—barring governmental bail-outs, philanthropically inclined investors, and similarly unlikely contingencies—it will ultimately become impossible to acquire the inputs to continue the routine on the existing scale and something will have to happen.

Under this pressure, a business firm may be expected to initiate some sort of search for a new routine that would be viable in the prevailing environment. The analysis of this sort of search runs roughly parallel to the analysis of imitation and innovation that will concern us later in this chapter, with the proviso that the initiation of the search under conditions of adversity has implications for the quantity and quality of the resources that may be devoted to it. But if the search is successful in the limited sense that the firm begins to attempt to carry out a new routine, then the old routine is no longer the target and has fallen victim to the condition of adversity. The firm itself may live on, at least temporarily.

Although some sort of search response to adversity is probably typical, it may happen that the organization remains firmly committed to its existing ways of doing things—a course of action that can be rationalized as an attempt to last out a period of adversity that is perceived or hoped to be temporary. In this case, the only "search" that goes on is for the resources to continue to finance the existing routine. A likely occasion for such attempts to fall short is when it comes time to replace a large, indivisible item of durable equipment. If unable to carry out such a replacement, the firm may simply shrink and carry on roughly as before, but on a diminished scale. This sort of response (in addition to the search response) is envisaged in the formal models that follow. After a series of scale reductions of this sort, the firm and its routine may ultimately disappear entirely.

In reality, a great many factors are involved in determining the consequences of sustained adversity—for example, the degree of owner versus management control, merger opportunities, tax and bankruptcy law considerations, the liquidity or illiquidity of the firm's assets, and the state of the firm's balance sheet when adversity began. It is beyond the scope of our present discussion to sort out these factors and relate them to the likely persistence or change of routines. One point perhaps is worth noting here: a firm without a viable routine is a firm without a viable truce in intraorganizational conflict. That consideration, by itself, affords abundant reason to doubt that firms behave in adversity "as if" they were under the rational control of a single actor.[13]

Imitation

As a final example of a routine serving as a target, let us consider the case in which the target is a routine of some other firm. The interest in this sort of situation arises, of course, because it often happens that a firm observes that some other firm is doing things that it would like to be able to do—specifically, making more money by producing a better product or producing a standard product more cheaply. The envious firm then attempts to duplicate this imperfectly observed success. We will consider here only the case in which the imitatee is not cooperating with the imitation effort, and will assume that non-cooperation implies, at a minimum, that the imitator's personnel cannot directly observe what goes on in the imitatee's plant.[14]

What distinguishes this situation from replication is the fact that the target routine is not in any substantial sense available as a template. When problems arise in the copy, it is not possible to resolve them by closer scrutiny of the original. This implies that the copy is, at best, likely to constitute a substantial mutation of the original, embodying different responses to a large number of the specific challenges posed by the overall production problem. However, the imitator is not directly concerned with creating a good likeness, but with achieving an economic success—preferrably, an economic success at least equal to that of the original. Differences of detail that are economically of no great consequence are perfectly acceptable.

By this economically relevant criterion, the prospects for successful imitation vary dramatically from one situation to another. At one extreme, the production in question may be a novel combination of highly standardized technological elements. If so, close scrutiny of the product itself—"reverse engineering"—may permit the identification of those elements and the nature of their combination, and

---

13. Philip Nelson's book (1981) provides fascinating details on the behavior of a number of business firms operating under adversity. One point that stands out is that, under severe adversity, the divergence of member interests contributes importantly to the inability of the organization as a whole to cope effectively with its problems.

14. There are cases intermediate between the categories of "replication" and "imitation"—cases of attempted near-replication in environments very different from the original one, or of imitation with the active support of the firm being imitated. These are usually addressed under the heading of "transfer of technology." Our own thinking in this general area has benefited particularly from the work on technology transfer of Hall and Johnson (1967) and Teece (1977).

this may suffice for an economically successful imitation. Indeed, even vague rumors about the nature of the product may suffice, perhaps permitting the copy to hit the market almost as soon as the original. At the other extreme, the target routine may involve so much idiosyncratic and "impacted" tacit knowledge that even successful replication is highly problematic, let alone imitation from a distance.

In the wide range of intermediate cases, the imitator's basic tactic is to follow the example of a replicator wherever possible (and not too expensive), and to fill in the remaining gaps by independent effort. One important application of this tactic is to try to hire away from the imitatee those employees that the imitatee would reasonably want to transfer to a new plant in an attempt to replicate the existing one. Another is to obtain, by whatever means may be available, indirect clues to the nature of the target routine.

An imitator working with an extremely sparse set of clues about the details of the imitatee's performance might as well adopt the more prestigious title of "innovator," since most of the problem is really being solved independently. However, the knowledge that a problem *has* a solution does provide an incentive for persistence in efforts that might otherwise be abandoned.

4. ROUTINES AND SKILLS: PARALLELS

As we observed at the start of the previous chapter, understanding of individual skills informs understanding of organizational behavior in two ways. First, because individuals exercise skills in their roles as organization members, the characteristics of organizational capabilities are directly affected by the characteristics of individual skilled behavior. We have noted some of these connections. For example, an organization's capabilities require the exercise of individual skills that may involve a large component of tacit knowledge; this directly implies limits on the extent to which the organization's capabilities can themselves be articulated, and there are attendant implications for the character of the replication task. Then, too, the inflexibility of behavior displayed by large organizations is attributable in part to the fact that individual skills become rusty when not exercised; it is therefore hard for an organization to hold in memory a coordinated response to contingencies that arise only rarely.

Here we make explicit the other sort of contribution that understanding of individual skills makes to understanding of organizational functioning: the contribution at the level of metaphor. Routines are the skills of an organization. The performance of an organizational routine involves the effective integration of a number of component subroutines (themselves further reducible), and is ordinarily accomplished without "conscious awareness"—that is, without requiring the attention of top management. This sort of decentralization in organizational functioning parallels the skilled individual's ability to perform without attending to the details. A routine may involve extensive direct interactions with the organization's environment and the making of numerous "choices" that are contingent both upon the state of the environment and the state of the organization itself, but these choices involve no process of deliberation by top management. The intervention of top management in the detailed functioning of lower levels is ordinarily symptomatic of an attempt to modify routine or of difficulties with the functioning of existing routines—just as conscious awareness of detail and attempts at articulation are symptomatic of new learning or of trouble in the case of individual skills.

In a number of respects, organizational behavior seems to be subject to magnified versions of problems and pathologies that afflict individual skilled behavior. The scale and complexity of a large organization make impossible the degree of centralization of control represented by the brain of an individual human being. This relative weakness of centralized analysis and control in organizations, when compared to individuals, is the obvious explanation for the relative severity of the difficulties that organizations encounter in areas where centralization is for some reason important. Thus, for example, we noted that limits on articulation in the case of individual skills derive partly from the "whole versus parts" problem of reconciling an exhaustive account of details with a coherent view of the whole. Much more severe limits on the articulation of organizational knowledge arise from the same cause, because although attending to details is something that can be shared and decentralized, the task of achieving a coherent view of the whole is not. Similarly, improvisation of a coordinated response from a system requires centralized control of the system. Organizations are poor at improvising coordinated responses to novel situations; an individual lacking skills appropriate to the situation may respond awkwardly, but an organization lacking appropriate routines may not respond at all.

Organizations can get a great deal accomplished that they do not know how to do, by drawing on the capabilities of other individuals and organizations. In doing so, however, they exercise planning routines that involve the manipulation of symbols representing highly complex entities. Like individuals, organizations may make ineffective use of the array of capabilities available in their environments, or be victimized by hucksters, because of limitations on their planning vocabulary—particularly when they do not themselves possess even the rudiments of the capabilities they seek to acquire.

The basic metaphor can be elaborated and extended in a number of other directions, but we will leave these byways unexplored. The important contribution of the metaphor is the insight it provides into the role of bounded rationality in organizational behavior. We observed in our discussion of individual skills that bounded rationality imposes a tradeoff between capability and deliberate choice. That tradeoff exists for organizations as well, but the relative weakness of centralized control in an organization makes the terms of the tradeoff much less favorable to deliberate choice. One cannot infer from the fact that an organization functions smoothly and successfully in a particular range of observed environments that it is a rational and "intelligent" organism that will cope successfully with novel challenges. If anything, one should expect environmental change to make manifest the sacrifice of flexibility that is the price paid for highly effective capabilities of limited scope.

5. OPTIMAL ROUTINES AND OPTIMIZATION ROUTINES

Orthodox economists ordinarily profess a complete lack of interest in the processes by which firms actually make decisions. From their perspective, the fact that our discussion to this point has been concerned with *how* organizations function means that it offers no clue as to "whether firms really maximize profits," since that question relates to "what they do"—that is, to the transactions they engage in, not to how they decide to do it. Insofar as their point relates to the possible optimality of particular actions in particular circumstances, we agree with it. Indeed, the evolutionary model of the following chapter illustrates the possibility that firms modeled according to the spirit of our own view of decision process may wind up taking profit-maximizing actions in selection equilibrium. However, if their claim is that firms *consistently* optimize, even under completely unanticipated circumstances, then we obviously disagree. And we would argue that evidence relating to decision processes is highly relevant to that issue.

We will not go into the subtle questions of methodological principle involved in this area. However, one rather simple point illuminates the nature of the clash between the orthodox view that firms optimize and the evolutionary view that they function according to routine. Imagine a firm that functions with a completely inflexible routine, totally unresponsive to its changing environment. It purchases inputs at constant flow rates and converts them into outputs which it sells at constant rates. The profitability of this operation varies as the environment changes, but imagine that it is always positive. Orthodoxy can accept this firm's behavior as profit maximizing, since the behavior is interpretable as reflecting optimization over a production set that contains only the single input-output list corresponding to the firm's routine—or perhaps that list and some others that are strictly inferior to it.

The key point here concerns the empirical basis of the claim that only that one pattern of behavior is available to the firm. If one accepts the methodological principle that "what the firm actually does" in market transactions is the only relevant evidence on the alternatives available, then the orthodox claim that this inflexible firm is an optimizer is safe from refutation. But if other sorts of evidence are admissible—for example, evidence that the firm's inflexibility reflects the existence of a delicate truce in an extremely severe case of latent intraorganizational conflict, or evidence on what other firms do—then the claim that this very rigid firm is an optimizer may well be refuted. More generally, the hypothesis that routinized behavior patterns really reflect optimization after all is likely to be more vulnerable to evidence that provides some sort of independent check on the alternatives that might be considered available than it is to evidence on the market transactions arising from the routine itself.[15]

Although a highly defensive and skeptical stance toward decision process evidence is typical, occasionally evidence of this sort is put forward in support of orthodox theory. Thus, for example, the fact that a particular firm has sophisticated accounting techniques, employs formal optimization procedures in some part of its decision making, or has a permanent in-house operations research unit may be adduced as evidence corroborative of the general proposition that firms optimize. Of course, the first question to be raised about this evidence is how representative it is, and whether orthodox analysis is to be understood as relevant only to the historical periods, economies, industries, and firm-size ranges in which these features of firm decision processes are typical. Beyond that, we emphasize that this sort of evidence fits into the evolutionary framework as useful information on the details of the routines that some firms follow.

We would conjecture, for example, that firms that have operations research (OR) groups not only go about making decisions in different ways from firms that do not, but that the decisions themselves are likely to differ. Whether a firm has an OR group and systematically does OR as part of its higher-order decision making is a question

---

15. We return to these issues in Chapter 7. The questions of methodology are addressed more extensively in Winter (1975).

that we view very much in the same light as the question of whether a firm does or does not use the oxygen process for making steel. Both questions are about the routines employed by firms. The exercise of an OR capability indicates that a firm has that capability in very much the same way that exercise of the oxygen process for making steel means that the firm has that particular capability.

However, the fact that a firm has an OR group that builds models and that this group is influential in decision making does not imply that the firm's actual decisions are "truly" optimal. Indeed, we would view particular attention of the OR group on a certain area of decision as an indication that the firm presently is not satisfied with its current routines in that area. Presuming the OR group comes up with a proposal for reform, we would regard it meaningless to say that the new policy is truly optimal; only God knows what policy truly would be optimal. There is no guarantee that the policy that would be optimal within the operations research model is even superior in the actual economic environment to the policy that is being replaced.

Also, and relatedly, knowledge of the fact that the firm goes through explicit maximization calculations to guide its decision making does not mean that the orthodox economist can on the basis of his own model make good predictions of what the firm will do. His model and that used by the operations research group may differ in important respects. It does mean, however, that if the economist knew the model used by the firm's operations research group, that information might help him predict and explain the firm's actions. The economist would then have direct information on the *routine* employed in decision making by the firm. And that, of course, is the heart of our theoretical proposal: the behavior of firms can be explained by the routines that they employ. Knowledge of the routines is the heart of understanding behavior. Modeling the firm means modeling the routines and how they change over time.

6. ROUTINES, HEURISTICS, AND INNOVATION

Both in customary usage and in our technical use of the term, "innovation" involves change in routine. We have stressed the uncertainty that inevitably surrounds technical innovation—the implementation of a design for a new product, or of a new way to produce a product. A similar uncertainty surrounds other kinds of innovation—the establishment of a new marketing policy, or a new decision rule for restocking inventories. In general, two kinds of uncertainty surround these innovations. The precise nature of the innovation actually arrived at is usually not closely predictable at the start of the endeavor that culminates in the innovation. And the consequences of employing the innovation—changing the routine—in general will not be closely predictable until a reasonable amount of actual operating experience with it has been accumulated. There is, however, more to be said about the relations of routine behavior and innovation than to observe that these concepts are commonly (and appropriately) regarded as opposed ideas. Our final task in this chapter is to explore some of the subtler connections between routinization and innovation, and ultimately to indicate how the existence of innovative activity relates, in our evolutionary theory, to the general image of firm behavior as governed by routine.

Puzzles from Prevailing Routines

It is sometimes remarked of an important research achievement that the hard part was in locating the right question; finding the answer to that question then proved to be relatively easy. One way in which the routine functioning of an organization can contribute to the emergence of innovation is that useful questions arise in the form of puzzles or anomalies relating to prevailing routines. The concreteness of such questions and the obvious existence of an application for the answers is an important point in their favor as guides to problem-solving activity.

Consider the foreman of a work team responsible for a particular operation (set of routines) who observes that a machine is not working properly. He routinely calls in to the maintenance department, which in turn routinely sends out a machine repairman. The machine repairman has been trained to diagnose in a particular way the troubles that such a machine might have. He goes down a list of possible problems systematically, and finds one that fits the symptoms. He fixes the part so that the machine again may play its role in the overall work routine. He may also, however, report to the foreman that this particular kind of trouble has become very common since the supplier started using aluminum in making the part in question and that perhaps the machine should be operated in a different manner to avoid the difficulty.

Or consider a sales manager who observes a significant and sustained decrease in total sales of a particular item. He routinely calls in his young assistant—a recent graduate of a master's program in management—to do a study of the problem. The assistant, with a bit of clerical help, scans what has been happening to sales in particular regions and by particular salesmen. He ascertains that almost all of the decrease has occurred in the Southeast. He may go on to check up on the activities of the salespeople concerned with the Southeast and may recommend some replacement of personnel. He may suspect that some important change in demand conditions has occurred and propose a new market survey to discover its nature. Or he may propose that a new advertising campaign, addressed to customers in the Southeast, may be needed.

These examples illustrate, on the one hand, the routine functioning of organizations. The responses described fall into the typical pattern in which a crisis or "exception" condition in one part of the organization is part of the routine content of jobs of other personnel. On the other hand, it is significant that the problem-solving responses routinely evoked by difficulties with existing routines may yield results that lead to major change. The effort triggered by the repairman's suggestion may lead to a radical improvement in the method of operation of the machine, or to a decision to switch to machines of quite a different sort, requiring numerous adaptations elsewhere in the routine. The market survey proposed by the young assistant may indicate that the trouble in the Southeast is only a symptom of a market change that is likely to become pervasive, and may thus trigger redesign of the product to meet the specific challenge that the survey identified. Problem-solving efforts that are initiated with the existing routine as a target may lead to innovation instead.

Existing Routines as Components

Schumpeter identified innovation with the "carrying out of new combinations" (Schumpeter, 1934, pp. 65–66). This phrase gives useful emphasis to the fact that innovation in the economic system—and indeed the creation of any sort of novelty in art, science, or practical life—consists to a substantial extent of a recombination of conceptual and physical materials that were previously in existence. The vast momentum of scientific, technological, and economic progress in the modern world derives largely from the fact that each new achievement is not merely the answer to a particular problem, but also a new item in the vast storehouse of components that are available for use, in "new combinations," in the solution of other problems in the future.

Innovations in organizational routine similarly consist, in large part, of new combinations of existing routines. An innovation may involve nothing more than the establishment of new patterns of information and material flows among existing subroutines. It may involve the replacement of an existing subroutine by a new and different one that performs, in relation to the rest, the same function that the old one did. Some parts of the innovative routine may rely on physical principles only recently discovered and now implemented through novel types of equipment and newly developed skills—but surrounding this novel core there may be many layers of complementary activity governed by the same routines that have prevailed for many years.

When an effort is made to incorporate an existing routine as a component of innovative routines, it is helpful if two conditions are satisfied. One is that the routine be reliable—that is, fully under control. The attempt to develop an effective new combination ordinarily involves a substantial amount of trial-and-error search, in which obstacles to effective performance are detected, diagnosed, and solved. It is helpful if the familiar elements of the new combination do not themselves contribute problems, particularly if the problems from that source would complicate the task of detecting and solving the problems arising from the novel elements. The second condition is that the new application of the existing routine be as free as possible from the sorts of operational and semantic ambiguities of scope that we discussed in connection with individual skills. Ideally, the existing routine may require only symbolic representation in the design effort for the new combination. For example, the existing routine for shipping the product to wholesalers may be as unambiguously applicable to the new product as it was to the old. In that case, the design effort for the new routine can handle the transportation problem simply by using the phrase "ship to warehouses," and the details of the shipment process need not be examined. But perhaps the new product is in some way more delicate than the old—more vulnerable to temperature extremes or to vibration. Then ambiguity may arise as to whether the existing shipping routine will suffice. If there is reason to doubt that it will, the problem of getting the product to the warehouses in good condition becomes interdependent with the rest of the design problem, and the simple symbolic reference to shipment will have to give way to consideration of details. The existing shipping routine may have to be tried out to see how it affects the new product; it may require modification, or perhaps the design of the product will have to be altered to make it less delicate.

These two conditions suggest an important qualification to the general notion of an opposition between routinization and innovation. Reliable routines of well-understood scope provide the best components for new combinations. In this sense, success at the innovative frontier may depend on the quality of the support from the "civilized" regions of established routine.

Heuristics and Strategies as Routines

Our final point concerning the relationship of routine behavior to innovation is centered on a simple distinction between organizational *activity* directed to innovation (or problem-solving more generally) and the *results* of such activity. The fundamental uncertainty surrounding innovative activity is uncertainty about its results. True, there may be considerable uncertainty, when the activity is initiated, about the details of the activity itself—particularly since those details may ultimately be recognized as an approach to some type of success that is not knowable in advance. But there may also be strong patterns of a highly predictable nature in the activity—and to the extent that this is so it seems reasonable to describe the activity as "routinized." A particularly clear illustration of the significance of the distinction is the case of systematic sequential search of a well-defined population for an element with attributes that make it the solution to a well-defined problem. When and whether a solution will be found may be quite uncertain, but the search itself follows a routine with a simple structure: select element, test for desired attributes, terminate with success if attributes are present, select next element if they are not.

Routinized arrangements for producing innovations and solutions to problems take a variety of forms, among which are some very familiar features of the organizational scene. Given a problem, direct a subordinate to look into it—or appoint a committee or a task force, or bring in a consultant with a good reputation. Given a decision to devote 4 percent of $100 million of sales to R&D, it is almost certainly possible to acquire some sort of facility, a research director, and some scientists, and go to work. In broad terms, at least, the art of deploying resources to *try* to bring about some result or other is not esoteric. Whether useful results are actually achieved is another matter. In fact, results that are more or less useful are often achieved—and it is an important feature of these problem-solving situations that the superior results that in some sense "could" have been achieved are usually not available as a standard of comparison.

The theory of heuristic search provides a helpful framework for thinking about these issues.[16] A *heuristic* is "any principle or device that contributes to the reduction in the average search to solution" (Newell, Shaw, and Simon, 1962, p. 85). Some heuristics are applicable across very wide ranges of problems—"work backward from the goal"—while others are relevant only in highly specific problem contexts. Devices like directing a subordinate to look into a problem,

---

16. See Newell, Shaw, and Simon (1962) and Newell and Simon (1972).

or appointing a committee, can be viewed as general types of managerial problem-solving heuristics. But every field of specialized competence contains a wide range of heuristics that are particularly appropriate to that field. The operations researcher will build an optimization model of the problem. The mechanical engineer will look at the mechanized aspects of the production process, and look for ways to mechanize it further. The chief executive officer whose background is in finance will bring a different set of heuristics to his job than one whose background is in production. The manager who transfers to a new organization will bring with him some of the heuristics that seemed to work in his previous employment.

The broad ideas that shape the most critical high-level decisions of a business enterprise may also be viewed as heuristics—they are principles that are believed to shorten the average search to solution of the problems of survival and profitability. Much discussion of heuristics of this sort has been carried on under the rubric "corporate strategy." Indeed, according to the concept of strategy that has been developed by a number of investigators associated with the Harvard Business School,[17] the fundamental heuristic imperative for top management is: "Develop a strategy." Other heuristics are involved in the implementation of that basic one—for example, "Assess the company's strengths and weaknesses in relation to the competition." A related idea is that the firm should adopt an organizational structure appropriate to its strategy.[18] More generally, principles that offer guidance for the selection of organizational structures may be viewed as another class of high-level managerial heuristics.

We propose to assimilate to our concept of routine all of the patterning of organizational activity that the observance of heuristics produces, including the patterning of particular ways of attempting to innovate. To the extent that such patterning persists through time and has implications for profitability and growth, it is part of the genetic mechanism underlying the evolutionary process. But we emphasize, once again, that viewing innovative activity as "routine" in this sense does not entail treating its results as predictable.

In many ways our position regarding these matters is consistent with that of Whitehead (1938), who proposed that sometime during the nineteenth century man invented the art of inventing, and is also consistent with the Schumpeter of *Capitalism, Socialism, and Democracy* (1950), who proposed that sometime during the twentieth century the modern corporation "routinized innovation." Neither Whitehead nor Schumpeter, we think, would deny the role of genius

---

17. See Caves (1980).
18. This idea is particularly associated with Alfred Chandler (1962).

or luck, or argue that systematic differences in innovative competence do not exist. But their views are quite compatible with the proposition that organizations have well-defined routines for the support and direction of their innovative efforts.

7. SUMMARY: ROUTINES AS GENES

Theorists should aim to tell the truth in their theorizing, but they cannot aim to tell the whole truth. For to theorize is precisely to focus on those entities and relationships in reality that are believed to be central to the phenomena observed—and largely to ignore the rest. To advance a new theory is to propose a shift of focus, to recognize as central considerations that were previously ignored.

In this chapter, we have focused upon the realities of organizational functioning that form the foundation of our evolutionary theory. Foremost among those realities are the factors that tend to limit the individual firm to the exercise of a distinctive package of economic capabilities that is of relatively narrow scope. Essential coordinating information is stored in the routine functioning of the organization and "remembered by doing." As in the case of individual skills, the specificity of the behavior involved is simply the obverse of its effectiveness; also, much of the knowledge that underlies the effective performance is tacit knowledge of the organization, not consciously known or articulable by anyone in particular. These cognitive factors are reinforced by motivational ones associated with the control of intraorganizational conflict. Prevailing routines define a truce, and attempts to change routines often provoke a renewal of the conflict which is destructive to the participants and to the organization as a whole.

As a first approximation, therefore, firms may be expected to behave in the future according to the routines they have employed in the past. This does not imply a literal identity of behavior over time, since routines may be keyed in complex ways to signals from the environment. It does imply that it is quite inappropriate to conceive of firm behavior in terms of deliberate choice from a broad menu of alternatives that some external observer considers to be "available" opportunities for the organization. The menu is not broad, but narrow and idiosyncratic; it is built into the firm's routines, and most of the "choosing" is also accomplished automatically by those routines. This does not mean that individual firms cannot be brilliant successes for a short or long period: success and failure depend on the state of the environment. As long as the world rewards great tennis playing, great tennis players will succeed in the world, regardless of their talents as physicists or pianists. Efforts to understand the functioning of industries and larger systems should come to grips with the fact that highly flexible adaptation to change is not likely to characterize the behavior of individual firms. Evolutionary theory does this.

As a second approximation, firms may be expected to behave in the future in ways that resemble the behavior that would be produced if they simply followed their routines of the past. Just what "resemble" means here is an important and complex question. It is a question that is particularly illuminated by inquiry into the factors that hold behavior to the channels of routine, since whatever change takes place may be expected to follow the path of least resistance. But to assess where the resistance is likely to be least requires a discriminating analysis of the relative strengths of different sources of resistance. This is the great challenge of the subject of "organizational genetics"—to understand how the continuity of routinized behavior operates to channel organizational change. Our discussion of routines as targets and as components addresses this problem in a preliminary way, but the subject has barely been defined and the real work remains to be done. The particular models that follow are built on very simple assumptions regarding these matters, particularly the assumption that capacity expansion can be achieved with faultless replication of routine, and similarly that contraction of a firm is simply a scaling down of the same routinized pattern of operation. The discussion above provides support for these assumptions as a starting point for model building, but it contains some important caveats that should be kept in mind in future work. It also makes even more suspect the assumption that imitation of another firm's routines can be accomplished perfectly. However, for the limited purposes of these particular models, use of a weaker assumption would do more to complicate the analysis than to change its substantive content. The important consideration captured by the models is that imitation, though costly and imperfect in the individual instance, is a powerful mechanism by which new routines come to organize a larger fraction of the total activity of the system.

In the contemporary economy, some portion of business behavior is closely calculated by sophisticated optimization methods. Another portion is innovation activity shaped by the creative problem-solving insights of scientists, engineers, and managers. A full account of business behavior has to deal with these sophisticated portions, and the imagery of routinized behavior does not have the clear validity and power here that it has in discussing, say, a family firm whose product mix has remained unchanged for generations. We have argued, however, that the notion of routine behavior does have application in this sophisticated realm, though in a qualfied sense. For example, the skills of the highly trained operations researcher, scientist, or manager are reflected in characteristic, highly patterned forms of problem-solving activity. The scope of the expertise involved in each case is defined by a certain class of problem-solving techniques and heuristics. For this and other reasons, even the sophisticated problem-solving efforts of an organization fall into quasi-routine patterns, whose general outlines can be anticipated on the basis of experience with previous problem-solving efforts of that organization. But the patterning of the problem-solving activity is reflected only vaguely in the immediate outcomes of that activity and even less clearly in the gross changes in firm behavior that these problem solutions may trigger. From the viewpoint of an external observer who has no access to the sophisticated workings within the organization, the results are hard to predict and on that ground are best regarded as stochastic. This is the approach we take in the evolutionary models that follow.

TEXTBOOK ECONOMICS REVISITED

6

Static Selection Equilibrium

WE BEGIN our explorations in formal evolutionary modeling by considering selection equilibrium and examining the characteristics and behavior of firms that survive under equilibrium conditions.[1] The selection equilibrium concept has some natural connections with the profit-maximizing, zero profit, long-run equilibrium concept in orthodox theory, and many economists have noted these. But economists have been divided on the right way to look at evolutionary arguments in economics. In some treatments the idea of a selection equilibrium has been used to provide support for the propositions of orthodoxy. In other treatments there is at least a hint that there is a separate and distinct theory here that may have significant differences from as well as similarities with orthodoxy.

The belief that competitive selection forces will drive from an industry all but the efficient profit maximizers is widespread in economics, and often has been put forth as a reason for adherence to the orthodox theory that assumes profit maximization. Perhaps the best-known articulation of this position is by Milton Friedman: "Let the apparent immediate determinant of business behavior be anything at all—habitual reaction, random chance or what not. Whenever this determinant happens to lead to behavior consistent with rational and informed maximization of returns, the business will prosper and acquire resources with which to expand; whenever it

---

1. The material presented in this chapter draws heavily on the earlier analyses presented in Winter (1964, 1971).

does not the business will tend to lose resources and can be kept in existence only by the addition of resources from outside. The process of natural selection helps to validate the hypothesis (of maximization of returns—N–W)—or, rather, given natural selection, acceptance of the hypothesis can be based largely on the judgment that it summarizes appropriately the conditions for survival" (Friedman, 1953, p. 22). There is no hint here that an evolutionary theory is an alternative to orthodoxy. Rather, the proposition is that selection forces may be the proper explanation of why orthodox theory is a good predictive engine.

Friedman's view of the proper theoretical place for evolutionary arguments seems quite different from the view put forth by Armen Alchian in his 1950 article "Uncertainty, Evolution, and Economic Theory." In it he sets forth a point of view regarding firm behavior that resembles ours in many ways, stressing the element of chance and luck in determining outcomes, the role of learning by trial and feedback and imitation in guiding firms to do better, and of selection forces in molding what firms and industries do. "What really counts is the various actions actually tried, for it is from these that success is selected, not from some set of perfect actions. The economist may be pushing his luck too far in arguing that actions in response to changes in environment and changes in satisfaction with the existing state of affairs will converge as a result of adaptation or adoption towards the optimum action that would have been selected, if foresight had been perfect" (Alchian, 1950, p. 218). This does not strike us as an argument that selection forces provide a reason for adherence to orthodox theory, but rather a suggestion that there may be some important differences between an orthodox and an evolutionary perspective.

In his *Three Essays on the State of Economic Science*, Tjalling Koopmans comments that Friedman's position, as well as Alchian's, would seem to imply a need for explicit evolutionary theorizing.

Friedman himself indicates an important step in this direction when he points out, in parallel with Alchian, that the postulate of profit maximizing behavior by entrepreneurs is supported by the fact that those who do not manage to maximize profits are likely to be eliminated by competition in the course of things. Here a postulate about individual behavior is made more plausible by making reference to the adverse effects of, and hence the penalty for, departures from the postulated behavior. The reality of the penalty is documented by technological and institutional facts, such as the reproductability of production processes and the operation of accounting procedures in bankruptcy laws, facts which are a degree less elusive to verification than mere behavioral postulates. But if this is the basis for our belief in profit maximization, then we should postulate that basis itself and not the profit maximization which it implies in certain circumstances. (Koopmans, 1957, p. 140)

Koopmans here identifies a serious weakness of most extant evolutionary theorizing in economics. The theoretical discussion proceeds exclusively at the informal level we have called appreciative theory, and is unconstrained by theoretical analysis of a more rigorous and formal sort. Thus, Friedman has not explored the assumptions that need to be made if economic selection forces are to force and sustain an equilibrium that closely resembles that of orthodox theory. We propose that the required assumptions are much more stringent than many economists seem to believe. Nor has Alchian explored rigorously the difference it might make that selection operates on "actions actually tried" and not "some set of perfect actions." We shall argue, through the vehicle of a variety of formal evolutionary models, that it does make a considerable difference.[2]

1. CHARACTERIZING ECONOMIC SELECTION PROCESSES

There is nothing about economic selection arguments that makes them peculiarly transparent, or otherwise obviates the need for careful logical analysis. Indeed, if anything is transparently obvious about the sort of casual argument typified by the Friedman passage quoted above, it is the existence of gaping holes in the logic. For example, the Friedman arguments neglect the fact that the process of prospering and acquiring resources with which to expand does not occur instantaneously; some time is required for the greater profitabilities of the firms that approach maximizing behavior to be manifested in a significantly greater relative importance of these firms in

---

2. In one of his more specific suggestions, Alchian proposed that an increase in the wage rate would tend to decrease the labor intensity of techniques used by survivors of the evolutionary struggle, just as it decreases labor intensity when firms optimize. Suppose, however, that all firms initially are less than optimally labor-intensive and are clustered around the lowest labor intensity consistent with nonnegative profits. Since a wage increase reduces profits at every labor intensity, it *increases* the smallest labor intensity at which nonnegative profits are earned. Thus, if firms that incur losses tend to search for alternative policies, the cluster of approximately zero-profit firms may be centered at a higher labor intensity after the wage increase than before.

Becker (1962a) similarly neglects to focus on the "actions actually tried." In a simple analysis, he assumes that production at minimum average total cost is a necessary condition for firm survival—failing to notice that if no firm ever chooses to produce at minimum average total cost, there is no mechanism to drive price to that level, and higher-cost production can be viable.

the economy. If the immediate determinant of behavior is "random chance or what not" there is no reason to believe that the firms that take actions consistent with profit maximization at one time will also take actions consistent with such maximization at all subsequent times; hence, there is no obvious reason to believe that there will be any cumulative tendency for the firms that are maximizing profits at any given time to grow relative to firms that are not maximizing. To the extent that behavior is random, there may be no systematic selection at all.

On the other hand, the idea that the immediate determinant of business behavior is "habitual reaction" provides a useful starting point for evolutionary modeling. We have argued in detail the view that organizational capabilities consist largely of the ability to perform and sustain a set of routines; such routines could be regarded as a highly structured set of "habitual reactions" linking organization members to one another and to the environment. The tendency for such routines to be maintained over time plays in our theory the role that genetic inheritance plays in the theory of biological evolution. But sweeping claims that economic selection forces drive individual firms and whole systems to optimal behavior cannot be defended merely by adducing a plausible genetic mechanism. There is no reason to believe that at any time the "habitual reactions" of extant firms include the reaction patterns that are the best in a broader set of possibilities. As Alchian has stated, selection works on what exists, not on the full set of what is feasible. Further, even habitual reactions that are close to maximizing under one set of economic conditions may not be under another. Thus, in models involving an extended process of selection among an initial set of behavioral routines, firms whose behavior would be profit maximizing under conditions of a given time may be eliminated by competition at an earlier stage, under conditions for which their behavior was not optimal.

To fill in the ranks of behavior patterns decimated by competitive struggles of earlier times, or to make possible the appearance of entirely new patterns, some mechanism analogous to genetic mutation must be posited. Otherwise, selection can only bring about the dominance of the best of the patterns that started the contest, or even the less maladapted of the survivors of some early stage. Innovation resulting from search by extant firms, and entry of new firms following new routines, play this role in our models.

In biological evolution, differential reproduction rates of phenotypes possessing different genetic inheritances drive the selection dynamics. In models of economic selection, expansion of profitable firms relative to unprofitable ones plays an analogous role. But in cultural selection systems, as contrasted with purely biological ones, there is as well the possibility of imitation. In the selection dynamics of the models we shall build, often both mechanisms will be at work.

That processes of innovation and imitation bring about change in firms' routines should be kept in mind when thinking about economic selection: it is important to distinguish between selection on firms and selection on routines. In an exploration of the possible correspondence between economic selection equilibrium and more orthodox equilibrium concepts, presumably the fates of firms as such are of no great interest. The focus is on behavior—that is, on the routines. But this raises the question: How should the set of routines that are candidates for selection be characterized? The problem does not arise in the simplest model, in which there is no entry by new firms and extant firms are locked into their particular routines. Nor are there particular complications if the model permits entry, so long as the set of all extant firms and potential entrants is finite, and firms do not change their routines. The problem arises when existing firms or those contemplating entry engage in search. Then the set of potential routines that can be reached by search becomes a major analytic concern. If the end in view is to explore the problem of developing a rigorous evolutionary argument that could serve as a partial prop for orthodoxy, one must accept in some form the orthodox assumption of a sharply defined opportunity set taken as a datum, and also the supposition that the properties of this set are such as to assure that the notion of a "best" routine for any set of market conditions makes sense. For more ambitious purposes, and particularly for analysis of economic growth and Schumpeterian competition, these orthodox commitments are unacceptable for reasons explained in Chapters 3 and 5. But since the former, limited concern occupies us here, we will make the necessary concession to orthodoxy and consider a given, finite set of possible routines that search may uncover.

It is similarly in the interest of evaluating the evolutionary defense of orthodoxy that we put forward in the following section a model that settles into a *static* selection equilibrium, in which the only continuing change takes the form of a futile search for routines profitable in that equilibrium. Such a focus on static equilibrium is plainly unnatural in the context of an evolutionary theory, and to generate such an equilibrium in an evolutionary model requires some delicate contrivances that have no independent rationale. Also, it is probably not entirely fair to those who have advanced the evolutionary defense of orthodoxy to impute to them the view that selection processes inevitably drive the system to a *static* equilibrium *exactly* like an orthodox equilibrium: they probably had in mind that there is (at most) a strong "tendency" for selection mechanisms to mimic orthodox theoretical predictions. Unfortunately, the limitations of orthodox formal theory make it impossible to do full justice in this particular discussion either to the proper development of evolutionary formalism or to the appreciative insights of Friedman and others. As we argued in Chapter 1, it is not really possible to be fully rigorous and fully orthodox and still admit disequilibrium as a theoretical possibility—and only by entirely suppressing the question of how equilibrium is achieved can one attempt to understand continuing change with the tools of equilibrium analysis. Thus, if we are to subject the evolutionary defense of orthodoxy to scrutiny in the context of a formal model, it must be a model of static equilibrium. Orthodoxy offers no other target.

2. A PARTICULAR MODEL OF ECONOMIC SELECTION

We now describe and analyze a simple evolutionary model that inevitably settles eventually into a static equilibrium that closely resembles the competitive equilibrium of orthodox theory. After completing the formal analysis, we review the critical assumptions that underlie its orthodox conclusions, and in so doing identify some of the limitations of informal arguments of the sort advanced by Friedman.

The focus here is on selection of two different kinds of routines. One is the "technique" that a firm uses in production. The other is the "decision rule" that determines a firm's rate of capacity utilization and thus its output level.

The industry in question produces a single homogeneous product. All firms in the industry face the same set of technical alternatives for producing their product. All feasible techniques are characterized by fixed input coefficients for variable inputs and constant returns to scale. All techniques have the same ratio of capacity output to capital stock; for convenience, let that ratio equal one. Techniques differ however, in terms of their variable inputs. A firm at any time employs only one technique.

The second routine employed by a firm is its capacity utilization rule. Such a rule relates the extent of capacity utilization to the ratio of price to unit variable cost of production. Thus,

$$q = \alpha\left(\frac{P}{c}\right) k,$$

where P and c are product price and unit variable production cost respectively, and q and k are output and capital (capacity). It is assumed that function $\alpha(\cdot)$ is continuous, monotone nondecreasing, positive for sufficiently large values of its argument, and satisfies $0 \leqq \alpha(\cdot) \leqq 1$. A capacity utilization rule may be interpreted as describing the percentage profit margin over variable cost needed to induce the firm to operate at various capacity utilization levels.

Factors of production are supplied perfectly elastically to the industry, and all factor prices are positive and constant over the course of the analysis. Thus all techniques can be characterized and ranked by variable unit production costs. Of course, for any technique total unit production cost is negatively related to the level of capacity utilization. For expositional convenience we assume that there is a unique best technique with unit variable production cost $\hat{c}$. We should call attention to the fact that there is not necessarily a unique best (profit-maximizing) capacity utilization rule. It is true that no other rule can beat the rule flagged by orthodox theory:

$$
\left.\begin{array}{l}
q = 0 \\[2em]
0 \leqq q \leqq k \\[2em]
q = k
\end{array}\right\} \quad \text{for} \quad
\left\{\begin{array}{l}
\dfrac{P}{c} < 1 \\[1.2em]
\dfrac{P}{c} = 1 \\[1.2em]
\dfrac{P}{c} > 1
\end{array}\right.
$$

But for any particular P/c value, any rule that calls for the same output as this one yields the same profit.[3]

The industry faces a strictly downward-sloping, continuous demand price function that relates the price of the product produced to total industry output. The function is defined for all nonnegative output levels. It is assumed that if total industry output is small enough, some technique and capacity utilization rule will yield a positive profit. If industry output is large enough, no technique and utilization rule will be profitable.

Formally, the system can be characterized as follows. Assuming that all the capacity possessed by a firm employs the same technique and is operated according to the same capacity use rule, the state of firm i at time t can be characterized by the triple $(c_{it}, \alpha_{it}, k_{it})$.

---

3. Strictly speaking, the fact that a range of output levels are equally acceptable when $P = c$ means that this orthodox rule is not a function but an upper semicontinuous correspondence. We admit this rule to our analysis as the sole exception to a general requirement that capacity utilization rules be continuous functions. No complication arises from this source; the important requirement is that profitability be a continuous function of the output price, and the orthodox rule satisfies this requirement. (It should be noted that the orthodox rule is unambiguously best only on the assumption that price is a parameter not affected by the firm's output decision.)

Together, the states of all firms at t determine a short-run supply function for period t:

$$q_t = \sum q_{it} = \sum \alpha_{it}\left(\frac{P_t}{c_{it}}\right) k_{it}.$$

Together with the demand-price function

$$P_t = h(q_t),$$

this determines P_t and q_t for the short-run period. The above as-sumptions concerning $h(\cdot)$ and the $\alpha_{it}(\cdot)$ guarantee that such a short-run equilibrium always exists. Net profit for firm i is

$$\pi_{it} = \left[(P_t - c_{it})\, \alpha_{it}\left(\frac{P_t}{c_{it}}\right) - r\right] k_{it},$$

where r is the cost of capital services.

Orthodox Equilibrium

It is apparent that, given the usual assumptions of orthodox theory, a conventional long-run equilibrium exists in this model. The ortho-dox assumptions are that firms are faultless profit maximizers, and that there are enough firms in the industry so that firms treat prices as parameters (our capacity utilization rules implicitly presume they do).

It is clear that if an equilibrium exists, profit maximization in that equilibrium requires that all operating firms employ the technique with the lowest unit cost. Thus, for all firms with $q_i > 0$, $c_i = \hat{c}$. For profits to be nonnegative, equilibrium price, P^*, must exceed $\hat{c}$. Then profit is maximized with an output determination rule that calls for full capacity utilization at P equals P^*. Of course, the orthodox rule has this property.

Equilibrium price P^* must equal $\hat{c} + r$, else profit-maximizing firms would see incentives to change capacity. The assumptions about the demand-price function guarantee that there is a q^* such that $h(q^*) = \hat{c} + r$. This is an equilibrium output and price. At that price, with all firms operating at full capacity $\sum q_i = \sum k_i$, equilibrium capital stock equals equilibrium output. Since there are constant re-turns to scale, the total industry capacity can be divided up in any way among the firms in the industry. With this total capacity and output, and all firms using the optimum techniques and decision rules, profits are maximized, profits are zero, and we have an ortho-dox long-run equilibrium.

Selection Dynamics

Is there a selection equilibrium as well—that is, a situation that is a stationary position for an appropriately defined dynamic process in-volving expansion of profitable firms and contraction of unprofitable ones? If there is such an equilibrium, does it have the same proper-ties as the orthodox one? To answer these questions, we obviously need to specify the dynamics of the selection process.

Our analysis will rely on the mathematical tools of the theory of finite Markov chains. In order to exploit these tools, there is need to modify and constrain the assumptions made above about production methods and capacity utilization policies. We assume the set of all feasible production techniques is finite, and the set of possible capacity utilization rules finite as well. (The orthodox, profit-maximizing capacity utilization rule is included in that finite set.) We further assume that capital comes in discrete packets; thus, at any time a firm possesses an integer-valued number of machines. All ma-chines used by a firm at any time operate with the same technique and according to the same utilization rule. Thus, as above, the state of a firm at any time can be characterized by a triple—the technique it is using, the capacity utilization policy it is using, and the number of machines it possesses. Each of these components is a discrete vari-able.

It is also assumed that the total number of firms actually or poten-tially in the industry is finite and constant, though the mix of extant firms and "potentials" may change. This number, M, is assumed to be large enough not only to make price-taking behavior on the part of firms plausible, but also to support the arguments made below about search. Note that because capacity utilization can vary contin-uously, it is still true that a short-run equilibrium always exists. We will abstract from the processes by which it is achieved.[4]

Because the number of machines is integer-valued, the standard argument presented above that a long-run equilibrium exists, based on continuity both of the demand function and of the (profit-

---

4. An alternative formulation of the model would recognize that output is ordinar-ily produced in anticipation of an imperfectly estimated future price. This could be done, for example, by introducing an expected price state variable as a state variable of each firm, and then specifying transition rules linking the expected price to the experi-ence of actual prices. At least for some choices of the expectation transition rule, the conclusions of the analysis here carry over to this modified model.

maximizing) supply correspondence, no longer can be employed with this model. However, it is clear that the orthodox market equilibrium "almost" exists if the capacity output of a machine is small enough relative to industry output. Pleading substantive rather than mathematical plausibility, we will assume that there is an orthodox equilibrium—that is, that the output level q^* determined by $\hat{c} + r = h(q^*)$ is an integer.

We make the following assumptions about investment. For firms with positive capital stock, if profit is zero, then investment is zero. Extant firms making positive profits expand probabilistically. There is zero probability that they will decline in size. With positive probability they remain the same size. With positive probability they add one machine to their stock. It also is possible that they add more than one machine, but there are bounds on their feasible expansion. Extant firms making negative profits contract probabilistically in the same sense; they certainly do not expand, there is a positive probability of no change, a positive probability of decline by just one unit, and a positive probability of a greater decline (but the magnitude of the decline is bounded by the firm's prevailing capital stock). Potential entrants, firms with zero capital stock, with positive probability (less than one), enter the industry with just one machine, if the routine pair they are contemplating would yield a positive profit at P_t if put into practice. Potential entrants with contemplated routine pairs that yield zero or negative profits do not enter.

The foregoing assumptions are expressed formally as follows.

For extant firms just breaking even:

$$k_{t+1} = k_t;$$

for extant firms making positive profit:

$$k_{t+1} = k_t + \delta \text{ with probability } \begin{bmatrix} 0 \\ >0 \\ \geqq 0 \\ 0 \end{bmatrix} \text{ for } \begin{cases} \overline{\delta < 0} \\ \delta = 0, 1 \\ 1 < \delta \leqslant \Delta' \\ \delta > \Delta \end{cases};$$

for extant firms making negative profits:

$$k_{t+1} = k_t - \delta, \text{ with } \delta \text{ having same distributional}$$
characteristics as above, with $\Delta = k_t$;

for potential entrants contemplating routines that yield positive profit:

$k_{t+1} = 0$ or 1, each with positive probability;

and for potential entrants contemplating routines that do no better than break even:

$k_{t+1} = 0.$

A feature that sharply distinguishes our evolutionary models from orthodox ones is that we do not impute to firms the ability to scan instantaneously a large set of decision alternatives. However, our model firms do engage in groping, time-consuming search. In this particular model we make the following assumptions about search. First, the outcome of the search, presuming that a firm is actively searching, is defined in terms of a probability distribution of routines which will be found by search, perhaps conditional upon a firm's prevailing routines. Second, regardless of the prevailing routines, there is a positive probability that any other technique, decision-rule pair will be found in a search. Third, there is positive probability that a searching firm will find no new routines and will thus necessarily retain its prevailing routines.

To complete our characterization of the dynamic system, we need to specify when search occurs. Two sets of considerations, partially opposed to each other, are involved. If the system is to wind up in an equilibrium that resembles an orthodox one, firms must search actively enough to assure that the orthodox actions—such as the use of the lowest-cost production technique—are ultimately found and tried. On the other hand, search must not be so active as to dislodge the system from what would otherwise be a reasonable equilibrium. A variety of assumptions can meet these requirements. Here we assume that firms with positive capacity do not search at all if they are making positive or zero profits; they "satisfice" on their prevailing routines. Potential entrants to the industry (firms with zero capacity) are assumed to be searching always, but when they enter they do so with routines that have passed the profitability test.

Selection Equilibrium

In the context of the present model, we shall define a (static) selection equilibrium as a situation in which the states of all extant firms remain unchanged, and the roster of extant firms also remains unchanged. It should now be clear that an orthodox market equilibrium (with an integral number of machines) constitutes such an equilibrium for the selection process just described. All firms in the industry with positive capacity are just breaking even; therefore, they are neither expanding nor contracting. Potential entrants continue to search, but no routines can be found that yield a positive profit in orthodox market equilibrium; thus, no actual entry occurs and the orthodox equilibrium values of price and industry output persist indefinitely.

It is also clear that under the prevailing assumptions, a selection equilibrium must display most of the significant properties of the orthodox equilibrium. All firms in the industry must be breaking even; otherwise one or more firms will be probabilistically expanding or contracting. P must equal $\hat{c} + r$. Price cannot be less than $\hat{c} + r$; under such conditions no firm can possibly be breaking even. Price cannot be greater than $\hat{c} + r$; otherwise, if some firm finds the best technique and the orthodox best capacity utilization rule, it can make a positive profit. Our assumptions about search guarantee that, sooner or later, some firm, if not an extant firm then a potential entrant, will find that pair of routines. If they are found under market conditions that generate a positive profit, an extant firm will probabilistically expand or a potential entrant will probabilistically enter. And at price $\hat{c} + r$ only firms with the best technique and a decision rule that calls for full capacity utilization at that price will break even; and no firm can do any better than that. Note, however, that there may be selection equilibria in which no firm follows the orthodox capacity utilization rule. If firms follow rules that yield full capacity utilization at the equilibrium price $P^* = \hat{c} + r$, equilibrium will not be disrupted by the search process. It does not matter what responses the rule yields at other prices.

The remaining question is: Will the selection process move the industry to such an equilibrium state if it is not there initially? Our assumptions imply that it will. The key step in the demonstration involves showing that there is a finite sequence of positive probability state transitions leading from any initial state to an equilibrium state. By a result in Feller (1957, pp. 352–353, 364), this suffices to establish that, with probability approaching one as time elapses, the industry will achieve an equilibrium state. But there are some preliminaries to be disposed of before giving the central argument.

The first thing needed is a precise characterization of the equilibrium states. By an "industry state" we simply mean the list of M firm states, where each firm state is characterized by the triple $(c_{it}, \alpha_{it}, k_{it})$ of unit variable cost, capacity utilization rule, and capacity. Call a capacity utilization rule "eligible" if it yields full capacity utilization at price $\hat{c} + r$—that is, if $\alpha[(\hat{c} + r)/\hat{c}] = 1$. The finite set of possible

rules contains, by assumption, at least one eligible rule—the orthodox one. An "equilibrium state" is one in which aggregate industry
capacity is $k^* = q^*$, such that $h(q^*) = \hat{c} + r$, and all firms with positive capacity have eligible capacity utilization rules and variable cost
$\hat{c}$. It is easily seen that in an equilibrium state the price is $\hat{c} + r$ and
the only sort of change that can occur is continuing futile search for
profitable routines by potential entrants, so selection equilibrium
prevails. In the language of the theory of Markov processes, the set E
of equilibrium states is a "closed set of states": Once a state in E
occurs, all subsequent states must also be in E.

We now show that from a given initial condition, only finitely
many industry states can be reached. Since there are finitely many
possible routines, the only issue here is whether industry capital can
increase indefinitely; we show that it cannot. Note first that for any
pair of routines (c, α) there is a capacity level $K(c, \alpha)$ that is the *largest*
value of capacity k for which the relations

$$(P - c) \, \alpha \left(\frac{P}{c} \right) - r \geqq 0$$

$$P = h \left[\alpha \left(\frac{P}{c} \right) k \right]$$

can both be satisfied. The first relation implies that $\alpha(P/c)$ is positive; the assumption that all routines are unprofitable at sufficiently
high industry output levels then implies that there is a maximum k
consistent with the two relations together. As a corollary, note that in
any industry state in which the aggregate capacity of firms with routines (c, α) exceeds $K(c, \alpha)$, routine pair (c, α) is unprofitable—the
possible existence of other firms producing positive output with
other routines only makes it clearer that price must be too low for
(c, α) to be profitable.[5] Now consider $\bar{K} = \text{Max } K(c, \alpha)$. Consistent
with the transition rules above, no firm can increase its capital to a
level in excess of $\bar{K} + \Delta$ from any lower level. Since Δ bounds the
possible capital increase $k_{t+1} - k_t$ in a single period, the starting
value k_t for such a transition would itself have to exceed $\bar{K}$. However,
since the firm must have *some* technique (c, α) and $k_t > \bar{K} \geqq K(c, \alpha)$,

---

5. It is not the case however, that a particular routine is necessarily unprofitable
when total industry capacity is extremely large. For price might be low enough so that
a large amount of capacity is entirely shut down, yet high enough so that a small
amount of capacity operated with an appropriate technique and rule would be profitable. In fact, given one industry state of this type, the short-run equilibrium is preserved if an indefinitely large amount of capacity is added to the firms that are shut
down.

the firm must be unprofitable and expansion is ruled out. Finally, since no firm can increase its capital to a value in excess of $\bar{K} + \Delta$, in any specific realization of the process the capital of firm i is bounded above by Max $(k_{i1}, \bar{K} + \Delta)$, where k_{i1} is firm i's capital in the initial industry state. There are, therefore, only finitely many industry states reachable from any initial state. We henceforth confine our discussion to this finite set of states.

It is now possible to be specific as to what constitutes a "large enough" number of firms: the number M of actual and potential firms exceeds $\bar{K}$. Thus, when aggregate industry capacity is no greater than $\bar{K}$, there are necessarily some firms with zero capacity—that is, some potential entrants. On the other hand, if aggregate capacity exceeds $\bar{K}$, at least one firm is making losses and searching. Either way, there is a positive probability that new routines with cost $\hat{c}$ and an eligible capacity utilization rule will be adopted. And all firms (extant and potential) displaying such routine pairs—which we may call the eligible firms—can retain them with positive probability for any finite period.

We now show that, given a state in which there is at least one eligible firm, it is always possible to take, with positive probability, "a step toward" the set E of equilibrium states. The number of "steps" that separate a given state from E may be counted as $k_n + |k_e - k^*|$, the aggregate capacity of noneligible firms plus the absolute value of the discrepancy between the capacity of eligible firms and k^*. Clearly, over a finite set of industry states this number of steps is bounded. Suppose that the given state is one in which price exceeds $\hat{c} + r$. Then clearly $k_e < k^*$, and a one-machine increase in capacity by an eligible firm, with no other change in firm states, is a positive probability step that reduces the distance to E. Suppose on the other hand that the state is one in which price is less than or equal to $\hat{c} + r$. The noneligible firms necessarily make losses, and if there are any such with positive capacity, a one-machine decrease in capacity by one of them is a positive probability step that reduces the distance to E. If $k_n = 0$, this sort of step is not possible, but in this case we necessarily have $k_e \geqq k^*$. If the strict inequality holds, a one-machine capacity reduction by an eligible firm is an appropriate positive probability step, while, if the equality holds, the given state is already in E. Iteration of this argument shows that, from any initial state, E is reachable by finitely many steps of positive probability under the stated assumptions on transition probabilities.

Thus, according to the previously cited passages in Feller (1957), there is probability one that E will eventually be reached.

Unorthodox equilibria. To underscore the point that it matters what rules are tried, consider what would happen if neither the orthodox rule nor any other eligible rule were included in the set of possible capacity utilization rules. Then orthodox equilibrium with full utilization would be impossible, for a price high enough to induce full utilization would be more than high enough to induce firms to expand capacity. There might, however, be a selection equilibrium, as the following proof sketch shows.

Maintain all of the assumptions of the above analysis except the assumption that at least one capacity utilization rule is eligible. For every rule α, there is a lowest price consistent with breaking even when variable cost is $\hat{c}$—that is, a lowest price consistent with

$$(P - \hat{c}) \, \alpha\!\left(\frac{P}{\hat{c}}\right) - r \geqq 0.$$

Denote by P^{**} the lowest such price over all possible rules α, and by $\hat{a}$ the capacity utilization rate at which this minimum price is achieved. Adapting the earlier convenience assumption for dealing with the indivisibility of capital, we now assume that there is an integral value of capital, k^{**}, that satisfies

$$P^{**} = h(\hat{a} \, k^{**}).$$

Call a capacity utilization rule "pseudo-eligible" if it yields capacity utilization rate $\hat{a}$ when $P^{**}/\hat{c}$ is the prevailing price/cost ratio. Now the argument simply follows the path of the foregoing analysis, with "pseudo-eligible" replacing "eligible" and p^{**}, k^{**}, and $\hat{a} \, k^{**}$ replacing p^{*}, k^{*}, and q^{*} respectively. The conclusion is that a selection equilibrium with capacity utilization rate $\hat{a}$ will ultimately be achieved.

Commentary

Even under our original assumption that the orthodox rule is among those tried, a selection equilibrium does *not* correspond to an orthodox market equilibrium. Since an issue of considerable generality and conceptual importance is involved, the point deserves emphasis.

The class of "eligible" capacity utilization rules does not consist merely of the orthodox optimal rule, but includes all rules whose action implications agree with those of the orthodox rule at the equilibrium ultimately achieved. Nothing precludes the achievement of a selection equilibrium in which some or all firms display eligible but nonoptimal capacity utilization rules—a proposition that follows from the observation that nothing would disrupt such an equilibrium if it happened to be achieved. Indeed, if the orthodox rule were not included in the feasible set, but other eligible rules were, neither the character of the equilibrium position nor the argument concerning its achievement would be affected. An example of an eligible but not optimal rule would be the capacity utilization counterpart of "full-cost pricing"—a rule that would shut down entirely whenever $P < \hat{c} + r$ and produce to capacity when $P \geqq \hat{c} + r$.

If interest attached only to the characteristics of an equilibrium achieved by a single once-and-for-all selection process, the fact that surviving rules might yield nonoptimal behavior out of equilibrium would be of no more consequence than the fact that the rules of potential entrants might be nonoptimal if actually employed. But orthodox theory is much concerned, and properly so, with the analysis of *displacements* of equilibrium—the problem of what happens if some parameter of the equilibrium position changes. There is also the question, less emphasized by orthodoxy, of the characteristics of adjustment paths between equilibria. For these purposes, it matters that nonoptimal rules may survive in selection equilibrium. A change in demand or cost conditions that shakes the system out of an orthodox-type selection equilibrium does not necessarily initiate the sort of adjustment process contemplated by orthodoxy, for the process might well be dominated by rules that produce, under disequilibrium conditions, actions much different from the orthodox ones. And if the orthodox rules are not included among those actually tried, the fact that the system achieves an orthodox-type equilibrium at one set of parameter values does not assure that the orthodox result would also be mimicked for another set. For example, the capacity utilization rule "Produce to capacity only if price is at least fifteen percent in excess of unit variable cost" is not eligible if r is less than $.15\hat{c}$.

The general issue here is this. A historical process of evolutionary change cannot be expected to "test" all possible behavioral implications of a given set of routines, much less test them all repeatedly. It is only against the environmental conditions that persist for extended periods (and in this loose sense are "equilibrium" conditions) that routines are thoroughly tested. There is no reason to expect, therefore, that the surviving patterns of behavior of a historical selection process are well adapted for novel conditions not repeatedly encountered in that process. In fact, there is good reason to expect the opposite, since selection forces may be expected to be "sensible" and to trade off maladaptation under unusual or unencountered conditions to achieve good adaptations to conditions frequently encountered. In a context of progressive change, therefore, one should not expect to observe ideal adaptation to current conditions by the products of evolutionary processes.

3. Complications and Snags

The simple formal model we have presented and analyzed above hardly does justice to the sweep of intuition that has led some economists to propose that selection forces provide support for the assumptions and conclusions of orthodox theory. In this sense, the model is almost a parody of those intuitive arguments. We would be the first to insist that there is more to the evolutionary perspective than this model captures. On the other hand, the exercise does have the virtue of provoking an explicit confrontation with the question of what sorts of assumptions actually suffice to generate strictly orthodox conclusions. Obviously, our basic model above is only one member of a very large class of economic evolutionary models having the property that a selection equilibrium exists and having basically the properties of an orthodox competitive equilibrium. We maintain, however, that all members of this class would have to contain assumptions that bear a family resemblance to those incorporated in the particular model just examined.[6] Here we treat the assumptions of that simple formal model as a point of departure and standard of comparison in a less formal discussion of the issue of evolutionary support for orthodoxy.

Search and the Set of Feasible Routines

The model contains very strong assumptions about the set of feasible routines and the effectiveness and persistence with which firms search that set. These assumptions are clearly at odds with our analysis in the previous chapters. We argued strenuously that there is no set of blueprints that completely describes available production technologies. In the first place, much of the knowledge of a particular technique is not published information, and firms often exert considerable effort to keep knowledge of their production techniques private. Second, aside from efforts to preserve privacy or legally to block access to a technique through such devices as patents, there is the issue that much production technology is tacit, not explicit, and not that easy to imitate even with the cooperation of the firm that possesses the technique in question. In many industries, furthermore, the set of production techniques is not fully known at any

---

6. That model may also be viewed as a member of the much broader class of evolutionary models generally, in which the issue of correspondence with orthodox results is not necessarily a central concern. In this perspective, the model may be seen to illustrate a number of generic structural features, but its detailed assumptions reflect its narrow purpose.

time; exploration is continually finding new regions that have not been described or much thought about before. In a sense, no "best" is ever found by anybody. We have argued that explicit recognition of this is an essential characteristic of models examining contexts and industries in which technical advance is important.

Regarding the search for a capacity utilization rule, the assumption that the "best" could soon be found by intelligent searchers may seem more acceptable. Surely it does not require great insight to recognize that if price is a parameter, it is profitable to produce whenever variable cost is covered. This assessment ignores, however, the realistic complications of the problem. Decisions on production for the market must ordinarily be based on past price data that provide an imperfect guide to the price at which the output will actually be sold. The problem of predicting the market price is thus intertwined with the problem of deciding what to do on the basis of any given prediction; this should be reason enough to warn economists against assuming that the problem is trivial and already conclusively solved. More broadly, it is important to avoid the fallacious supposition that, because a decision problem is simple in the context of an economic model (by virtue of the modeler's own choices), it is permissible to argue as if it were simple in the real situation modeled. For example, the model may abstract from small and variable amounts of market power possessed by firms in the real situation—amounts trivial enough to neglect for some analytical purposes, but not so trivial as to make the choice of an output level entirely straightforward.

The simple model follows orthodoxy in abstracting from the costs of search, whether for techniques or capacity utilization rules. To recognize that positive search costs of some magnitude are always a feature of real situations is to recognize the shakiness of the model's assumption regarding persistent search by potential entrants. Who is paying the bill for all this search?

There is no problem in developing evolutionary models that reflect in various ways these features of search that are neglected or distorted by the simple model. Some of the possibilities are illustrated by models appearing later in this volume. The only problem is one faced by those who would invoke selection arguments in support of orthodoxy: the plausible models thus constructed do not, in general, support orthodox conclusions. For example, it is possible to specify a model incorporating costly, groping search that will achieve a "pseudo-orthodox" equilibrium in which all surviving routines are optimal relative to the set of alternatives displayed along the evolutionary path. But any disruption of that equilibrium will reinitiate search, and, in general, the search will uncover new routines superior to those in the previous equilibrium. For both positive and normative analytical purposes, therefore, the "optimality" of routines in the pseudo-orthodox equilibrium is only pseudo-optimality.

Investment

Regarding investment, the model contains both some rather technical assumptions and some that are typical of evolutionary models generally. In the former category are those that are needed to support the particular argument used to prove that static selection equilibrium is achieved, such as the assumption that firms that are expanding or contracting can do so, with positive probability, by a single machine, and the assumption that firms making zero profit maintain their capacity with probability one. Closely related, of course, is the technical assumption that asserts the existence of an integral industry capacity level at which eligible firms precisely break even.

As we have already suggested, the model's focus on the precise achievement of static equilibrium involves an element of artificiality, and the technical assumptions reflect that artificiality. Absent a viable orthodox analysis of disequilibrium, it would be more to the point to ask whether selection mechanisms tend to move the industry rather promptly to the neighborhood of orthodox equilibrium and hold it there with reasonable consistency. For an affirmative answer to that question to be possible, it certainly is not necessary that a break-even firm never change capacity, or that break-even conditions be precisely achievable. On the other hand, that question cannot be addressed without first focusing on a number of essentially *quantitative* questions about investment, search, the elasticity of demand, and, indeed, everything bearing on the quantitative stability characteristics of the selection mechanism. Then it would be necessary to establish an appropriate metric for "closeness" to equilibrium, which for substantive relevance should presumably involve the rate at which economic surplus is generated. Finally, the terms "promptly" and "with reasonable consistency" would have to be given precise and objective meanings. Although this may define a feasible approach for a simulation study, it hardly seems to be the sort of thing that can be accomplished by analytic methods or with any great generality. In spite of the artificiality, the static equilibrium approach seems more fruitful, at least as a starting point.

The more general qualitative features of the investment assumptions seem reasonable, and we will make identical or highly similar assumptions repeatedly. But they nevertheless warrant some critical scrutiny. The model assumes that firms that lose money tend to decline. While this seems plausible, it ignores the possibility (remarked on but not explored by Friedman) that such firms might be sustained by resources "from the outside." Temporarily, at least, an individual firm may be sustained by funds supplied by stockholders or creditors rather than by customers. Contexts in which entry is (or appears to be) easy may be ones in which these sources of support are of continuing importance to industry functioning. In other contexts, the existence of economies of scale or of tendencies for efficiency to be improved through learning provide affirmative reasons for a firm in current difficulty to seek its salvation through growth, as well as arguments with which to support appeals to investors for additional funds.

There are similarly a number of circumstances in which the assumption that firms making positive profits tend to expand might not be warranted. In many industries, successful small proprietors seem to be quite content with being small; consider chef-owned French restaurants, for example. And, contrary to the model's assumption that all firms are price takers, large firms may consciously constrain their growth of capacity in recognition of the effect of this growth on price. If profitable firms *do* expand, there is the question of whether they behave like simple multiples of their former selves, as the model assumes they do. Larger size confers opportunities for economies and the threat of diseconomies—but to the extent that either of these is significant in reality, the simple evolutionary story about growth in the relative importance of the more profitable routines requires qualification.

Endogenous Profitability Rankings and Transient Environments

The above discussion of complications relating to the assumptions about search and investment has been quite general. Although we have not seen much discussion of the particular issues that we raise, we have reason to believe that many economists are at least roughly familiar with them. There are, however, two less obvious snags for evolutionary arguments that aim to provide a prop for orthodoxy, and to which we wish to draw particular attention. These are, first, that the relative profitability ranking of decision rules may not be invariant with respect to market conditions. And, second, that profitable survival in equilibrium may require that a firm first survive an extended episode of unprofitability.

In the model examined above, there was an unambiguous best production technique, more profitable than any other technique for any capacity utilization rule employed, and for any market price. Moreover, the complete ranking of techniques, not merely the identity of the best, was insensitive to market conditions and to the identity of the capacity utilization rule employed. Similarly, one could easily identify a best (profit-maximizing) capacity utilization rule: produce zero output if price is less than variable costs, and produce at full capacity output if price equals or exceeds the variable costs. However, the situation was more complicated regarding the ranking of capacity utilization rules. As noted earlier, in equilibrium there was a whole class of capacity utilization rules that did as well as the orthodox best one. And out of equilibrium, the ranking of various capacity utilization rules, other than the orthodox best, was not invariant with respect to the technique being employed by the firm or to product price. Thus, if growth is assumed to be related to profitability, it is not true in this model that eligible firms necessarily grow relative to noneligible firms in disequilibrium states.

More generally, sensitivity of the profitability ranking of routines to market conditions may stymie the selection process in an evolutionary model, and very likely in the dynamic processes of the real economic world as well. The problem is particularly serious when the routines that would be viable in equilibrium are dominated by other decision rules out of equilibrium. If the system is not initially in equilibrium, the selection forces operating in disequilibrium states may prevent it from ever reaching equilibrium.

For example, it is possible that, at equilibrium prices, techniques that employ little labor and a considerable amount of semiprocessed materials may entail lower costs than a more labor-intensive technique. However, at low levels of industry output, labor may be cheaper relative to semiprocessed inputs. If firms start out small and take time to grow, firms initially employing processed material-intensive techniques may be out-competed in the early stages of the industry's evolution by labor-intensive firms, and driven out of business. This story presumes an upward-sloping labor supply curve and a flat or downward-sloping processed material supply curve to the industry. But a comparable phenomenon may obtain if returns to scale are not constant, and techniques that are efficient at relatively low levels of output are very different from those that are efficient at high levels of output. If firms are small in the early stages of industry growth, those that start with techniques that are efficient only after the firm has grown considerably may be defeated in the evolutionary struggle by firms whose techniques are better suited to low levels of output—unless, of course, they can persuade potential lenders of their long-run strength. Clearly, adequate evolutionary models of cases in which the best techniques are sensitive to industry and firm size must include careful modeling of capital markets as an important component of the analysis.

Even if the initially disadvantaged firms do not survive, as the industry grows larger and the surviving firms grow along with it, firms that have techniques suitable to low industry and firm size may search and find techniques more appropriate to the new conditions. But to assume such "rediscovery" of techniques that would be optimal in equilibrium is to make a strong commitment about search processes.

There is also the problem that certain episodes of an industry's evolution may be characterized by negative profits for virtually all firms. For example, assume that there is a once-and-for-all drop in the demand for a product, or an increase in factor prices. Even if the profit ranking of routines were invariant with respect to prices, the firms that would have survived in equilibrium may drop out of business before equilibrium is achieved. For example, they might be small firms with limited access to credit. Here again, assumptions about investment and capital markets, or assumptions about search, can salvage the selection argument (and the "best" routines). But this only underlines the critical nature of these assumptions.

There are two analytically distinct problems here. The first is that the routines of extant firms determine, to some degree at least, the environment that selects on routines. The second is that in order to play a role in an actual equilibrium, a routine must be consistent with survival in a previous disequilibrium. In the biological literature on evolution, the first problem was for a long while imperfectly recognized. The second has been recognized by biologists, but we do not think it has been adequately recognized in economic evolutionary arguments.[7]

It is interesting that the first difficulty appears to have been neglected until relatively recently in the biological literature on evolution.[8] The problem stated for the two contexts in parallel, is this: the comparative fitness of genotypes (profitability of routines) determines which genotypes (routines) will tend to become predominant over time. However, the fitness (profitability) clearly depends on the characteristics of the environment (market prices) confronting the species (collection of firms with similar routines). The environment (price vector) in turn depends, however, on the genotypes (routines) of all the individual organisms (firms) existing at a time—a dependency discussed in the subdiscipline called ecology (market theory). Therefore, no theory of long-run evolutionary change logically can

---

7. See, for example, Wilson and Bossert (1971).

8. The sociobiological analysis of "altruism" is an example of recent moves to correct this neglect. See, for example, Maynard-Smith (1976), Boorman and Levitt (1980), and Hirshleifer (1977a, 1977b).

take the environment of the individual species (collection of firms) as exogenous. Hence, the notion of fitness (profitability) contributes much less to the understanding of the long-run pattern of change than might at first glance appear. What does play a crucial though obscure role is the character of the whole evolving system's interactions with the truly exogenous features of the environment, represented in the current model by product demand and factor supply curves, and in the context of biology by considerations that have not, to our knowledge, been specified in biological theory. A theory that omits to explain how significant properties of that interaction affect the changing requirements for fitness (profitability) over time cannot be regarded as an adequate explanation of the evolution of the system.

That organisms often face an environment in which there is some variation, including some occasions in which the environment is unusually harsh, has been recognized in the biological literature on biological evolution. Two different "strategies" for a species in coping with a varied environment and occasional hardship have been analyzed.

According to the first strategy, the behavior patterns (presumably built in by the genes) of the organism are quite flexible so that the organism can, for example, shift from one source of food to another, survive in dry seasons and in wet, and so forth. In a fluctuating environment, a flexible organism may survive where organisms better suited to the modal environment will not. In terms of the model under consideration here, a better "policy" regarding capacity utilization can help a firm with a poor technique survive when prices are low (by shutting down to minimize losses), whereas a firm with a better technique but an inflexible decision rule (always produce at capacity output) might fail under adverse market conditions.

The second strategy is to have a high mutation rate. Existing genotypes of such species may be able to survive only in a limited range of conditions, but if their offspring are variegated there is a high likelihood that some of the next generation will be capable of coping with environments that would kill their parents. In the context of the model under consideration here, prevailing decision rules can be quite inflexible in themselves, yet the industry may respond quite flexibly to changed market conditions if there is a lot of search either by extant firms or by potential entrants.

These strategies are ones that are favored by a changing environment. The characteristics of such strategies—flexibility, and considerable continuing exploration of alternatives to prevailing routines—are not virtues of the type considered in most economic analyses employing the selection metaphor.

We argued earlier that most interesting problems of economic analyses have to do with change—change either in external market conditions or resulting from innovation within the industry itself. If the analytic task is to deal with change, then analysis of static selection equilibrium of the sort considered in this chapter is not a direction that one can fruitfully pursue very far. Evolutionary economic theorizing must deal explicitly with dynamics, and not get drawn into spending undue time considering selection equilibrium as a counterpart to more orthodox economic equilibrium concepts. This is certainly so when the focus is on processes of long-range economic growth or on Schumpeterian competition. But it is also true when the analytic focus is on the canonical positive problem of the price theory textbooks—the problem of the response of firms and the industry to changed market conditions. To this analysis we now turn.

7

Firm and Industry Response to Changed Market Conditions

THEORY about the characteristics of equilibrium plays two connected but distinct roles in contemporary economics. One is to characterize and rationalize any prevailing constellation of inputs, outputs, and prices—thus the conclusion that in competitive equilibrium, firms will earn zero profits; thus also the normative analysis of modern welfare economics, which explores the social merits and demerits of competitive equilibrium.

The second role is to explain or predict how firms and industries react to changed market conditions. A major concern of microeconomic theory texts is: How will industry inputs, output, and price respond to a rightward shift in the demand curve for the product of the industry, or to changes in the terms under which different factors of production are available? Of course, as we noted in Chapter 2, "How will industry respond?" is not *precisely* the question that contemporary positive theory analyzes. Rather, the analysis compares equilibrium configurations of inputs, output, and prices under the two market conditions.

It is possible to do comparative statics analysis of the selection equilibria of evolutionary theory, as well as of equilibria of the more orthodox sort. But the thrust of our central concern about contemporary orthodox theory is exactly that that theory deals inadequately with change. Even if it were a reasonable assumption that equilibrium configurations change seldom and discretely, the economic system still might be out of equilibrium the bulk of the time; hence, explanations of observed configurations and their movements, based on simple comparative statics, would be at best incomplete and probably quite misleading. Explicit consideration of the way in which an industry moves from one equilibrium configuration to another should be, in our view, an essential part of any positive theory of firm and industry response to changed market conditions. And since there is in general no guaranteeing that the character of the equilibrium achieved is independent of the time path to it, we do not think that an adequate theory can be achieved merely by adding to traditional equilibrium theory a disequilibrium adjustment dynamic.

In this chapter we develop an explicitly evolutionary analysis of firm and industry response to changed market conditions.[1] As we remarked at the start of this book, in a way our approach represents a formalization of ideas that long have been present in economics, and indeed were dominant before contemporary formalism took over. Many earlier writers clearly meant to include, as an important component of the response of firms to changed market conditions, the phenomenon that contemporary economists would call "induced innovation." And in many of the classical statements, competition was viewed as a dynamic process involving uncertainty, struggle, and disequilibrium, not as a tranquil equilibrium state. The language about "tendencies," so frequent in Marshall's prose, was meant to signal that he believed that an equilibrium analysis of economic conditions was misleading in many ways. But his formal analysis in the footnotes and appendixes stressed equilibrium, and the economics profession followed the ideas of his footnotes, not of his prose.

Important issues are at stake here. First, we suspect that most economists, if asked where economics has been most successful as a positive science, would point to explanations and predictions of the way in which industry output and input respond to shifting product and factor prices—the stuff of textbook positive economics. Although we wonder if many economists may not be exaggerating the strength of the evidence confirming the "standard" predictions, the evidence is considerable and weighty. Contemporary orthodox theory does provide a way of formally deducing observed relationships. To be credible as a general theory of firm and industry behavior, an evolutionary theory must show itself capable of similarly predicting the standard responses.

In the second place, the textbook theory of firm and industry response to changed market conditions is employed by the profes-

---

1. The analysis of this chapter is based on Nelson and Winter (1975, 1980). Thanks are due to Donald Brown for his assistance with early versions of the appendix.

sion not merely as a special theory about the phenomenon, but as defining the ingredients of the general theory of firm and industry behavior—that is, as defining legitimate ways of modeling such diverse phenomena as long-run economic growth in a market economy, and the response of firms to regulatory constraints. Further, the content of positive theory defines the focus of normative theory. We take it as a challenge that our evolutionary modeling of the particular relationships under consideration in this chapter should define the general way that we look at a broader range of questions. Thus, just as textbook microeconomic theory forms the basis not only for analysis of factor substitution in response to changed factor prices, but also for analyses of the way in which a growing capital-labor ratio affects both factor prices and labor productivity, so our evolutionary analysis of response to factor price change will likewise be consonant with our analysis later in this book of long-run economic growth fueled by technical advance. And just as contemporary welfare economics is defined so as to link with the prevailing orthodox theory of firm behavior, so we will later attempt to develop a way of looking at normative economic questions consonant with our positive evolutionary theory of firm behavior.

1. ACCOUNTING FOR FIRM AND INDUSTRY RESPONSE

The following propositions about the behavior of firms are consistent with both an orthodox and an evolutionary view, although the emphasis and connotations of each would be different: at any time, firms in an industry can be viewed as operating with a set of techniques and decision rules (routines), keyed to conditions external to the firm, prominently prices, and to various internal state conditions, in particular the firms' capital stocks. Expansion or contraction of firms is related to the profitability of such moves. Firms also may have procedures for hunting for better techniques.

   In the orthodox formulation, the decision rules are assumed to be profit-maximizing over a sharply defined opportunity set that is taken as a datum, the firms in the industry and the industry as a whole are assumed to be at equilibrium size, and innovation (if it is treated at all) is absorbed into the traditional framework rather mechanically. In evolutionary theory, decision rules are viewed as a legacy from the firm's past and hence appropriate, at best, to the range of circumstances in which the firm customarily finds itself, and are viewed as unresponsive, or inappropriate, to novel situations or situations encountered irregularly. Firms are regarded as expanding or contracting in response to disequilibria, with no presumption that the industry is "near" equilibrium. Innovation is treated as stochastic and as variable across firms.

These differences in perspective mean that when analysis deals with the effects of changed market conditions upon behavior, the focus is on different things. The following analysis of the behavior of firms and the industry is at once general enough to encompass both perspectives and designed to highlight the differences.

Let x_i be the vector of firm i's outputs and variable inputs, the latter taken as negative. Assume for simplicity that the levels of inputs that are fixed in the short run can be represented by a scalar, k_i, the size of the firm's capital stock. And assume that firm i's decision rule governing output and variable input levels has the following general form:

(1) $\left(\dfrac{x_i}{k_i}\right) = D(P, d_i).$

Here P is the vector of output and variable input prices corresponding to x_i, and d_i is a vector of decision rule parameters. (For notational convenience we treat all differences among alternative possible decision rules, among firms and over time, as parameter differences.)

In a behavioralist view, the complex multidimensional rule of equation (1) should be considered as a collection of simpler rules guiding particular input and output decisions, with the simpler rules regarded as but loosely connected. An orthodox view also admits a decomposition of the global rule into a collection of subrules, while ordinarily presuming strong linkages among these subrules.[2] But from either perspective, it is legitimate to consider separately different kinds of subrules. Thus, in the customary textbook treatment, sometimes the focus is on the rules used by firms to determine variable input and the analytic concern is with the mix among variable inputs used (with a given stock of capital) as a function of factor prices. Of course, in considering input mix rules, it must be understood that output also may be varying as a function of input prices. It is customary to limit the analysis, at least at a preliminary stage, to the choice of a cost-minimizing input mix with output level constant. Sometimes the focus is on output decisions. Here x_i refers to an out-

---

2. For example, it would ordinarily be assumed that all information about the environment (P) that is available to any part of the firm's decision-making process is available to all parts of that process. Some models in the theory of teams (Marschak and Radner, 1972) depart from this pattern.

put, and the analysis relates to the nature of the firm's rule connecting the quantity of output that will be produced (given a capital stock) to output price. It is understood that variable inputs will (normally) rise as output rises. In strict logic, of course, the input and output levels of the orthodox competitive firm are simultaneously determined optimal values at each vector of prices for all inputs and outputs. In that context, the vector function $D(\cdot)$ in equation (1) should be interpreted as expressing the general solution of that simultaneous equation problem, and the values of the parameters d_i are the optimal ones. The generality of the formulation, in the orthodox perspective, is qualified only by the fact that the solution is expressible as inputs and outputs per unit capital stock, which implicitly assumes constant returns to scale and a unidimensional capital stock.

Let $X = \Sigma x_i$ and let $K = \Sigma k_i$ (all summations here are over the index i). Then, for the industry:

$$(2) \quad \left(\frac{X}{K}\right) = \sum D(P, d_i) \left(\frac{k_i}{K}\right).$$

Under any market regime X/K may evolve over time. The traditional comparative statics approach of price theory represses what happens to X/K over time for a given set of market conditions and focuses on the variation associated with different market conditions. In what follows, we will be explicit about *both* kinds of differences.

Consider two different market regimes. In regime zero, prices are at P_0 forever. Under regime one, prices are at P_0 until time t and at P_1 after that time. Consider some time T greater than t. Then, under regime zero we can "account for" X/K at time T as follows:

$$(3) \quad \left(\frac{X}{K}\right)_0^T = \sum D(P_0, d_i^t) \left(\frac{k_i}{K}\right)^t$$

$$+ \sum [D(P_0, d_{i0}^T) - D(P_0, d_i^t)] \left(\frac{k_i}{K}\right)^t$$

$$+ \sum D(P_0, d_{i0}^T) \left[\left(\frac{k_i}{K}\right)_0^T - \left(\frac{k_i}{K}\right)^t\right].$$

The superscripts T and t identify the time at which the variables are measured. The subscript zero has been used to tag variables that may be different at time T under regime zero than under regime one. Given this notation, the first term is, of course, $(X/K)^t$. The second term accounts for the effects of the evolution of rules between t and T, weighted by capital stocks initially (at time t). The final term accounts for selection effects that change capital share weights on the final rules.

Under regime one, X/K at time T can be accounted for as follows:

(4)
$$\left(\frac{X}{K}\right)_1^T = \sum D(P_1, d_i^t) \left(\frac{k_i}{K}\right)^t$$
$$+ \sum [D(P_1, d_{i1}^T) - D(P_1, d_i^t)] \left(\frac{k_i}{K}\right)^t$$
$$+ \sum D(P_1, d_{i1}^T) \left[\left(\frac{k_i}{K}\right)_1^T - \left(\frac{k_i}{K}\right)^t\right].$$

By subtracting equation (3) from equation (4) one can "account for" the difference in X/K at time T under the two market regimes.

(5)
$$\left(\frac{X}{K}\right)_1^T - \left(\frac{X}{K}\right)_0^T = \sum [D(P_1, d_i^t) - D(P_0, d_i^t)] \left(\frac{k_i}{K}\right)^t$$
$$+ \sum [D(P_1, d_{i1}^T) - D(P_1, d_i^t) - D(P_0, d_{i0}^T)$$
$$+ D(P_0, d_i^t)] \left(\frac{k_i}{K}\right)^t$$
$$+ \sum \left[D(P_1, d_{i1}^T) \left[\left(\frac{k_i}{K}\right)_1^T - \left(\frac{k_i}{K}\right)^t\right] \right.$$
$$\left. - D(P_0, d_{i0}^T) \left[\left(\frac{k_i}{K}\right)_0^T - \left(\frac{k_i}{K}\right)^t\right]\right].$$

The first term (or, properly, the terms under the first summation) can be viewed as the result of firms' moving along the decision rules at time t in response to a change in price from P_0 to P_1. The second term reflects the fact that decision rules may evolve differently under the two regimes. The final term accounts for the difference in selection effects.

The above decomposition of the difference made by a price change could be regarded as merely a matter of accounting, without causal significance. We believe, however, that the separation we propose is useful analytically, because the three terms correspond to the operation of analytically distinguishable mechanisms. Thus, in what follows we will analyze separately *along-the-rule effects, search effects,* and *selection* effects of a change in price regimes. Although what is essential to the *theorizing* is that separable mechanisms are involved, we put forth as a tentative *empirical* proposition that the three effects occur at different speeds and that it is convenient to think of the along-the-rule effect as occurring promptly, followed by the appearance of differential innovation effects, followed in turn by differential selection effects. Our identification of the three terms in our particular accounting of distinct causal mechanisms rests on this image of the sequence of events. But our discussion of the individual mechanisms is relevant whether they are assumed to operate in this sequence, some other sequence, or—realistically—concurrently.

In any case, the prototypical question of positive economic theory is: What is the sign of the difference analyzed in equation (5)—say, the sign of the response of intensity of use of an input to a rise in its price? In deference to tradition and the weight of empirical evidence, we shall call the results that accord with orthodox qualitative predictions "standard" and results that fail to accord "perverse."

Orthodox theory derives its "standard" results from the assumption of profit maximization over a given choice set. In terms of the accounting framework above, orthodox theory may be interpreted as a theory about responses governed by decision rules. The second and third terms are not considered. Our analysis involves both rejection of the orthodox view of the derivation of decision rules, and emphasis on the likely importance of the second and third terms. For overall industry response to be standard, it would be sufficient for each of the three terms in our accounting to carry the sign of standard response. We shall consider each mechanism in turn.

Consider the movements along prevailing decision rules, accounted for in the first term. It is implicit in both the behavioralist and the orthodox notion of a "decision rule" linking input and output quantities to prices that at any particular time there is a certain set of action alternatives open to the firm. For an orthodox economist this set is a technological "given" and the decision rule is derived by optimization over it. For us, the rules are what they are because they have evolved that way over time. The concept of known "possible actions" has no standing independent of the actions invoked by decision rules. These rules are themselves observable (in principle) by looking "inside" the firm. Indeed, this may be the only way to actually find out what they are. Since some of the responses invoked by rules take time to work out, and since over time the rules may change, it is risky to try to infer rules from observed market responses that take place over time. In any case, under an orthodox interpretation of decision rules or under ours, it is implicit that if a firm takes one action under one market condition and another action under another market condition, it could have done exactly the reverse.

Given this interpretation, a prediction of a standard sign of along-the-rule change can be derived from the assumption that the rules reflect sensible profit-seeking behavior. The specific assumption is that routinized responses to price changes are not worse, in profitability terms, than no change at all. Let $(x/k)_{i0} = D(P_0, d_i^t)$ denote the full vector of input and output flows "per unit capital" under regime P_0. Holding the decision rule constant but changing the price, $(x/k)_{i1} = D(P_1, d_i^t)$. Treat k as a constant. Then (repressing both k and the i subscript) profit under regime one equals $P_1 \cdot x_1 \geq P_1 \cdot x_0$, or else the firm would have done better to stick with x_0. Similarly, $P_0 \cdot x_0 \geq P_0 \cdot x_1$. Familiar algebra yields the conclusion $\Delta P \cdot \Delta X \geq 0$. Hence, if ΔP has a single nonzero component, the corresponding element of Δx cannot carry the opposite sign from that component.

Although the conclusion and its derivation are familiar and orthodox, the interpretation is not. This is a hypothesis about decision rules, involving no commitments regarding the existence of an independently specified set of "known" or "possible" production methods, or about the characteristics of the processes that introduced these methods in the firm and established the decision linkages between them and the prices. The argument rests on the assumption that x_0 is an "available" behavior when P_1 prevails, and similarly for x_1 and P_0. The hypothesis is that the decision rules are plausibly responsive to changed conditions, not that they are "optimal" among the set of all "possible" decision rules (whatever that might mean).

To illustrate, consider again the decomposition of the global decision rules customarily employed in conventional textbooks. Thus, the analysis above can be specialized to refer to the proposition that, for a given quantity of output produced, a change in inputs induced by a change in input prices will be such that the cost of producing output at the new input prices is not increased. In the neoclassical analysis, changes in inputs reflect changed points of tangency of an isocost line with an isoquant; in our formulation, although changes in input proportions reduce unit costs, there is no underlying isoquant to which an isocost can be made tangent. Another common specialization, of course, is that a change in output price will induce a change in output in the same direction. Here the neoclassical analysis presumes movement along a marginal cost curve, and our more general proposition does not.

The hypothesis that the along-the-rule response is standard certainly is not true by definition. There are several reasons why it might prove false. It could be that the firm does not consider changing its inputs in response to changing prices; then decision rule "response" would not be strictly perverse but it would not be strictly standard. It could be that the profit calculation does not adequately reflect the structure of the firm's goals. For example, the firm (or rather its managers) might have a distaste for a relatively profitable activity that employs a particular input intensively, but might be bound by a minimum profit constraint. Then a rise in the price of the input might, by decreasing the profitability of its current mix of activities, lead the firm perversely to undertake its disliked activity more intensively. It could be that there are minor errors built into the rules, that one behavior is employed when another is slightly more profitable; or it could be that really major blunders are built in. However, the proposition that the routinized component of response to price change is standard seems likely to be of sufficiently broad validity to warrant its tentative acceptance as a theoretical commitment. (For the purposes of equation (5), the relevant question is whether the appropriately weighted *average* of routinized response is standard, so there is room for some exceptions.)

The second term of our accounting reflects the consequences of changes in decision rules under regime P_1 compared with what would have happened under P_0. We use the term "search" as a rubric for the variety of processes, mostly intentional but some not, by which rule changes take place. The question is: Will the effect of the changed price regime on search be standard?

Search differs from routinized response in three fundamental respects. First, inasmuch as it involves the acquisition of information, it is intrinsically an irreversible process. The irreversibility is rooted in the familiar economic fact that the costs of retention and use of a given item of information are typically much lower than the costs of initial acquisition or production. An immediate implication of irreversibility is that a prediction of a standard response of search outcomes to price changes cannot be derived by the same theoretical argument just used for the case of rule-governed response. Although it remains plausible that rule changes will tend to enhance profitability, there is no reason why the new decision rules yielded by search should not dominate the old, and be more profitable at the old prices as well as at the new.

The second fundamental characteristic that distinguishes search is uncertainty. The scene surveyed by a decision maker inside the firm may well include identifiable "alternatives" that could be explored, but these are only dimly perceived and it may not be at all clear which will turn out to be best. The process of exploring perceived alternatives, or exogenous events, may bring to light other alternatives not even contemplated in the original assessments. As argued earlier, uncertainty and individual differences are structural aspects of search. It is clearly appropriate to conceptualize and model search as a stochastic process. And it is clearly *inappropriate* to apply uncritically, in the analytical treatment of that process, formalisms that posit a sharply defined set of perceived alternatives, to which no behavioral reality corresponds.

Last, search is distinguished by what we may term its *contingent* character. Real search processes take place in specific historical contexts, and their outcomes clearly depend in part on what those contexts contain in the way of problem solutions that are available to be "found." What there is to be found consists in large part of the fruits, by-products, and residues of information-producing activities elsewhere in the society. The flow of general social history thus impinges directly on the firm through its search activities, and searching at t is not the same thing as searching at $T > t$.

We have probably exaggerated here the extent to which the conceptual distinctions among irreversibility, uncertainty, and contingency are clear-cut. Rather, these are three interrelated aspects of the single central fact that search processes are historical processes, not repetitive and not readily separable from other processes of historical change. Awareness of that central fact should perform the valuable function of keeping the ambitions and pretensions of economic theorizing under realistic control; there is reason not to expect too much.

Distinguishing among the three characteristics is helpful in a more specific sense: it provides the basis for a taxonomy that clarifies the contribution and limitations of particular modeling approaches. For example, one approach to modeling the firm's search for superior techniques involves taking input coefficients (or changes therein) as the objects of the search. This approach suppresses the contingent aspect of search at the outset; it loses contact immediately with the fact that the realities of search for techniques involves questions of improved machine design, work arrangement, and so on, and that answers or partial answers to such questions are generated by processes external to the firm. But at the price of accepting this rather extreme abstraction, we can construct simple models that illustrate the "tendency" for search outcomes to be deflected in the "standard" direction by input price changes. We shall demonstrate below that "standard" results are obtainable in a simple "search-and-test" model in which the direction of search is not influenced by factor prices. A searching firm draws on a random distribution of technological coefficients in the neighborhood of its current techniques; it compares the cost of the alternative technique it "finds" with costs associated with the status quo, and it switches if the alternative is less costly. The distribution may be such that there is a coefficient drift in one direction or another under a wide range of factor prices. However, the expected change in input coefficients resulting from search is deflected in the standard direction by a change in relative input prices.

It is plausible, of course, to assume that input prices affect the search process in more subtle ways than merely by providing parameters of a test applied to a discovered result. For example, the expected gains from an array of different R&D projects may be reordered by a change in prices so that the nature of what is attempted by the firm is changed. This too can be modeled, and the standard result may again be obtained. There are also relevant mechanisms traceable to certain descriptive regularities of behavior. Cyert and March (1963) advanced the generalization that organizational search is "problemistic": it is stimulated by a particular problem, and the symptoms of the problem define a neighborhood in which the search takes place. If the "problem" is a profit reduction associated with the rise of a price of an input, and if the symptoms (cost increases) show up most vividly in certain activities or product lines that make intensive use of that input, one might expect that the firm's problem-solving activities will be directed to those areas. It is also plausible that search will be structured by the question "How can we reduce our use of this input?" If a search process thus directed and structured is successful, it will probably reduce use of the input.[3]

So the hypothesis that price change–induced changes in search outcomes are standard is plausible. But proper interpretation of the hypothesis requires some delicacy. First, insofar as the model treats search (appropriately) as stochastic, the hypothesis necessarily relates to "tendencies," or average results. An individual outcome may easily be perverse. Second, since search may take place even in a constant market regime, the hypothesis about the consequences of a change in regime necessarily involves a comparison with "what might have been"—that is, the path of technique change that would have occurred under the original regime. There is no reason why search outcomes might not be strongly biased in one way or another, reflecting the relative ease or visibility of certain kinds of innovations. For example, under some circumstances it may be that ways to save labor are obvious to see and easy to develop, relative to other kinds of innovation, and that the evolution of technology (decision rules) will show a labor-saving bias under a wide range of possible factor price ratios. Under these circumstances, search may reduce labor input over time in a regime of constant wage rates, and lower wages would simply mean a slower drift in that direction than would higher ones.

Even when delicately posed, the hypothesis that the results of

---

3. For a model in this spirit, see Winter (1981).

search are standard is not of self-evident validity; intelligent profit-seeking behavior does not necessarily imply it. Consider, for example, the following scenario. A metal fabricating firm confronts a sudden rise in the price of its raw material. It makes routine adjustments to this change by, say, making greater use of odd-shaped pieces of material that were formerly treated as scrap. After this adjustment, a severe profit pinch remains, and triggers off a search for ways to deal with this situation—a search that would not have been undertaken had the price increase and cost crisis not occurred. The result of the quest is the discovery that new types of *labor*-saving machinery, adaptable to the firm's problems, have become available. The firm buys such machinery and eases its profit problem—but the new machinery is less tolerant of odd-shaped pieces of material than were the workers who previously performed the relevant operations. As a result, the raw material intensity of the output increases. Search triggered by the price rise has contributed a perverse component to the total response of the firm. The decision rule change moved the firm in the direction opposite to that in which its routine decision rule moved it. Because search would have been less, the firm would not have discovered this decision rule change in the different factor price regime.

The third term in the decomposition captures the effect of different price regimes on the growth or decline of firms that have different time T decision rules. Again, under a variety of assumptions selection effects will be standard. For example, assume that routinized and search responses occur sufficiently rapidly so that capital shares can be considered as practically constant while these changes are going on. Then the reweighting effect is a pure selection effect on decision rules that have been established shortly after t and that are constant over the selection period. It can be shown that under these assumptions the selection effect of a change in the price of a single input is standard, if firm growth rates are linearly related to gross rents per unit of capital and the slope coefficients are the same for all firms.[4]

Again, there is nothing tautological about this. Timing effects can make the selection term perverse. For example, if the firms that by time T have most adapted their decision rules to accommodate the change in prices do their adapting late in the game relative to firms that only adapt a little, the selection term can have the wrong sign. Or a perverse effect is possible if the marginal relationship between

---

4. A model of this selection effect, in the simple case in which search and along-the-rule effects are absent, may be found in Chapter 10. The "equal slopes" condition is imposed there by an assumption that all techniques have equal capital-output ratios and that all gross profits are reinvested.

(quasi-rent) returns to capital and the firm growth rate is different for different firms, and systematically related to interfirm differences in intensity of use of the input whose price has changed. Imagine, for example, that there are two groups of firms, the first with a labor-capital ratio that is 10 percent lower than the second. Suppose that initial total capital in the two groups is the same, but investment by labor-intensive firms hardly responds to profitability at all, while in the other group half of any "excess return" on capital is reinvested. A fall in the wage rate will encourage investment by both groups. Although the capital-intensive group enjoys a smaller increase in profitability, its investment policies translate this into a larger increase in growth rate. Thus, abstracting from rule-induced changes and the effects of the wage rate decline on search, considering only selection effects, the average labor-capital ratio in the industry falls with a decline in the wage.

Obviously, our accounting scheme does not do full justice to the richness of the possible behavioral relationships and dynamic interactions linking routinized response, search, and selection. Formal dynamic models incorporating these mechanisms can be constructed, and explored analytically or with simulation. In the exploration of a particular dynamic model, our accounting scheme may retain heuristic value, but the specific assumptions of the model would necessarily take over the center of the stage.

The discussion above has been quite general. We have demonstrated that it is plausible to think of "along the rule," "search," and "selection" as involving different aspects of firm behavior and that under plausible models the effects of each of these mechanisms would be standard. Although specific perverse cases can be constructed, it seems unlikely that it would be possible to produce a plausible model in which an overall perverse result would hold in general, independent of particular initial conditions and parameter values. The qualitative predictions of orthodox comparative statics analysis may well describe the typical patterns of firm and industry response in the dynamic, evolving economy of reality. However, evolutionary analysis probes more deeply into the explanations for these patterns and warns of possible exceptions. Also, the explicit recognition of the search and selection components of adjustment brings a whole new range of phenomena into theoretical view.

2. A Markov Model of Factor Substitution

In this section we focus on one aspect of firm and industry response to changed market conditions—factor substitution induced by changed factor prices. A model of technique choice by the individual firm is set forth, and its implications for the phenomena of factor substitution at the firm and industry level are explored. The conclusions are "standard," but the mechanisms involved are very different from those of orthodox theory. To highlight the contrast with orthodox theory, we assume here that the routinized decision rules of firms produce absolutely no factor substitution; only search and selection effects exist. The model rests on a very simple abstract representation of the idea that firms search for cheaper production techniques.

The analytical framework here is similar to that of the previous chapter. In each time period, each firm has a given capital stock and operates a single production technique (fixed coefficients). We assume for simplicity that there is no flexibility to the output decision rule; the technique and capital stock of a firm thus determine its output and variable inputs in a time period. The industry faces a downward-sloping demand curve for output. From period to period, firms expand or contract according to their profitability, and firms search for better techniques. When a firm finds a new technique through search and adopts it, all of its capital is shifted costlessly to that technique. Output, inputs, and average input proportions in the industry evolve over time as firms change their capital stocks and techniques.

To avoid complications, we will assume that all techniques have the same capital-output ratio, and focus on substitution among variable factors. Two regimes of constant prices for variable factors, involving differing relative prices, will be compared. The formal analysis is confined to the case of two inputs, though it may be interpreted as concerned with the consequences of a change of the price of one factor as against the aggregate of all others whose prices remain constant.

At the center of the model is the technique search process for the individual firm. Let q, k, x_1, x_2, be respectively the levels of the firm's output, capital stock, and two variable inputs. As noted above, we assume that k/q is constant over all possible techniques. Techniques differ in input coefficients $a_1 = x_1/q$ and $a_2 = x_2/q$ for the two variable inputs. Firm search involves a draw on a distribution of alternative techniques a_1', a_2' near its prevailing technique. When a technique is found that is cheaper than the current one at prevailing prices w_1 and w_2—that is, when $w_1 a_1' + w_2 a_2' < w_1 a_1 + w_2 a_2$, the firm changes to the alternative (a_1', a_2'); otherwise, it sticks with (a_1, a_2).

Our basic assumption concerning the distribution of alternatives found through search is that proportional changes in input coefficients are distributed independently of the prevailing coefficients. It is convenient, therefore, to characterize the process in the space of logarithms of input coefficients. And, since we are particularly concerned with the evolution of factor ratios, it is also convenient to characterize a technique by the logarithm of its factor ratio,

$$U = \log\left(\frac{a_2}{a_1}\right) = \log(a_2) - \log(a_1).$$

To locate a technique in the two-dimensional space of logarithms of input coefficients, we need one other coordinate besides U. It is convenient to measure the second coordinate perpendicular to the first—that is, to choose it to be

$$V = \log(a_1 \, a_2) = \log(a_1) + \log(a_2).$$

Obviously, for a given U coordinate, a technique with a smaller V coordinate is better than one with a large V coordinate. A locus in the (a_1, a_2) space on which V is constant may be thought of as an isoquant of a Cobb-Douglas production function characterized by equal exponents for the two factors—but this is only a formal correspondence and has nothing to do with out economic argument.

We will consider a denumerable array of possible techniques that involves finitely many values of U, indexed from 1 to N, and infinitely many values of V, indexed from $-\infty$ to $+\infty$. More specifically, possible techniques differ in their U and V values by integral multiples of a constant Δ. This constant is arbitrary (except as noted in the discussion below), and its effect could equally well be represented by an appropriate choice of the base to which the logarithms are computed. Let $u_1, u_2, \ldots, u_N$ and $\ldots, v_{-2}, v_{-1}, v_0, v_1, v_2, \ldots$ represent the different possible values of U and V. By technique (i, j) we mean the technique characterized by the pair

$$U = u_i = u_0 + i\Delta,$$
$$V = v_j = j\Delta.$$

Here, u_0 is a constant that anchors the range of factor ratios under consideration, and Δ corresponds essentially to the proportional difference in the size of adjacent input coefficients in the array. It is easily seen that the input coefficients of technique (i, j) are

$$a_1 = \exp[(v_j - u_i)/2]$$
$$a_2 = \exp[(u_i + v_j)/2]$$

Figures 7.1 and 7.2 illustrate such an array of techniques in both the (a_1, a_2) and $(\log(a_1), \log(a_2))$ spaces; Δ has been chosen to be $\log(2)$ for illustrative purposes.

The search scheme may now be characterized. Let the technique of a particular firm at time t be technique (i, j); that is,

$$U_t = u_i$$

$$V_t = v_j$$

The search outcome is determined by an integer-valued random pair (G_t, H_t) that essentially represents the number of steps the firm takes in the U and V dimensions, subject to the qualification that the U values can only range from u_1 to u_N:

$$U'_{t+1} = u_{i+G_t} = u_0 + (i + G_t)\Delta \qquad \text{for } 1 < i + G_t < N$$

$$U'_{t+1} = u_1 = u_0 + \Delta \qquad\qquad \text{for } i + G_t \leq 1$$

$$U'_{t+1} = u_n = u_0 + N\Delta \qquad\qquad \text{for } N \leq i + G_t$$

and

$$V'_{t+1} = v_{j+H_t} = (j + H_t)\Delta.$$

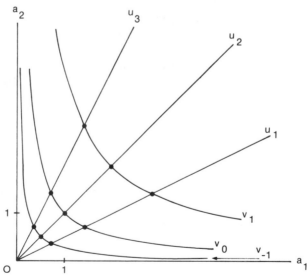

7.1   Technique array in input coefficient space.

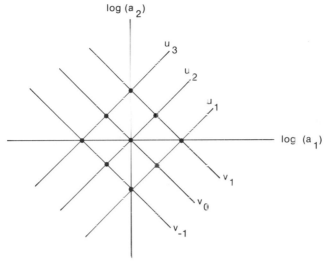

7.2   The same array in $\log(a_1)$, $\log(a_2)$ space.

Random variables (G_t, H_t) are independent of (U_t, V_t) and all prior values of (U, V), are jointly distributed in a bounded region $-B \leqq (G, H) \leqq B$, and should be thought of as indexed by firm number as well as by time periods. They are independently and identically distributed over firms and time. If the technique implied by search outcome (U'_{t+1}, V'_{t+1}) passes the cost reduction test described above, then $U_{t+1} = U'_{t+1}$ and $V_{t+1} = V'_{t+1}$. Otherwise, $U_{t+1} = U_t$ and $V_{t+1} = V_t$. Note that the distribution of alternatives discovered through search has been assumed to be independent of factor prices, but the distribution of alternative techniques adopted is affected by factor prices through the cost reduction test.

  This search-and-test scheme determines a probability distribution for period $(t + 1)$ technique conditional on the period t technique, a distribution that depends on the distribution of (G, H) and on the factor prices. (We assume here that probability "piles up" at the boundary values of u_1 and u_N; for example, all of the probability associated with G values such that $G \geqq N - i$ is assigned to the outcome $U'_{t+1} = u_N$.) The independence assumptions made above imply that the sequence of techniques employed by a firm over time forms a Markov chain. A significant feature of this chain is that the sequence of factor ratios of the firm, $\exp(U_t)$, is *itself* a Markov chain—in fact, a finite Markov chain with transition probabilities that are constant over time. This follows from the easily verified fact that $\exp(V_t)$ cancels out of the cost comparison inequality. The same (G, H) pairs that produce, for example, a u_3 to u_7 transition when $V_t = v_{21}$ also do so when $V_t = v_{-57}$ or for any other value of V_t.[5]

The behavior of a firm's factor ratio over time may therefore be characterized by an N by N transition probability matrix $F = [f_{ik}]$, i, $k = 1, \ldots, N$, where state i is associated with factor ratio $\exp(u_i)$ and f_{ik} is the probability that state i follows state k. This transition matrix is constant over time, but depends on the factor prices used in the cost comparison.

Two properties of matrix F are central to the argument that follows. The first is that a rise in the price ratio w_1/w_2 increases the probability of higher-numbered states (higher a_2/a_1) conditional on each and every initial value of a_2/a_1. Specifically, if $\hat{f}_{ik}$ are the coefficients following the increase in the relative price of variable factor 1, we have

$$(6) \quad \sum_{i=1}^{n} \hat{f}_{ik} \leq \sum_{i=1}^{n} f_{ik}, \text{ for } n = 1, \ldots, N-1$$

$$\text{and } k = 1, \ldots, N$$

In the form stated, this property holds with full generality given that the matrices F and $\hat{F}$ derive from the search-and-test scheme described above. This may be verified simply by comparing, for a given initial pair (a_1, a_2), the regions in the input space that satisfy the cost comparison test for two different input price ratios; the assumption that makes such a comparison relevant is that the search-generated distribution of alternatives does not depend on the prices. The second property is that the columns of matrix F are ordered by a relation similar to that above:

$$(7) \quad \sum_{i=1}^{n} f_{iK} \leq \sum_{i=1}^{n} f_{ik} \text{ for } n, k = 1, \ldots, N-1$$

$$\text{and } K > k.$$

That is, conditional on a higher-numbered state the probability of going to a low-numbered state is smaller than it is conditional on a lower-numbered state. This mathematical property is a plausible translation of the economic idea that search is "local"—that is, that it

---

5. Note, however, that the value of V_{t+1} is not independent of U_{t+1}, given U_t and V_t. For example, suppose that U_t is such that the share of factor two is substantially less than that of factor one: $(w_2/w_1) \exp(U_t) < 1$. Then a small increase in U is cost-reducing if V is held constant. A larger value of U_{t+1} makes larger values of V_{t+1} consistent with passing the cost reduction test.

involves incremental modifications of existing techniques. Local search is not likely to change the factor ratio very much and ratios near the initial one are the most probable. The probability of winding up at a ratio lower than any particular value is thus higher if the initial ratio is itself low. Here we will simply assume that (7) holds for matrix F. However, at the price of some additional assumptions on the search-and-test scheme, and some tedious argument, this property can be established as a theorem. What is required is a stronger form of the concept that search is "local": Δ is very small and the integer B is large but still small enough to leave $B\Delta$ much smaller than one; also, it is required that the probability distribution of (G, H) not be too irregular.[6] On these same assumptions, the inequalities in (6) and (7) will hold as strict inequalities (except that, in the case of relations (6), the fact that we are dealing with a discrete probability distribution makes it possible that a very small price change might leave the outcome of the cost reduction tests unchanged at some or all points of the array). We assume that the relations are in fact strict.

Analysis of the dynamic behavior of the factor ratio in a given firm is now a straightforward application of the mathematical results set forth in the appendix to this chapter. At the time of the increase in the relative price of factor one, the firm will be characterized by a particular a_2/a_1 ratio $= \exp(u_i)$. Its probability distribution over the N states of the Markov chain is at that point characterized by the unit vector δ_i; with one in the ith place and zeroes elsewhere. From time τ on, the evolution of the firm's factor ratio is governed by transition matrix $\hat{F}$ rather than by F. In the notation of the appendix we have assumed $\hat{F} > F$, which means that every column of F shows some displacement of probability toward higher-numbered states relative to the corresponding column of F. The ordering property we have assumed to hold among the columns of F is called condition (*) in the appendix. Theorem 3 of the appendix (and the following discussion) says that under these conditions $\hat{F}^t > F^t$. This obviously entails for $t > \tau$

$$\hat{F}^{t-\tau} \delta_i > F^{t-\tau} \delta_i.$$

---

6. More precisely, the result holds for the case in which G and H are uniformly distributed over the integers $-B$ to $+B$, provided $B\Delta \ll 1$. Also, the more tightly clustered is the distribution of alternatives around the initial value (the smaller is $B\Delta$), the more irregular the distribution can be and still have the result hold. A small $B\Delta$ implies a small rate of change of the factor ratio *per period*, but one can, of course, think of a "period" as a short time interval. These considerations suggest that an analogue of the property in question holds with high generality in an analogous process in continuous time and a continuous state space.

That is, the change in the price ratio at time τ has shifted the probability distribution of the factor ratio at every time after τ in the direction of higher values of a_2/a_1. The same shift holds in the limit, when the probability distribution of the state has converged to a stationary distribution that is independent of the initial condition (see Theorem 4 of the appendix).

Consider now what happens to the average factor ratio displayed by the industry. The foregoing analysis applies to each individual firm, with the proviso that different firms will in general have time τ factor ratios $\exp(U_\tau)$ as well as different values of V_τ. The factor price change displaces the post-τ probability distribution for each and every firm in the direction of higher values of a_2/a_1; looking into the remote future from time τ, one sees the distributions for all firms converging to the stationary distribution associated with transition matrix $\hat{F}$. Thus, it is clear that the probability distribution of the unweighted average of firm factor ratios for every time $t > \tau$ is displaced in the standard direction by the price change, and that the expected value of the (unweighted) average ratio for large t is increased from

$$\sum_{i=1}^{N} s_i \exp(u_i) \quad \text{to} \quad \sum_{i=1}^{N} \hat{s}_i \exp(u_i)$$

where s and $\hat{s}$ are respectively the stationary probability vectors associated with matrices F and $\hat{F}$.

Of course, the actual industry aggregate x_2/x_1 ratio is the *capital weighted* average of individual firm ratios. This means that selection effects are involved in the change of the industry ratio, along with the search effects already analyzed, and this introduces some complications. Formally, let $I_{im}(t) = 1$ if at time t firm m has $U_t = u_i$, and $I_{im}(t) = 0$ otherwise. That is, $I_{im}(t)$ is simply, for each m, the random N-vector indicating which state of the factor ratio Markov process firm m is in at time t. Let $Z_m(t)$ be the capital share of firm m:

$$Z_m(t) = \frac{K_m(t)}{\sum_{j=1}^{M} K_j(t)}.$$

Then the factor ratio of the industry as a whole may be written as

$$\alpha(t) = \sum_{i=1}^{N} \sum_{m=1}^{M} Z_m(t)\, I_{im}(t)\, \exp(u_i).$$

Take the expectation of $\alpha(t)$:

$$E(\alpha(t)) = \sum_{i=1}^{N} \sum_{m=1}^{M} \exp(u_1)[E(Z_m(t)) \cdot E(I_{im}(t)) + \text{Cov}(Z_m(t), I_{im}(t)].$$

The analysis above implies that for large t (and for all m), $E(I_{im}(t))$ is approximately equal to $\hat{s}_i$ as compared to the value s_i it would have if the factor price change did not take place. Since the capital shares sum to one, this means that $E(\alpha(t))$ differs from the unweighted average characterized previously by the sum of the covariance terms $\text{Cov}(Z_m(t), I_{im}(t))$. The substantive questions posed by the presence of these covariance terms are whether a change in factor prices can produce a perverse *change* in the covariance, and, if so, whether that constitutes a significant nonstandard effect on the behavior of the industry aggregate factor ratio. Our answers to these questions are not as sharp as we would like.

Our assumption that search is local means that the positions of firms in the range of possible factor intensities tend to be roughly persistent over time. This being the case, it is clear that a change in factor prices impinging on the particular industry state of $t = \tau$ tends to produce, in the following periods, selection effects in the standard direction. (As we noted earlier in this chapter, the relevant comparison here is with what would have happened absent the price change.) For a major price change, there may be a prolonged transient phase during which search effects gradually move the bulk of the weight in the factor ratio distribution into an entirely new range. If, in a particular realization of the process, a particular firm gets ahead of the pack in moving its factor ratio in the right direction during this transient, it will, in that realization, have an episode of better cost reduction experience and relatively more growth than it would have in a realization in which it chanced to lag. Thus, looking into the near future from the time of the price change, the covariance between capital shares and factor ratios may be seen as a partial reflection of the role of the selection mechanism in the response to the price change.

Looking into the more remote future, however, all individual firms are seen as distributed across factor ratios according to the stationary probabilities $\hat{s}$. Although cost reduction experience is related to factor ratios and factor ratio changes from time period to time period, the capital share of a firm reflects its entire history, in which the most recent periods play a negligible role. It therefore seems a plausible conjecture that the covariance between factor ratios and capital shares tends to zero in the limit as time goes to infinity. A proof of this conjecture could only be set forth in the context of a more explicit formal model of the firm growth process than we have provided here. We have verified the conjecture only for some models that have the somewhat objectionable feature that the industry is a near monopoly almost all of the time—although not always with the same firm in the dominant role. The tendency for industry structure to be degenerate in the long run, in this sense or even in some stronger sense, is a characteristic feature of industry models that involve or approximate the "Gibrat's law" property of independent random growth rates that are independent of firm size. Such models have considerable substantive importance as well as technical interest. We will return to these issues in Part V.

3. What Difference Does It Make?

What difference does it make if one takes an evolutionary perspective or an orthodox one on firm and industry response to changed market conditions? By an evolutionary perspective here we mean the broadly defined point of view we discussed earlier in the chapter, rather than the particular model presented above. Just as the case for orthodox theory should not stand or fall on the evaluation of a particular model (say, one that involves a Cobb-Douglas production function and a linear demand curve), so our particular model of Section 2 should be regarded as a member of a class of models. It is a comparison of the class of evolutionary models with the class of orthodox ones that we want to consider here.

The theory of firm and industry response to changed market conditions plays a double role in economic theory. It is at once a theory with its own specific focus and a building block for larger structures. We contend that even if regarded as a special theory aimed at exploring the effect of changed market conditions on firm behavior, orthodox theory is inadequate. Some of the predictions it yields tend to be qualitatively correct, but a central argument of this chapter is that other broadly defined theories (in particular an evolutionary theory) also can generate the correct qualitative predictions. The quantitative reliability of models drawn from orthodox theory is not high. Since an evolutionary theory contains all the elements of an orthodox theory and more, presumably the econometric equations consistent with an evolutionary approach should predict at least as well as more narrowly based predictive equations.

If one backs off from debating the merits of orthodox versus evolutionary theory in terms of accuracy of prediction, the consonance of the formal version of the theory with the appreciative theory of the phenomenon in question would seem to be an important criterion of merit; after all, the former purports to be an abstracted version of the latter. And appreciative theory is very often revealed when economists do applied research or engage in policy-oriented analysis. Economists doing applied work with the intention of influencing policy choices often find it necessary to stray far beyond the boundaries of orthodox formal theory. They recognize, implicitly or explicitly, all of the mechanisms described in our evolutionary accounting for response.

Consider, for example, the argument in favor of letting petroleum or natural gas prices rise to induce substitution or conservation by energy-consuming firms. Few economists really believe, or have stated, that firms have built-in optimizing decision rules that will achieve the most efficient possible substitution. Although a number of utilities (for example) are capable of using different fuels and switch fuels routinely as prices vary, it seems apparent that these built-in decision rules are not expected to account for the bulk of the response of the economy to higher prices. Rather, it is presumed that higher fuel prices will stimulate firms (and consumers) to think more about possibilities for substitution, conservation, or doing without. Discussion of the supply-response aspects of energy pricing is similarly eclectic. Many economists have argued that higher prices will induce greater supply, over both the short and long runs. It is apparent that many suppliers do have built-in procedures guaranteeing positive short-run response. However, long-run supply response is explicitly understood to involve search, in a literal sense. The expectation is that higher prices will induce more search for new oil and gas fields, more R&D on ways to get more oil out of the ground, and so forth. It is not, of course, assumed that all oil companies will make the same adaptations, search in the same directions, and succeed or fail together. Rather, some will be smarter, luckier, or have more favored initial positions than others; they will tend to prosper, to grow, and to be at the focus of the imitative efforts of others. Clearly, a story about firms responding to changed prices by picking a different point in a given choice set is an inadequate metaphor for all of this activity, and few economists, if any, would rely entirely on that metaphor to structure the analysis.

It is not merely that formal orthodox theory is not helpful in guiding thinking about concrete cases, and that a broader conceptualization is in fact used. The problem is that because the broader conceptualization tends to be implicit and *ad hoc*, rather than explicit and systematic, a number of important issues tend to be neglected. As a prominent example, consider concepts like "elasticity of substitution" or "elasticity of supply." Contemporary formalism takes these as "technologically determined data" and not variables that themselves can be "explained" by a deeper structural analysis that may also reveal them to be manipulable. An evolutionary theory of firm and industry response would suggest that substitution and supply responsiveness would be a function of the quantity and quality of "searching" and "innovating" that higher prices draw forth. Some of the key parameters of orthodox theory thus become endogenous in an evolutionary theory.

This and other differences between orthodox and evolutionary ways of theorizing lead to different perspectives on the policy issues involved. Suppose that the policy question is how to induce desirable levels of substitution and supply response. An orthodox approach would examine the relationship between the price signals received by the relevant economic actors and the social objectives that ultimately determine the desirability of various responses. The elasticities of supply and substitution would be regarded as technological data. From an evolutionary point of view, since these variables are not taken as given, the analyst can begin to think about how they can and perhaps should be manipulated by governmental policies. In particular, the question of the appropriate role of government in facilitating or guiding the R&D endeavor might become a topic of inquiry. Questions such as whether certain important R&D projects generate significant externalities, or require support on a scale beyond the resources of the firms in the industry, are naturally called forth. This is not to say that these issues are easy to think through. But one of the advantages of evolutionary theory is that they are signaled, and both general and specific research would tend to be focused upon them. A serious indictment of the orthodox perspective is that in almost all analyses by economists of the energy policy question they are ignored.

Relatedly, R&D receives awkward treatment in some of the more formal energy models, focused on identifying the optimal mix of technologies over time. Many of the "technologies" in the model are recognized as not now operational. Yet these technologies are assumed somehow to become operational at the appropriate or assumed time. The uncertainty about the cost of developing these technologies and their economic attributes is disregarded. As a result, the possible desirability of developing and exploring multiple alternatives is obscured. The heart of the R&D-innovation problem is that reasonable people will disagree about what technologies will be best when. This is a major reason why it makes sense to have R&D largely conducted by competitive business firms who make their own bets, rather than place it under centralized control. But in such a system there is the question of R&D incentives and the R&D portfolio that the incentives will draw forth. The technologies that will get developed at various times depend on that portfolio. Thinking about the role of government should hinge on assessing the way in which active policies can modify incentives or fill out the R&D endeavor so that the portfolio makes sense from a social point of view, given both the "best bet" characteristics of the technologies and the uncertainties. Orthodox formalism does not lead applied researchers to build applied models that explore these questions.[7]

The case for orthodox theory is even weaker in view of its inadequacies as a basic building block in modeling firm and industry behavior generally. Earlier we noted that the requirement for abstraction means that models—little theories—aimed at different phenomena will stress different things. Given the inevitable diversity of special-purpose models, it is of great value that the different models be recognized as special cases of a broader "master theory." The theory of firm and industry response to changed market conditions is viewed by the profession not merely as a special theory but as in some sense the master theory. As such it has been proving structurally adequate. We noted earlier the failure of models within orthodox theory to deal adequately with growth or with Schumpeterian competition. One of the great advantages of the evolutionary theory we propose is its extendability to explicitly dynamic problems, like growth and dynamic competition. In Parts IV and V we will explore these topics with the aid of models that closely resemble the ones used here to study more conventional problems. And the problems that have plagued the extensions of orthodox theory to these arenas will not be present.

Appendix

In this appendix, all vectors are understood to be vectors in R^N, and all matrices N by N matrices. Subscripts identify components of vectors and matrices; superscripts distinguish different vectors. If A is the matrix with typical element a_{ij}, then a_j denotes the jth column of A.

We shall be concerned with a partial ordering of vectors in R^N denoted by $\geq$ and defined as follows. Consider two vectors $x = x_1$, $x_2, \ldots, x_N$ and $y = y_1, y_2, \ldots, y_N$. Then $y \geq x$ if and only if

---

7. We return to these policy questions in Chapter 16.

$\sum_{i=1}^{n} x_i \geqq \sum_{i=1}^{n} y_i$ for $n = 1, 2, \ldots, N$. Define the strict relation $>$ by $y > x$ if and only if $y \geq x$ and not $x \geq y$. Then the statement $y > x$ is seen to be equivalent to $\sum_{i=1}^{n} x_i \geqq \sum_{i=1}^{n} y_i$, with the strict inequality holding for at least one n.

In our applications, the vectors x and y are probability vectors—that is, they are nonnegative and their components sum to one. More specifically, they are probability distributions over the states of a finite Markov chain. To interpret the relation $\geq$, imagine that the states of the chain are identified with the points $1, 2, \ldots, N$ on the real line. Then the partial sum of the components, $\sum_{i=1}^{n} x_i$, corresponds to the value of the cumulative distribution function at the point n. The relation $y > x$ then says that the cumulative distribution function corresponding to y lies to the right of that corresponding to x, and its algebraic definition is the equivalent statement that the cumulative distribution function for y is nowhere above, and, for at least one point below, that for x. Thus translated, $\geq$ is seen to be identical with the standard idea of first-order stochastic dominance,[8] with, however, the proviso that the ordering of the state indices is identified with an ordering of the states on the line. The fact that the state indices would not ordinarily have such an interpretation, and that some additional assumptions are required to support such an interpretation, is exactly what the analysis here is about.

The relation $\geq$ may be extended to matrices in the following manner. Given two matrices A and B, write $B \geq_c A$ if $\geq$ holds column by column—that is, if $b_j \geq a_j$ for $j = 1, 2, \ldots, N$. The corresponding strict relation $>_c$ then holds if $B \geq_c A$ and $b_j > a_j$, for at least one j. The geometrical interpretation for transition probability matrices is formulated in terms of what those matrices do to the unit vectors. More generally:

Theorem 1: If $B \geq_c A$ and $x \geq 0$, then $Bx \geq Ax$.

Proof: Let $y^a = Ax$, and $y^b = Bx$, and define $d_n = \sum_{i=1}^{n} (y_i^a - y_i^b)$. Then

$$d_n = \sum_{i=1}^{n} \left(\sum_{j=1}^{N} a_{ij}x_j - \sum_{j=1}^{N} b_{ij}x_j \right).$$

By reversing the order of summation and passing x_j through, we find

$$d_n = \sum_{j=1}^{N} x_j \left(\sum_{i=1}^{n} (a_{ij} - b_{ij}) \right)$$

8. The primary application of the concept of stochastic dominance in economic theory has been in the theory of optimal choice under uncertainty. See, for example, Quirk and Saposnik (1962) and Hadar and Russell (1969).

or

$$d_n = \sum_{j=1}^{N} x_j c_{nj},$$

where

$$c_{nj} = \sum_{i=1}^{n} (a_{ij} - b_{ij}).$$

By definition of $B \gtrsim_c A$, $c_{nj} \geq 0$ for every i and n. Since $x_j \geq 0$, $a_n \geq 0$ also for every n, and this is equivalent to $Bx \geq Ax$.

Note that if $B >_c A$, then $c_{nj} > 0$ for some n and j. If also $x > 0$, then $d_n > 0$ for some n, and $Bx > Ax$. Alternatively, suppose that x is semipositive—that is, $x \geq 0$ and $x \neq 0$. If $b_j > a_j$ for *every* j, $j = 1, 2, \ldots, N$, then we again have $Bx > Ax$. This last strong condition on the columns of two matrices is sufficiently important to our argument that we reserve for it the denotation $B > A$. If A and B are transition probability matrices and x is any probability vector, then $B > A$ implies $Bx > Ax$.

In the text, we are concerned with a situation in which a single application of the transition probability scheme does not shift a probability distribution very far in terms of the state ordering on the real line. Thus, for example, if the probability distribution of the state at period t is concentrated on high-numbered states, the distribution at period $t + 1$ will be similarly concentrated on the high-numbered states. More specifically, suppose at t the probability is entirely concentrated on state N. Then the distribution at $t + 1$ must be concentrated "far to the right"—in particular, it must be farther to the right than it would be if the period t probability had been concentrated at state $N - 1$, or $N - 2$, and so on. This line of reasoning leads to condition (*) below, which relates to the $\gtrsim$ ordering of the columns of a transition probability matrix A.

$$(*) : a_N \gtrsim a_{N-1} \gtrsim \cdots \gtrsim a_1$$

Theorem 2: If $y \gtrsim x$, and matrix A satisfies condition (*), then $Ay \gtrsim Ax$.

Proof: Proceeding as in the previous proof, let $z^x = Ax$ and $z^y = Ay$ and form $d_n = \sum_{i=1}^{n} (z_i^x - z_i^y)$. Then

$$d_n = \sum_{i=1}^{n} \left(\sum_{j=1}^{N} a_{ij} x_j - \sum_{j=1}^{N} a_{ij} y_j \right) = \sum_{i=1}^{N} \sum_{j=1}^{N} a_{ij} (x_j - y_j)$$

$$= \sum_{j=1}^{N} (x_j - y_j) \sum_{i=1}^{n} a_{ij}.$$

Let

$$c_{nj} = \sum_{i=1}^{n} a_{ij},$$

then

$$d_n = \sum_{j=1}^{N} (x_j - y_j)c_{nj}.$$

Now condition (*) on matrix A implies that, for $n = 1, 2, \ldots, N$,

$$c_{n1} \geqq c_{n2} \geqq \ldots \geqq c_{nN} \geqq 0.$$

The sum that is d_n may be rewritten as follows:

$$d_n = c_{nN} \sum_{j=1}^{N} (x_j - y_j) + (c_{n(N-1)} - c_{nN}) \sum_{j=1}^{N-1} (x_j - y_j)$$

$$+ (c_{n(N-2)} - c_{n(N-1)}) \sum_{j=1}^{N-2} (x_j - y_j) + \ldots$$

$$+ (c_{n1} - c_{n2}) (x_1 - y_1).$$

That the sums of $x_j - y_j$ and $x_1 - y_1$ are all nonnegative is the direct implication of $y \geq x$. The system of inequalities involving c_{nj} yields $c_{nN} \geqq 0$ and $c_{nj} - c_{n(j+1)} \geqq 0$ for $j = 1$ to $N - 1$. Hence, d_n has been expressed as a sum of products of nonnegative factors, and is nonnegative (for every n). The desired conclusion follows.

To obtain the strict result $Ay > Ax$, it is sufficient that $y > x$ and that all the relations in condition (*) be strict.

In the context of the application, Theorem 2 states that when the transition probability matrix A satisfies condition (*), the application of the transition probabilities to two vectors ordered by $\geq$ preserves that ordering. The mth power of matrix A represents the probabilities for m step transitions in the process, and is of course obtained by repeated multiplications of A into its own columns. If those columns are ordered by $\geq$, which is what (*) says, then the ordering will be preserved in the powers of A. Further, if two matrices are related columnwise by $\geq_c$, then that relation also prevails between powers of the matrices. This is the content of the following theorem.

Theorem 3: If A and B are nonnegative matrices, and A satisfies condition (*) of Theorem 2, and $B \geq_c A$, then $B^t \geq_c A^t$ for every positive integer t.

Proof: The case $t = 1$ is covered by hypothesis. Proceeding by induction, assume that the proposition is true for $t = m$. Let a_j^m denote the jth column of A^m, and so forth. Then

$$a_j^{m+1} = Aa_j^m.$$

By the induction hypothesis, $b_j^m \geq a_j^m$. By Theorem 2, therefore,

$$Ab_j^m \geq Aa_j^m.$$

Since B is nonnegative, so is B^m. Theorem 1 therefore implies that

$$b_j^{m+1} = Bb_j^m \geq Ab_j^m.$$

We have shown, therefore, that $b_j^{m+1} \geq a_j^{m+1}$, and hence that

$$B^{m+1} \geq_c A^{m+1}.$$

Thus, the proposition is true for every integer t.

To obtain the conclusion $B^t >_c A^t$, it suffices that the strict relations hold either in $Ab_j^m \geq Aa_j^m$ or in $Bb_j^n \geq Ab_j^m$ in the above proof. This conclusion, therefore, follows if $B >_c A$, and either relation (*) holds strictly in A or B is positive. If (*) holds strictly in A and $B > A$ then $B^t > A^t$ for all t.

Theorem 4: Let A and B be Markov matrices—that is, nonnegative matrices with all column sums equal to one. Assume that A has a unique vector of stationary probabilities, x^A—that is, a unique nonnegative characteristic vector associated with the dominant characteristic root of one. Let x^B be a vector of stationary probabilities for B. If condition (*) holds for A and $B \geq_c A$, then $x^B \geq x^A$.

Proof: By Theorem 1, $x^B = Bx^B \geq Ax^B$. By repeated application of Theorem 2,

$$Ax^B \geq A(Ax^B),$$
$$A(Ax^B) \geq A(A^2x^B), \text{ etc.}$$

That is, $A^{t-1}x^B \geq A^tx^B$ for $t = 1, 2. \ldots$ But $\lim_{t \to \infty} A^tx^B = x^A$, and, therefore,

$$x^B \geq x^A$$

Suppose that the relations of condition (*) hold strictly for A, and that $x^B > Ax^B$. Then $x^B > x^A$. For condition $x^B > Ax^B$ to hold, it suffices either that $x^B > 0$ and $B >_c A$, or that x^B is semipositive and $b_j > a_j$ for every j.

Intuitively, Theorem 4 says the following. Suppose that transition matrix A differs from B in that, conditional on each individual state, A attaches higher probability to the lower-numbered states. Then the stationary probability distribution for A attaches higher probability to the lower-numbered states than does stationary distribution for B. So expressed, the result has so much intuitive appeal as to appear trivial, and condition (*) on A may seem to be of doubtful necessity. (Theorem 2 has a very similar intuitive appeal that is similarly misleading with regard to the importance of condition (*).) It may, therefore, be useful to supply here an example of two matrices A and B such that $B >_c A$ and yet it is not the case that $x^B > x^A$. It is easily verified that this is impossible for $N = 2$. However, for $N = 3$, consider

$$A = \begin{bmatrix} 0.8 & 0 & 0.8 \\ 0.2 & 0.8 & 0.2 \\ 0 & 0.2 & 0 \end{bmatrix} \qquad B = \begin{bmatrix} 0.75 & 0 & 0.75 \\ 0.25 & 0.25 & 0.25 \\ 0 & 0.75 & 0 \end{bmatrix}.$$

Clearly $B >_c A$, and it is easily verified that

$$x^A = \begin{bmatrix} 0.4 \\ 0.5 \\ 0.1 \end{bmatrix} \qquad \text{and} \qquad x^B = \begin{bmatrix} 0.5625 \\ 0.25 \\ 0.1875 \end{bmatrix}.$$

Although B leads to a higher stationary probability on state 3, as intuition suggests, it also drastically reduces the probability on state 2 and increases that on state 1. As a consequence, if one assigns numerical values to the state as an increasing function of the state index, it is, of course, quite possible for the stationary expectation of this random variable to be lower in B than in A, although each and every conditional expectation is higher in B. For example, assigning values 1, 2, and 3 to states 1, 2, and 3, respectively, illustrates this point.[9]

---

9. Subsequent to our original publication of these mathematical results (Nelson and Winter, 1975), the paper by O'Brien (1975) was brought to our attention. It contains comparison theorems for stochastic processes of considerably greater generality than ours, and cites a 1962 paper by Kalmykov as the original source for theorems relating, as ours do, to the case of the finite Markov chain.

IV

GROWTH THEORY

Neoclassical Growth Theory:
A Critique

MUCH OF THE ECONOMIC THEORY developed by the great classical economists was concerned with exploring patterns of long-run economic change. Their thinking was strongly influenced by their recognition of technological advance and capital formation as important aspects of the historical transformations they witnessed. Whereas Ricardo and Malthus were (in some respects) pessimistically inclined, Smith before them and most of the classical tradition following them tended to believe that, at least for a considerable time into the future, long-run economic change meant economic progress.

The sharp focusing of microeconomic theorizing on the behavior of firms operating with *given* technologies (in a variety of different market constellations) developed relatively late in the history of economic thought, and came to dominate the textbooks and treatises only after World War II. It is not easy to understand exactly why microeconomic theory was purged of serious concern with long-run change. One reason was that it proved easier to provide a satisfactory mathematical statement of a static theory than a dynamic one. It also seems to have been the case that during the period when these intellectual developments were occurring, economists tended to lose their interest in economic growth, although this may have been a result of the trend that theory was taking, just as much as it was a cause.

In any case, the consequence was that in the 1950s, when many economists again became interested in patterns of long-run economic growth, they found themselves without a well-developed growth theory. First attempts at constructing one appeared in efforts to introduce a more explicit dynamics into Keynesian analysis, through recognition that investment is at once a source of demand for goods and services and a source of increased capacity to produce goods and services. However, the Harrod-Domar growth model, based on an assumption of fixed input coefficients, proved a poor tool for facilitating thinking about rising capital-labor ratios and increasing real incomes per head, which obviously were salient features of observed growth patterns. By the late 1950s, growth theorists had responded to the need to understand these features by borrowing heavily from the intellectual tool kit of static neoclassical microeconomics.

Inevitably, the nature of those neoclassical tools profoundly influenced the approach taken to the explanatory tasks of growth theory. We take it that there is at least rough agreement among economists as to the nature of that task. The minimal set of phenomena to be explained are the time paths of output, inputs, and prices. National economies have grown at various rates over time, and in given eras nations have grown at different rates. Output per worker and capital per worker have grown together. Real wages have risen relative to interest rates. Once one disaggregates the growth experience of particular countries, it is apparent that certain sectors have developed much more rapidly than others and that the sectoral pattern of growth has varied over time. Relative price changes have been correlated with relative productivity growth rates. Although different theories may define and delineate these central phenomena somewhat differently and economists also may divide on questions of the relevance of data of other types (such as productivity differences among firms), almost all economists would agree that a satisfactory theory must be able to explain the above phenomena.

We also take it that most economists would agree that the following are essential elements of the neoclassical explanation.[1] The dominant theme derives from the theory of the firm and production in a competitive industry. At any time, firms are viewed as facing a set of alternatives regarding the inputs and outputs they will procure and produce. Firms choose so as to maximize profits or present value, given the external conditions they face. The economy or sector is assumed to be in equilibrium in the sense that demand and supply are balanced on all relevant markets and no firm can improve its position given what other firms are doing. If we think of a "macro" economy with one sector and with no Keynesian difficulties, growth occurs in the system because over time factors of production expand in supply and production sets are augmented: in an "industry" growth model,

---

1. Much of the following discussion was first presented in Nelson and Winter (1973). The analysis of growth accounting follows Nelson (1973).

changes in demand must be considered as well. The time path of output, input, and prices is interpreted as the path generated by maximizing firms in a moving equilibrium driven by changes in factor demand, factor supply, and technological conditions.

As a glance at Solow's concise survey of growth theory testifies (Solow, 1970), this theory comprises a diverse collection of specific models. The empirical work generated by the theory is similarly diverse. Various neoclassical econometric models have "explained" growth reasonably well on the basis of input growth and technical change, if the criterion is a high R^2. Growth accounting has proceeded apace and has provided an intellectual format for enriching our understanding of the factors that have influenced growth. The theory has been robust in the sense that it continues to survive and to spawn a considerable amount of research that has enhanced our understanding of economic growth. This is a strong plus for neoclassical theory.

However, there is a peculiarity about the success story, which we noted earlier. By the late 1950s it had become apparent that it was impossible to explain very much of the increase in output per worker that had been experienced over the years in developed countries by movements along a production function resulting from increases in capital and other inputs per worker, if constant returns to scale and the other assumptions employed in traditional microeconomic theory were accepted. The "residual" was as large as that portion of total output growth explained by growth of factors of production. For the growth of output per worker, the residual was almost the whole story. The researchers working within the theory found a way to resolve this problem. Earlier, Schumpeter (1934) and Hicks (1932) had proposed that innovation (technical change) could be viewed as a shift in the production function. In the late 1950s Solow's work (1957) made this notion an intellectually respectable part of neoclassical thinking about economic growth. In the empirical work, the residual was simply relabeled "technical advance." Instead of reporting to the profession and the public that the theory explained virtually none of experienced productivity growth, the empirical researchers reported their "finding" that technical change was responsible for 80 (or 85 or 75) percent of experienced productivity growth.

1. THE RESIDUAL EXPLANATION OF ECONOMIC GROWTH

Technological Change as a Residual "Neutrino"

This type of intellectual sleight of hand is not peculiar to economic analysis, and reasonable toleration for it is not necessarily inimical

to the progress of science. The neutrino is a famous example in physics of a "labeling" of an error term that proved fruitful. Physicists
ultimately found neutrinos, and the properties they turned out to
have were consistent with preservation of the basic theory as
amended by acknowledgement of the existence of neutrinos. A major
portion of the research by economists on processes of economic
growth since the late 1950s has been concerned with more accurately
identifying and measuring the residual called "technical change,"
and better specifying how phenomena related to technical advance
fit into growth theory more generally. The issue in question is the
success of this work.

Considerable effort has gone into developing the concept of technical change within a production function framework and into modifying that framework to make technical change endogenous to the
neoclassical system rather than exogenous. Regarding the first part of
the task, the effort can be viewed as augmenting the specification of
the production function so as to include more terms—for example, a
term that can be interpreted as "total factor productivity" or terms
that can be interpreted as the "efficiency" of labor or of capital. These
terms are then treated as variables, not constants, within the system.
Technical advance is brought into the standard neoclassical format
for economic behavior by postulating that these terms are a function
of past investments (in activities called research and development)
aimed specifically to advance them. The standard profit maximization hypothesis has been employed regarding these investments.

A variety of empirical studies have proceeded guided by the
above conceptual structure, and have come up with conclusions that
are qualitatively consistent with it. For example, if one assumes that
the profitability of an invention is proportional to the sales of an industry, one would expect that changes over time in the amount of inventing directed toward different industries would be correlated
with changes in the sizes of industries, and that at any moment in
time there would be more inventing going on relevant to "large" industries than to small ones. These are exactly Schmookler's conclusions, based on his use of patents as an indicator of inventing
(Schmookler, 1966).

A special version of the theory focuses on technical advance to
"save" or increase the efficiency of various factors of production used
in producing a particular product. In this version of the theory a rise
in the price of one factor relative to another should, other things
equal, lead to an increase in efforts aimed to augment the efficiency
of that factor relative to others. Recent work by Hayami and Ruttan
(1971) and others, directed toward agriculture, shows that both time
series and cross-country data are roughly consistent with that theory.

The Identification Problem

In the case of the neutrino, the characteristics of the unobserved particle were relatively well pinned down by prevailing theory (assuming that the theory itself was viable). In the case of technical change, neoclassical theory did not specify very well how "large" or important technological change must be—only that there was "something" there. To see the problem, consider these familiar "stylized facts." Output (gross national product) has been growing at roughly the same rate as capital and at a faster rate than labor; hence, the capital-output ratio has been constant and output per worker and the capital-labor ratio have risen in the same proportion. Factor shares have remained constant; thus, the rate of return on capital has been constant and the wage rate has risen. These "facts" very roughly characterize the Western economic experience that the growth accounting exercises seek to explain.

The facts are inconsistent with an explanation that interprets growth solely in terms of movement along a neoclassical production function. The rise in output per worker would have been less than the rise in the capital-labor ratio, whereas in fact worker productivity has grown at the same rate as capital intensity. And the returns to the factor increasing in relative supply—capital—would have fallen, not remained roughly constant. Thus, the production function must have shifted.

But within the broad framework of interpretation provided by the idea of a shifting production function, there is a wide range of qualitatively different explanations available. Consider the following two, both consistent with the time series data. One is that the underlying production function is Cobb-Douglas (unitary elasticity of substitution) and that technical change has been neutral in the sense of Hicks. The second is that the underlying production function has an elasticity of substitution less than one and that technical change has been labor-saving. The first interpretation is depicted in Figure 8.1, the second in Figure 8.2. Points a and b in the two figures are identical and the slopes of the curves (the marginal productivity of capital) at those points also are identical. Thus, both interpretations are consistent with the input, output, and factor price data.

The two interpretations are different in the following "growth accounting" sense. In the case of Figure 8.1, output would have grown by Δ_{11} if capital per worker had grown as it did, but the production function had not shifted. Δ_{12} represents the increase in output per worker not explained by growth of the capital-labor ratio and due, in some sense, to technical change. In Figure 8.2, Δ_{21} can be attributed to growth of capital per worker and Δ_{22} to technical change

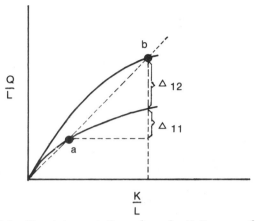

8.1   One interpretation of productivity growth.

in the sense above. In the latter interpretation the lower elasticity of substitution means that less of the productivity growth can be attributed to growing capital intensity; hence, more must be attributed to improved technology. Since both interpretations are equally consistent with the time series data, there is no way to choose between them without *a priori* assumptions or other data.

One could view this identification problem as posing difficulties for statistical estimation but as not raising any major theoretical issues; most economists look at the problem this way. For example, it has been proposed that if one had access to cross-section data showing firms operating at the same moment in time using different input coefficients, as well as time series data, one might be able to

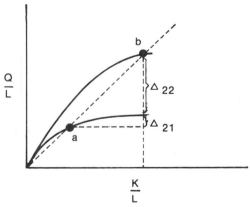

8.2   Another interpretation of productivity growth.

disentangle the two sources of growth. Contemporaneous observations would be presumed to reflect the same underlying store of technical knowledge. However, if these firms are within the same economy, these differences in choice of inputs must reflect either the fact that they face different factor prices at the same time, or the fact that they are making different technological choices given the same factor prices; either assumption presents difficulties for the neoclassical formulation that have not really been confronted.

Some Major Conceptual Issues

There are deeper theoretical and conceptual issues behind the scenes. The neoclassical formulation rests on the assumption that at any given time there is a wide range of technological possibilities from which firms may choose, including alternatives that no firm has ever chosen before. The initial period production functions in Figures 8.1 and 8.2 are drawn so as to extend a considerable distance to the right of point a, to depict production possibilities employing capital-labor ratios significantly greater than any firm had up to that time experienced. What is the meaning of that? What does one mean when one says that a production possibility exists even though no one is using it or has ever used it? As stated earlier, we do not think it realistic to assume that a sharply defined body of technical knowledge exists that governs production possibilities at input combinations remote from actual experience. Exploration of technologies that have not been used before involves in an essential way the characteristics of "innovation" that we described earlier. If this position is accepted, it is not merely that movements along preexisting production functions explain little of experienced growth. It is that the idea of movements along the production function into previously unexperienced regions—the conceptual core of the neoclassical explanation of growth—must be rejected as a theoretical concept.

The problems with rectifying the production function at remote input combinations are not satisfactorily resolved by grafting onto the theory a neoclassical model of induced innovation. The graft assumes that "inventing" or "doing R&D" is an activity whose outcome can be predicted in advance in fine detail. In effect, there is no difference in the amended theory between moving along the production function by increasing one kind of capital (plant and equipment) through physical investment, and "pushing outward" the production function by increasing another form of capital (knowledge?) through investing in R&D. Both kinds of investments are explained by the same behavioral model. The distinction between innovation and routine operation is totally repressed.

It is repressed at the level of description of the activities involved. There is no room in the neoclassical formulation for nontrivial uncertainty, or for differences of opinion regarding what will work best, or for recognition of the fact that the set of innovation alternatives is shrouded in fundamental ambiguity.

It is repressed in the characterization of the "output" of the activities involved. The models discussed above, which view "shifts" in production functions as resulting from investment undertaken by firms as part of the profit-maximizing portfolio of investments, rest on the presumption that the outcome of research and development is a "private good." Yet certainly there is often an important degree of "publicness" about new knowledge, whether that knowledge is in the form of "blueprints" or in the form of experience. This is so even if the innovating firm tries to restrict access to that knowledge. At the least, knowledge that another firm has done something successfully changes the thinking of other firms regarding what is feasible. And, in some cases, enough knowledge is published or is evident to the sophisticated observer to provide very good clues as to how to proceed.

It could be that the neoclassical induced innovation models implicitly postulate a system of patents. But this certainly is not built specifically into the theoretical formulation. If it were, the theory would need to take account of the fact that firms at any time differ in terms of the technologies they can use, or would have to postulate a perfect system of patent licensing. However, in either case, as long as firms differ in terms of what they come up with as a result of their research and development activities, firms will differ in terms of their profitability.

Inconsistency with Micro Data

The amended neoclassical formulation represses the uncertainty associated with attempts to innovate, the publicness of knowledge associated with the outcomes of these attempts, and the diversity of firm behavior and fortune that is inherent in a world in which innovation is important. Thus, it is unable to come to grips with what is known about technological advance at the level of the individual firm or individual invention, where virtually all studies have shown these aspects to be central. This has caused a curious disjunction in the economic literature on technological advance, with analysis of economic growth at the level of the economy or the sector proceeding with one set of intellectual ideas, and analysis of technological advance at a more micro level proceeding with another.

Over the years economists, other social scientists, and historians have done an enormous amount of research on the more micro aspects of technological change. We shall discuss this literature in some detail in Chapter 11. Suffice it to say here that studies by historians like Landes (1970), Habakkuk (1962), David (1974), and Rosenberg (1972), and by students of industrial organization and technical change like Schmookler (1966), Jewkes, Sawers, and Stillerman (1961), Peck (1962), Griliches (1957), Mansfield (1968), and Freeman (1974) have revealed extremely interesting facts about the technological change process. While some of these are in harmony with neoclassical themes, others are quite discordant. We have, for example, much evidence of the role of insight in the major invention process, and of significant differences in ability of inventors to "see things" that are not obvious to all who are looking. Yet once one has made a breakthrough, others may see how to do similar, perhaps even better, things. The same patterns apparently obtain in innovation. Relatedly, there are considerable differences among firms at any time in terms of the technology used, productivity, and profitability. Although these studies show clearly that purpose and calculation play an important role, the observed differences among persons and firms are hard to reconcile with simple notions of maximization unless some explicit account is taken of differences in knowledge, maximizing capabilities, and luck. The role of competition seems better characterized in the Schumpeterian terms of competitive advantage gained through innovation or through early adoption of a new product or process than in the equilibrium language of neoclassical theory.

It is not possible to reconcile what is known about the phenomena at a micro level with the intellectual structure used to model technical advance at the macro or sectoral level by arguing that the macro model deals with the average or the modal firm. The differences among firms and the disequilibrium in the system appear to be an essential feature of growth driven by technical change. Neoclassical modeling cannot avail itself of this insight.

There have been a few noteworthy if neglected attempts to square the neoclassical theory of industry production and growth with the observed facts of very considerable diversity of techniques and profitability of firms within an industry at any time. Houthakker (1956) developed a model in which firms at a given time are endowed with different techniques, with each firm being profitable under some sets of product and factor prices but not under others. These techniques are fixed and given, as are the capacities of the various firms. Firms either produce at capacity or produce nothing, depending on the vector of prices. Within such a model it is possible that the aggregate industry data from different periods and different prices will have a form that resembles that of orthodox neoclassical theory. But the model would predict that in a given time there would exist considerable diversity across firms in productivity levels and profitability.

The Houthakker model does not explain why the techniques in existence (with positive capacity) at any time are what they are, and in his model the distribution of capacity over techniques is treated as a constant. There are several different models that "explain" cross-industry diversity of techniques at any time as a result of the dates at which various plants were put in place. See notably Solow, Tobin, von Weizsäcker, and Yaari (1966), Salter (1966), and Johansen (1972). But in these vintage models new investment is always in "best practice" technology, and firms are never uncertain about the characteristics of new technologies. And the evolution of "best practice" is unexplained. Thus, the neoclassical vintage models, at least their present versions, abstract away much of what scholars of the microeconomics of technical advance have learned about the topic.

Theoretical schizophrenia thus forces economists to keep their understandings in different boxes. A central purpose of a theoretical structure—to enable one to see links between apparently disparate phenomena and thus to enable knowledge to be superadditive—is thwarted by this neoclassical partitioning of technical advance. Relatedly, the structure of contemporary formal theory drives a wedge between the analysis of those economists who take the theory seriously, and those, such as economic historians, who pay more attention to the phenomena involved.

The tension has been recognized in the profession. For example, Nordhaus and Tobin have remarked: "The [neoclassical] theory conceals, either in aggregation or in the abstract generality of multisectoral models, all of the drama of events—the rise and fall of products, technologies, and industries, and the accompanying transformation of the spacial and occupational distributions of the population. Many economists agree with the broad outlines of Schumpeter's vision of capitalist development, which is a far cry from growth models made nowadays in either Cambridge, Massachusetts or Cambridge, England. But visions of that kind have yet to be transformed into a theory that can be applied to everyday analytic and empirical work" (Nordhaus and Tobin, 1972, p. 2).

2. The Need for an Evolutionary Approach to Growth Theory

The issue then is this. Following upon the discovery that there was a large "residual" involved in neoclassical explanations of economic growth, and the identification of that residual with technical change, economists undertook a considerable amount of research aimed toward pinning down what technical change actually is. This is just what happened after physicists discovered the neutrino. But what we now know about technical change should not be comforting to an economist who has been holding the hypothesis that technical change can be easily accommodated within an augmented neoclassical model. Nor can the problem here be brushed aside as involving a phenomenon that is "small" relative to those that are well handled by the theory; rather, it relates to a phenomenon that all analysts (or virtually all) acknowledge is the central one in economic growth. The tail now wags the dog. And the dog does not fit the tail very well.

The neoclassical approach to growth theory has taken us down a smooth road to a dead end. If an evolutionary approach has advantages as a way of analyzing traditional textbook questions, the arguments for such an approach to growth theory seem overwhelming.

9

An Evolutionary Model of
Economic Growth

THE STRENGTHS of the neoclassical approach to economic growth are considerable. Neoclassical theory has provided a way of thinking about the factors behind long-run economic growth in individual sectors and in the economy as a whole. The theoretical structure has called attention to the historical changes in factor proportions and has focused analysis on the relationship between those changes and factor prices. These key insights and the language and formalism associated with them have served effectively to guide and to give coherence to research that has been done by many different economists scattered around the globe. The weakness of the theoretical structure is that it provides a grossly inadequate vehicle for analyzing technical change. In particular, the orthodox formulation offers no possibility of reconciling analyses of growth undertaken at the level of the economy or the sector with what is known about the processes of technical change at the microeconomic level.

The challenge to an evolutionary formulation then is this: it must provide an analysis that at least comes close to matching the power of neoclassical theory to predict and illuminate the macroeconomic patterns of growth. And it must provide a significantly stronger vehicle for analysis of the processes involved in technical change, and in particular enable a fruitful integration of understanding of what goes on at the micro level with what goes on at a more aggregated level.

The key ideas of evolutionary theory have been laid out. Firms at any time are viewed as possessing various capabilities, procedures, and decision rules that determine what they do given external conditions. They also engage in various "search" operations whereby they discover, consider, and evaluate possible changes in their ways of doing things. Firms whose decision rules are profitable, given the market environment, expand; those firms that are unprofitable contract. The market environment surrounding individual firms may be in part endogenous to the behavioral system taken as a whole; for example, product and factor prices may be influenced by the supply of output of the industry and the demand for inputs. In Part III this broad conceptual scheme was incorporated in specific models of selection equilibrium and of the response cf firms to changed market conditions. The task now is to devise particular models, consistent with the broad theory, that are especially well suited to analysis of economic growth.

The model presented in this chapter is embodied in a computer simulation program.[1] Simulation techniques have been employed in economic analysis for a variety of different reasons. In some cases (probably comprising the best-known applications) the model is believed to be based on good understanding of a large number of different components of the overall problem. In large-scale macroeconomic models, these may be of the form of estimated behavioral relationships. What is desired is to analyze the effect of various hypothesized changes (the elapse of time, an increase in the tax rate) on a set of variables representing the interactive outcome of a large number of these processes (gross national product, employment, consumption expenditure). The problem is too complicated and constrained, however, to work through analytically. Therefore, the analyst puts the overall model on the computer and "experiments" with the variables whose impact he wants to assess. In cases like this, the analyst has clearly in mind the "structure" of the model he wants to analyze. Although he can analyze a highly simplified form of that model with more conventional techniques, simulation is dictated by an unwillingness to bear the costs of such "oversimplification."

Our situation here is not quite the same. We have some strong qualitative beliefs about a number of components of the model we want to build, but certainly are not rigid about the precise form they should take. We are very flexible about other components, and will choose these so as to enhance the tractability of the model. Our central objective is to build a model that admits, and will likely generate, considerable diversity of behavior at the level of the individual firm. At the same time we want the model to generate aggregative time paths of certain variables, and want to be able to manipulate certain

---

1. The model and most of the subsequent discussion was presented earlier in Nelson and Winter (1974) and Nelson, Winter, and Schuette (1976).

variables of the model so that these time paths are broadly consistent with historical experience. Also, we want to be able to explore the way in which certain variables defined at the microeconomic level influence these macroeconomic time paths. These requirements naturally lead us to a simulation format.

Needless to say, there are costs involved in working with a simulation rather than an analytic model. For one thing the results are of uncertain generality. If there is a large domain of interesting independent variables and parameters to explore, it is virtually impossible to explore all parts of it. The problem is compounded if the model is stochastic; one is then unsure about the representativeness of the result, even for the parts of the domain explored. In our view, however, the most serious problem with many simulation models is lack of transparency: the models yield results that are not easy to understand. Although this danger is more obvious in simulation than in other modeling strategies, it would be a mistake to believe either that simulation models are inherently opaque or that the results of more traditional analytic techniques are inherently transparent. A random sample of articles from contemporary economics journals is likely to include a substantial proportion of cases in which "conclusions" ground out by traditional analytic techniques take the form of complex mathematical expressions whose substantive economic rationale is extremely difficult (perhaps impossible) to discern.

Also, one can aim for and achieve a considerable amount of transparency in a simulation model by keeping it relatively simple and clean. And this will create opportunities to use simulation and analytic techniques in tandem.

Analysis is, in our view, an important complement of a good simulation study. Special cases of a simulation model (for example, where certain variables are set at zero) may be analytically tractable. It may be possible to construct simple analytic models that capture certain features of the more complicated simulation model; for example, in Chapter 10 we present such a simple analytic model that has much in common with the more complicated simulation model developed here. More generally, simple analytic arguments often can provide an economically meaningful interpretation of the results of simulation experiments.

Simulation, on the other hand, can be a useful adjunct to an analytic approach. Simulation models are not bound by some of the constraints imposed by the requirement for analytic tractability. But the simulation format does impose its own constructive discipline in the modeling of dynamic systems: the program must contain a complete specification of how the system state at $t + 1$ depends on that at t and on exogenous factors, or it will not run. In contrast, in orthodox analytic modeling the stress is on equilibrium conditions, and time paths may be treated in an *ad hoc* way or completely ignored.

The opportunity for fruitful exploitation of the complementarity can, however, be largely foreclosed if it is not treated as an important consideration in the design of the simulation model. Most important, the freedom associated with the relaxation of tractability constraints must be exercised with restraint if the output is to be susceptible to analytic checking and interpretation. To introduce complexity in the name of "realism" alone, disregarding the added costs of checking and interpretation, is no more appropriate in the one theoretical endeavor than in the other. It is, in short, a very pernicious doctrine that portrays simulation as a nontheoretical activity, in which the only guiding rule is to "copy" reality as closely as possible. If reality could be "copied" into a computer program, that approach might be productive—but it cannot, and it is not.

1. The Model

An evolutionary model of economic growth must be able to explain the patterns of aggregate outputs, inputs, and factor prices that neoclassical theory "explains." In the exercise here, the standard of reference is provided by Robert Solow's classic article "Technical Change and the Aggregate Production Function" (Solow, 1957). The data addressed in that article comprise gross national product (GNP), capital input, labor input, and factor prices, over a forty-year period. Data beneath these macro aggregates is ignored. Our simulation model must be capable of generating those macro aggregates, but through the route of "building them up" from microeconomic data. And our model must eschew neoclassical analytic components based on well-specified production functions and profit-maximizing behavior and employ in their place the evolutionary theory components of decision rules, search, and selection.

The model involves a number of firms, all producing the same homogeneous product (GNP), by employing two factors: labor and physical capital. In a particular time period, a firm is characterized by the production technique it is using—described by a pair of input coefficients (a_l, a_k)—and its capital stock, K. As in the model presented in Chapter 6, to enable us to exploit the mathematics of finite Markov chains, capital stock is assumed to come in discrete packets. A firm's production decision rule is simply to use all of its capacity to produce output, using its current technique—no slow-down or shut-down decision is allowed for. Thus, at any time, the "state" of a firm can be characterized by a triple (a_l, a_k, K) indexed by time and the identification number for a particular firm. The industry state at time t is the (finite) list of firm states at time t. Given the basic behavioral assumption, aggregate output and labor demand are directly determined by the industry state. The wage rate is endogenous, and is determined in each time period by reference to a labor supply curve. The gross returns to capital are simply output (at price equal to one) minus labor payments. Thus, the model can generate or explain the macroeconomic data that Solow addressed.

Changes in the industry state are generated by applying probabilistic transition rules, independently, to the individual firm states. These transition rules result from our specification of search processes and investment rules. In turn, the way we characterize particular transition mechanisms reflects our desire to capture, in stylized form, some of the salient aspects of technical advance and Schumpeterian competition as they have been identified by microeconomic studies. We discuss, first, the transition rules for firms "in business"—that is, with a positive capital stock. Assumptions governing entry will be mentioned later. In the following discussion, a parenthetical delta (δ) will identify parameters that have been varied in the experimental runs. The assumptions below, which determine the form of the general model, reveal the kinship of this model with that analyzed in Chapter 6. Yet they differ in important ways.

Technical Change

Use of the term "search" to denote a firm's activities aimed at improving on its current technology invokes the idea of a preexisting set of technological possibilities, with the firm engaged in exploring this set. This connotation seems natural when one is considering R&D aimed to find, say, a seed variety with certain properties or a chemical compound with certain characteristics. It seems less natural when one is considering R&D aimed to develop a new aircraft, or, more generally, R&D activities where the terms "invention" or "design" seem appropriate. Instead of exploring a set of preexisting possibilities, R&D is more naturally viewed in these contexts as creating something that did not exist before. And surely modern research on hybrid seeds and pharmaceuticals involves creating as much as discovering.

But for the purposes of our evolutionary modeling, the distinction here is one of semantics not substance. The R&D activities of our firms will be modeled in terms of a probability distribution for coming up with different new techniques. We will discuss this in terms of sampling from a distribution of existing techniques. But alternatively we could discuss it in terms of a distribution of things that a firm might "create." In either case, that distribution might be a function of time (opportunities might evolve over time), a firm's R&D policy (some firms might spend more or perform different kinds of R&D than others), the firm's existing technique (search may be largely local), and other variables.

In the particular model explored in this chapter, time *per se* is not an element; there is a given set of techniques to be found; a firm's R&D "policy" is modeled as involving "satisficing." And what a firm comes up with as a result of its R&D is much influenced by its prevailing technique and the prevailing techniques of other firms.

Satisficing. To highlight the similarity of the model employed here to the equilibrium-seeking model of Chapter 6, we assume that if firms are sufficiently profitable they do no "searching" at all. They simply attempt to preserve their existing routines, and are driven to consider alternatives only under the pressure of adversity. Their R&D activity should thus be conceived as representing an *ad hoc* organizational response rather than a continuing policy commitment. This satisficing assumption is a simple and extreme representation of the incentives affecting technical change at the firm level. We dispense with this assumption in the dynamic competition models in Part V, in which the differential profitability of alternative levels of commitment to R&D expenditure is a major focus of concern, but we believe it is adequate for our present purposes. In fact, it seems useful to demonstrate that in an evolutionary model with such conservative firms, there can be continuing innovation in the economy as a whole.

In the simulation runs here, only those firms that make a gross return on their capital less than the target level of 16 percent engage in search. Given that a firm is searching, it either seeks incremental improvements to its present methods or looks to what other firms are doing, but not both at the same time.

Local Search. There is a given constant set of technological possibilities, and each technique is characterized by coefficients a_l and a_k. Technical progress occurs as this set gradually is explored and discovered. For any firm engaging in such exploration, search is "local" in the sense that the probability distribution of what is found is concentrated on techniques close to the current one. The formula used for the distance between techniques h and h' is

$$D(h, h') = WTL \left|\log a_l^h - \log a_l^{h'}\right| + WTK \left|\log a_k^h - \log a_k^{h'}\right|, \text{ where } WTL + WTK = 1.$$

That is, distance is a weighted average of the absolute differences in the logs of input coefficients. This gives rise to diamond-shaped equal-distance contours in the space of logs of input coefficients. Employment of different values of WTL (δ) permits us to treat search with differing degrees of "bias" toward discovering labor- or capital-saving technologies. Probabilities for transitions from a given technique to others are then determined as a decreasing linear function of distance, subject to obvious nonnegativity conditions, an appropriate normalization, and introduction of a probability that no alternative technique will be found. The slope of this linear function is IN(δ), where IN stand mnemonically for "ease of INnovation." The larger (less negative) the value of IN, the more likely it is that the search process will uncover technologies with input coefficients significantly different from the initial ones.

Imitation. A searching firm may look to what other firms are doing. If it does, the probability that it will find a particular technique is proportional to the fraction of total industry output produced by that technique in the period in question. Alternatively we might have assumed that imitation is focused on "best practice," and we do so in models presented later. The assumption here is more consonant with models of diffusion, where what is best practice is not obvious to a firm *ex ante* but where widely used techniques attract attention.

The actual probabilities of "finding" different techniques for a firm that is searching are, then, a weighted average of the probabilities defined by "local search" and the probabilities defined by "imitation." The relative weights on local search and imitation are characterized by the parameter IM (δ), where IM is a mnemonic for "emphasis on IMitation." A high value of IM denotes a regime where search is more likely to be over what other firms are doing and less likely to be of the "local search" type than it would be in regimes where the value of IM is low.

An alternative rule turned up by the search process is adopted by the firm only if it promises to yield a higher return, per unit capital, than the firm's current rule. (Since the firm's capital stock is independently determined, the return-per-unit-capital criterion gives the same result as a test based on anticipated total profit.) The wage rate employed in this comparison is the one associated with the current industry state. There is an element of random error in the comparison: the capital and labor input coefficients employed in the test are not the true values for the alternative technique, but the products of the true values and realizations of independent normal deviates. A firm in business misjudges the input coefficient of an alternative technique by an amount that exceeds 20 percent about a third of the time.

Investment

Our characterization of the determinants of changes in the sizes of firms can be described much more compactly. The capital stock of a firm with positive capital in the current state is first reduced by a random depreciation mechanism; each unit of capital is, independently, subject to a failure probability of $D = 0.04$ each period. The capital stock, thus reduced, is then increased by the firm's gross investment in the period. Gross investment is determined by gross profit, where gross profit πK is revenue Q minus wage bill WL minus required dividends RK. (More precisely, gross investment is gross profit rounded to the nearest integer, the rounding being necessary because capital stock is integer-valued and gross profit is not.) This rule is applied even when gross profit is negative, subject only to the condition that the resulting capital stock not be negative. The higher the value of R (δ), the smaller the investment the firm is able to finance.

Entry

As indicated above, we make special assumptions about entry. A firm with zero capital in the current state is a potential entrant and "contemplates" the use of a production decision rule. If its decision rule implies a gross rate of return to capital in excess of 16 percent calculated at current prices, it becomes an actual entrant with probability 0.25. If it does enter, its capital stock is determined by a draw on a distribution that is uniform over the integers from five to ten. (Entry is relatively infrequent, and the contribution it makes to gross investment is minor when averaged over several periods.) Other firms (those contemplating rules that do not meet the rate-of-return test) remain at capital stock zero with probability one. The assumptions about search by potential entrants differ slightly from the assumptions about search by firms already in the industry; these will be mentioned when needed.

The Labor Market

The price of labor is endogenous to the model, being determined by the exogenous supply and endogenous demand for labor. The prevailing wage rate influences the profitability of each firm, given the technique it is using, and, in turn, the behavior of the industry as a whole is a powerful, but not unique, influence on the wage rate. The simulation program admits all wage determination equations of the form

$$w = a + b\left(\frac{L_t}{(1 + g)^t}\right)^c,$$

where t is the time period, L_t is the aggregate labor use in the period, and a, b, c, and g are constants. When $g = 0$, labor supply conditions are constant over time, and the model as a whole is a Markov process with constant transition probabilities. A nonzero g corresponds to changing labor supply conditions; the model as a whole remains a Markov process, but with time-dependent transition probabilities.

The Markov process defined by the above relations may be summarized as follows. At any moment the capital stocks of extant firms, together with their techniques, determine their required labor inputs and their outputs. Industry output and total labor employment then are determined. Total labor employment determines the industry wage rate. Given the wage rate, the gross profitability of each firm is determined.

Firms that make a gross rate of return of less than the target level engage in search. Of those firms that are searching, some attempt to innovate and others to imitate the techniques used by more profitable firms. Firms screen the techniques that they have uncovered by search, and if they deem them more profitable they are adopted and the old ones discarded. Firms that had been earning more than the target level, or that do not come up with techniques they deem better than the ones they had, keep their old techniques.

Extant firms invest in the purchases of new capital the earnings they have left after paying wages and required dividends. Their net investment equals gross investment minus depreciation. New firms may enter the industry at positive capital stock if the profitability of the technique they were contemplating exceeds the target level.

Thus, the next-period techniques of all firms are determined (probabilistically), and so are the next-period capital stocks. The "industry state" for the next period then has been established.

Calibration

The model will generate a time path of firm and industry inputs and output, and a time path of the industry wage rate and firm and industry rates of the return on capital, the labor share, and the capital share. One central question we are exploring is whether a model of the sort described above is capable of generating time paths of the macroeconomic variables that are similar to the actual observed time paths of these variables (in particular to those displayed in the data analyzed by Solow).

The initial conditions of the model were set so that they roughly corresponded to the conditions revealed in Solow's data for 1909.[2] Thus, we initially endowed our firms with techniques that, on average, had roughly the input coefficients displayed by the Solow data for 1909. We assigned an initial amount of capital to each firm and positioned the labor supply curve so that, given the implied labor requirements for the initial period, the wage rate equaled the 1909 wage rate and the initial capital-labor ratio roughly matched the 1909 data. (For reasons of convenience we chose an initial total capital stock of three hundred units.) Given that wage rate and the choice of input coefficients, the initial average rate of return on capital of our firm must be roughly equal to that in the Solow data for 1909. And labor's and capital's shares of income under initial conditions of the model also will be consonant with the actual Solow data for 1909.

The data analyzed by Solow also determined the set of possible techniques (input coefficient pairs) built into the model. The techniques were determined by random choice from the uniform distribution over a square region in the space of logarithms of input coefficients.[3] The region includes, with room to spare, all of the historical coefficients implied by Solow's data. We judged that distinguishing one hundred possible techniques in this region would permit adequate representation of cross-sectional diversity and historical change. This scatter is displayed in Figure 9.1, along with the actual time paths of input coefficients from the Solow data. An important question being explored is whether the (average) input coefficients of our simulation model can be induced to display a time path that is similar to the actual one.

The time path of the input coefficients, and of related variables like the capital-labor ratio, obviously will depend on how labor and capital grow over time in the model. Given the broad specification of the model's logic, this will depend on the particular parameter settings of some of the key variables. Thus, in the runs reported here we have assumed that the labor supply curve shifted to the right over the period of time at a rate of 1.25 percent per year. This is roughly consistent with the observed historical rate.

---

2. More precisely, the attempt was made to set initial values so that period 5 of the simulation run would approximately agree with the 1909 values.

3. A slight compromise of the random choice procedure was made: the scatter chosen was one of four generated, and it was selected because it was most free of "holes"—areas of the square in which no techniques occurred.

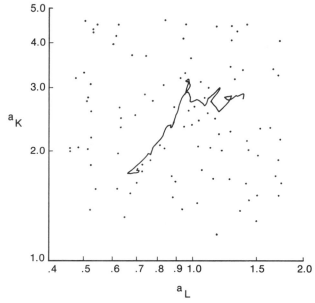

9.1   Input coefficient pairs for unit output, with Solow's historical input coefficient values.

Varying Some Key Parameter Values

One question we are asking about the model is whether, under plausible parameter settings of the sort described above, it can generate time paths of the macroeconomic variables comparable to those actually observed. Another range of issues being explored involves the connections between variables defined at the microeconomic level and the macroeconomic time path.

The "localness of innovative search" assumption built into the model implies that, at a microeconomic level, most innovations are relatively minor. It is possible, however, to vary the localness of search—to make it easier (more likely) or harder (less likely) for a firm to discover a technique significantly different (far away) from the one it has. (Specifically, the relevant parameter here is the slope of the relationship between the distance of an alternative technique from the current one and the probability that the alternative will be discovered.) If search is less local, if major innovation is easier, a firm is more likely to come up with innovation that is markedly inferior. But given that its profitability checks are reasonably reliable, it will not adopt such innovations. On the other hand, the innovations that it does adopt are likely on average to be bigger (involving a larger decline in the input coefficients). To what extent would the ease of major innovation, in the above microeconomic sense, show up in, say, a faster rate of growth of labor productivity or of total factor productivity? One's faith in the model's ability to represent micro-macro links would be severely strained unless there were some such association. By choosing different settings of the "ease of major innovation" parameter, it is possible to explore this question.

It also is possible to vary the parameter that determines what fraction of a firm's "searching" will be directed to what other firms are doing, rather than toward possible innovations. What differences would this make? The logic of the system at the micro level would suggest that if more search is directed toward imitating and less toward innovating, the production techniques of firms will tend to be bound together more closely. The competitive race would be "closer." And one implication of this might be that firms tend to remain together in size, as well as in technology. By calculating some measure of industry concentration at the beginning and end of the simulation runs, one can explore the effect of different degrees of emphasis on imitation on the extent to which concentration evolves over time in the model economy, and perhaps on some other variables. If interesting and plausible connections show up in the simulation results, these might form hypotheses to be tested against real-world data.

One can also vary the required dividend rate. If the dividend payout is low, the rate of growth of the capital stock ought to be higher than it would be if the payout were higher. This higher capital stock might be expected to lead to higher labor demand, thus to higher wages and to a tendency to adopt less labor-intensive techniques, when the cost of capital is low than it would when the cost is high. Another influence on the evolution of the capital-labor ratio might come from the extent to which search is easier in a capital-saving direction or in a labor-saving direction. One can vary this within the model by choosing different weights on the distance measure regarding innovative search.

In our simulation models we employed two different settings for each of the variables discussed above: the ease of major innovation, the emphasis on imitation, the cost of capital, and the labor-saving bias of search. That is, we undertook runs (of fifty periods each) with sixteen different sets of parameter settings. The sixteen runs comprise all possible combinations of levels of the four experimental factors, with two levels for each factor.

All of the experimental runs were initiated with the same assignments of techniques to thirty-five firms. In the eight runs with a high dividend payout rate, the fifteen firms in business each had twenty units of capital. In the runs with low required dividends, firms in business each had twenty-two units of capital. These initial capital values were chosen to put the system in approximate "equilibrium"—that is, with roughly zero expected net investment in the initial period. To have started all runs at the same industry state, ignoring the implications of the different parameter values, would have been a straightforward but naïve approach to the problem of achieving "identical" initial conditions for the different runs. Drastic differences in the aggregate outcomes in the early periods would then have been implied by the differences in parameter values; no such strong effects are visible in the results as they stand.

2. THE GROWTH RECORD OF THE SIMULATED ECONOMY

The computer output describing the experimental simulation runs contains abundant quantitative detail and is rich in qualitative patterns. Firms thrive and decline; new techniques appear, dominate the scene briefly, and then fade away. Time series for most aggregate data display strong trends, and also a good deal of short-period fluctuation. The stack of paper containing the description of the total of eight hundred years of synthetic history is over eight inches high. It is clear that it must be summarized fairly drastically for the purpose of this discussion.

How do the aggregative time series look? In a word, plausible. In Table 9.1 the results of one simulation run and the real data addressed by Solow are displayed side by side. There is, of course, no reason to expect agreement between the real and simulated data on a year-to-year basis. The simulation run necessarily reflects nonhis-

Table 9.1.   Selected time series from one simulation run, compared with Solow data, 1909–1949.

Year	Q/L^a		K/L^b		W^c		S_k^d		A^e	
	Sim	Solow	Sim	Solow	Sim	Solow	Sim	Solow	Sim	Solow
1909	0.66	0.73	1.85	2.06	0.51	0.49	0.23	0.34	1.000	1.000
1910	0.68	0.72	1.84	2.10	0.54	0.48	0.21	0.33	1.020	0.983
1911	0.69	0.76	1.83	2.17	0.52	0.50	0.25	0.34	1.040	1.021
1912	0.71	0.76	1.91	2.21	0.50	0.51	0.30	0.33	1.059	1.023
1913	0.74	0.80	1.94	2.23	0.51	0.53	0.31	0.33	1.096	1.064
1914	0.72	0.80	1.86	2.20	0.61	0.54	0.15	0.33	1.087	1.071
1915	0.74	0.78	1.89	2.26	0.56	0.51	0.24	0.34	1.108	1.041

Table 9.1   continued.

Year	Q/L[a] Sim	Solow	K/L[b] Sim	Solow	W[c] Sim	Solow	S_k[d] Sim	Solow	A[e] Sim	Solow
1916	0.76	0.82	1.89	2.34	0.60	0.53	0.21	0.36	1.136	1.076
1917	0.78	0.80	1.93	2.21	0.59	0.50	0.23	0.37	1.159	1.065
1918	0.78	0.85	1.90	2.22	0.62	0.56	0.21	0.34	1.169	1.142
1919	0.80	0.90	1.96	2.47	0.57	0.58	0.29	0.35	1.190	1.157
1920	0.80	0.84	1.94	2.58	0.64	0.58	0.19	0.32	1.192	1.069
1921	0.81	0.90	2.00	2.55	0.61	0.57	0.25	0.37	1.208	1.146
1922	0.83	0.92	2.02	2.49	0.65	0.61	0.21	0.34	1.225	1.183
1923	0.83	0.95	1.97	2.61	0.70	0.63	0.17	0.34	1.243	1.196
1924	0.86	0.98	2.06	2.74	0.64	0.66	0.26	0.33	1.274	1.215
1925	0.89	1.02	2.19	2.81	0.59	0.68	0.33	0.34	1.293	1.254
1926	0.87	1.02	2.07	2.87	0.74	0.68	0.15	0.33	1.288	1.241
1927	0.90	1.02	2.16	2.93	0.67	0.69	0.25	0.32	1.324	1.235
1928	0.91	1.02	2.18	3.02	0.70	0.68	0.23	0.34	1.336	1.226
1929	0.94	1.05	2.27	3.06	0.68	0.70	0.28	0.33	1.370	1.251
1930	0.98	1.03	2.47	3.30	0.62	0.67	0.37	0.35	1.394	1.197
1931	0.99	1.06	2.46	3.33	0.70	0.71	0.29	0.33	1.408	1.226
1932	1.02	1.03	2.57	3.28	0.69	0.62	0.32	0.40	1.435	1.198
1933	1.02	1.02	2.46	3.10	0.85	0.65	0.16	0.36	1.452	1.211
1934	1.04	1.08	2.45	3.00	0.85	0.70	0.19	0.36	1.488	1.298
1935	1.05	1.10	2.44	2.87	0.87	0.72	0.17	0.35	1.500	1.349
1936	1.06	1.15	2.51	2.72	0.82	0.74	0.22	0.36	1.499	1.129
1937	1.06	1.14	2.55	2.71	0.83	0.75	0.22	0.34	1.500	1.415
1938	1.11	1.17	2.74	2.78	0.76	0.78	0.32	0.33	1.543	1.445
1939	1.10	1.21	2.66	2.66	0.88	0.79	0.20	0.35	1.540	1.514
1940	1.13	1.27	2.75	2.63	0.84	0.82	0.25	0.36	1.576	1.590
1941	1.16	1.31	2.77	2.58	0.90	0.82	0.23	0.38	1.618	1.660
1942	1.18	1.33	2.78	2.64	0.95	0.85	0.20	0.36	1.641	1.665
1943	1.19	1.38	2.79	2.62	0.93	0.91	0.22	0.34	1.652	1.733
1944	1.20	1.48	2.80	2.63	0.97	0.99	0.20	0.33	1.672	1.856
1945	1.21	1.52	2.82	2.66	0.97	1.04	0.20	0.31	1.683	1.895
1946	1.23	1.42	2.88	2.50	0.96	0.98	0.22	0.31	1.694	1.812
1947	1.23	1.40	2.89	2.50	0.98	0.94	0.21	0.33	1.701	1.781
1948	1.23	1.43	2.87	2.55	1.01	0.96	0.18	0.33	1.698	1.809
1949	1.23	1.49	2.82	2.70	1.04	1.01	0.15	0.33	1.703	1.852

a. Q/L = Output (1929 dollars per man-hour; Solow data adjusted from 1939 to 1929 dollars by multiplying by 1.171, the ratio of implicit price deflators for GNP).

b. K/L = Capital (1929 dollars per man-hour).

c. W = Wage rate (1929 dollars per man-hour; Solow data adjusted from 1939 to 1929 dollars).

d. S_k = Capital share (equals one minus the labor share).

e. A = Solow technology index. (Recalculation on the basis of figures in other columns will not check exactly, because of rounding of those figures. Solow figures shown for 1944–49 are correct; the values originally published were in error.)

Note: These data are from run 0001; see Table 9.2 for key to run numbering.

torical random influences. But more than that, and of particular importance to this comparison, the simulation model, unlike Solow's analysis of the real data, generates its own input history on the basis of very simple assumptions about behavior and institutional structure. The real period in question involved eposides of economic depression and war, and while these episodes might be considered as historical random events, the simulation model is not prepared to deal with them realistically. The same trend in the labor force, the same Say's Law assumption, the same link of investment to retained earnings persist year by year. Since the model's historical accuracy is so sharply limited by these considerations we have not attempted to locate parameter settings that would, in any sense, maximize similarity to the real time series. For example, it would have been easy to assure a better match of initial conditions.

Rather, the question we think should be addressed is whether a behavioral-evolutionary model of the economic growth process, of the sort described in the preceding section, is capable of generating (and hence of explaining) macro time series data of roughly the sort actually observed. So considered, we regard the simulation as quite successful. The historically observed trends in the output-labor ratio, the capital-labor ratio, and the wage rate are all visible in the simulated data. The column headed A in the table shows the Solow-type index of technology, computed on the contrafactual assumption that the simulated time series were generated by a neutrally shifting neoclassical production function. The simulated average rate of change in this measure is about the same as in the Solow data (indicating, essentially, that we have chosen an appropriate value in this run for our localness-of-search parameter). It is interesting to note, however, that our simulated world of diverse simple-minded firms searching myopically in a continuing disequilibrium generates a somewhat smoother aggregate "technical progress" than that found by Solow in the real data for the United States. For example, our series shows only five incidences of negative technical progress, whereas Solow's series shows eleven—and the run shown is typical in this respect.

Table 9.2 presents data on each run for each of several variables, observed at period forty of the run.[4] Also displayed are the corresponding figures, where these exist, for the thirty-sixth period (1944)

---

4. The reason for focusing on values observed late in the run is to allow plenty of time for the different parameter settings to display their distinctive influences on the industry state. The reason for observing at period 40 rather than, say, at period 50 is that a few of the runs display, in the late periods, clear "boundary effects" associated with proximity of average input coefficients to the edge of the region from which the decision rules were chosen.

and the fortieth period (1948) of the Solow data. Given the experimental design, it is convenient to distinguish the runs by numbering them in the binary system. The interpretive key to this numbering is explained in the note to Table 9.2.

It is plain that the simulation model does generate "technical progress" with rising output per worker, a rising wage rate, and a rising capital-labor ratio, and a roughly constant rate of return on

Table 9.2.   Values of aggregative variables at period forty.

Run	$\dfrac{K}{L}(40)^a$	$A(40)^b$	$a_L(40)^c$	$a_k(40)^d$	$C_4(40)^e$	$\Delta w(40)^f$	$\Delta Q(40)^g$
0000	2.796	1.727	0.832	2.326	0.560	1.4	3.6
0001	3.129	2.391	0.592	1.851	0.521	2.5	5.0
0010	2.519	1.712	0.846	2.131	0.383	1.6	3.4
0011	4.242	2.716	0.477	2.025	0.387	3.2	3.6
0100	2.035	1.855	0.825	1.678	0.645	1.8	3.8
0101	2.695	2.106	0.679	1.829	0.404	2.4	4.5
0110	2.686	1.658	0.841	2.258	0.405	1.4	6.0
0111	2.703	2.123	0.672	1.817	0.388	2.1	4.6
1000	3.015	1.746	0.800	2.411	0.476	2.1	4.7
1001	4.511	2.359	0.524	2.364	0.457	2.4	5.6
1010	4.332	2.098	0.600	2.599	0.443	1.9	4.4
1011	4.258	2.450	0.514	2.190	0.325	2.8	4.3
1100	3.212	1.835	0.705	2.265	0.491	1.9	4.3
1101	3.391	2.190	0.600	2.034	0.518	2.6	5.1
1110	3.031	1.963	0.705	2.136	0.394	1.9	5.3
1111	3.315	1.913	0.682	2.260	0.327	1.9	4.1
Solow (1944)	2.63	1.856	0.675	1.776	—	—	—
Solow (1948)	2.55	1.810	0.699	1.784	—	1.7	—

a. K/L = Capital-labor ratio.
b. A = Solow technology index. (Solow figures for 1944 and 1948 are correct; the values originally published were in error.)
c. a_L = Average labor input coefficient, L/Q.
d. a_k = Average capital input coefficient, K/Q
e. C_4 = Four-firm concentration ratio. (Initial value = 0.206.)
f. Δw = Rate of change of wages, percent per period.
g. ΔQ = Rate of change of output, percent per period.
Note: Runs are numbered in binary, $X_{WT}X_RX_{IM}X_{IN}$. When $X_{IN} = 0$, the probability of discovery of a technique declines with distance with slope −6.0; when $X_{IN} = 1$, the slope is −4.5. In the $X_{IM} = 0$ setting, search activity involves imitation with probability .2 for extant firms; when $X_{IM} = 1$, that probability is .4. When $X_R = 0$, the required dividend rate $R = .02$; when $X_R = 1$, $R = .06$. With the $X_{WT} = 0$ setting, there is no bias in search, whereas when $X_{WT} = 1$, $WTL = .4$ and $WTK = .6$.

capital. The rates of change produced correspond roughly to those in the Solow data. Also, some individual runs produce values quite close to the Solow values for the variables measured—for example, runs 0101 and 0111.

Figures 9.2–9.5 display the time paths of the average input coefficients generated by the sixteen runs. To keep the figures relatively uncluttered, the values are plotted for the initial period and at periods 5, 10, and so on thereafter. In Figure 9.6 the input coefficient track for one run (1110) is compared with the track implied in the Solow data. The case shown is one in which there is close agreement at the initial point, and also forty periods later, but there is a wide divergence in between. The divergence is associated with the fact that, while the simulated track gives the impression of taking a relatively constant direction, there is a sharp turn in the track of the real data, suggestive of a change in the underlying regime. The apparent break occurs between 1929 and 1934. Perhaps it would be asking too much of the simulation model, committed as it is to full employment, to reproduce that break.

It seems interesting to ask: If a neoclassical economist believed the aggregative time saving generated by the simulation model to be real data, and tested his theory against the data, what would he conclude?

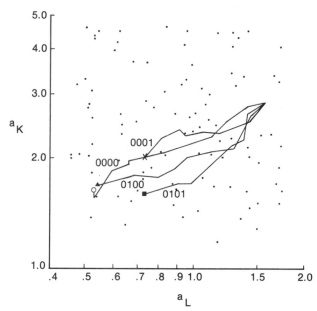

9.2   Average input coefficient paths for four runs with low emphasis on imitation and no bias in search.

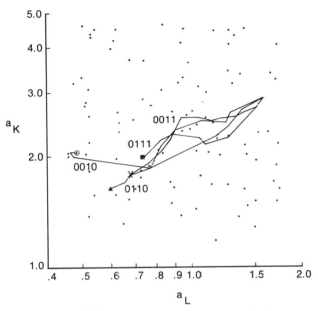

9.3   Average input coefficient paths for four runs with high emphasis on imitation and no bias in search.

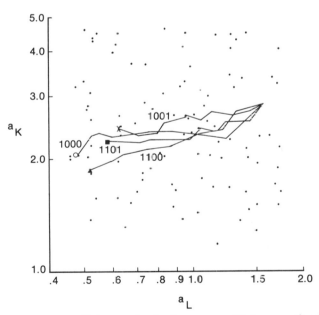

9.4   Average input coefficient paths for four runs with low emphasis on imitation and labor-saving bias in search.

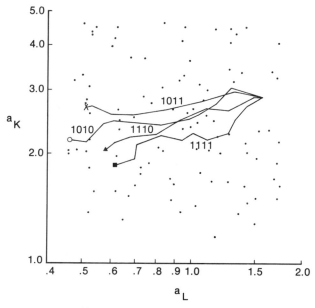

9.5   Average input coefficient paths for four runs with high emphasis on imitation and labor-saving bias in search.

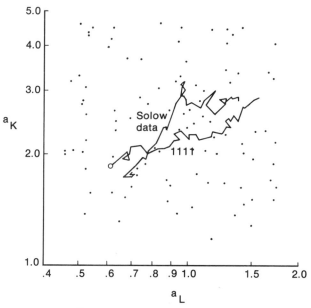

9.6   Average input coefficient paths: Solow data compared with run 1111.

Table 9.3.   Cobb-Douglas regressions, Solow method.

$$\log \left(\frac{Q(t)/A(t)}{L(t)} \right) = a + b \log \left(\frac{K(t)}{L(t)} \right)$$

Run	b	R^2	Run	b	R^2
0000	0.195	0.993	1000	0.211	0.968
0001	0.184	0.990	1001	0.268	0.991
0010	0.244	0.996	1010	0.261	0.994
0011	0.214	0.993	1011	0.256	0.986
0100	0.219	0.985	1100	0.325	0.999
0101	0.248	0.988	1101	0.241	0.987
0110	0.301	0.998	1110	0.249	0.978
0111	0.193	0.942	1111	0.313	0.997

The answer depends on the particular simulation run from which the data are taken and on the particular test. But by and large it seems that he would believe that his theory had performed well. (Of course, if he also looked at the microeconomic data and observed the inter-firm dispersion of techniques and differential growth rates, he might ponder a bit whether his theory really characterized what was going on. But the pondering would likely conclude with the consoling thought that macro theories need not square with micro observations.)

Tables 9.3 and 9.4 display the results of fitting Cobb-Douglas production functions, by each of two methods, to the aggregate time

Table 9.4.   Cobb-Douglas regressions with time trend.

$$\log Q(t) = a + b_1 \log K(t) + b_2 \log L(t) + b_3 t$$

Run	b_1	b_2	b_3	R^2	Run	b_1	b_2	b_3	R^2
0000	0.336	0.649	0.012	0.999	1000	0.505	0.550	0.008	0.998
0001	0.681	0.541	0.011	0.999	1001	0.648	0.360	0.011	0.999
0010	0.201	0.764	0.016	0.998	1010	0.723	0.336	0.009	0.999
0011	0.728	0.158	0.017	0.997	1011	0.532	0.505	0.015	0.998
0100	0.281	0.654	0.016	0.999	1100	0.637	0.444	0.008	0.999
0101	0.222	0.833	0.017	0.999	1101	0.669	0.448	0.010	0.999
0110	0.405	0.593	0.009	0.998	1110	0.479	0.545	0.013	0.999
0111	0.075	0.658	0.013	0.999	1111	0.641	0.547	0.007	0.998

series data for each experimental run. The Solow procedure was followed in generating Table 9.3. The percentage neutral shift in the hypothetical aggregate production function was calculated in each period, and the technology index $A(t)$ constructed. The index was then employed to purge the output data of technological change, and the log of adjusted output per labor unit was regressed on the log of capital per labor unit. The observations were taken from periods 5–45 of the simulation run, to give us a sample size the same as Solow's and to minimize possible initial-phase and terminal-phase effects on the outcomes. The regressions in Table 9.4 are based on an assumed exponential time trend in the technology index and involve the logs of the absolute magnitudes rather than ratios to labor input. The same sample period was employed.

The most noteworthy feature of these results is that the fits obtained in most of the cases are excellent: half of the R^2 values in Table 9.3 exceed 0.99, and more than half of those in Table 9.4 equal 0.999. The fact that there is no production function in the simulated economy is clearly no barrier to a high degree of success in using such a function to describe the aggregate series it generates. It is true that the fits obtained by Solow and others with real data are at least as good as most of ours, but we doubt that anyone would want to rest a case for the aggregate production function on what happens in the third or fourth decimal place of R^2. Rather, this particular contest between rival explanatory schemes should be regarded as essentially a tie, and other evidence consulted in an effort to decide the issue.

Thus, a model based on evolutionary theory is quite capable of generating aggregate time series with characteristics corresponding to those of economic growth in the United States. It is not reasonable to dismiss an evolutionary theory on the grounds that it fails to provide a coherent explanation of these macro phenomena. And the explanation has a certain transparency. As we discussed earlier, many of the familiar mechanisms of the neoclassical explanation have a place in the evolutionary framework.

Consider, for example, the empirically observed nexus of rising wage rates, rising capital intensity, and increasing output per worker. Our simulation model generated data of this sort. In that model, as in the typical neoclassical one, rising wage rates provide signals that move individual firms in a capital-intensive direction. As was proposed in Chapter 7, when firms check the profitability of alternative techniques that their search processes uncover, a higher wage rate will cause to fail the "more profitable" test certain techniques that would have "passed" at a lower wage rate, and will enable to pass the test others that would have failed at a lower wage rate. The former will be capital-intensive relative to the latter. Thus, a higher wage rate nudges firms to move in a capital-intensive direction compared with that in which they would have gone. Also, the effect of a higher wage rate is to make all technologies less profitable (assuming, as in our model, a constant cost of capital), but the cost increase is proportionately greatest for those that display a low capital-labor ratio; thus, a rise in wages tends to increase industry capital intensity relative to what would have been obtained. And output per worker will be increased; a more capital-intensive technology cannot be more profitable than a less capital-intensive one unless output per worker is higher.

While the explanation here has a neoclassical ring, it is not based on neoclassical premises. Although the firms in our simulation model respond to profitability signals in making technique changes and investment decisions, they are not maximizing profits. Their behavior could be rationalized equally well (or poorly) as pursuit of the quiet life (since they relax when they are doing well, and typically make only small changes of technique when they do change) or of corporate growth (since they maximize investment subject to a payout constraint). Neither does our model portray the economy as being in equilibrium. At any given time, there exists considerable diversity in techniques used and in realized rates of return. The observed constellations of inputs and outputs cannot be regarded as optimal in the Paretian sense: there are always better techniques not being used because they have not yet been found and always laggard firms using technologies less economical than current best practice.

On our reading, at least, the neoclassical interpretation of long-run productivity change is sharply different from our own. It is based on a clean distinction between "moving along" an existing production function and shifting to a new one. In the evolutionary theory, substitution of the "search and selection" metaphor for the maximization and equilibrium metaphor, plus the assumption of the basic improvability of procedures, blurs the notion of a production function. In the simulation model discussed above, there was no production function—only a set of physically possible activities. The production function did not emerge from that set because it was not assumed that a particular subset of the possible techniques would be "known" at each particular time. The exploration of the set was treated as a historical, incremental process in which nonmarket information flows among firms played a major role and in which firms really "know" only one technique at a time.

We argue—as others have before us—that the sharp "growth accounting" split made within the neoclassical paradigm is bothersome empirically and conceptually. Consider, for example, whether it is meaningful to assess the relative contribution of greater mechanization versus new technology in increasing productivity in the textile industries during the Industrial Revolution, of scale economies versus technical change in enhancing productivity in the generation of electric power, or of greater fertilizer usage versus new seed varieties in the increased yields associated with the Green Revolution. In the Textile Revolution the major inventions were ways of substituting capital for labor, induced by a situation of growing labor scarcity. It could plausibly be argued that in the electric power case, various well-known physical laws implied that the larger the scale for which a plant was designed, the lower the cost per unit of output it should have. However, to exploit these latent possibilities required a considerable amount of engineering and design work, which became profitable only when the constellation of demand made large-scale units plausible. Plant biologists had long known that certain kinds of seed varieties were able to thrive with large quantities of fertilizers and that others were not. However, until fertilizer prices fell, it was not worthwhile to invest significant resources in trying to find these varieties. In all of these cases, patterns of demand and supply were evolving to make profitable different factor proportions or scales. But the production set was not well defined in the appropriate direction from existing practice. It had to be explored and created.

We argued in Part II that at any given time the set of techniques that an individual can control skillfully, or that an organization can control routinely, likely does not extend very far beyond those that are being more or less regularly exercised. Relatedly, we proposed that an attempt to employ a technique significantly different from those likely involves a nontrivial amount of deliberation, research, trial and feedback, and innovation. But in Chapters 6 and 7, and here again, models in which only a small part of changed input-output relations could be regarded as "routine" (moving along a production fraction) displayed patterns over time that had many of the qualitative properties of movements along the production functions of orthodox theory. The model in this chapter is somewhat extreme in endowing a firm with only one technique that it can operate routinely at any time. It would not be inconsistent with evolutionary theory to assume that a firm at any time is capable of operating a small number of alternative techniques, with various decision rules employed to determine the mix. In this case a larger share of factor substitution in response to changing prices would have been accounted for by along-the-rule movements. But it is interesting that even with along-the-rule responses excluded completely, an evolutionary model is capable of generating, and hence explaining, data that orthodox theory explains only by recourse to the unrealistic assumption that firms have large, well-defined production sets that extend well beyond the experienced range of operation.

The question of the nature of "search" processes would appear to be among the most important for those trying to understand economic growth, and the evolutionary theory has the advantage of posing the question explicitly. In the simulation model, we assumed that technical progress was the result strictly of the behavior of firms in the "sector" and that discovery was relatively even over time. However, it is apparent that the invention possibilities and search costs for firms in particular sectors change as a result of forces exogenous to the sector. Academic and governmental research certainly changed the search prospects for firms in the electronics and drug industries, as well as for aircraft and seed producers. In the simulation, the "topography" of new technologies was relatively even over time.[5] However, various studies have shown that often new opportunities open up in clusters. A basic new kind of technology becomes possible as a result of research outside the sector. After a firm finds, develops, and adopts a version of the new technology, a subsequent round of marginal improvements becomes possible. This appears to be the pattern, for example, in the petroleum-refining equipment and aircraft industries. However, this pattern does not show up in the manufacture of cotton textiles (after the Industrial Revolution) or in the automobile industry, where technical advance seems to have been less discrete. The search and problem-solving orientation of an evolutionary theory naturally leads the analyst to be aware of these differences and to try somehow to explain or at least characterize them.

The perspective on the role of the "competitive environment" is also radically different in the evolutionary theory, and leads one to focus on a set of questions concerning the intertwining of competition, profit, and investment within a dynamic context. Is the investment of a particular firm strictly bounded by its own current profits? Can firms borrow for expansion? Are there limits on firm size, or costs associated with the speed of expansion? Can new firms enter? How responsive are "consumers" to a better or cheaper product? How long can a firm preserve a technically based monopoly? What kind of institutional barriers or encouragements are there to imitation? The answers to these questions are fundamental to under-

---

5. Here and subsequently, we use the term "topography" in a metaphorical sense to suggest the role of the cognitive conditions under which the search for new methods takes place. The topography of innovation determines what possibilities can be seen from what vantage points, how hard it is to get from one spot in the space of possibilities to another, and so forth.

standing the workings of the market environment. The specifics of their treatment, like that of the nature and topography of "search," is an empirical issue within our theory.

These kinds of questions can be illuminated by some of the findings of the vast literature on the micro aspects of technological change. Chapter 11 will be concerned specifically with such an exploration. However, some interesting micro-macro links appear in our simulation model.

3. THE EXPERIMENTS

In our discussion above of the logic of the model, we introduced four variables that tie macroeconomic performance to microeconomic behavior and that were varied experimentally in the simulation runs. These variables were the ease of innovation, the emphasis on imitation, the cost of capital, and the labor-saving bias of search. What effect do different settings of these variables have on the macroeconomic time paths in the model?

We adopted a linear regression approach to this question. We considered three different macroeconomic variables: the Solow technology index in year forty, the capital-labor ratio in year forty, and the four-firm concentration index. Our four experimental variables we designated X_{IN}, X_{IM}, X_R, and X_{WT}. We assigned the value one to these variables when (respectively) major innovation was relatively easy, search emphasis was on imitation, the required dividend rate was high, and the search was somewhat biased in a labor-saving direction.[6]

The effects on the period-forty value of the Solow technology index are characterized by the following regression equation:

$$A(40) = 2.335 + 0.456\ X_{IN} + 0.0529\ X_{IM} - 0.194\ X_R + 0.034\ X_{WT}$$
$$(0.006) \qquad (0.59) \qquad\quad (0.07) \qquad\quad (0.73)$$
$$R^2 = 0.705.$$

Figures in parentheses are significance levels. The conjecture that easier major innovation at a microeconomic level should lead to a faster rate of growth of total factor productivity at a macroeconomic level is strongly confirmed. This lends additional confidence that the model provides plausible and understandable connections between the microeconomic phenomena and macroeconomic phenomena of

---

6. For the explanation of the parameter settings corresponding to the two levels of our experimental factors, see the footnote to Table 9.2.

economic growth. Note that this is not a trivial result, since the rate of growth of total factor productivity and the level of the Solow technology index late in an economy's evolution here are simply macro statistics, and do not correspond directly to features of the model.

Some interesting results also come out of regression analysis of the determinants of the capital-labor ratio in year forty.

$$\frac{K}{L}(40) = 3.353 + 0.577\ X_{IN} + 0.288\ X_{IM} - 0.717\ X_R + 0.7825\ X_{WT}$$

$$(0.017) \qquad (0.19) \qquad (0.005) \qquad (0.003)$$

$$R^2 = 0.766.$$

The hypothesized effects of factors three and four are strongly confirmed. A higher price of capital, considered as a return that must be paid out and that is not available for reinvestment, does lead to a substantially less capital-intensive mode of production after a period of time. Considered as a growth rate effect, the rise in R from 0.02 to 0.06 produces a decrease of 0.3 percentage points per period in the rate of change of the capital-labor ratio. The effect of the labor-saving search bias introduced by factor four is of comparable magnitude but, of course, in the opposite direction.

The magnitude and significance level of the coefficient of X_{IN} comes as something of a surprise. Why should the capital-labor ratio be higher in a system in which search is less local? On reflection, one possible answer to this question seems to be the following. The general direction of the path traced in input coefficient space does not depend on the localness of search. However, the rate of movement along the path is slower if search is more local. Therefore, given that the path is tending toward higher capital-labor ratios (as a consequence of the level chosen for R and the neutrality or labor-saving bias of search), the capital-labor ratio that results after a given number of periods is lower when search is more local.

Another possible answer is more Schumpeterian. A high rate of technical progress may produce a high level of (disequilibrium) profits, which in turn are invested. The resulting increase in the demand for labor results in a higher wage and deflects the results of profitability comparisons in the capital-intensive direction. These possible answers are not, of course, mutually exclusive.

The regression result regarding concentration is:

$$C_4(40) = 0.495 - 0.058\ X_{IN} - 0.127\ X_{IM} + 0.0028\ X_R - 0.033\ X_{WT}$$

$$(0.04) \qquad (0.0004) \qquad (0.91) \qquad (0.22)$$

$$R^2 = 0.741.$$

Here, C_4 is the four-firm concentration ratio. The imitation effect is clearly the most pronounced. We have suggested an explanation for this effect in terms of the "closer race." There are actually two distinct mechanisms in the simulation model by which a closer technical race tends to keep concentration down, and both are quite plausible as hypotheses about economic reality. First, as among firms in business, similarity in technique implies similarity in cost conditions, hence in profit rates, and hence in growth rates. Thus, a closer race implies a smaller dispersion of firm growth rates and lower concentration. But, second, potential entrants also stay closer to the technical leaders when imitation is easy and perceived opportunities for profitable entry thus occur more frequently. Since entry tends to occur in a particular (and relatively low) scale range, the amount of capacity added by entry is higher when entry is higher. Considerations of overall industry "equilibrium" imply that the infusion of capacity through entry is partially offset by lower investment by the firms previously in business. Since the latter are typically larger than the entrants, concentration is reduced.

The above analysis of the influences on the concentration of firms is illustrative of a fundamental difference between the neoclassical and evolutionary approaches to growth theory. Neoclassical growth theory is aimed at macro phenomena, and its micro details are instrumental to its macro purposes. Evolutionary theory treats the micro processes as fundamental and treats the macro aggregates as aggregates. Hence, it encompasses a wider range of phenomena; its treatment of the micro details is intended to be subject to test. Thus, for example, we can treat our simulation model not only as an abstract account of the phenomena of aggregate economic growth, but also as an abstract account of the size distribution of firms. This we will do in a later chapter.

4. SUMMARY AND CONCLUSIONS

We return now to our opening theme. Neoclassical theory has provided a fruitful way of looking at certain macroeconomic patterns of growth. However, it has been strikingly unsuccessful in coming to grips with the phenomena of technological change, and relatedly that theory stands as an obstacle in thinking about microeconomic phenomena and macroeconomic phenomena within the same intellectual frame. In this chapter we have shown that a model based on evolutionary theory can come to grips with the macro phenomena, although at the cost of somewhat greater complexity than that usually involved in neoclassical models. With that increased complexity has come some loss of transparency, although we have argued that the model involves readily discernable relationships between input growth and output growth, and between changes in factor prices and changes in factor proportions. And the gain has been in terms of a characterization of the technological change phenomenon that is much closer to the accounts of those who have studied it carefully, and in terms of the ability to encompass microeconomic phenomena and macro phenomena within the same intellectual framework. We have produced an account of economic growth in technical change that is simultaneously consistent (1) in quantitative terms, with the broad features of a certain body of aggregated data; (2) qualitatively, with such phenomena as the existence of cross-sectional dispersions in capital labor ratios and efficiency, and patterns of innovation and diffusion of techniques; and (3) metaphorically, with the empirical literature on firm decision making. These fragments of economic reality (at least) need not be regarded as posing isolated problems to be addressed through special-purpose assumptions. The model's consistency with disparate types of data indicates that it is not merely consistent with the data of any one type, but rather bears a fairly intimate relationship to "what is really going on out there."

10

Economic Growth as a Pure Selection Process

THE MODEL DEVELOPED in the preceding chapter was quite complex, containing a number of interacting analytic components. Several of the components themselves incorporated rather complicated structural equations. One consequence was the need to employ simulation methods to analyze the model.

In this chapter we simplify the analysis in two (related) ways. First, we eliminate the new-technique generation or finding process and focus the analysis on selection of techniques that are initially "in being"—that is, being used at a positive (if perhaps very small) level. Second, we eliminate the stochastic element of the analysis. These simplifications make it convenient to work with a continuous-time rather than a discrete-time model.

We explore two versions. In the first, instead of one hundred possible techniques, as in the preceding model, there are only two. The focus is on changes over time in the relative employment of two known techniques, one "old" and one "new." Individual firms have no identity in this model; aggregation is over all firms using a particular technique.

In the second model we allow a multitude of techniques initially in being, rather than just two. The selection process thus is more complicated. However, many of the conclusions of the simpler model will prove to hold within this more complex version.

1. DEVELOPMENT AND BACKWARDNESS IN A TWO-TECHNOLOGY EVOLUTIONARY MODEL

The two-technology model would seem appropriate to the study of the processes by which a particular new technology replaces an older one within an industry, and of the associated effects of this on such industry variables as productivity. A large number of empirical studies have been concerned with the first part of this question: Griliches (1957) analyzed the diffusion of hybrid corn, Mansfield (1973) examined the diffusion of a wide variety of new manufacturing processes, and so forth. The effects of diffusion on such variables as productivity and factor shares have been less studied, and there is virtually no work that has attempted to tie together analysis of diffusion patterns and productivity changes. The model that will be developed here is well suited for this purpose.

Our model has been designed for studying certain important aspects of the processes involved in economic development of low-income countries. The problem can be posed as follows. A striking feature of the international economic landscape is the great disparity among countries in levels of per capita income, which largely reflect differences in output per worker. One of the key tasks of economic development theory is to explain these differences and in particular to facilitate understanding of why productivity in the low-income countries is so far below the level in high-income countries. Answering this question would appear to be a necessary precursor to answering a question of more direct policy concern: How can the rate of growth of income in the currently less developed countries be effectively augmented? The central questions of economic development theory are similar to those of the theory of economic growth in high-income countries, which were discussed in the preceding two chapters. What differentiates the economic development problem from the general economic growth problem is that the more productive technologies that the less developed country will be adopting in the course of its development are (usually) known and have been employed before in other (high-income) countries.

As was the case with respect to post–World War II theorizing about processes of economic growth in advanced countries, economists interested after the war in economic development problems (after a brief flirtation with models that assumed fixed coefficients in production) reached into the tool kit of neoclassical microeconomic theory for their analytic ideas. The attempt was to explain differences in output per worker between low- and high-income countries as representing different points along a common production function. High-income countries simply had more capital per worker than low-income countries. To the extent that this is the appropriate explanation for productivity and income differences, the prescription for development follows immediately: productivity will grow as the capital-labor ratio is increased.

A considerable volume of research was guided by these theoretical ideas. Since adequate measures of the capital stock in less developed countries seldom were available, various proxy measures for capital and other factors believed associated with labor productivity had to be used in the empirical research. That research did verify some qualitative aspects of the theory. However, relatively early in the game a problem became apparent, analogous to that which signaled the importance of technical change in the work guided by neoclassical growth theory. If the normal assumptions about the shapes of production functions are made, it is highly dubious if not theoretically impossible that differences in the quantities of capital and other complementary factors of production per worker can explain the whole, or even the bulk, of differences across countries in productivity levels. The analytic problem was depicted in Figures 8.1 and 8.2. The high-income countries possess more capital and other inputs per worker than do low-income countries, but they also seem to be operating on a "higher" production function.

This discovery not only undermined the neoclassical explanation of differences across countries, but it also signaled that the neoclassical characterization of the development process was at best incomplete. A good part of that process seems to involve less developed countries learning about and adopting the superior (as well as more capital-intensive) technologies of the more developed ones.

An evolutionary approach to development theory seems called for. From an evolutionary perspective economic growth in any economy, developed or less developed, would be viewed as a disequilibrium process involving a mix of firms employing different vintages of technologies. Over time, these mixes change. In the more developed countries, new technologies enter the mix as invention occurs. In the less developed countries, new technologies enter the mix as the technologies of high-income countries are borrowed. At any time, differences across countries can be explained by differences in the mixes of the technologies used, as well as by factor proportions.

Using this interpretation, there are several different reasons for the fact that there is no worldwide production function of a simple neoclassical sort. One is that new technology needs to be embodied in new, specially designed equipment, and the capital stock of the less developed countries is older than the capital stock of advanced countries; the relative mix of technologies in a country reflects the relative importance of new capital compared with old. A second reason is that it takes time for labor in a less developed country to acquire the skills to operate modern technology; thus, the use of modern technology is constrained by skill shortages as well as by limitations on physical investment. Both of these propositions are consistent with a worldwide production function involving a large number of inputs of closely specified characteristics.

Although the above almost certainly are part of the reason why it has proved impossible to explain productivity differences among countries in terms of different points along a simple production function, there is much more to it. It is time-consuming and costly for a firm to learn about, and learn to use, technology significantly different from that with which it is familiar. Further, firms will differ in their awareness, competence, and judgments in choosing to adopt or not adopt new techniques.

Let us play out the metaphor sketched above as a model of unequal economic development across economies.[1] The specific assumptions are as follows. The phenomena of interest are the paths of outputs, inputs, and factor prices in an economy as a whole or an important sector (say, manufacturing), and differences in these across countries. There is an old technology, characterized, as technologies were in the preceding chapter, by constant returns to scale and fixed coefficients. There is a new technology as well. In comparison with the old technology, it is characterized by higher output per worker but the same output per unit of capital. Note that at any set of factor prices, unit costs are lower and the rate of profit on capital is higher if the new technology is employed rather than the old one. As in the preceding chapter, expansion or contraction of capital is assumed to be proportional to revenues minus wages minus required dividends, all per unit of capital. In this model we repress the identity of firms using particular technologies; it is the technologies (or rather the capital embodying them) that are viewed as expanding or contracting.

Imagine a country in which the bulk of economic activity employs the old technology, but in which there is some use of the new technology. Within this model, the great development traverse can be characterized as follows. At any time, labor input per unit of output in the economy or sector will be the weighted average of labor input per unit of output in the two technologies, the weights being the proportion of output produced by each of the technologies. Given the assumption that the capital-output ratios of the two technologies are the same, these weights are the same as the fractions of capital embodying the technologies. Let unit labor input using the new

---

1. The model is a revised version of that first presented in Nelson (1968).

technology be $l_2 = \alpha l_1$ (with $\alpha < 1$), and K_1/K and K_2/K denote the fraction of capital embodying the old and the new technologies. Then:

(1) $\quad \dfrac{L}{Q} = l_1\left(\dfrac{K_1}{K}\right) + \alpha l_1\left(\dfrac{K_2}{K}\right).$

The assumptions about investment, then, can be formalized as follows. Let the price of the product be P, and the (common) capital-output ratio be one. Assuming that there is no depreciation and that investment is proportional to excess profits:

(2) $\quad \dfrac{\dot{K_i}}{K_i} = \lambda(P - r - wl_i).$

where r is the cost of capital services and w is the wage rate.

In general, w will not be assumed constant over the course of the traverse but will itself evolve. We assume that at the start of the traverse (where virtually all capital is in the "old" technology), aggregate capital, labor supply, and the resulting wage w are at levels such that the old technology just breaks even. Then the new technology must be making a profit and expanding.

It is apparent that for the system to reach a new equilibrium, either the price of the product must fall or w must rise (or some combination of these must occur). In an industry or sectoral model it would be natural to complete the specification above by postulating a strictly downward sloping demand curve for the product of the industry, and by assuming that the wage rate is constant or is subject to an autonomous drift. When the focus is on pervasive developmental processes and the sector in question is viewed as comprising a large share or even all of economic activity, it is more natural to complete the model along the lines employed in the preceding chapter. The product itself is taken as the *numéraire*; hence, its price is constant. There is an upward-sloping labor supply curve:

(3) $\quad w = w(L).$

Thus, it is wage rate increases that bring the system back into equilibrium. This is the analytic route taken here. For expositional simplicity, we will assume a constant population and an upward-sloping supply curve that does not shift over time. The analysis easily can be augmented to admit a growing labor force, although then the equilibrium concept is somewhat different.

In any case it is easy to see that, in the new equilibrium, output per worker has risen from the level associated with the old technology to that associated with the new. The capital-output ratio has remained constant over the traverse; thus, the capital-labor ratio has been rising and ultimately achieves the level associated with the new technology. If the price of capital services remains constant, capital's share (as well as that of labor) is the same in the new equilibrium as in the old. All this is obvious.

What is interesting about this model is what it tells us about the path to the new equilibrium and the characteristics of the industry (or the economy) along the path. The relative importance of the old and the new technologies will be changing as follows:

$$(4) \quad \frac{d}{dt} \log\left(\frac{K_2}{K_1}\right) = \frac{\dot{K_2}}{K_2} - \frac{\dot{K_1}}{K_1}$$
$$= \lambda w(l_1 - l_2)$$
$$= \lambda w(1 - \alpha)l_1.$$

The rate of growth of K_2/K_1 (and of Q_2/Q_1) will be greater, the greater is λ, and the greater the productivity of labor using the new technology relative to the old. If there were no change in w over the traverse, K_2/K and Q_2/Q would trace out a logistic curve. With a rising w, the rate of takeover of the new technology would exceed that predicted by a logistic curve. The path of output per worker would be similar at the start of development: it would rise slowly, then accelerate, then slow again as its new higher equilibrium is approached.

What will be happening to factor prices and shares? Given the assumptions of the model, in the new equilibrium the share of capital must be the same as it was in the old equilibrium. The capital-output ratio is the same in the new technology as in the old one; hence, if the return to capital is to equal the price of capital services (a necessary condition for equilibrium), equilibrium defines a unique share for capital. In the new equilibrium, the wage rate has grown in proportion to the growth in productivity over the traverse, and labor's share is the same as it was initially. However, in the course of the disequilibrium traverse, capital's share will be above its equilibrium rate if the returns to capital are defined to include quasi-rents. During the diffusion process, positive quasi-rents will be made by the sector employing the new technology and pulling its expansion, and negative quasi-rents by the subsector employing the old technology and forcing its contraction. But if there is net growth of capital during development (and there will be, relative to labor), the former will outweigh the latter.

$$(5) \quad S_k = \left[P - wl_1\left(\frac{K_1}{K}\right) - wl_2\left(\frac{K_2}{K}\right) \right]\Big/ P$$

$$= \left[r\left(\frac{K_1}{K}\right) + r\left(\frac{K_2}{K}\right) + (P - wl_1 - r)\left(\frac{K_1}{K}\right) \right.$$

$$\left. + (P - wl_2 - r)\left(\frac{K_2}{K}\right) \right]\Big/ P$$

$$= \left(\frac{r}{P}\right) + \left(\frac{\dot{K}}{K}\right)\Big/ \lambda P, \text{ from equation (2)}.$$

Notice that the quasi-rents (the second term of the equation above) will be largest when capital and output growth are most rapid.

Let us now shift attention away from development within a particular country and focus, instead, on a cross-section of countries. Some started development (in the sense of adopting the "new technology") earlier than others, or developed more rapidly. In these the "old" technology has been almost entirely eliminated. In others development started late or has proceeded slowly; in these a sizable fraction of economic activity still involves the old technology. In the "less developed countries" average productivity is lower, and so is the average wage rate. The capital-labor ratio is lower, but almost any neoclassical analysis also would show differences in levels of "total factor productivity." In the less developed countries, one would find considerable dispersion among firms in productivity levels, wage rates paid, and profitability. Furthermore, capital's share is likely to be larger in the less developed countries than in the more developed ones, mainly reflecting the presence of large quasi-rents in that part of the economy employing the modern technology. In fact, this is not a bad characterization of a number of the more salient differences between the less developed countries of today and the advanced ones.

2. Many Techniques and Many Variable Inputs

In the preceding analysis, there were only two techniques and one variable input (labor). We now generalize the analysis to consider selection on many techniques, each involving many variable inputs. We preserve the other assumptions above, including that all techniques have the same capital-output ratio, and that relative expansion or contraction of use of a technique is proportional to unit profit using that technique. There are two kinds of complications to the earlier analysis that need to be considered. First, selection no longer can be characterized as the growth of one technique relative to a single other, but rather involves a more complex expression of changing weights. Second, with more than one variable factor of production, the fact that one technique uses less of one input per unit of output than does another technique no longer is decisive, but rather the relative advantage of different techniques depends on all the input coefficients (a_{ij}) and on factor prices.

Profit (over and above the normal return to capital) using technology j now is

$$(6) \quad \pi_j = P - r - \sum_{i=1}^{n} w_i a_{ij}.$$

If the amount of capital employing technique j is K_j, the industry's overall profit rate is

$$(7) \quad \bar{\pi} = \sum_{j=1}^{M} \left(\frac{K_j}{K}\right) \pi_j = \sum_j S_j \pi_j,$$

where $S_j = K_j/K$. If the rate of net investment in a technology is equal to excess returns, then

$$(8) \quad \dot{S}_j = S_j\left(\frac{\dot{K}_j}{K_j} - \frac{\dot{K}}{K}\right)$$

$$= S_j (\pi_j - \bar{\pi})$$

$$= S_j\left(\sum_i w_i \bar{a}_i - \sum_i w_i a_{ij}\right),$$

where $\bar{a}_i$ is the industry average coefficient for input i.

$$(9) \quad \frac{d}{dt} \log S_j = \sum_i w_i \bar{a}_i - \sum_i w_i a_{ij}.$$

Integrating from zero to T gives

$$(10) \quad \log S_j(T) - \log S_j(0) = \int_0^T \sum_i w_i \bar{a}_i dt - \left(\sum_i w_i a_{ij}\right) T.$$

Define $\alpha(T) = \int_0^T \Sigma w_i \bar{a}_i dt$, an expression that depends on all the w's, the a's, and initial conditions.

$$(11) \quad S_j(T) = S_j(0) \exp\left(\alpha(T) - \left(\sum_i w_i a_{ij}\right) T\right).$$

Assume that, given factor prices, technique j is the unique most profitable technique. Then for $T > 0$, $\alpha(T) > (\Sigma w_i a_{ij})T$ unless $S_j(T) = 1$. But then $S_j(T)$ goes to one as T goes to infinity. If there are other techniques that tie technique j regarding profitability, the sum of the weights on the set of most profitable techniques approaches one as time progresses.

Given the selection process as characterized above, it is possible to analyze what happens over time to the quantity of any input per unit of output for the industry as a whole.

$$(12) \quad \bar{a}_k(T) = \sum_j S_j(T)a_{kj}$$

$$= \sum_j \left[S_j(0) \exp\left(\alpha(T) - \left(\sum_i w_i a_{ij} \right) T \right) \right] a_{kj}.$$

If there is a single dominant technique, the industry average input coefficient approaches its coefficient; if there is a set of dominant techniques, the industry average approaches some average of these.

Given the assumptions of constant returns to scale and constant factor prices, there is a dominant technique or set of techniques in this model whose identity (or identities) does not change over the selection traverse. None of the problems pointed out in Chapter 6 plague the selection mechanism.

However, in the model of this section, in contrast with the simpler version set forth earlier in the chapter, the identity of the least-cost technique or techniques is sensitive to factor prices. What is the effect upon the selection path, and on its ending point, if the price of one factor (say, labor) jumps? Alternatively, what about changes over time in the average industry labor input coefficient under two different regimes where, after common initial conditions, the wage rate is higher in one than in the other? From virtually all the analyses presented thus far in this book, one is led to conjecture that the standard conclusion would hold in the selection model. With some slight complications, it does.

$$(13) \quad \frac{\partial}{\partial w_k} \bar{a}_k(T) = \sum_j S_j(0) a_{kj} \frac{\partial}{\partial w_k} \left[\exp\left(\alpha(T) - \left(\sum_i w_i a_{ij} \right) T \right) \right]$$

$$= \sum_j S_j(0) a_{kj} \exp\left(\alpha(T) - \left(\sum_i w_i a_{ij} \right) T \right) \left(\frac{\partial \alpha(T)}{\partial w_k} \right.$$

$$\left. - a_{kj} T \right).$$

To evaluate this expression we note that

(14) $\sum_j S_j(T) = \sum_j S_j(0) \exp\left(\alpha(T) - \left(\sum_i w_i a_{ij}\right) T\right) \equiv 1.$

Differentiating the identity with respect to w_k yields

(15) $\sum_j S_j(0) \exp\left(\alpha(T) - \left(\sum_i w_i a_{ij}\right) T\right)\left(\frac{\partial\alpha(T)}{\partial w_k} - a_{kj} T\right) \equiv 0.$

Thus,

(16) $\dfrac{\partial\alpha(T)}{\partial w_k} = \sum_j S_j(T)\, a_{kj}\, T = \bar{a}_k(T)\, T.$

Substituting in equation (13):

(17) $\dfrac{\partial}{\partial w_k} \bar{a}_k(T) = \sum_j S_j(0)\, a_{kj} \exp\left(\alpha(T) - \left(\sum_i w_i a_{ij}\right) T\right) (\bar{a}_k T - a_{kj} T)$

$= -\sum_j S_j(T)\, a_{kj}\, (a_{kj} - \bar{a}_k)\, T$

$= -T \sum_j S_j(T)(a_{kj} - \bar{a}_k)^2,$

since $\Sigma_j S_j(T) a_k(a_{kj} - \bar{a}_k) = 0$. Thus,

(18) $\dfrac{\partial}{\partial w_k} a_k(T) = -T\, \mathrm{Var}(a_{kj}),$

where $\mathrm{Var}(a_{kj})$ is the share-weighted cross-sectional variance of a_{kj} at time T. The value of $a_k(T)$ varies inversely with w_k if there is positive variance.[2]

---

2. This result reminded us of R. A. Fisher's "fundamental theorem of natural selection": "The rate of increase in fitness of any organism at any time is equal to its genetic variance in fitness at that time" (Fisher, 1929, p. 37). A more direct analogue for Fisher's theorem in the present model is the proposition that the rate of reduction in industry average unit cost is equal to the share-weighted cross-sectional variance of unit cost. This proposition is indeed a theorem under the assumptions of the present model, a fact we were led to verify by the parallel with Fisher's result. We are not aware of any counterpart in the biological literature for our result on the deflection of the selection process by a parameter change.

The standard conclusion applies, of course, only when there is a positive variance. If, at the moment of the increase in the price of labor, all but one technology already have been eliminated, then an increase in the price of labor can have no effect. Of course, in this model no technique initially in the set is ever completely eliminated; however, if initially only one technique employs nonnegligible capital, it will take a long time for any change in factor prices to have a noticeable effect.

If there initially are several technologies with positive capital with one of these ultimately dominant, and if the change in factor prices does not change the dominant technology, then the variance approaches zero as T approaches infinity. An increase in the price of labor then speeds up or slows down the rate at which the dominant technology takes over, depending on whether that technology has, respectively, a lower than average or higher than average labor input coefficient. The time path of the industry labor input coefficient is influenced, but not the limiting value of the coefficient, as T approaches infinity.

If a change in factor prices changes the dominant technology or, more generally, modifies the dominant set, there is a discontinuity at that point in the function relating the asymptotic input coefficients as T approaches infinity to the factor prices. Thus, assume that initially techniques with different input coefficients are all cost-minimizing. Then $\mathrm{Var}(a_{kj})$ does not tend to zero and, at that w_k,

$$\lim_{T \to \infty} \frac{\partial}{\partial w_k} \bar{a}_k(T) = -\infty.$$

We can complicate the model slightly to admit the possibility that techniques may be operable with different mixes of variable factor inputs. Assume that each technique is associated with a neoclassical isoquant, and that for any set of factor prices the firms using a technique cost-minimize. Let $\phi_j(w)$ be the minimized unit variable cost of technique j. Then

(6a) $\pi_j = P - r - \phi_j(w)$.

All the analysis goes through as before, with $\phi_j(w)$ replacing $\Sigma w_i a_{ij}$, and $\bar{\phi}(w) = \Sigma S_j \phi_j(w)$ replacing $\Sigma w_i \bar{a}_i$. In analyzing $(\partial / \partial w_k) \phi_j(w)$, duality theory assures that this expression equals a_{kj}, as before.

Of course, an additional term is involved in analysis of the effect of changing prices on industry input coefficients.

$$(19) \quad \frac{\partial}{\partial w_k} \bar{a}_k(T) = -T \operatorname{Var}(a_{kj}) + \sum S_j(T) \frac{\partial a_{kj}}{\partial w_k}.$$

Thus, there are along-the-rule effects as well as selection effects.

Compared with the modeling of Chapter 9, the analysis in this chapter has been highly simplified and stylized. The gain was ability to explore analytically certain properties of the model that, in the most complex version, could only be studied by simulations. Thus, in the two-technologies model, it was possible to derive analytically an expression for the time path of productivity and the factors on which it depended. In the model incorporating many technologies and many variable inputs, it was possible to analyze the effect of a change in factor prices on the time path of average industry input coefficients.

Which is the more appropriate level of abstraction—that of the simulation model or that of the models in this chapter? We do not think this is a useful question. Both are appropriate, each for the different kinds of understanding they lend. Both are appropriate because the understanding gained in one often helps to illuminate questions about the other.

11

Further Analysis of Search and Selection

THE MODELS PRESENTED in Chapters 9 and 10 were highly abstract and simplified. These characteristics suited their purpose—to address phenomena at a macro level in a way metaphorically consistent with more microscopic phenomena, and to illuminate some of the micro-macro links. With the model of Chapter 9, for example, one could examine the connection between the probability distribution of technical advances at a micro level and the rate of productivity growth at a macro level. One could explore how the ease or difficulty of imitation influenced the extent to which an originally unconcentrated industry tended either to stay that way or to become concentrated.[1]

While the simple models served their purpose, they are too simple and stylized to address much of the micro data or to facilitate examination of some of the more subtle connections. Our objective in this chapter is to enrich and variegate the characterization of search and selection—the two major modeling components—so that these concepts can illuminate and structure what is known about the micro phenomena relating to technological advance.[2]

Studies aimed at exploring technological advance at a microeconomic level comprise a vast and heterogeneous lot. Economists, other

---

1. It obviously is of interest to consider the causal linkage running in the opposite direction, from industry structure to innovation. This we will do in the following chapters.

2. This chapter draws heavily from Nelson and Winter (1977b) and Nelson (1979).

social scientists, historians, psychologists, and natural scientists all have contributed. Reflecting the diversity of the topics explored and the backgrounds of the researchers, the studies do not link together very well. Knowledge of technological advance at a micro level is in the form of semi-isolated clusters of facts organized by special-purpose theories, rather than in the form of a consistent intellectual structure. The challenge is to develop such a structure, capable of providing some coherence for these congeries of research tradition, so that the relationships among them can be seen and so that each can help support the others more effectively.

An important part of the challenge is to structure the theoretical framework so that it is capable of encompassing and characterizing considerable diversity. The neoclassical perspective on economic growth and technical advance tends to divert attention from important aspects of diversity. Of course, it is recognized that growth rates in the same country may vary over time and that countries at any given time may vary in their growth rates. And there is limited recognition of the fact that there are significant differences across industries in their rates of achieved technical progress — a theme to which we shall return.

But the neoclassical formulation sets one's mind to see diversity in only a limited number of dimensions. The micro studies concerned with technical progress reveal great intersectoral differences in who does R&D, the criteria employed, and the key processes involved in advancing a technology. They reveal significant differences in the mechanisms involved in screening and selecting new technologies. Technologies and industries have evolved in dramatically different ways. These differences in technical change at a micro level are presumably connected with the interindustry differences in rates of technical progress and productivity growth. Ultimately, these connections should be explored in formal models.

But the purpose of this chapter is more modest. We aim to develop a richer characterization of search and selection as a vehicle for exploring some of the micro literature on technical progress — an endeavor worth undertaking in its own right.

1. SEARCH STRATEGIES AND TOPOGRAPHIES

Earlier we argued that the key features distinguishing search are irreversibility (what is found is found), its contingent character and dependency on what is "out there" to be found, and its fundamental uncertainty. The statement is open regarding both the topography over which search proceeds and the decision rules guiding the level and direction of search. In Chapter 9 we employed a special model of search that assumed a quite regular and constant topography of technological alternatives. The decision rules guiding search were stylized and simplified. Firms searched only when they were not earning target returns. They chose no particular direction of search, although the nature of their searching made it likely that if they found anything it would be in the neighborhood of their current technologies. Market conditions affected search only by influencing whether a firm was searching or not and by determining whether what was found was profitable or not. There was no reference to the "state of knowledge" or other factors that might influence whether and how firms search. In order to link with the rich literature on R&D and invention, it is essential to consider more complex strategies and topographies.

Elements of an Enriched Search Model

Our proposal for a more general model of search has several major elements. The first is a set of not yet discovered or invented technologies. Any technology can be described under two different headings. One involves economic parameters, such as input coefficients or certain product attributes. If these are known, then for any given set of product demand and factor supply conditions, one can directly calculate the economic merit of the technology—unit production costs (at various levels of output) or the price at which the product can profitably be sold. A technology also can be described in certain "technological" dimensions, such as size, chemical composition, or thermodynamic cycle employed. While these are not of economic interest in themselves, knowledge of them may be very important in R&D decision making.

The economic attributes of members of the set are not, in general, known to the R&D decision maker. What he does know includes some of the technological attributes of the technologies (these may provide the "name" or the description of the technological alternative in question), and also some general stochastic relationships between technological attributes and economic attributes. Thus, it is known that a plane with a higher-pressure and higher-temperature engine will fly faster and that this offers certain advantages to a potential purchaser of the plane, but the engine will cost more to produce. It is known, too, that certain classes of chemicals are much more likely to include effective pain-killers than other classes of chemicals. However, these relations are not known sufficiently well so that economic attributes can be perfectly predicted from technological ones.

There is a set of activities that may be used for finding out more about the technological and economic attributes of a technology. This "finding out" can be considered as "doing research," "testing," or "making a study." There is a related but different set of activities that is involved in working out the details and developing a technology so that it can be employed in practice. The decision maker can predict, to some degree but not perfectly, the outcomes of conducting these various activities at various levels of input utilization.

The R&D decision maker is viewed as having a set of decision rules that guide the employment of the above activities; these rules determine the direction of "search," in the general sense in which we are using the term, and may be termed a "search strategy." A strategy may be keyed to such variables as the size of the firm, its profitability, what competitors are doing, assessment of the payoff of R&D in general and of particular classes of projects in particular, evaluation of the ease or difficulty of achieving certain kinds of technological advances, and the particular complex of skills and experience that the firm possesses.

The outcome of the actions taken by any firm can be described stochastically in terms of two variables. One of these corresponds to invention; probabilistically there will be certain previously undiscovered or uninvented technologies that become known and certain previously undeveloped technologies that have been developed sufficiently to permit their implementation. But there will be, as well, a change in the knowledge possessed by the firm that in general will involve information much more broadly useful than merely the knowledge about the particular new technology. Something will be learned about a class or "neighborhood" of technologies (not merely the particular one developed) that may involve the technological or economic attributes associated with that class. In principle, the distributions of these stochastic outcomes can be deduced if one knows the other three components of the model: the topography, the search activities, and the decision rules. In practice, unless the model is kept quite simple, deductions may be difficult or impossible.

The search model of Chapter 9 can be regarded as a very simple truncated special case of the above broader model, involving regular topography, very simple search procedures, naïve decision rules, and no explicit advance of knowledge except for the new technologies found. The "neighborhood" search characterization was a simple formalization of the idea that knowledge at a given technology is partially transferable to related ones. Many of the contemporary neoclassical models of invention also can be reconciled with this framework. We diverge from the neoclassical formulation in rejecting the supposition that the decision rules employed by the firm can be literally optimal, and in placing emphasis on the uncertain, stochastic nature of the processes involved. As usual, the problem with the neoclassical metaphor here is not that it connotes purpose and intelligence, but that it also connotes sharp and objective definition of the range of alternatives confronted and knowledge about their properties. Hence, it misleadingly suggests an inevitability and correctness in the decisions made, represses the fact that interpersonal and interorganizational differences in judgment and perception matter a lot, and ignores the fact that it is not at all clear *ex ante* what is the right thing to do.

In the following subsections we shall employ this broad framework to consider certain common decision rules, strategies, and paths taken by technological advance that have been revealed by empirical research. These "facts" about invention or R&D will be given an interpretation within the model.

Decision Rules Guiding the Level of R&D Effort

In Chapter 7 we argued that one would expect decision rules that have stood the test of time to be plausibly responsive to variables to which firms should attend if they are to achieve their purposes. This will be our hypothesis about decision rules guiding R&D behavior.

Many different kinds of organizations do R&D. The objectives of a university laboratory certainly differ from those of an applied laboratory of a government agency, and the objectives of an R&D laboratory in a profit-seeking business firm are likely different from either of these. Here we will focus on R&D done by business firms and private inventors and will assume that profit is a dominant or at least an important goal—and the more profit the better. Our hypothesis about decision rules, then, is that their "form" can be explained in terms of how different variables impinge on the profitability of various levels and allocations of R&D. One would expect, therefore, that decision rules would be linked both to factors relating to the demand for or payoff of R&D and to factors relating to the supply or cost of R&D.

Numerous studies have documented quite strikingly to what extent the amount of inventive effort is sensitive to the level of demand for or sales of the product in question. At the sectoral or industry level, Schmookler (1966) powerfully argued the proposition that the anticipated size of the market for a product is a consideration that influences the amount of R&D effort directed toward improving that product or reducing its cost. At least within manufacturing industry, R&D expenditure, direct and indirect (done by input suppliers), is correlated with the sales of the industry. And shifts in the pattern of sales tend to pull the allocation of R&D inputs in the same direction. There are certain analytical subtleties in the connection between the size of the market for a product and the amount of R&D that it pays to perform; these subtleties have tended to be overlooked by some of the researchers who have argued the important role of product demand. In particular, a whole set of problems that is associated with "externalities" from R&D needs to be analyzed in assessing the strength of the connection. We will pay special attention to the externalities problem in Chapter 13. It is very plausible, however, that the size of the market is positively related to the amount of research and development that it pays to do.

This plausible relationship seems to have been built into the decision rules that individual firms use to guide the level of their research and development spending. Several studies have documented that many firms have as a decision rule that R&D expenditures should be a roughly constant fraction of sales. Decision rules of this type at the firm level will generate the observed empirical relationships at the industry or sectoral level if systematic interindustry differences in target R&D/sales ratios are not too large.

In contrast with demand-side factors whose influence on the level of R&D spending is reasonably well understood, the effect of variables that influence the ease or difficulty of inventing in particular product fields upon the amount of R&D effort directed to those fields is quite uncertain. Part of the reason for the uncertainty is that it has proved difficult to get a firm conceptual grip on how one would measure differences in the ease of inventing across fields or on the variables that would influence the ease of inventing. A number of conjectures have been put forth. Several scholars have proposed that "knowledge" relating to certain technologies is stronger than that relating to others and that a strong knowledge base facilitates technical invention. However, it is difficult to state precisely just what "stronger knowledge" means in this context. Some writers have associated knowledge with formal science and have attempted to classify certain industries (for example, electronics and chemicals) as more closely based upon science than other industries (for example, textiles). But even when there has been an agreement regarding classification, there has been dispute regarding the effect of a stronger scientific base upon the research and development inputs and outcomes. Some economists, notably Schmookler, have argued that the relationship between the strength of the scientific base in an industry and the amount of research and development that goes on is much weaker than the connection between the level of product demand and the amount of research and development spending. Others, such as Rosenberg (1974), have argued that the pace of technical advance is much higher in industries that are close to science than in those that are not. Notice that these positions are not necessarily inconsistent, the former relating to inputs to research and development and the latter to outputs from research and development.

Let us employ a variant of the schematic search model outlined above to try to bring a little order to this chaos. Assume, for the present, that product attributes are constant over the set of all possible production methods and that all these technologies have constant returns to scale and fixed input coefficients. The R&D decision maker does not know the economic characteristics of as yet uninvented or undiscovered technologies, but he knows certain technological attributes. These enable him to divide up the set of possibilities into subclasses—a set of "blue" technologies, a set of "yellow" ones, and so on. At the existing set of factor prices he may know, for example, that the blue technologies are more promising ones for exploration than any of the others in the sense of stochastic dominance of the distribution of unit cost reductions.

The research and development process can be stylized as follows. The decision maker can "sample" from any of the subpopulations and "study" or "test" the elements of his sample. A study will exactly identify the economic attributes, and hence the cost saving (if any) associated with the use of that technology if developed. Development consists of making a known technology usable in practice. Suppose that the cost of the study is the same for all technologies and independent of the number of technologies tested. Development cost is the same for all technologies.[3]

For the present, let us consider a single period and assume that at most one technology will be developed. The decision maker will draw a sample of given size determined by his level-of-effort decision rule. He will direct his sampling to a particular subclass; in this case a sensible allocational decision rule will obviously indicate "blue." If the "best" of the sample, when compared to the prevailing technology, has a cost reduction that more than offsets development costs, that technology is developed.

Assume that the level-of-effort rule is plausibly responsive to the relevant variables in the sense discussed above. Consider the effect of an increase in the "size of the market." An increase in the volume of production that would be undertaken with a new technology increases the total cost saving associated with any reduction in input

---

3. There are a number of extant models of R&D that treat R&D as search. See, for example, Evenson and Kislev (1976), Roberts and Weitzman (1981), Weitzman (1979), and Dasgupta and Stiglitz (1980a, 1980b).

coefficients. In this model of search, there are decreasing but positive returns to increasing the number sampled before commitment to development. The magnification of economic advantage from a "better technology" shifts upward the marginal returns schedule. Thus, a "plausibly responsive" decision rule would tie the amount of search monotonically to the level of expected production or sales.[4]

Suppose there is an increase in the strength of the knowledge base, in the following sense. It suddenly is learned that the set of all blue technologies can be partitioned into a set of blue-striped technologies and a set of blue technologies without stripes, with the former a better set than the latter in the sense of stochastic dominance. Drawing a given number of elements from the striped blue set will lead to a probability distribution of the expected unit cost saving of the "best" of the elements sampled that stochastically dominates the expected value of a cost saving of the best element of a sample of comparable size drawn from the whole set of blue elements. Stronger knowledge (in this sense) leads to a lower expected cost (smaller number sampled) of achieving an advance of given magnitude or to a larger expected advance from a given search expenditure (given number sampled). However, if one could compute an optimal strategy, there is not necessarily any more sampling (R&D input) in the case where knowledge is stronger than in the original case.[5] Just as in more traditional cases, a decrease in the cost of achieving something increases the amount it pays to achieve, but not necessarily the inputs applied to achieving. The connection between the strength of knowledge and the amount of research and development that one "ought to do" is more complicated and difficult to see through than the connection between the level of demand for a product and the amount of research and development it pays to do. There is no reason to expect a plausibly responsive decision rule to link R&D spending closely to "the state of knowledge."

This model, then, does provide some theoretical support for Schmookler's conclusions about the loose connection between the strength of the scientific base and research and development spending. But it also provides support for Rosenberg's argument. The "effectiveness" of R&D input is directly related to the strength of knowledge in the sense modeled above. Even if R&D input is no greater in industries where the scientific base is strong than in those

---

4. It is a well-known fact of order statistics (see Lippman and McCall, 1976; or Nelson, 1961 or 1978) that the value of the maximum element of a sample of size n increases with n, but at a diminishing rate. The value in the context here is simply unit cost reduction. The analysis above follows immediately.

5. See Lippman and McCall (1976) or Nelson (1978).

where it is weak, one might expect the pace of technical advance to be faster.

Factors Influencing the Allocation of Effort, Given the Overall Budget

In contrast with the situation regarding the level of effort where there is a certain asymmetry in the effects of factors influencing payoff and factors influencing cost, there ought to be more symmetry in decision rules guiding the allocation of effort. Assume that the product in question (being sold by the firm) can have different attributes; cars or television sets can be big or small, models can be deluxe or plain, and so forth. An R&D decision maker ought to have a pretty good (though not infallible) idea regarding what subclasses of "new technologies" will lead to a product with one or another set of attributes. A shift in consumer demand toward one set of attributes and away from another changes the mix of production that would be dictated by plausibly responsive production decision rules. But such a shift also ought to influence the allocation of research and development effort in the same direction.

Exactly the same demand or payoff argument enables the model to generate the qualitative conclusions that come out of many neoclassical models relating the direction of inventing, in the sense of factor saving, to factor prices. If the R&D decision maker can identify, *ex ante*, classes of technology that are relatively rich in elements that will save considerably on labor per unit of output or on capital per unit of output, a "plausibly responsive" decision rule ought to link his search direction to the relative prices of labor and capital. The empirical work that started with Habakkuk (1962) and that was significantly extended by Hayami and Ruttan (1971) and Binswanger and Ruttan (1976) has empirically documented the effect of factor prices on the factor bias displayed by innovation. This linkage is as well explained by our "search" model as by the neoclassical formulation, which assumes a highly unrealistic ability on the part of the inventors to calculate and foresee.

A good decision rule for allocating research and development resources obviously must attend both to factors on the demand side and to factors that influence the ease or cost of invention. It is no good to pick out projects that are technically exciting and doable but that have no demand, or to undertake a project that if successful would have a high payoff but that would have no chance for success. The question is: What kinds of decision rules have evolved that are responsive to these criteria?

In view of the great size and uneven topography of the set of all possible projects, R&D decision makers must have some simple guidelines for homing in on plausible regions. A widely used procedure seems to begin by developing lists of projects that if successful would have high payoff, and then screening this list to find those projects that look not only profitable if they can be done, but doable at reasonable cost. In a sense, payoff-side factors are examined first, and those relating to cost or feasibility are looked at second. It appears that certain firms, however, proceed with their sorting quite the other way, focusing first on exciting technological possibilities and then screening these to identify the ones that might have high payoff if achieved. Studies suggest that the first of these two strategies not only is more common but is more likely to result in a commercially successful project than the second strategy. However, the strategy that looks at interesting technological possibilities first tends to pay off handsomely when it pays off at all.[6]

Neither of these two approaches, of course, is literally optimal. Our basic point is that firms cannot hope to find optimal strategies. Since all alternatives cannot be considered, there must be some rather mechanical procedures employed for quickly narrowing the focus to a small set of alternatives and then homing in on promising elements within that set. It is noteworthy that both of the strategies mentioned above pay attention to factors both on the demand or payoff side and on the cost and feasibility side. We interpret the widespread use of strategies of this sort as confirmation of our hypothesis that policies in use, although in no sense optimal, tend to be plausibly responsive to the key variables influencing profitability.

Cumulative Technological Advance

The discussion thus far has focused on R&D activity at a single moment in time. It is possible to explain continuing technological progress over time within a simple search model of the sort discussed above, under the assumption that tomorrow's round of projects is independent of what happens today except for the fact that what is achieved today imposes a higher standard of success for tomorrow's efforts. Under plausible assumptions, in the absence of increased knowledge there would then be diminishing returns to R&D. These can be offset, however, by growing demand for product. Thus, R&D may grow and technical advance be sustained. This characterization may capture what is going on in some technologies, but it fails to explain the cumulative nature of technological advance in many sectors. In many technological histories the new is not just

---

6. For a discussion, see Pavitt (1971) or Freeman (1974).

better than the old; in some sense the new evolves out of the old. One explanation for this is that the output of today's searches is not merely a new technology, but also enhances knowledge and forms the basis of new building blocks to be used tomorrow.

For example, today's research and development may be searching for a new technology (say, a chemical compound) with certain economic attributes and may be focusing on alternatives with certain technological attributes: the blue technologies. Tests prove that a particular blue-striped technology indeed does have desirable economic attributes. As a result, the hypothesis that the set of blue technologies contains some good ones is reinforced, and the subhypothesis might be formulated that the subclass of blue-striped technologies is particularly attractive.

Or consider the set of technological possibilities defined by various mixes of ingredients. On the basis of past experience, the decision maker believes that a significant increase in the amount of one of these relative to others will yield an economically superior product. But he is not sure, and does not know how much more to add. A sensible R&D strategy might involve first testing the economic attributes of a mix somewhat richer than the prevailing one, and, if the results are favorable, trying out an even richer mix, and so on—in effect, hunting for the top of the hill. In general, a good strategy will stop the R&D project somewhere short of the top of the hill because the economic attributes achieved are good enough and because the gains from varying the mix in one way or another are not expected to be worth the cost of performing another test. But the knowledge acquired in the course of the project may have implications for the next round of R&D projects, perhaps involving a different ingredient.[7]

In many hardware-producing industries such as the aircraft industry, R&D may be represented as a gradual filling-in of the details of an overall rough design idea, with the course of the design work being guided by a series of studies and tests. In the later stages these involve prototype versions of the actual new hardware. In endeavors of this sort the metaphor of "alternatives out there waiting to be found" is somewhat forced. Researchers are building a technological variant that was not in existence before and are finding out how it works. Information is being acquired not only in activities that are incidental to discovery but also in the course of creating and learning about something new. In general, the new design will involve a large number of subdesign elements or components. Regarding each of

---

7. Box and Draper (1969) have proposed a simple procedure for using analysis of variance techniques to guide this sort of search for improvements in manufacturing processes, particularly chemical processes.

these there may be certain "design problems" to solve, in the sense that certain performance goals need to be achieved. Knowledge can facilitate the problem solving by guiding the effort toward promising design alternatives. And knowledge can facilitate overall design by indicating what problems may be hard or easy and by guiding strategy toward configurations that do not require that the former kind be solved. As was the case with the search for a better chemical mix, a successful development project creates more than a discrete practical invention. Today's new hardware represents a set of solutions to design problems and provides a new starting point for the next round of research and development efforts.

In all of these examples, the result of today's searches is both a successful new technology and a natural starting place for the searches of tomorrow. There is a "neighborhood" concept of a quite natural variety. It makes sense to look for a new drug "similar to" but possibly better than the one that was discovered yesterday. One can think of varying a few elements in the design of yesterday's successful new aircraft, trying to solve problems that still exist in the design or that were evaded through compromise.

This formulation appears to explain relatively satisfactorily certain aspects of what has become known as the "product cycle." The history of many technologies seems to be characterized by occasional major inventions followed by a wave of minor ones. Part of what is going on is product design evolution. As Miller and Sawers (1968) tell the story, the original Douglas DC-3, the result of the confluence of a number of R&D strands, represented a radically new civil aircraft package: all-metal skin, low wing, streamlining of body and engine configuration, more powerful engines. Over the subsequent decade, the basic design was improved in a variety of models, designed by other manufacturers as well as by Douglas. Each successive generation of plane was faster, had longer range, and was more comfortable. The original basic design was stretched to achieve additional performance and was differentiated to meet a variety of different demands and conditions. The DC-4 represented the start of a series of four-engine versions. By the mid 1950s the potentialities of this design concept appear to have been largely exploited. The advent of the Boeing 707 and Douglas DC-8 represented the start of another technological product cycle within the civil aircraft industry. Enos (1962) reported a similar pattern in petroleum-refining technology. Again, technical change was marked by the periodic introduction of major new technologies (the batch thermal process in 1931, catalytic cracking in 1936, and so on), followed by a wave of improvements. The flow of subsequent improvements in petroleum refining appears to have been even more important than that in aviation. Enos reports that in many cases the first versions of the new technology tended to be only marginally superior to the most recent versions of the older technology and were sometimes not superior at all. The advantages of the new were achieved largely through the wave of improvements that were possible with the new design, compared with the difficulty of finding further major improvements in the old one.

As the product evolves, so do the processes of production. Hirsch (1952), in one of the earliest but still among the most illuminating of the studies of "learning curves," pointed out three different kinds of mechanisms at work: workers are learning to do their jobs better, management is learning how to organize more effectively, and engineers are redesigning the product to make the job easier and to replace labor where it is possible and economical to do so. Hirsch in his study of machinery and Asher (1956) in his research on aircraft noted that different kinds of costs are affected differently over the learning process. In particular, unit labor costs tend to be reduced dramatically, unit materials costs are reduced to a lesser degree, and unit capital costs may rise. This corresponds closely to events that Enos observed during the design improvement process for petroleum-refining equipment. In addition, the detailed studies of the "learning process" do not treat learning as somehow an inevitable and uninfluenceable consequence of doing. Rather, learning is viewed more actively, and it is apparent that resources can be applied to learning.

In some cases this hunting for marginal improvements involves exploring in a variety of different directions. But in some cases a few directions seem much more compelling of attention than others. Particularly in industries where technological advance is very rapid, advance seems to follow advance in a way that appears almost inevitable. Rosenberg (1969) writes of "technological imperatives" as guiding the evolution of certain technologies: bottlenecks in connected processes and obvious weak spots in products form clear targets for improvement. In other cases, the directions taken seem "straighter" than is suggested by Rosenberg's emphasis on the shifting focus of attention. We term these paths "natural trajectories."

Natural trajectories are specific to a particular technology or broadly defined "technological regime." We use "technological regime" in much the same way as Hayami and Ruttan (1971) use "meta production function." Their concept refers to a frontier of achievable capabilities, defined in the relevant economic dimensions, limited by physical, biological, and other constraints, given a broadly defined way of doing things. Our concept is more cognitive, relating to technicians' beliefs about what is feasible or at least worth attempting. For example, in the case discussed by Miller and Sawers (1968), the advent of the DC-3 in the 1930s defined a particular technological regime; metal skin, low wing, piston-powered planes. Engineers had notions regarding the potential of this regime. For more than two decades innovation in aircraft design essentially involved better exploitation of this potential: improving the engines, enlarging the planes, making them more efficient.

In many cases the promising trajectories and strategies for technological advance, within a given regime, are associated with improvements of major components or aspects thereof. In aviation, engineers can work on improving the thrust-weight ratio of engines or on increasing the lift-drag ratio of airframes. General theoretical understanding provides clues as to how to proceed. In jet engine technology, thermodynamic understanding relates the performance of the engine to such variables as temperature and pressure at combustion. This naturally leads designers to look for engine designs that will enable higher inlet temperatures and higher pressures. In airframe design, theoretical understanding (at a relatively unsophisticated level) always has indicated that there are advantages to getting planes to fly at higher altitudes, where air resistance is lower. This leads designers to think of pressurizing the cabin, demanding aircraft engines that will operate effectively at higher altitudes, and so forth.

Often there are complementarities among the various trajectories. Advances in engine power and the streamlining of aircraft are complementary. The development of seeds that germinate at the same time and grow at the same rate facilitates mechanical harvesting.

While natural trajectories almost invariably have special elements associated with the particular technology in question, in any era there appear to be certain natural trajectories that are common to a wide range of technologies. Two of these have been relatively well identified in the literature: progressive exploitation of latent economies of scale and increasing mechanization of operations that have been done by hand.

In a wide variety of industries and technologies, the advance of equipment technology involves the exploitation of latent economies of scale. In chemical process industries, in power generation, and in other sectors where equipment of larger capacity will permit output expansion without a proportional increase in capital or other costs, the objectives of cost reduction apparently lead designers to focus on making equipment larger. Hughes (1971) documented the way in which designers of electric power equipment have aimed progressively to push forward the scale frontier. Levin (1974) provided a general theoretical discussion of the phenomenon as well as case studies of the process in the manufacture of sulfuric acid, ethylene, and ammonia and in petroleum refining. Exploitation of scale economies is an important part of the story of the improvement of refining equipment as told by Enos. In the development of aircraft technology, designers long have understood that larger planes could in principle operate with lower costs per seat-mile. Of course, in aviation, as in electric power, the possibilities for exploiting latent economies of scale are limited by the market as well as by engineering. In aviation, high volumes and long hauls provide the market's targets of opportunity. And historically these have tended to grow in importance over time. This has permitted engineers to follow their design instincts. As a rule, each generation of commercial aircraft has tended to be made up of larger vehicles than those in the preceding generation.

Another quite common natural trajectory is toward the mechanization of processes previously done by hand. This shows up strikingly in the Hirsch and Asher studies of learning. Mechanization seems to be viewed by designers of equipment as a natural way to reduce costs, increase reliability and precision of production, gain more reliable control over operations, and so on. This point has been stressed by Rosenberg (1972) in his study of nineteenth-century innovation in American industry. That this tendency to mechanize still exists has been suggested by Piore (1968) and documented in considerable detail by Setzer (1974) in her work on the evolution of production processes at Western Electric. Inventors and research and development engineers, operating under a higher-order objective to look for inventions and design changes that will reduce costs, look for opportunities to mechanize. Engineers, through training and experience, apparently acquire heuristics that assist the design of machinery. For this reason, hunting for opportunities for mechanization, like trying to exploit latent economies of scale, can serve as a useful focus for inventive activity.

David (1974), in a fascinating and important essay, proposed a different but complementary hypothesis. Whereas the studies above point to "easy invention" in directions that increase the capital-labor ratio, David suggested that in the late nineteenth century technologies that already were capital-intensive were easier to improve in a "neutral" direction than were technologies that involved a lower degree of capital intensity; at that time there was "a lot of room" for improving mechanized operations, and engineer-designers had some clever ways of moving in that direction.

Exploitation of latent economies of scale and opportunities for further mechanization are important avenues for technological advance in many sectors at the present time, just as they were in the nine-

teenth century. Many of the studies cited above are of relatively contemporary examples. However, there is no reason to believe, and
many reasons to doubt, that the powerful general trajectories of one
era are the powerful ones of the next. For example, it seems apparent
that in the twentieth century two widely used natural trajectories
opened up that were not available earlier: first, the exploitation of an
understanding of electricity and the resulting creation and improvement of electrical and later electronic components, and, second, similar developments regarding chemical technologies. As with the case
of mechanization during the 1800s, these developments had several
different effects. For example, a greater understanding of electrical
phenomena and growing experience with electrical and electronic
equipment led to a substitution of these kinds of components for
others. And technologies that had many and important electronic
components were better able to benefit from the improvements in
these components than were other technologies.

It is apparent that industries differ significantly in the extent to
which they can exploit the prevailing general natural trajectories,
and that these differences influence the rise and fall of different industries and technologies. During the nineteenth century, cotton
gained ascendancy over wool in large part because its production
processes were easier to mechanize. Quite possibly both Rosenberg
trajectories and David trajectories were involved. In the twentieth
century, Texas cotton drove out southeastern cotton mainly because
the area was amenable to mechanized picking. In the current era,
where considerable skill has developed regarding the design and
improvement of synthetic products, synthetic fibers have risen in
importance relative to natural ones.

One aspect of natural trajectories, whether specific to a particular
technology or more general, whether of the nineteenth century or
contemporary, is that underlying the movement along them is a body
of knowledge held by the technicians, engineers, and scientists involved in the relevant inventive activity. The knowledge may be
quite specific, such as an understanding of the tactics for hybrid
development of seeds or an understanding of the operating characteristics of jet engines. The knowledge may involve more art and
intuition than science; this certainly was so of the knowledge behind
the mechanization and scale economies trajectories during the 1800s.
But in the middle to late twentieth century, many scholars have been
strongly tempted by the hypothesis that underlying the technologies
that have experienced the most rapid advance (or built into a key
component of these) is a relatively well-articulated scientific knowledge. This does not mean that the "inventors" are active scientists or
that "inventing" exploits knowledge produced by recent science. But

the fact that college-educated scientists and engineers now comprise the dominant group doing applied research and development indicates that, at the very least, scientific literacy is an important background factor.

The interpretation given here of product cycles and of trajectories within classes of technology is useful for organizing thinking about certain irregularities in the pace and pattern of technical progress. Consider a set of technological possibilities that consists of a number of quite different classes of technology—say, engines employing different thermodynamic cycles, or different technologies for the generation of electric power. Within any of these classes of technology, technological advance may follow a particular trajectory. At any given time all the R&D may be focused on one class of technologies (the blue ones), with no attention being paid to the yellow technologies because the structure of knowledge (the ability effectively to explore within that subset) is weak in that area. Along the prevailing trajectory there will be a tendency for returns to fall. Assume, however, that knowledge occasionally is created (perhaps from basic research done at universities) that significantly improves the structure of understanding regarding portions of the set in which knowledge previously had been weak and hence that applied research tended to ignore (striped yellow technologies tend to be very effective, dotted yellow ones ineffective). Then one would expect that a significant shift would occur in the nature of the R&D that goes on and that old experience and knowledge would become obsolete. The R&D game would become very different, perhaps requiring people of different kinds of backgrounds, different kinds of firms, and so on. And technical progress would surge forward as solutions appeared to problems suddenly made relatively easy by the strengthening of the knowledge base—only to slacken again as the new areas of search become, in their turn, relatively well explored.

2. THE SELECTION ENVIRONMENT

Elements of a Selection Model

As was the case with search, the model presented in Chapter 9 incorporated a highly simplified and stylized characterization of "selection." In order to make good contact with the microeconomic studies of technological advance, a more complex and subtle formulation is needed, and significant intersector differences need to be recognized. A general model of the selection environment can be devised, we propose, by specification of the following elements: (1) the nature of the benefits and costs that are weighed by the organizations that will decide to adopt or not to adopt a new innovation; (2) the manner in which consumer or regulatory preferences and rules influence what is "profitable"; (3) the relationship between "profit" and the expansion or contraction of particular organizations or units; and (4) the nature of the mechanisms by which one organization learns about the successful innovations of other organizations and the factors that facilitate or deter imitation. Given a flow of new innovations, the selection environment thus specified determines the way in which relative use of different technologies changes over time. And, of course, the selection environment also generates feedback that influences strongly the kind of R&D that firms in an industry will find it profitable to undertake. In this section we shall try to organize within this theoretical scheme some of the diverse literature concerned with what happens to an innovation. Before proceeding, however, there is an important conceptual issue that needs to be clarified.

In much of the literature on technological change a sharp distinction has been drawn between "inventing" and "innovating" (where the latter term is used, more narrowly than we are using it, to refer to a decision to try out technology in practice). The distinction harks back to Schumpeter's *Theory of Economic Development*. Although technological invention was not the centerpiece in his analysis regarding invention, he described a world in which independent inventors had to link up with extant firms, or with entrepreneurs seeking to establish new firms, in order to implement their inventions. In the current institutional environment, in which much innovation comes from internal R&D, the old Schumpeterian distinction is much less useful than it used to be. Although there are examples of inventions that were economically viable without further R&D— inventions that simply lay around waiting for someone to try them out—this nowadays seems a rare occurrence. Further, the earlier experimental use of a new technology often is integrated with the last stages of the research and development process.

There is, however, a significant distinction that has some of the flavor of the old Schumpeterian one. Often an innovation is produced by a firm for sale to customers who will use it. Thus, there are two acts of innovation (in the narrow sense of the term) that are involved. In the case of the advent of jet passenger aircraft, DeHaviland, the company that produced the first commercial jet, was an innovator. But so was the airline that bought the plane. More generally, if the focus is on any economic sector, it is useful to distinguish between two kinds of innovation. Some of these may bubble out of the research and development activities of the firms in the sector.

Others may be largely in the form of materials, components, or equipment offered by supplying firms. However, for the moment let us pass over that distinction and focus on an economic sector that is experiencing a flow of new innovations, some of which may be viable and others not. While the range of possible innovations and of the characteristics of the sectors obviously is extremely broad, the analytic task is to develop a conceptual framework that at once identifies commonalities and enables the differences to stand out.

Consider, then, the following diverse set of innovations and industries: the first model 707 aircraft produced by the Boeing Aircraft Company, the first use of the oxygen process on a commercial basis by a steel company in Austria, a new seed variety tried by a farmer, a pioneering doctor trying an anticancer drug, a district court experimenting with releasing on their own recognizance without bail a select group of people accused of crime, and a school experimenting with open classrooms. The range of possible innovations and of the characteristics of the organizations that introduce them is enormous.

A necessary condition for survival of an innovation is that after a trial it be perceived as worthwhile by the organizations that directly determine whether it is used or not. If the innovation is to persist and expand in use, the firm must find a new product or process profitable to produce or employ, the doctor must view the treatment as efficacious, the school system must be persuaded that the new classroom technique is good educational practice and worth the cost. We shall call all of these primary organizations "firms" and use the term "profitable" to indicate value in the eyes of the firms, without implying that the objectives are monetary profit rather than something else or that the organization is private not public. Neither do we imply any social merit in firms' objectives. Firms may be motivated by little more than the prestige of being first. Sectors obviously differ in terms of the objectives of the firms.

The question of whether or not the firms find the innovations profitable depends not only on the objectives of the firms. In almost all economic sectors the firms—profit-seeking private organizations, public agencies, individual professionals—are subject to monitoring mechanisms that at least influence which innovations score well or poorly according to the objectives of the firms and that may impose more direct constraints on firm behavior. A key part of this monitoring mechanism involves the individuals or organizations that are the demanders or beneficiaries of the goods or services produced by the firms in the sectors. Thus, the profitability to Boeing of producing 707-type aircraft depends on how the airlines react to these planes. Consumers must be willing to buy the new strain of corn, which the new seed produced, at a price that covers cost. Patients must agree to the new treatment. School systems and legal systems are constrained by budgets that are proposed by higher authorities and voted by legislatures. In some sectors there are additional constraints imposed on firms by agencies that are assigned a legal responsibility to monitor or regulate their activity. Thus, the Boeing 707, before it could be put into commercial use, had to pass tests devised by the Federal Aviation Administration; new pharmaceuticals are regulated by the Food and Drug Administration; and so forth. Selection environments differ greatly in the structure of demanders and monitors and in the manner and strength in which these mold and constrain the behavior of firms.

There are, roughly speaking, two distinct kinds of mechanisms for the spread of a profitable innovation. One of these is greater use of an innovation by the firm that first introduces it. If the firm produces a variety of products or undertakes a variety of activities, this may occur through substitution of the new activity for older ones. Or the firm may grow both absolutely and (if there are competitors) relatively by attracting new resources. In sectors that involve a number of administratively distinct organizational units on the supply side, there is a second innovation-spreading mechanism that needs to be considered: imitation. Imitation of certain innovations may be deliberately spurred by the institutional machinery. Thus, the agricultural extension service encourages widespread adoption by farmers of new seed varieties. If the innovation is produced by a supplying firm, its sales agents will try to encourage rapid adoption. Or the institutional machinery may deter or block imitation, as the patent system blocks the adoption by one firm of patented innovations created by a competitor.

The relative importance of these mechanisms differs from sector to sector. Dieselization of a nationalized railroad system proceeds largely through substitution of diesels for other kinds of locomotives within that one system, although improvement in the service may enable a nationalized railroad to gain funds to finance some growth. If, on the other hand, there are several organizationally separate railroad systems, successful innovation is likely to spur the relative growth of the innovator, but full dieselization almost certainly must await imitation by other railroads. The success of the 707 encouraged and enabled Boeing to expand its production facilities. And other aircraft producers were spurred, at their peril, to design and produce comparable aircraft. Bail reform has spread in part by greater use within particular districts, but since one jurisdiction is not permitted to expand relative to another, and since there are many thousands of jurisdictional districts, the ultimate spread of innovations in the criminal justice system depends upon imitation.

We propose that a rigorous general model of the selection environment can be built from the specification of these four elements: the definition of "worth" or profit that is operative for the firms in the sector, the manner in which consumer and regulatory preferences and rules influence what is profitable, and the investment and imitation processes that are involved. In the remainder of this section we shall discuss some important qualitative differences in sectoral selection environments that become the focus of attention once one poses the theoretical problem in the way we have. Market sectors differ significantly among themselves. And many sectors involve important nonmarket components that have special characteristics.

The Market as a Selection Environment

The perception that market competition in a sector constitutes a particular sort of selection environment was explicit in the writings of many of the great nineteenth- and early twentieth-century economic theorists. Schumpeter was well within this classical tradition. In a stylized Schumpeterian evolutionary system, there is both a carrot and a stick to motivate firms to introduce better production methods or products. "Better" here has an unambiguous meaning: lower cost of production, or a new product that consumers are willing to buy at a price above cost. In either case the criterion boils down to a higher monetary profit. Successful innovation leads to both higher profit for the innovator and to profitable investment opportunities. Thus, profitable firms grow. In so doing they cut away the market for the noninnovators and reduce their profitability, which, in turn, will force these firms to contract. Both the visible profits of the innovators and the losses experienced by the laggers stimulate the latter to try to imitate.

The Schumpeterian dynamics differ somewhat depending on whether the innovation is of a new product or a new process. For product innovation, the profitability to the firm depends strongly on the uncertain reactions of potential consumers. For process innovation, which does not change the nature of the product, the market constraints are far more blunt. The firm can make an assessment of profitability by considering the effects on costs, with far less concern for consumer reaction. Further, and reinforcing these differences, product innovation usually comes from a firm's own R&D; significant process innovations often come from the R&D done by suppliers and are embodied in their products. To the extent this is so, imitation by a competitor of a process innovation is likely to occur relatively rapidly and to be encouraged by a marketing supplier, rather than retarded by a patent.

Both expansion of the innovator and imitation by competitors are essential to the viability of the Schumpeterian process. In the standard descriptions of dynamic competition, expansion of the innovator is likely to be stressed. It is surprising, therefore, that the relationship between innovation and investment has hardly been studied empirically at all. The principal studies of firm investment have been based on neoclassical theory modified by Keynesian considerations and tend to ignore the relationship between innovation and expansion of a firm. The Meyer-Kuh (1957) retained earnings–capacity pressure theory would imply that successful innovators tend to expand. Presumably a successful innovation both yields profits and attracts demand, which may, initially at least, exceed capacity. A more straitlaced neoclassical theory also would predict that firms that come up with better processes and products ought to want to expand their capacity to produce. But the major studies of firm investment have, virtually without exception, ignored the influence of innovation on investment.

The exceptions are studies in which the author's basic hypothesis is oriented toward the Schumpeterian interactions. Mueller (1967) does find that lagged R&D expenditure by a firm has a positive influence on its investment in new plant and equipment. In a later study, Grabowski and Mueller (1972) used lagged patents as a measure of R&D output, but find that the influence on plant and equipment investment is weak statistically. Mansfield's studies (1968) give stronger support for a Schumpeterian view. In examining investment at an industry level, Mansfield found that the number of recent innovations is a significant explanatory variable, augmenting more traditional variables. But perhaps his most interesting results involve comparisons of firm growth rates, where he found that innovating firms in fact tend to grow more rapidly than the laggers. However, although the advantage of the innovators may persist for several periods, the advantage tends to damp out with time, apparently because other firms have been able to imitate or to come up with comparable or superior innovations.

In contrast to the spareness of studies of the relationship of investment to successful innovation, a large number of studies have focused on the spread of innovation by diffusion (imitation) in profit-oriented sectors. These have ranged across a variety of sectors, including agriculture (study of the diffusion of hybrid corn among farmers), railroads (diesel engines), brewing, and steel. Many have documented the role of profitability of an innovation in influencing the speed at which that innovation spreads. However, other studies have concluded that the calculations made by firms tend to be haphazard and that even *ex post* the firms had little idea, quantitatively, how profitable the innovation turned out to be (Nasbeth and Ray, 1974). Several have found that, for innovations that are costly to put into operation, large firms (with greater financial resources) tend to adopt a new technology earlier than do smaller firms, although there are exceptions. Most of the studies show an S-shaped pattern of use of the new innovation over time. In many cases this has been attributed to the fact that the later users are observing the behavior (and perhaps the performance) of the earlier adopters before making their own decisions. In some instances the innovations were inputs provided by a supplier, and the early adopters of the innovation were not in a position to block subsequent use of their competitors. In other instances this was not the case. For example, a glass-producing company, Pilkington, holds the basic patents on the float glass process and presumably had an interest in limiting diffusion to other firms except where Pilkington was blocked from the market. It is interesting that the analysts of diffusion have not in general been cognizant of these differences.

It also is quite surprising that in no study of which we are aware has there been an attempt to examine together the dual roles of expansion of the innovator and imitation of the imitator. It would seem that in order for a market selection environment to work effectively, a rather fine balance is required between the two mechanisms. We will return to this issue later.

Nonmarket Selection Environments

While economists have concentrated their attention on market sectors, research on the selection environment of nonmarket sectors has been undertaken principally by anthropologists, sociologists, and political scientists. This in itself would have led to some significant differences in focus and analysis. But to a considerable extent the differences in analysis appear to reflect real differences in the selection environments.

An essential element in most theorizing about market selection environments is a relatively clear separation of the "firms" on the one hand, and consumers and regulators on the other. Consumers' evaluation of products—versus their evaluation of other products and versus price—is presumed to be the criterion that ought to dictate resource allocation. Firms can be viewed as bidding and competing for consumer purchases, and markets can be judged as working well or poorly depending on the extent to which the profitability of a firm hinges on its ability to meet consumer demands as well as or better than its rivals. The viability of an innovation should depend on consumers' evaluation of it.

A hallmark of nonmarket sectors is that the separation of interests between firms and customers is not as sharply defined as in market sectors. The relationship between a public agency, such as a school system, and its clientele (students and parents) and sources of finance (mayor, council, and voters) simply does not have the arm's-length-distance quality that marks the relationship between seller and potential buyer of a new car. Relatedly, the question of how legitimate values are to be determined is much more complex in nonmarket sectors than in market sectors. The public agency is expected to play a key role in the articulation of values and to internalize these and work in the public interest of its own volition. This is so in many nominally private-sector activities, such as the provision of medical services by doctors. The doctor is not supposed to make his decisions regarding the use of a new drug on the basis of whether this will profit him, but rather on his expectation of how this will benefit his patients. Further, he is supposed to know more about that than do his patients. This is not to say that interests of firms and consumers are in fact consonant. In most nonmarket sectors (as in market sectors where competition is lax) the firm has a good deal of discretionary power regarding what it is to provide, and the customer may have little direct power to reward or to punish performance. For example, the specific view of the public interest articulated by a public agency often seems to be highly consonant with the requirements for the survival and growth of the agency itself. But in general the appropriate "control" mechanism over a provider of goods and services in a nonmarket sector is not viewed as competition among providers for the consumer dollar.

For these reasons, one cannot assume that the firms in a nonmarket sector are motivated solely by monetary profit. This makes it difficult to analyze the operative values relating to acceptance or rejection of an innovation. As in the theory of consumer behavior, as contrasted with the textbook theory of the firm, tastes matter; they may be hard to analyze and may not be stable. Even in situations where there is a relatively clear-cut goal and where the decision to employ an innovation or not hinges on assessment of efficacy relative to that goal, it has proved hard to identify relevant criteria. Thus, in the Coleman, Katz, and Menzel (1957) study of the diffusion among physicians of a new pharmaceutical, the authors did not even attempt to specify quantitatively the ways in which the new product was superior medically to preexisting alternatives. In Warner's (1974) study of the decision by doctors to use new chemotherapeutic techniques for the treatment of cancer, for several of the cancer varieties that were treated with this method there was no quantitative evidence that the therapy had any effect. The physicians made their decisions on hope, with no objective evidence. Friedman (1973), in his study of the acceptance and spread of a certain program of bail reform, was able to identify a few rather specific reasons why the key agencies might find the reform attractive. But the reasons were largely qualitative and it is interesting that, after adopting the reform, there was no real monitoring to check that the programs were performing as hoped. In fact, the performance of the program eroded over time in at least one key dimension, and no one noticed.

Political and regulatory control over firms cannot provide the pervasive, if not always coercive, set of value signals and incentives that is provided by consumer sovereignty in market sectors. Thus, there is greater room left for autonomous and discretionary behavior on the part of suppliers. However, the employment of regulatory and political mechanisms of governance, as contrasted with consumer sovereignty, means that in many cases several different parties may have to go along before an innovation can be operative. In Friedman's study of bail reform, the police and the courts both had to agree to the proposal, and legislative agreement was necessary where budget considerations were involved. Government agencies often have to gain specific agreement from both political chief executives and a legislature before they can proceed with a new program.

Nonseparation of suppliers and demanders leaves little room for firms to compete with one another for consumer dollars. Where there is a single supplying entity—such as the United States Postal Service or the Department of Defense—diffusion of an innovation is a matter of internal decision making constrained and pressured to some degree by the higher-order political processes. Where there is a range of suppliers—as in medicine or in state and local governmental agencies—innovations must spread largely through imitation across the spectrum of noncompeting firms. At the same time, there is no incentive for the innovating firm to deter imitation. Organizations that cannot expand into the terrain of others and know that others cannot encroach on their territory have little to gain from preventing others from adopting their successful innovations. Indeed, in most of the sectors under consideration here, there are formal arrangements for cooperation and flow of information across firms. In many, professional organizations set values and judge the merit of new innovations. The professional stamp of approval, and the adoption pattern it stimulates, often are the only criteria of merit available to a nonprofessional.

Consider the quasi-market for the provision of physician services. Without strong constraints afforded by consumers or outside regulators, consumer welfare is guarded (perhaps not so securely) largely by professional standards of efficacy of treatment. To assess the efficacy of new treatments, doctors consult with each other and apparently aim for professional consensus guided by the judgment of certain key experts. Mohr's study (1969) of the spread of new practices and policies across local public health services reveals a similar professionalism at work. Walker's (1969) study of the lead and lag pattern among state governments in the adoption of new programs indicates the presence of regional groups with intraregional leaders (generally in populous, urban, and wealthy states) to which officials in departments in other state governments look for references and models.

Professional judgments are moderated by political constraints on spending limits and by other governmental regulatory processes that impinge on decision making in a more detailed way. Thus, in Mohr's study the speed with which a local public health service adopted new practices was found to be positively related to the extent to which public health professionals were in control of the key office. However, the professional bias toward adoption of new techniques was moderated by political and budgetary constraints. These, which had to do with the composition and presumably the attitudes of the local "consuming" populations, did limit, if in a loose way, the innovations that local public health services could afford to adopt. Similarly, Walker's study showed that budgetary constraints imposed by state political systems significantly moderated the proclivity of state officials to adopt progressive programs (read: programs adopted by other states whose judgments they admired).

Crain's (1966) study of the spread of fluoridation among American cities is perhaps the most revealing example of a sector in which the "firms" have a bias toward adopting an innovation based on notions of professional or technical appropriateness but in which "consumers" tend to resist it. He notes that the spread of fluoridation first occurred quite rapidly, in a context in which local health professionals were in charge of the decision. As time elapsed, fluoridation became a more openly political issue, and mayors began to take the decision-making authority out of the hands of the professionals. The spread of fluoridation slowed significantly. Still later, it became common for citizen referendum to become the vehicle for decision. This development brought the spread of fluoridation to a virtual halt.

The pattern in all of these cases is quite different from that in the market sectors studied by economists. It is, however, easy enough to see the same broad elements of modeling that need to be stressed: motivations of the firms in the sector (in general, not characterizable in terms of monetary profit), the ways in which consumers (often voters) and financers (often legislatures) may constrain firm behavior, and the mechanisms of information and value sharing among firms in the imitation process (which is the dominant mechanism by which an innovation spreads).

3. SUMMARY

In contrast to preceding chapters, which developed and analyzed a formal model, the strategy here was to elaborate the language and concepts of our proposed theoretical framework in order better to see, understand, and link together the numerous but disjoint fragments of knowledge about technological change that exist in the micro literature on the topic. In earlier chapters the stress was on the importance of explicit recognition and sophisticated modeling of the fundamental uncertainty involved in invention and innovation, and on the consequent pervasive disequilibrium that characterizes the economic growth process. In this chapter we preserved this perspective, but complicated it further by calling attention to the significant differences among sectors in the nature of the key search processes and selection mechanisms involved. The challenge was somehow to encompass this diversity, in the sense of being able to see it sharply and analytically. To see sharply is to recognize that agriculture is not like aircraft, which in turn is not like medical care. To see analytically is to go beyond merely listing differences and to be able to treat these as in some sense parametric differences within a general model.

To this end, the characterization of "search" was enriched so as to be able to comprehend a wide range of topographies, techniques for exploration, and decision rules guiding the application of various techniques. The characterization of "selection environment" was similarly generalized.

In principle, any broad theoretical structure is consistent with a wide range of models at different points along the tractability–descriptive verisimilitude tradeoff spectrum. One can build more complex, more "realistic," less tractable models within a neoclassical theory just as one can within an evolutionary theory. But to explore the fine structure of technical advance with a neoclassical model requires an enormous amount of "*ad hoc*-ery" that is uncongenial to the basic neoclassical theoretical viewpoint. It is therefore virtually inevitable that, if a neoclassical perspective is preserved for the analysis of the macro phenomena of economic growth, a scholar working on micro phenomena and a scholar working on macro phenomena will be unable to talk to each other using a common language. And an individual scholar interested in both aspects of the problem will find his knowledge compartmentalized. A major advantage of an evolutionary theory is that it provides a way to avoid this difficulty.

V

SCHUMPETERIAN COMPETITION

12

Dynamic Competition and Technical Progress

THE MODELS PRESENTED in Part IV were aimed at some of the central issues of growth theory. Innovation by private business firms was placed centrally in the analysis, and profits were viewed as at once the lure to motivate innovative activity and the vehicle by which successful innovators grow relative to other firms. Competition was represented as an active dynamic process.

However, two features were absent from those models that must be addressed in any serious analysis of dynamic competition. Firms were viewed as identical with regard to their *ex ante* prospects for technical advance. But, as Schumpeter emphasized, a central aspect of dynamic competition is that some firms deliberately strive to be leaders in technological innovations, while others attempt to keep up by imitating the successes of the leaders. In general, the former policy entails costs that the latter does not, and it is important to examine the conditions under which an innovative strategy will prove profitable or at least viable. Second, the model did not focus upon the connections among market structure, R&D spending, and technical advance. Of course, it was noted that the pattern of technical advance strongly influenced the market structure that developed over time. But market structure lacked its usual implications for industry performance because the firms in the model acted as price takers even if they grew very large relative to the market as a whole. And the effect of the evolving market structure on the R&D and technical advance generated was not considered at all.

The model that we will treat in Part V explicitly considers a range of R&D policies open to firms in an industry and focuses on the complicated interactions among market structure, R&D spending, technical change, and other aspects of industry performance. The model is of the same general character as those considered in Parts III and IV. Firms are treated as behavioral entities. Firms search to find alternatives to techniques they presently are using. Their profitability is presumed to determine whether they expand or contract. The mathematical form of the model is that of a Markov process in a set of industry states. However, the specific structure of the model considered here differs considerably from the structure of the earlier models. In part, this is because the focus is different. But in part, also, it is our intention to demonstrate the wide range of specific models that is compatible with our general theoretical scheme.

Unlike the analysis in Parts III and IV, where it was possible and important to compare an evolutionary treatment of the topics with an orthodox one, in the analysis that follows this cannot be done. As we stressed in Chapter 2, analysis of Schumpeterian competition has proved a difficult task using orthodox theoretical premises. In recent years there has developed a small class of models attempting to formalize Schumpeter's contribution but preserving some variant of the orthodox premises of profit maximization and equilibrium. Although these models have yielded some illuminating insights, they ignore essential aspects of Schumpeterian competition—the fact that there are winners and losers and that the process is one of continuing disequilibrium. An evolutionary analysis seems required if the model is to recognize those facts.

In an evolutionary theory of the sort that we develop, the nature of the "economic problem" is fundamentally different from that depicted in contemporary orthodox theory. The latter views choice sets as known and given. The economic problem is to pick the best possible production and distribution, given that set of alternatives. The function of competition is to get—or help to get—the signals and incentives right. In evolutionary theory, choice sets are not given and the consequences of any choice are unknown. Although some choices may be clearly worse than others, there is no choice that is clearly best *ex ante*. Given this assumption, one would expect to see a diversity of firm behavior in real situations. Firms facing the same market signals respond differently, and moreso if the signals are relatively novel. Indeed, one would hope for such a diversity of response in order that a range of possible behaviors might be explored. One function of competition, in the structural sense of many firms, then would be to make possible that diversity. Another function of competition, in this more active sense, is to reward and enhance the choices that prove good in practice and to suppress the bad ones.

Over the long run, one hopes, the competitive system would promote firms that choose well on the average and would eliminate, or force reform upon, firms that consistently make mistakes.

In this view, the market system is (in part) a device for conducting and evaluating experiments in economic behavior and organization. The meaning and merit of competition must be appraised accordingly. This is very much the position taken by Schumpeter more than seventy years ago in *The Theory of Economic Development* (Schumpeter, 1934; first published, in German, in 1911).[1] We should understand as "development," he wrote, "only such changes in economic life as are not forced upon it from without but arise by its own initiative, from within" (p. 63). The key development process he identified as the "carrying out of new combinations," and in the competitive economy "new combinations mean the competitive elimination of the old" (pp. 66–67). It is the entrepreneur who carries out new combinations, who "'leads' the means of production into new channels" and may thereby reap an entrepreneurial profit. "He also leads in the sense that he draws other producers in his branch after him. But as they are his competitors, who first reduce and then annihilate his profit, this is, as it were, leadership against one's own will" (p. 89).

Schumpeter's concept of innovation, or "carrying out new combinations," was a broad one. His five identified cases were: "(1) The introduction of a new good . . . (2) The introduction of a new method of production . . . (3) The opening of a new market . . . (4) The opening of a new source of supply . . . (5) The carrying out of the new organization of any industry, like the creation of a monopoly position" (Schumpeter, 1934, p. 66). Clearly, these examples range well beyond the narrowly defined territory of scientific and engineering knowledge where orthodoxy locates both the phenomena of technical change and the capabilities of business firms. And if the point is not clear enough from the list of cases itself, it is certainly driven home by Schumpeter's treatment of the distinction between invention and innovation (p. 88), and by his emphasis on the organizational aspect of changes in methods of production (p. 133). In other words, Schumpeter's treatment of innovation prefigures our own emphasis on the error of overdrawing the related distinctions between technological and organizational considerations, between capabilities and behavior, between doing and choosing.

---

1. Although Schumpeter is particularly noteworthy for his emphasis on this point, most of the great economists, from Adam Smith to the onset of the modern period of formalization, gave some weight to the experimental role of competitive markets.

Here we are concerned, however, with the narrower range of issues. We focus on "technological progress," as that term is commonly understood, and put aside the phenomena of organizational innovation. This narrower focus is consistent with Schumpeter's own analysis in *Capitalism, Socialism, and Democracy* (1950), where it is the industrial research laboratory that is represented as central to the innovation process and that threatens to render the entrepreneurial function obsolete. That analysis is, of course, the *locus classicus* of the discussion of market structure and innovation that forms an important part of the background of our present inquiry. It includes, in particular, the passages that advance what has come to be called "the Schumpeterian hypothesis": the claim that a market structure involving large firms with a considerable degree of market power is the price that society must pay for rapid technological advance.

A substantial body of research by contemporary economists explores various aspects and implications of this hypothesis, and the issue is certainly an important one. We think it important, however, to distinguish between Schumpeter's general propositions about the nature and social value of competition in technologically progressive industries and the particular viewpoint on the role of market structure represented by the Schumpeterian hypothesis. One can accept the value of the former while remaining open-minded or even skeptical about the latter. And one can regard the analysis of Schumpeterian competition as constituting a promising research agenda on which a start has barely been made, while considering that sharply diminishing returns may have set in some time ago for certain lines of effort directed to the narrower question.

1. The Complex Structure of the Schumpeterian Arguments

It is important to emphasize that the particular view of technological change under consideration here involves considerable abstraction, even apart from its problematic separation of the technological and organizational aspects of innovation. A large number of variables clearly influence the pace and pattern of technological progress in an industry. There are many different sources of innovation, and many kinds of policies impinge upon them. However, it is characteristic of discussion relating to the Schumpeterian arguments to focus on one class of innovators—firms in the industry—and on policy influencing the structure (in some sense) of the industry. We will stick with these conventional ground rules.

The Relationship between Market Structure and Innovation

Much of Schumpeter's discussion in *Capitalism, Socialism, and Democracy* stressed the advantages for innovation of large firm size, and was not focused on market structure *per se*. When he referred to the "monopoly level of organization," the particular advantages addressed were mostly innovation "capability advantages" of large firm size stemming from economies of scale in R&D and management, greater capabilities for risk spreading, finance, and so on.

There are superior methods available to the monopolist which either are not available at all to a crowd of competitors or are not available to them so readily: for there are advantages which, though not strictly unattainable on the competitive level of enterprise, are as a matter of fact secured only on the monopoly level, for instance, because monopolization may increase the sphere of influence of the better, and decrease the sphere of influence of the inferior, brains, or because the monopoly enjoys a disproportionately higher financial standing . . . There cannot be any reasonable doubt that under the conditions of our epoch such superiority is as a matter of fact the outstanding feature of the typical large-scale unit of control, though mere size is neither necessary nor sufficient for it. These units not only arise in the process of creative destruction and function in a way entirely different from the static scheme, but in many cases of decisive importance they provide the necessary form for the achievement. They largely create what they exploit. (Schumpeter, 1950, p. 101)

He almost certainly also had in mind "appropriability advantages" of large firms over small ones. In the economic world of *Capitalism, Socialism, and Democracy*, as in that of his earlier work, the returns to innovation stem from the transient monopoly of a new product or process provided by imitator lag. Where patent protection is spotty and imitation may occur rapidly, the payoff to an innovator may depend largely on his ability to exploit that innovation over a relatively short period of time. Large firms have a level of production, productive capacity, marketing arrangements, and finance that enables them quickly to exploit a new technology on a relatively large scale.

The argument that large firms can be more efficient in R&D and can quickly reap the advantages of large-scale use of an innovation has been countered by arguments that the bureaucratic control structure of large firms may partially or even fully offset these latent advantages. While there are extant theoretical models that have tried to capture the roles of scale economies in R&D and of the appropriability advantages of large size, to our knowledge there has been no explicit modeling that tries to come to grips with the internal control issues. This remark applies to the model we shall present here, as well as to other models of Schumpeterian competition.

In the argument above, what is required for innovation is firm size, not market power *per se*. To the extent that some minimal scale is necessary for innovation, it is of course possible that the necessary scale may be achievable only by a monopolist in a product field or by a structure involving just a few firms. But arguments that market power in itself is important to induce innovation must be of a different stripe.

One such argument is that the absence of competitors, and the ability to block imitation by competitors, are factors that in their own right influence appropriability. Put another way, market structure influences the speed with which transient quasi-rents are eroded away by imitators. This relationship is presumably what Schumpeter had in mind when he declared that perfect competition was incompatible with innovation. "The introduction of new methods of production and new commodities is hardly conceivable with perfect— and perfectly prompt—competition from the start. And this means that the bulk of what we call economic progress is incompatible with it. As a matter of fact, perfect competition is and always has been temporarily suspended whenever anything new is being introduced —automatically or by measures devised for the purpose—even in otherwise perfectly competitive conditions" (Schumpeter, 1950, p. 105). A related but distinguishable argument is this: absence of competition or restrained oligopolistic competition, by leading to high rates of return in the industry generally, can serve to shelter firms that do innovative R&D in circumstances where, if competition were more aggressive, firms that aim for a "fast second" would drive the real innovators out of business.

Of course, as a number of commentators remarked, weak competition may reduce the spur to innovation. A permissive environment for an activity like R&D neither guarantees that the activity is in fact undertaken nor provides the discipline to assure that what is done is done well. Absent opportunities to increase market share significantly, and absent a threat that someone else may drive you out of business if you are a laggard, the incentives and pressures to do innovative R&D are dulled; managerial whim may decide whether resources are devoted to a quest for technical leadership or to other forms of managerial consumption. This argument, like the one about bureaucratic obstacles to innovation in large firms, has not yet been adequately modeled.[2] Nor do we treat it in our model.

---

2. More precisely, this issue of the "spur" to innovation provided by more competitive market structure has been formally treated in the context of models that assume profit *maximization*. We do not think that this is what the "spur" discussion is all about.

Finally, whereas most analyses of the connections between market structure and innovation have viewed the causation as flowing from the former to the latter, under Schumpeterian competition there is a reverse flow as well. Successful innovators who are not quickly imitated may invest their profits and grow in relation to their competitors. Similarly, a firm that plays an effective "fast second" strategy may come ultimately to dominate the industry. Market structure should be viewed as endogenous to an analysis of Schumpeterian competition, with the connections between innovation and market structure going both ways. It is surprising that studies concerned with the Schumpeterian hypothesis typically neglect this reverse causal linkage. An important exception is Phillips' (1971) study of the aircraft industry.

Beyond the problem of the relations between market structure and innovation lie two sets of questions of more direct policy consequence. The first involves the nature of the possible tradeoffs between static efficiency and technological progressiveness that may be implicit in the links between market structure and innovation. The second relates to the policy tools available and their influence over time on structure and progressiveness. We will turn our attention to these issues in Chapter 14. In the remainder of this chapter we present a formal model of Schumpeterian competition and report the results of some preliminary experiments exploring its important causal links.

2. The Model

The connections that link market structure and technical progress with other aspects of industry performance clearly are very complex. The modeling challenge is to devise a simple formal structure that enables the exploration of some of the more interesting of these connections and that is transparent enough so that the results of the model can be understood and reconsidered in the context of the more complicated reality.

Our model is of an industry in which a number of firms produce a single homogeneous product. The industry faces a downward-sloping demand curve. At any particular time, each firm operates a single technique—the best it knows. All techniques are characterized by constant returns to scale and fixed input coefficients. A firm will use its best technique to the maximum level permitted by its existing stock of capital, purchasing needed complementary inputs on factor markets. It is assumed that factor supplies are perfectly elastic and that factor prices are constant over the period in question. The technique used by each firm thus determines its unit costs. Given each firm's capital stock and its technique, industry output and product price are determined. The price-cost margin for each firm, then, is determined as well.

Each technique requires the same complementary inputs per unit of capital; techniques differ in terms of output per unit of capital. Input prices facing the industry are constant; thus, costs per unit of capital are constant across firms and over time. But the cost of a unit of output is a variable in the model, since productivity will in general vary across firms and increase over time as better techniques—ones that produce more output per unit of capital—are discovered and implemented. A firm can discover a more productive technique, one that enables output to be produced at lower unit cost, by two methods: by doing R&D that draws on a general fund of relevant technological knowledge or by imitating the production processes of other firms. Either method involves expenditures on R&D, and such expenditures yield uncertain outcomes.

Firms may differ in their policies toward innovation and imitation. Both innovation and imitation policies are defined in terms of expenditure on these kinds of R&D per unit of capital. Thus, as the firms grow or decline, so do their R&D expenditures on imitation and innovation. The innovation and imitation policies of the firms, together with their size, determine their R&D spending on these activities.

We model both kinds of R&D as a two-stage random sampling process. Within a given period the probability that a firm may take a "draw" on the set of innovation possibilities, or the set of imitation possibilities, is proportional to the firm's spending on these activities. Hence, over a run of many periods, the realized average number of innovation and imitation draws per period is proportional to the firm's average expenditures per period on these kinds of R&D. An innovation draw is a random sampling from a probability distribution of technological alternatives. Our specification of that probability distribution will be discussed below. An imitation draw will, with certainty, enable the firm to copy prevailing best practice. In this model, there are no economies of scale of doing R&D: big firms spend more on R&D than do small firms and thus have a greater chance each period of an R&D draw, but that increased chance is only just proportional to their greater spending. There are, though, "appropriability advantages" of large firm size. Once a firm has acquired access to a new technique through either innovative or imitative R&D, it can apply that technique to its entire capacity without further costs. Thus, we set aside issues relating to the embodiment of technical advance and assume away any possibilities that a large firm may be slower than a small firm to adopt a new technique found through R&D.

We will consider two different specifications of the distribution from which a firm samples if it has an innovation draw. These different regimes of technological change imply quite different relationships between industry productivity growth and industry R&D spending.

In one of these regimes, which we shall call the "science-based" case, we view the distribution sampled by an innovative R&D draw as improving over time as a result of events going on outside the industry—for example, advances in fundamental science occurring in universities. At any time, firms sample from a log normal distribution of values of the average productivity of capital. (Recall that all other inputs are proportional to capital in all feasible techniques.) The mean (log) of this distribution increases over time at a rate we call the rate of growth of "latent productivity." Under this specification, what a firm finds today as a result of an innovation draw is independent of what it might have found last year or the year before. And the population being sampled is richer in productive techniques than the one sampled earlier. Innovative R&D by a firm can be interpreted as its efforts to keep up with a moving set of new technological possibilities created outside the industry. Less R&D by a firm or by the industry as a whole means that that moving frontier is tracked less closely. In the other regime, as in the models employed in Chapters 7 and 9, the distribution of innovative R&D outcomes is centered on the prevailing productivity of a firm, and there is no exogenous determination of technological possibilities. An innovation draw is, in effect, a draw on a constant distribution of proportional increments to the firm's prevailing productivity level. Small increments are more likely than large ones. An innovative R&D success buys a firm not only a better technique, but a higher platform for the next period's search. We call this the "cumulative technology" case.

Market structure evolves endogenously. Given the capital stocks and techniques of the firms in a particular period, output for that period is determined. The demand curve then determines price, and productivity levels (given input prices) determine production cost. For each firm the ratio of price to unit production cost—which we call the "price-cost ratio"—is determined. (Given the assumption that all inputs are proportional to capital and all input prices constant, the rate of return on capital in production—abstracting from R&D costs—is monotonically related to the price-cost ratio.)

We assume that a firm's desire to expand or contract is governed by its price-cost ratio and its prevailing market share, within constraints set by the assumed physical depreciation rate of capital and the firm's ability to finance investment. For firms of a given size, the greater the ratio of price to production cost, the greater the desired proportional expansion. And the greater the price-cost ratio, the greater the firm's retained earnings and the greater its ability to persuade the capital market to provide finance. However, R&D expenditures, like production costs, reduce the funds available for investment.

Since this is an industry in which all firms produce the identical product, it makes better sense to see firms as having "quantity policies" rather than as having "price policies." Quantity policies are made operative through the firm's investment decisions. (Recall that we have assumed that a firm always operates at full capacity.) Firms with large market shares recognize that their expansion can spoil their own market. The larger a firm's current market share, the greater must be the price-cost ratio needed to induce a given desired proportional expansion. By varying the shape of this relationship, a spectrum of possible patterns of investment behavior may be represented. These patterns may be interpreted as reflecting the assumptions of the firm regarding the effect that an increase in its output will have on the industry price. In the simulation runs analyzed later in this chapter, the assumption involves a correct perception that the industry demand curve is of unitary elasticity and a belief that the remainder of the industry responds along a supply curve that is also of unitary elasticity. In the following chapters, we contrast two patterns, one of which reflects somewhat greater wariness about spoiling the market than the assumption just described and the other of which involves no wariness at all. The first may be termed a "Cournot" strategy: a firm picks a target capital stock on the basis of a correct appraisal of the industry demand elasticity and a belief that the other firms will hold output constant. In the second pattern the firm behaves as if it believed that the price would not be affected at all by its own output changes; that is, it behaves as a price taker.

More formally, the model has the following structure.

(1) $Q_{it} = A_{it}K_{it}$.

The output of firm i at time t equals its capital stock times the productivity of the technique it is employing.

(2a) $Q_t = \sum Q_{it} = \sum A_{it}K_{it}$;

(2b) $P_t = D(Q_t)$.

Industry output is the sum of individual firm outputs. Price is determined by industry output, given the product demand-price function, $D(\cdot)$.

(3) $\pi_{it} = (P_t A_{it} - c - r_{im} - r_{in})$.

The profit on capital of that firm equals product price times output per unit of capital, minus production costs (including capital rental) per unit of capital, minus imitative and innovative R&D costs per unit of capital,

R&D activity generates new productivity levels by a two-stage random process. The first stage may be characterized by independent random variables d_{imt} and d_{int} that take on the values one or zero according to whether firm i does or does not get an imitation or innovation draw in period t. Success in getting such draws occurs with respective probabilities:

(4) $Pr(d_{imt} = 1) = a_m r_{im} K_{it}$

(5) $Pr(d_{int} = 1) = a_n r_{in} K_{it}$.

(Parameters are chosen so that the upper-bound probability of one is not encountered.) If a firm does get an imitation draw, it then has the option of observing and copying industry best practice. If a firm gets an innovation draw, it samples from a distribution of technological opportunities, $F(A; t, A_{it})$. This distribution is a function of time and is independent of a firm's prevailing technique in the science-based case. It is independent of time *per se* but dependent on the firm's prevailing technique in the cumulative technology case.

For a firm that obtains both an imitation and innovation draw in the particular period, the productivity level of following periods is given by:

(6) $A_{i(t+1)} = \text{Max}(A_{it}, \hat{A}_t, \tilde{A}_{it})$.

Here $\hat{A}_t$ is the highest (best practice) productivity level in the industry in period t, and $\tilde{A}_{it}$ is a random variable that is the result of the innovation draw. Of course, the firm may fail to obtain an imitation draw, an innovation draw, or both, in which cases the menu from which next-period productivity is drawn is shorter.

A firm's desired expansion or contraction is determined by the ratio of price to production cost, $P/(c/A)$—or, equivalently, the percentage margin over cost—and its market share. But a firm's ability to finance its investment is constrained by its profitability, which is affected by its R&D outlays as well as by revenues and production costs.

(7) $K_{i(t+1)} = I\left(\dfrac{P_t A_{it}}{c}, \dfrac{Q_{it}}{Q_t}, \pi_{it}\right) + (1 - \delta) K_{it}$.

Here, δ is the physical depreciation rate, and the gross investment function $I(\cdot)$ is constrained to be nonnegative. It is nondecreasing in its first argument and nonincreasing in the other two. Also, we assume that

$$\lim_{s \to 0} I(1, s, 0) = 0.$$

In other words, a firm that has price equal to unit cost, negligible market share, zero R&D expense and hence zero profit will have zero net investment.

There are two key differences between our model and other recent formal models of Schumpeterian competition—for example, those surveyed in Kamien and Schwartz (1975, 1981) or that presented by Dasgupta and Stiglitz (1980) or Flaherty (1980). The strategies or policies assumed of our firms are not derived from any maximization calculations, and the industry is not assumed to be in equilibrium.

An essential aspect of real Schumpeterian competition is that firms do not know *ex ante* whether it pays to try to be an innovator or an imitator, or what levels of R&D expenditures might be appropriate. Indeed, the answer to this question for any single firm depends on the choices made by other firms, and reality does not contain any provisions for firms to test out their policies before adopting them. Thus, there is little reason to expect equilibrium policy configurations to arise. Only the course of events over time will determine and reveal what strategies are the better ones. And even the verdict of hindsight may be less than clear, for differences in luck will make the same policies brilliantly successful for some firms and dismal failures for others.

To understand the *process* of industry evolution, we have chosen to focus on cases in which firm R&D policies are strictly constant over time. This might be defended as an approximation of empirical reality by some combination of arguments involving high setup and adjustment costs in real R&D programs, bureaucratic sluggishness, and difficulties in distinguishing signal from noise in the feedback on a prevailing policy. But in our view a more fundamental justification for this approach is methodological. If competition is aggressive enough and the profitability differences among policies are large enough, differential firm growth will soon make the better policies dominate the scene, regardless of whether individual firms adjust or not. If, however, the model sets the stage for an evolutionary struggle that is quite protracted (as those in reality often are), then admitting policy change at the individual firm level is unlikely to change the general industry environment much—and it certainly complicates the task of understanding the dynamic process. To forgo the attempt to understand the process, as orthodoxy does, is to leave open the question of the promptness and efficacy of the forces pressing the system toward equilibrium. It is also to overlook the shaping role of differential firm growth as a determinant of the sort of equilibrium toward which the industry may be moving. While it would not be difficult to augment the model by admitting adaptive R&D policies, in order to clarify the evolutionary role of selection we have chosen not to do this. On the same ground, we have devoted our attention to cases in which entry is barred.

The model defines a stochastic dynamic system in which, over time, productivity levels tend to rise and unit production costs tend to fall as better technologies are found. As a result of these dynamic forces, price tends to fall and industry output tends to rise over time. Relatively profitable firms expand and unprofitable ones contract, and those that do innovative R&D may thrive or decline. In turn, their fate influences the flow of innovations.

3. BEHAVIOR OF THE MODEL IN SPECIAL CASES

Simulation will be the principal tool employed to explore the model. However, in certain simple cases it is possible to achieve analytic results.

Consider first the behavior of the model when firms make no efforts to obtain new techniques—that is, when r_{ia} and r_{im} are set to zero in all firms and all firms have the same unit production costs. If entry is impossible or is restricted to being strictly imitative of extant firms, the model's behavior becomes independent of latent productivity. Also, since the only stochastic features of the full model are associated with the occurrence of technical change, the circumscribed model is fully deterministic. Since R&D expenses are the only non-production costs, positive net investment can always be financed if price is above unit cost. If all firms have identical productivity and unit cost levels, there will be equilibria in which N firms share the market equally. The equilibrium price-cost ratio will be determined by the investment equation (7), when $K_{i(t+1)} = K_{it}$, $A_{it} = A$, and $Q_{it}/Q = 1/N$ for all firms.

The picture is more complex if the firms have different productivity levels A_{it} and hence different unit cost levels. If N different firms have N different cost levels but the differences are small, there can be equilibria in which all N firms survive but in which output shares are ranked inversely with unit cost levels. At the other extreme, suppose there are N_1 firms at the lowest-cost level. Consider this lowest unit cost marked up by the equilibrium margin determined in the manner just described, with $Q_{it}/Q = 1/N_1$. If this value is below the next-to-lowest unit cost, then the "natural selection" process will operate unimpeded by the output restraint of the lowest-cost firms: they will drive the others entirely out of the market and will wind up sharing the market among themselves. This result will necessarily occur if N_1 is sufficiently large, since the equilibrium price-cost ratio tends to one as Q_i/Q tends to zero.

Now suppose that r_{in} is zero but that all firms display the same positive r_{im}. The effects of the selection mechanism will be supplemented by imitative search. Ultimately, all surviving firms will display the same unit cost level, which will be the lowest of those displayed in the initial conditions (assuming that no mistakes are made in technique comparisons). The number of surviving firms (and hence the equilibrium margin) will depend on the exit specifications. If declining firms exit in finite time, the randomness of the imitation process may be reflected in a range of equilibrium results.

If we now admit positive values of r_{in}, the link to latent productivity comes into play and things become a great deal more complicated. Much depends, obviously, on the relation between initial firm productivity levels and latent productivity and on the time path of latent productivity. Radically different patterns of "historical" development of the industry are implied by the different assumptions, and we contend that these differences are worthy of analysis and suggestive of possible interpretations of real events. For present purposes, however, the temptations of steady-state analysis are irresistible. Let us discuss what happens when latent productivity is advancing at a constant exponential rate.

Consider, specifically, the simplified model that arises if the investment mechanism (as well as entry and exit) is suppressed and firms remain the same size forever. This makes productivity behavior independent of price and profitability. Each firm will have characteristic (positive) levels of R&D expenditure, constant over time. Asymptotically, the average rate of productivity increase in each individual firm will equal the rate of increase of latent productivity. In other words, each firm's productivity level will fluctuate around a particular long-run average ratio to latent productivity. Of course, the larger the firm's R&D expenditures, the higher that ratio will be. But any maintained rate of expenditure—no matter how small—will yield, asymptotically, the same growth rate. This is because the expected productivity gain from an innovation or imitation draw keeps increasing as the firm falls further behind latent productivity, or further behind other firms, and ultimately is sufficiently large to compensate for the long average interval between draws.

If we abandon the simplifying assumption that individual firms stay the same size, the phenomena that appear include not only those of differential firm growth—which are central to our evolutionary analysis—but also certain gross responses to demand by the industry as a whole. Assuming that demand is constant over time, a demand function of constant unitary elasticity has special significance: a given percentage increase in productivity produces the same percentage decrease in unit cost and price, leaving the industry capital stock in the same state of equilibrium or disequilibrium it was before. That is, with unitary elasticity of demand, the advance of productivity does not in itself produce a trend in industry capital. By contrast, if demand elasticity is constant and greater than unity, productivity advance raises the price-cost ratio (at a given capital stock) and thus leads to an increased capital stock. Since information-seeking efforts are proportioned to capital, this mechanism tends over time to produce an increase in the ratio of realized to latent productivity. The corresponding implications of inelastic demand, or demand growth or decline, are obvious.

4. SIMULATION OF COMPETITION BETWEEN INNOVATORS AND IMITATORS

In the remainder of this chapter we report and analyze certain results of a simulation experiment using the model. This experiment is a preliminary exploration of the influence of initial market structure on the innovative and price performance of the industry and on the evolution of industry structure over time. Other experiments that are focused on particular issues, some of which come into view as a result of this set of runs, are discussed in the following two chapters.

In the simulations reported here, five different sets of initial conditions were examined, with two, four, eight, sixteen, and thirty-two firms in the industry. In each condition half of the firms spend on R&D for innovation as well as for imitation, and the other half spend only on imitative R&D. For any given setting all the firms are of equal size initially and have the same productivity level, which is equal to the level of latent productivity. While all firms have the same initial production costs, the firms that spend on innovative as well as imitative R&D have higher total costs per unit of output, at least initially. The initial total capital stock (and the stocks of each firm) were chosen so that, for each initial structure, desired total net investment was zero. Since a smaller margin over production cost induces positive investment when a firm's market share is small compared to when it is large, this means that total capital is larger initially and initial price is lower, the larger the number of firms. The levels of r_{in}

and r_{im} are adjusted to compensate for the difference in initial capital, so that the initial levels of total innovation expense and total imitation expense are the same in all runs. Thus, the initial expected values of innovation draws and imitation draws are the same under all initial conditions; in this sense, the industry is initially equally progressive under all initial conditions.

In addition to differences in the number of firms and in initial industry output and price, we also explored differences between two regimes of finance for firm investment. Under one regime a firm can borrow up to 2.5 times its own net profits for financing investment. Under the other regime, firm's borrowings were limited to a matching of their profits.

Thus, there are ten experimental conditions in all—five market structures times two financial regimes. Each condition was run five times. The runs lasted 101 periods each—100 periods after initial conditions. For the particular parameter values chosen, a period can be thought of as corresponding to a quarter of a year; hence, the computer runs are of twenty-five years.

The runs here relate to an industry with science-based technology in which latent productivity advances at 1 percent a quarter or 4 percent a year. Values of r_{in} for the innovative firms correspond to an R&D-sales ratio of about .12, which by empirical standards is high. This high value was chosen so that the cost of doing innovative R&D would stand out clearly in the initial experiments. The probability of innovative R&D success was set so that the industry as a whole averaged about two innovative finds per year, at initial conditions. And at initial conditions, an imitation draw was about as likely for the industry as a whole as an innovative draw.

The elasticity of demand for the industry's product was set equal to one. This is an important fact in understanding the simulation runs, since it meant that total capital in the industry tended to stay relatively constant over the runs. Growing productivity meant falling prices and growing output, but relatively constant input (in this case, capital input). As a result, the average number of imitation draws per period tended to be roughly constant over the run. The average number of innovative draws tended to grow or decline as the share of industry capital accounted for by innovators grew or declined.[3]

With the vision of hindsight, we know that the parameter settings for this particular set of runs—in particular, the rate of growth of latent productivity, the productivity of innovative R&D in terms of the

---

3. A full quantitative statement of the model employed for the simulation runs of this chapter is contained in Appendix 1 at the end of this chapter.

probability of finding a new technique per dollar of expenditure, and the productivity of imitative R&D expenditure in terms of the probability of successful imitation per dollar—defined a regime in which innovative R&D is somewhat unprofitable on average. In Chapter 14 we will explore the conditions that determine whether or not innovative R&D is profitable and the difference it makes to overall industry performance. But here, keeping in mind that the climate is not favorable to innovative R&D, we can ask two sets of questions.

First, how does industry performance over a considerable number of periods depend on the initial concentration of the industry? There are several different performance variables worth examining. One is the time path of the best practice (highest productivity) in the industry. Another is the time path of average practice (average productivity). Also, it seems important to consider the effect of initial concentration on the average markup over production costs in the industry. And, finally, what happens to the price is obviously of considerable interest.

Second, it is interesting to explore the effects of initial concentration on the way in which industry structure evolves over time. In this context, where innovative R&D is not profitable, in what way does the survivability of firms that do innovative R&D depend on initial concentration? More generally, which initial structures tend to be stable and which unstable? Do the initially unconcentrated structures tend to concentrate over time? Do the initially concentrated structures tend to concentrate further?

These are the kinds of questions we will be exploring. Our preliminary answers will sharpen intuition regarding the processes of dynamic competition in our model industry and raise some specific questions that we will explore in subsequent runs.

Performance

Figures 12.1–12.6 show various performance variables as a function of initial structure. The solid line shows average performance of the five runs in which the firms had considerable access to bank credit (BANK = 2.5). The dotted line shows average performance when bank credit was more limited (BANK = 1.0).[4] All values shown are at the end of the run and are means over five runs.

Figure 12.1 shows best-practice productivity in period 101. In this model the evolution of best practice (or at least best practice at the end of the run) does not appear to depend upon initial concentration.

---

4. The numerical data underlying the figures, and some additional information on the runs, are presented in Appendix 2.

Figure 12.2 shows average productivity at the end of the run as a function of initial concentration. Figure 12.3 shows the "average productivity gap," defined as the geometric mean over time of the ratio of average productivity to latent productivity, minus one. Both of these indices show that average productivity toward the end of the run (and apparently over a considerable part of the run) was lower when there were many firms than when there were few. Thus, the small-numbers cases were marked by a considerably higher ratio of average productivity to best-practice productivity than were the large-numbers cases. Since the initial productivity levels of all firms were the same under all initial conditions, average productivity apparently rose more rapidly and average production costs declined more rapidly in the small-numbers cases than in the large-numbers cases.

While this latter result is consistent with the Schumpeterian hypothesis, the fact that growth of best-practice productivity apparently is invariant to initial industry structure suggests that something different might be going on. Figure 12.4 displays cumulative innovative R&D expenditure over the course of the run, for the different initial market structures. Neither end-period best-practice productivity nor average-practice productivity seems well correlated with innovative R&D outlays of the industry.

That the evolution of best-practice productivity is not strongly sensitive to total industry innovative R&D expenditures or to in-

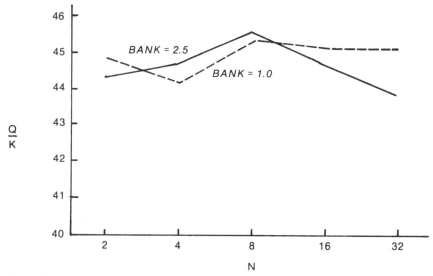

12.1   Best-practice productivity.

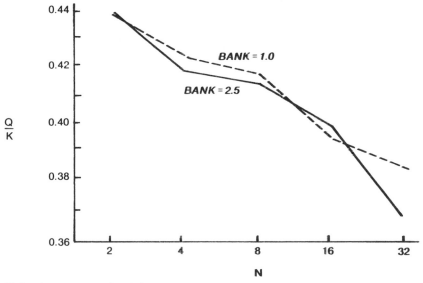

12.2   Average productivity.

dustry structure can be partially explained as follows. In the version
of the model under exploration here, the driving force of technological advance in the industry is growth of latent productivity,
which is occurring as a result of forces exogenous to the actions of the
firms in the industry. The innovative R&D efforts of the firms in the
industry take advantage, as it were, of new technological opportuni-

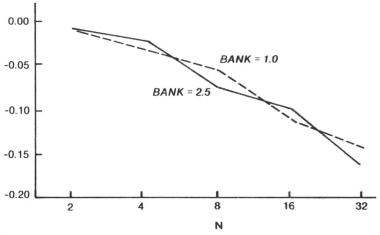

12.3   Average productivity gap.

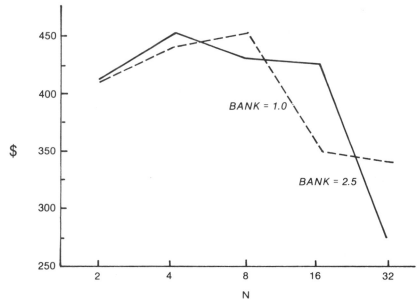

12.4   Cumulative expenditure on innovative R&D.

ties that have been created elsewhere. Greater R&D expenditure within the industry means that latent productivity is tracked more smoothly, but aside from that the path of best-practice productivity is unlikely to be much higher than it is when industry R&D expenditures are less. In the situation explored in these runs, which we have called the "science-based industry" case, there are sharply diminishing returns to industry R&D expenditure. The situation might be quite different when there is no exogenous growth of technological opportunities and when technological advance in the industry builds on itself—what we call the "cumulative technology" case. We shall explore the differences in Chapter 14. However, it is apparent that in the particular runs considered here, enough innovative R&D was going on even in the runs of sixteen and thirty-two firms so that latent productivity is being tracked reasonably well by best practice.

Why, then, is average productivity so sensitive to industry structure? The answer relates, ultimately, to the particular view of the nature of the firm that is implicit in our model—that is, to the theoretical significance of the firm as an institution. Within the boundaries of a firm, technical information that is available for use with one unit of capital is equally and costlessly applicable to all other units. On the other hand, scarce resources are consumed by the innovation and imitation processes that first bring new information into the firm. No doubt this contrast is overdrawn in our model, as theoretical contrasts usually are. But it is certainly broadly consistent with the view of the firm that we set forth in Part II.

More specifically, the effect on average productivity arises in the following way. Innovative R&D effort yields, from time to time, superior techniques that temporarily define "best practice." The larger the innovator relative to the industry, the larger the immediate effect of such a technical change on industry average productivity. Similarly, when a new technique is imitated, the larger the imitator relative to the industry, the larger the impact on industry average productivity of each successive imitation of the new technique. In the model, the rate at which acts of imitation (imitation draws) occur is roughly independent of industry structure. Thus the lessening of the effect of each individual draw, because of the smaller amount of capital affected when the number of firms is larger, is fully reflected in industry average productivity. For a given level of industry expenditure on innovative R&D, the productivity level associated with best-practice technique is independent of industry structure. But the gap between average and best-practice productivity is larger in the more fragmented structure because of the reduced scope of application of individual successes in innovation and imitation.

Since there will always be at least one innovating firm among those that have the best-practice productivity level at a given time, one might expect that a widening gap between best practice and average productivity would be associated with a widening gap between the average productivity of innovators as compared to imitators. Figure 12.5 shows that this expectation is borne out—up to a point. But the innovators' superiority in productivity is smaller in the case of thirty-two firms than it is in the eight-firm case. This result presumably reflects the fact that the selection forces are operating strongly against the innovators in the thirty-two-firm case. A small innovative firm that has not actually had a success recently is more likely to be using out-of-date techniques than is a larger imitator that successfully plays the "fast second" strategy.

Thus, in this model a more competitively structured industry does lead to a poorer productivity performance than does an industry that is more concentrated. But the reason is not the one commonly associated with the Schumpeterian hypothesis: that best-pricatice technology evolves more slowly in the many-firm case than in the few-firm case. It is that there is a much larger gap between best practice and average practice in the case where industry capital is fragmented than there is in the case where it is concentrated.

While average production costs are higher in the many-firm case, Figure 12.6 shows that the average price-cost margin is lower where

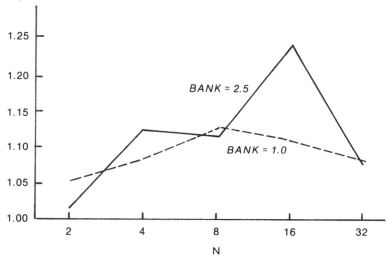

12.5   Ratio of average productivity: innovators/imitators.

industry structure is more competitive. Figure 12.7, which displays total net worth, shows the same thing: the excess-profit rate (and net worth) is higher when the industry starts concentrated than when it starts unconcentrated. The reason is right out of the textbooks: perceived market power associated with larger market shares has led to investment restraint and thus to higher prices and profit margins.

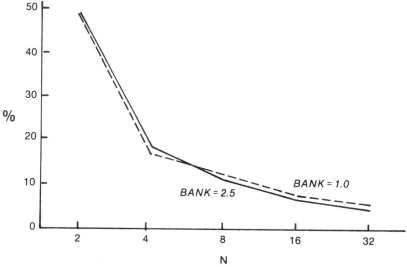

12.6   Percentage margin over average cost.

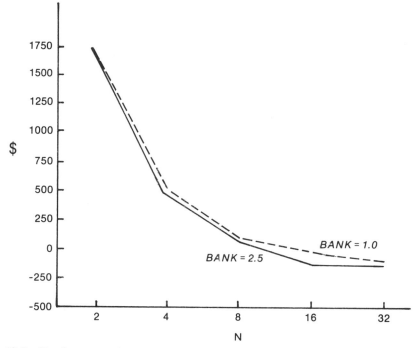

12.7   Total net worth.

Figure 12.8 shows end-of-run price in the industry as a U-shaped function of the number of firms. Up to a point, in these runs at least, the lower margin, which is associated with more competitive structure, more than offsets the higher unit production costs. However, the curve appears to turn upward as the industry gets very competitive. Beyond eight firms, the additional competition yields only limited gains in terms of lower margins, and further deconcentration entails costs in terms of lower average productivity.

Evolution of Structure

We already have remarked that the parameter settings of these runs define a context in which innovative R&D is not profitable. Figure 12.9 presents the research expense recovery rate. This is a simple descriptive measure of the extent to which firms that do innovative R&D recapture, in transient profits derived from superior productivity, the funds they spend on R&D. The measure is defined as the difference between the final net worths of innovators and imitators, divided by cumulative R&D expense, plus one. The value of 1.0 corresponds, obviously, to a case in which the final net worths of inno-

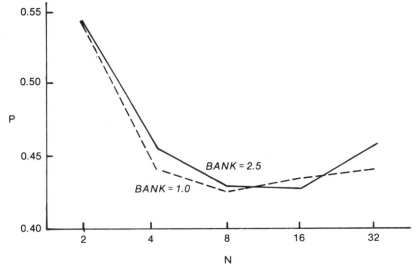

12.8   Price.

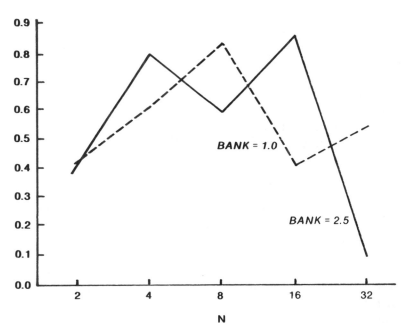

12.9   Innovation expense recovery rate.

vators and imitators are equal. In this case the productivity advantages gained from innovative R&D are worth just enough to be offset by the cost of R&D. A value of 0.5 indicates that the pecuniary benefit that innovators derive from their R&D amounts to only half of what they spend. Figure 12.9 shows that, in general, innovative R&D does not pay in these runs. The net worth differences between innovative firms and firms that do no innovative R&D are displayed in Figure 12.10. Essentially they mirror the results of the previous figure.

A straightforward application of the selection argument would lead one to expect, given the profitability differential, that the firms that undertook innovative R&D would be driven out of business. Figure 12.11 shows that this is too simple. Despite their relative unprofitability compared with firms that did only imitative R&D, in the small-numbers cases the innovators accounted for more than half of the industry's capital stock toward the end of the run. Only in the thirty-two-firm case was the unprofitability of innovative R&D clearly reflected in the innovators' capital share.

It is apparent that this is the consequence of two factors. First, in the small-numbers cases competition among firms was sufficiently restrained so that, even though the innovators were not as profitable as the imitators, they still made positive profits. The reluctance of large profitable firms to expand their capital stock and thus "spoil the market" provided a shelter for firms that were less profitable. Sec-

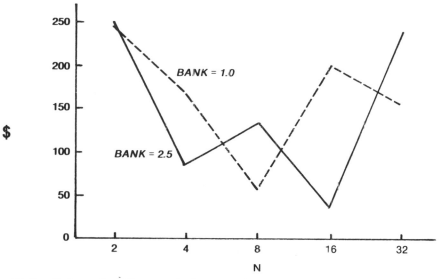

12.10 Net worth difference: imitators − innovators.

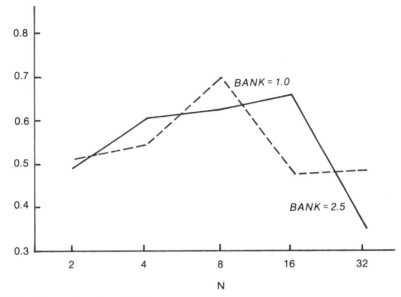

12.11 Innovators' capital share.

ond, we have assumed in this model that a firm's desire to expand its
capacity for production is tied to the margin between prices and production costs. For two firms with the same market share, the firm
with the lower production cost will have a higher target output and
capital stock than the firm with the higher production cost, even
though including R&D expenditures the former may have higher
total cost per unit of output than the latter. When profits are high,
there is no financial constraint to prevent the difference in targets
from being reflected in reality.

The latter mechanism is the explanation for the fact that the innovators' capital share actually exceeds 0.5 in most of the runs. But on
the more basic issue of the survival of the innovators, it is the investment restraint associated with the concentrated structure that is the
key. If the more profitable firms were more aggressive in expanding
their capacity even when they were large, it appears that the firms
that did innovative R&D would indeed be gradually run out of business. The consequences of this might not be too serious if the evolution of technology in the industry were science-based, as in the runs
here, but it might be serious if the technological regime were cumulative. We shall explore these questions in a later chapter.

What can one say about the evolution of economic structure more
generally? While runs that started out with a highly concentrated
market structure tended to remain concentrated, there was a marked

increase in concentration in the runs with an unconcentrated initial structure. Figure 12.12 displays end-of-run values of the "Herfindahl numbers equivalent." This is a measure of output concentration in the industry; intuitively it is the number of firms in an industry of equal-sized firms that has the same degree of concentration as the actual industry according to the Herfindahl-Hirschman measure. Thus, the fact that the numbers equivalent is very close to 2.0 in all the duopoly cases is a reflection of the fact that the two firms do remain very nearly equal in size in these cases. In the four-firm cases, there is a slight tendency for concentration to increase over the run. This tendency becomes pronounced beginning with the eight-firm cases. In the ten runs with thirty-two firms, the largest final value for the numbers equivalent is a level of concentration comparable to the consequences of the disappearance of well over half of the firms initially in business, if the remainder were of equal size. And, as we have seen above, the bulk of the concentration increase involved the decline of firms who had policies of investing in innovative R&D.

In this chapter we have explored the behavior of our model of Schumpeterian competition with various initial industry structures in a context where, in general, innovative R&D was not profitable. We considered both how industry performance was influenced by initial industry structure, and how industry structure evolved over time. In Chapter 13 we will consider in more detail questions relating to the evolution of industry structure. In Chapter 14 we will consider in more detail the structure-performance links.

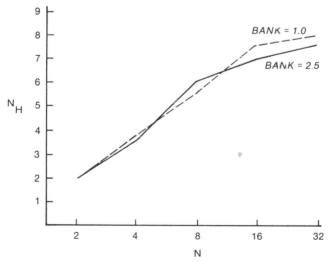

12.12   Herfindahl numbers equivalent.

APPENDIX 1

Table 12.1 displays the initial values for firm capital stocks, and the values of the parameters that govern firm expenditure on innovative and imitative R&D. As explained in the text, the latter are adjusted to compensate for initial differences in industry capital, which itself is adjusted to maintain zero desired net investment in the initial state. The result is that industry expenditures on R&D are constant across experimental conditions. Also, the initial value of latent productivity is .16 in all experimental conditions, and all firms have productivity level .16 initially.

Table 12.1.   Initial values of firm capital stocks and values of R&D parameters.

	Number of firms				
	2	4	8	16	32
K	139.58	89.70	48.85	25.34	12.89
r_{im}	0.00143	0.00112	0.00102	0.00099	0.00097
$r_{in}{}^a$	0.0287	0.0223	0.0205	0.0197	0.0194

a. Values shown are for innovators only; noninnovators have $r_{in} = 0$.

We set forth here a characterization of the simulation model that incorporates the parameter settings used in the particular runs reported in this chapter. Equation numbers below correspond to those in the text, and explanations provided in the text are not repeated.

(1) $Q_{it} = A_{it} K_{it}$

(2a) $Q_t = \sum Q_{it}$

(2b) $P_t = 67/Q_t$

(3) $\pi_{it} = P_t A_{it} - .16 - r_{im} - r_{in}$

(4) $Pr(d_{imt} = 1) = 1.25 \, r_{im} K_{it}$

(5) $Pr(d_{int} = 1) = .125 \, r_{in} K_{it}$

(6) $A_i(t + 1) = \text{Max}(A_{it}, d_{imt} \hat{A}_t, d_{int} \tilde{A}_{it})$, where $\hat{A}_t = \text{Max}_i(A_{it})$, and $\log(\tilde{A}_{it})$ has the normal distribution $N(\lambda(t), \sigma^2)$, with $\lambda(t) = .16 + .01t$, and $\sigma = .05$.

(7) $K_{i(t+1)} = I\left(\dfrac{P_t A_{it}}{.16}, \dfrac{Q_{it}}{Q_t}, \pi_{it}\right) K_{it} + .97 \, K_{it}$

where π_{it} is given by (3) above, and

$$I(\rho, s, \pi) = \mathrm{Max}\left[0, \mathrm{Min}\left(\left(1.03 - \frac{2-s}{\rho\,(2-2s)}\right), f(\pi)\right)\right]$$

$$f(\pi) = \begin{cases} .03 + \pi & \text{for } \pi \leq 0 \\ .03 + 2\pi & \text{for } \pi > 0 \text{ and BANK} = 1 \\ .03 + 3.5\pi & \text{for } \pi > 0 \text{ and BANK} = 2.5 \end{cases}$$

APPENDIX 2

The precise numerical values of the five-run means graphed in Figures 12.1–12.12 are set forth in the first twelve lines of Table 12.2. Also shown, in parentheses, are the standard deviations of the five-run samples. A noteworthy pattern in the standard deviations is that, for several variables, the run-to-run variability in results is much smaller in the duopoly cases than in other cases. The innovation expense recovery rate (variable 9) and the innovators' capital share (variable 11) are examples of this phenomenon.

Variable 13 is the industry rate of excess return at the end of the run, expressed as a percentage rate per quarter. Variable 14 is cumulative borrowing. It is apparent that the availability of financing is a much more significant consideration when the number of firms is large than when it is small. Under more nearly competitive conditions, firms have little in the way of excess returns to finance investment; also, firms with production cost advantages have large desired investment because they are essentially price takers. The last four variables in Table 12.2 are set forth here for purposes of comparison with results in Chapter 14. Variables 15 and 16 are the output shares of the first- and second-largest innovator firms, while variables 17 and 18 are output shares of the first- and second-largest imitator firms. It is interesting that the final size of the largest firms of each type is relatively insensitive to the initial firm sizes (or number of firms). For example, the eightfold increase in the number of firms from four to thirty-two is reflected in only a 15 percent decline in the average market share of the largest imitator at the end of the run, and a decline of roughly a third in the share of the largest innovator.

Table 12.2. Means and standard deviations of five-run samples (values at end of run).

	BANK	Number of firms				
		2	4	8	16	32
1. BEST PRAC A	1.0	0.449	0.442	0.454	0.451	0.451
		(0.0154)	(0.0127)	(0.0248)	(0.0254)	(0.0163)
	2.5	0.443	0.447	0.456	0.446	0.438
		(0.0137)	(0.0148)	(0.0263)	(0.0190)	(0.0184)
2. AV A	1.0	0.438	0.423	0.418	0.395	0.385
		(0.0096)	(0.0138)	(0.0066)	(0.0210)	(0.0126)
	2.5	0.439	0.417	0.414	0.398	0.368
		(0.0195)	(0.0130)	(0.0130)	(0.0107)	(0.0130)
3. AV A GAP	1.0	−0.009	−0.044	−0.057	−0.116	−0.145
		(0.0075)	(0.0121)	(0.0083)	(0.0095)	(0.0074)
	2.5	−0.007	−0.028	−0.069	−0.098	−0.157
		(0.0130)	(0.0086)	(0.0147)	(0.0090)	(0.0145)
4. IN R&D SUM	1.0	412.8	441.7	445.7	353.9	343.9
		(0.6)	(5.7)	(48.0)	(53.4)	(21.6)
	2.5	413.1	456.1	435.0	432.8	278.6
		(0.4)	(14.2)	(78.3)	(53.3)	(27.3)
5. AV A: IN/IM	1.0	1.054	1.086	1.130	1.111	1.088
		(0.085)	(0.067)	(0.051)	(0.102)	(0.054)
	2.5	1.018	1.129	1.120	1.246	1.085
		(0.037)	(0.090)	(0.098)	(0.177)	(0.108)

6. MARGIN AV COST (%)	1.0	49.2	17.5	11.5	7.3	6.8
		(3.41)	(1.32)	(0.91)	(1.43)	(2.03)
	2.5	49.6	18.8	11.0	6.1	4.4
		(1.01)	(1.63)	(1.39)	(2.58)	(1.59)
7. TOT NET W	1.0	1745	515	119	−21	−103
		(5.5)	(19.4)	(63.3)	(51.1)	(73.9)
	2.5	1741	500	71	−127	−159
		(4.9)	(40.2)	(75.4)	(26.3)	(38.7)
8. P	1.0	0.545	0.444	0.427	0.435	0.444
		(0.0235)	(0.0137)	(0.0059)	(0.0263)	(0.0190)
	2.5	0.546	0.456	0.429	0.427	0.456
		(0.0277)	(0.0173)	(0.0117)	(0.0168)	(0.0157)
9. IN EX RECOV	1.0	0.417	0.618	0.847	0.418	0.556
		(0.075)	(0.056)	(0.280)	(0.373)	(0.226)
	2.5	0.402	0.802	0.599	0.874	0.124
		(0.053)	(0.250)	(0.524)	(0.240)	(0.303)
10. NET W: IM − IN	1.0	240	169	59	191	152
		(30.8)	(22.7)	(114.6)	(123.4)	(72.1)
	2.5	247	87	133	45	238
		(21.7)	(114.2)	(175.4)	(82.9)	(63.6)
11. CAP SHR: IN	1.0	0.504	0.564	0.716	0.478	0.484
		(0.009)	(0.027)	(0.110)	(0.160)	(0.091)
	2.5	0.500	0.618	0.628	0.666	0.344
		(0.007)	(0.055)	(0.164)	(0.093)	(0.114)

Table 12.2 continued.

	BANK	Number of firms				
		2	4	8	16	32
12. H NUM EQV: K	1.0	1.998	3.816	5.560	7.574	7.991
		(0.002)	(0.203)	(0.693)	(0.278)	(1.152)
	2.5	1.999	3.662	6.123	6.991	7.599
		(0.000)	(0.155)	(1.063)	(0.760)	(1.071)
13. EX RET (%/QTR)	1.0	6.27	1.42	0.28	0.13	0.48
		(0.533)	(0.155)	(0.231)	(0.431)	(0.308)
	2.5	6.35	1.52	.37	-.43	.04
		(0.141)	(0.155)	(0.172)	(0.479)	(0.278)
14. CUM BORROW	1.0	55.1	100.7	135.4	186.4	212.4
		(12.45)	(8.80)	(22.84)	(11.73)	(12.33)
	2.5	65.2	136.4	207.8	289.3	326.6
		(11.16)	(19.47)	(34.97)	(15.02)	(26.16)
15. Q SHR: IN1	1.0	0.518	0.326	0.246	0.170	0.222
		(0.030)	(0.036)	(0.038)	(0.063)	(0.097)
	2.5	0.504	0.347	0.248	0.240	0.200
		(0.016)	(0.034)	(0.069)	(0.027)	(0.115)
16. Q SHR: IN2	1.0	n.a.	0.257	0.222	0.120	0.084
			(0.014)	(0.026)	(0.056)	(0.025)
	2.5	n.a.	0.299	0.198	0.198	0.057
			(0.039)	(0.061)	(0.030)	(0.040)

17. Q SHR: IM1	1.0	0.482 (0.030)	0.251 (0.033)	0.156 (0.048)	0.214 (0.069)	0.213 (0.040)
	2.5	0.494 (0.014)	0.242 (0.050)	0.122 (0.046)	0.132 (0.058)	0.214 (0.064)
18. Q SHR: IM2	1.0	n.a.	0.167 (0.055)	0.080 (0.060)	0.129 (0.055)	0.127 (0.049)
	2.5	n.a.	0.112 (0.024)	0.103 (0.042)	0.093 (0.040)	0.127 (0.058)

13

Forces Generating and Limiting Concentration under Schumpeterian Competition

A FEATURE of several of the models that have been developed thus far is that the distribution of firm sizes tends to evolve over time, reflecting the pattern of winners and losers in the game of dynamic competition. Thus, in the growth model explored in Chapter 9 there was a tendency for concentration to develop. In the model of Schumpeterian competition examined in Chapter 12 there was a noticeable tendency for industry structures that originally were unconcentrated to show growing concentration over the course of the runs. On the other hand, the structures that started out concentrated appeared to be more stable.

The basic causal mechanism is clear enough. Supranormal profits are the reward for successful innovation. To the extent that growth is keyed to profitability, successful innovators grow in relation to other firms. If a firm is a successful innovator frequently enough or if one of its innovations is dominant enough, the consequences of successful innovation may be a highly concentrated industry structure. However, the models we have explored thus far suggest that the growth of concentration is not inevitable, and we have identified a number of causal factors that appear to affect it. In Chapter 9, for example, growth of concentration was significantly smaller when firms focused their searches on imitating rather than on innovating. We shall explore these relationships systematically.[1]

A few studies have addressed the kinds of causal mechanisms we

---

1. Much of the analysis in this chapter was first presented in Nelson and Winter (1978).

are concerned with here. Mansfield (1962) examined empirically the question of whether or not successful innovators tend to grow faster than other firms and, if they do, the persistence of their advantage. He found that they do tend to grow faster, but that their advantage tends to decrease over time. Since his exploration was empirical and not theoretical, he did not explore the factors that would make the growth rate differential between innovators and noninnovators large rather than small or persistent rather than transient. Relatedly he did not consider the effect of these kinds of variables on the size distribution of firms that would evolve. There are some propositions about this. Phillips (1971) proposed that in an industry, such as commercial aircraft manufacturing, in which opportunities for major technological advance occur infrequently and in which there are significant and durable advantages to the firm that makes an advance first, a high degree of concentration is likely to develop. Williamson (1972) discussed antitrust problems that may result from a circumstance in which past innovativenesses of a firm lead to its market domination and to blockaded entry but in which that firm no longer is creative.

For the purpose of exploring the dynamic forces in Schumpeterian competition that affect concentration, it is useful to consider the model developed in the preceding chapter as a member of the class of stochastic models of the firm-size distribution. The basic point of departure for all such models is the simple stochastic process that in economics is associated with the term "Gibrat's law." If the population of firms is constant, if period-to-period firm growth rates are generated by probability distributions that are independent from firm to firm but the same for all firms and over all periods (in particular, if there is no relationship between firm size and the distribution of growth rates and no serial correlation), the distribution of firm sizes will approach a log normal distribution. Stochastic models aimed at "explaining" the distribution of firm sizes are all akin to Gibrat's law, but all have various departures built in to better match empirical observations about growth rates of firms or to better fit the actual size distributions.

The model presented in the preceding chapter deviates from Gibrat's law in a number of respects. Two are of special importance. First, the model involves mechanisms that may be expected to produce serial correlation of growth rates. Second, the distributions of firm growth rates and of firm size (market share) are not independent.

The serial correlation stems from the fact that a firm with a significantly better than average (worse than average) technology today also is likely to have a better (worse) one tomorrow. For this reason, profit rates and growth will be serially correlated. Such correlation would exist in our model even if it were assumed that R&D expenditure were insensitive to firm size and that desired markups also were unrelated to firm size. But in our model, neither R&D expenditures nor investment policies are insensitive to firm size. If all firms have the same R&D policy (which will be our assumption in this chapter) and if that policy is defined in terms of expenditure per unit of capital on innovation and imitation, large firms spend more on R&D than do small firms. The probability that a firm will come up with an innovation is proportional to its R&D spending and hence to its size; thus, large firms have a higher probability of coming up with a new technique in any period, and on average they tend to be closer to the frontier of techniques and tend to experience more steady progress than do smaller firms. Also, the chances that a firm will be able to imitate is proportional to its R&D spending. This further accentuates the tendency of large firms to stay close to the frontier and to experience relatively steady progress. Counteracting these advantages of size, and the consequent tendency of large firms to grow relative to small firms, is the fact that the perceived market power of large firms affects their desired investment: they restrain their plans for expansion because they recognize that one of the consequences of expansion will be to drive down price. Given this formulation, one might expect that the variance of growth rates would be smaller among large firms and that the average growth rate would first increase and then flatten out or decrease with firm size.

These departures from Gibrat's law seem to square with empirical evidence. As mentioned above, Mansfield found serial correlation and showed that this was related to successful innovation. He also showed that the variance of growth rates declines with firm size. Singh and Whittington (1975) reported serial correlation, smaller variance of growth rates for large firms than for small, and a positive correlation between growth rates and size for a large sample of firms in the United Kingdom. Although their study does not show the nonlinearity between average growth rates and firm size that is apparently built into our model, their "largest size" group has a considerable range. A number of researchers who have explored growth rate differences among quite large firms in some detail have proposed that after some point there is negative correlation between size and the growth rate. See, for example, Steindl (1965) and Ijiri and Simon (1964, 1974).

1. Hypotheses and Experimental Setup

Consider an industry that initially is relatively unconcentrated. Assume that the firms are involved in a process of Schumpeterian competition along the lines of that characterized in the model presented in the previous chapter. Under what conditions would one expect the industry to undergo a rapid increase in concentration? Alternatively, what conditions should be conducive to preserving the competitive structure?

The logic of the model makes it plausible that the more rapid the pace at which technological opportunities expand over time, the greater the propensity for the industry to become concentrated. Under a regime of rapid growth of latent productivity, an R&D success by one firm will give a bigger enhancement (on average) to its productivity level than would be the case when latent productivity growth is slower. The firms that have R&D successes therefore ought to be more advantaged relative to those firms that are experiencing dry runs. At any time, then, one would expect greater variation in productivity and profitability levels among firms and greater variance in their growth rates. Thinking by analogy with the Gibrat's law model, we would expect this to lead to growth of concentration.

Similar reasoning suggests that the greater the variance of a successful R&D outcome, the more spread out will be firm productivity levels at any time and the greater will be the variance in growth rates and the tendencies for concentration to develop. At least, this was our initial conjecture. It turns out that there are features of the model that significantly attenuate the extent to which variance in the outcome of research draws results in variance among firms' technology levels after completion of a research project. The reason for the attenuation is interesting in its own right and possibly is relevant to real situations. We will explore it shortly.

The ease of imitation would appear to be another factor influencing the tendencies of an industry to grow concentrated over time. The harder it is for other firms to imitate the technology of an innovator, the longer-lasting will be the advantage to the latter of its R&D success. On the other hand, if imitation is relatively easy (tends to occur quickly), even if R&D successes give the innovating firm a significant initial advantage over firms that are not successful in their R&D efforts, this advantage will not last very long.

Finally, one would expect concentration to grow rapidly in cases in which firms with a higher productivity level and greater profitability press their advantage hard over disadvantaged firms by expanding their capital stock. On the other hand, if firms as they grow large restrain their capacity growth even when they are very profitable, this behavior in effect provides a shelter over firms that at that time have lower productivity and profitability levels. Thus, the hypothesis is that the less the tendency of firms to restrain their further capacity growth as they grow larger, the greater the tendency of significant concentration to develop out of a situation that originally started with many equal-sized firms.

While these same factors would tend to operate in the same direction in an industry that originally started out with a few large equal-sized firms, there are considerations that lead us to expect greater stability in the latter situation. The fact that the firms originally are large means that more is spent on both research and imitation and thus that firms tend to stay close to each other in technologies, as well as close to the frontier. Further, output growth restraint is operative always, not just when a firm grows large.

Our experimental design was to set two different levels for each of the four experimental factors: pace of latent productivity growth, variance of innovative R&D draws around latent productivity, difficulty of imitation, and aggressiveness of investment policies. We ran each of the sixteen possible combinations in a context consisting first of four equal-sized firms and then of sixteen equal-sized firms. In this experiment all firms have the same R&D policies and spend on both innovation and imitation, and the technological change regime is science-based. To get some indication of the variability of outcomes for a given combination of factor settings, we ran each setting at least twice in the sixteen-firm cases.

For our measure of concentration (the dependent variable) we use the Herfindahl-Hirschman index of concentration of the industry's capital stock. There is a theoretical rationale for employing this index in the model being used here. In this context, the Herfindahl index is a measure of the expected fraction of the industry's capital stock that will be modernized by a successful R&D project.

Consider a successful R&D project occurring at a moment in time. The project could have been the work of any of the firms in the industry. The probability that any particular firm would come up with the successful project is proportional to its share of R&D spending in the industry's total; in turn, this is simply equal to the share of the firm's capital stock in the industry's total. The percentage of industry capital that can be "modernized" by that project is also the percentage of that firm's capital in total industry capital. Thus, the expected fraction of industry capital that can be modernized by a successful R&D project is simply:

$$H = \sum_i \left(\frac{K_i}{K} \cdot \frac{K_i}{K} \right) = \sum_i \left(\frac{K_i}{K} \right)^2.$$

This is the Herfindahl index of capital concentration. In much of our analysis we employ the inverse of the Herfindahl index or "Herfindahl numbers equivalent"—which has an interpretation as the

number of equal-sized firms that would have the same Herfindahl
index as the actual size distribution of firms.

2. RESULTS

There were striking differences between the runs that started out
with four equal-sized firms and those that started out with sixteen
equal-sized firms. We had conjectured that the initial distribution in
the former case would be more stable than in the latter case and that
the ultimate distribution of firm sizes would be less sensitive to such
factors as the rate of advance of latent productivity and the ease of
imitation. We were surprised at the strength with which these conjectures were confirmed.

Table 13.1 presents the figures for the Herfindahl numbers equivalent for period 101, for each of the runs that started out with four
equal-sized firms. The contrast with Table 13.2, which presents the
same data for the runs that started out with sixteen equal-sized
firms, is dramatic. Over a run of 101 periods (during which, even in
the runs with "slow" growth of latent productivity, average output
per unit of capital increased by more than half), for virtually every
parameter setting, the four initially equal-sized firms preserved close
to their initial shares of industry output. One principal factor that
bound the firms together was that all of them had numerous suc-

Table 13.1.   Final-period concentration in the four-firm runs.

Experimental condition binary number [a]	Herfindahl numbers equivalent	Experimental condition binary number [a]	Herfindahl numbers equivalent
0000	4.000	1000	3.976
0001	3.995	1001	3.719
0010	3.998	1010	3.611
0011	3.973	1011	3.794
0100	4.000	1100	3.701
0101	3.997	1101	3.849
0110	3.978	1110	2.353
0111	3.998	1111	2.489

a. *Binary code:* Experimental factors are represented by binary digits in the
following order (left to right): aggressiveness of investment policies, difficulty of
imitation, rate of latent productivity growth, variability of innovative outcomes. For
each factor, the "one" (or "high") setting is expected to lead to higher concentration
than the "zero" (or "low") setting. For example, 0101 denotes the condition in which
investment policies are unaggressive, imitation is difficult, the rate of latent productivity growth is low, and the variability of research outcomes is high.

Table 13.2. Final-period concentration in the sixteen-firm runs.

Experimental condition binary number	Herfindahl numbers equivalent	Experimental condition binary number	Herfindahl numbers equivalent
0000	14.925 15.060	1000	12.937 13.158
0001	14.347 14.286	1001	13.550 13.228
0010	12.005 12.019	1010	7.429 7.788
0011	12.516 13.514	1011	6.361 4.938
0100	13.072 13.495	1100	10.893 11.001
0101	14.045 10.741	1101	10.091 8.058
0110	10.776 9.579	1110	6.150 5.102
0111	11.050 8.418	1111	2.856 4.686

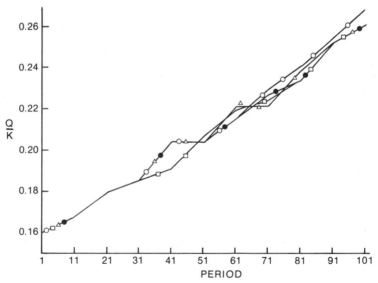

13.1 Time paths of firm productivity levels in one four-firm run (experimental condition 1000).

cesses in their R&D efforts looking at new technological possibilities and at the techniques their competitors were using. As a result, over time they tended to have roughly the same (in many cases identical) productivity levels. Figure 13.1 presents the time path of productivity for each of the four firms in a representative case (1000).

Another factor at work, in half the cases, was the investment restraint exercised by firms even when they gained a productivity advantage over their competitors. The Herfindahl numbers equivalent is systematically smaller in the right half of Table 13.1, which records runs in which firms viewed demand as infinitely elastic, than in the left half of the table, which records runs in which firms did restrain investment in new capacity. The last two runs—in which firms exercised no restraint, latent productivity growth was rapid, and imitation was difficult—show a markedly more concentrated end structure than the other runs. Figure 13.2 presents the productivity time paths associated with run 1111. Clearly there is more dispersion among firms than is displayed in Figure 13.1. This, plus aggressive investment policies, clearly led to the growth of concentration. But this case was rather exceptional. To our eyes the most striking feature of the four-firm runs was that, through thick and thin and in spite of the fact that long-run output policies were noncooperative or even competitive, productivity levels of the firms tended to stay close and the initial division of the market tended to be preserved.

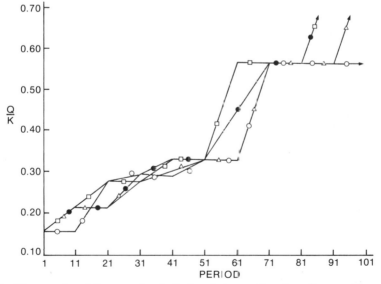

13.2   Time paths of firm productivity levels in another four-firm run (experimental condition 1111).

In the sixteen-firm runs, the situation was quite different. Two runs at each parameter setting are reported in Table 13.2. As the table indicates, there was variation between the two runs at the same parameter settings, but for the most part these differences were small compared with those related to different parameter settings.

One simple but powerful way to test the hypotheses about the model that we put forth in the previous section is to make a set of binary comparisons of the Herfindahl numbers equivalent in the period 101 for runs that are identical in their parameter settings except for one variable. Thus, one can compare final concentration in runs with the same parameter settings for ease of imitation, rate of latent productivity growth, and distribution of a successful research outcome about the mean, but with different investment policy parameters and similarly for other differences.

While these comparisons can be made by scanning Table 13.2, it is hard to get good impressions this way. Table 13.3 arrays in a more visually convenient way the binary comparisons relevant to assessing the effect of the rate of latent productivity growth. In every single comparison in which a run with a low rate of latent productiv-

Table 13.3.   Concentration: comparisons of runs differing in latent productivity growth.

Experimental condition binary number (low rate)	Herfindahl numbers equivalent	Experimental condition binary number (high rate)	Herfindahl numbers equivalent
0000	14.925 15.060	0010	12.005 12.019
0001	14.347 14.286	0011	12.516 13.514
0100	13.072 13.495	0110	10.776 9.579
1000	12.937 13.158	1010	7.429 7.788
1001	13.550 13.228	1011	6.361 4.938
1100	10.893 11.001	1110	6.150 5.102
1101	10.091 8.058	1111	2.856 4.686

ity growth is compared with one in which there was a high rate, the end concentration is greater in the latter. Similarly, in every binary comparison in which a run in which firms expressed investment restraint was compared with a run with aggressive investment policies, or a run in which easy imitation was compared with one in which imitation was harder (all other factors being held constant), the results went in the predicted direction.

In contrast, comparison among runs that differed only in terms of the variance of research draws around latent productivity yields ambiguous results. It now is apparent to us that we did not fully think through the implications of an important fact: before a firm adopts a new technique that it has "found" through research, it compares the productivity of that technique against the productivity of the technique it already is using. One implication of this is that an increase in the dispersion of research outcomes always increases the expected productivity advance associated with a research draw: outcomes inferior to existing practice are irrelevant regardless of the margin of inferiority, and the increased likelihood of large advances always makes a positive contribution to the expectation. Table 13.4 shows that this implication is reflected in substantial end-period

Table 13.4. Geometric average ratio of industry productivity to latent productivity: comparisons of some runs differing in innovative R&D outcome variance factor only.

Experimental conditions	Geometric average ratio
0000[a]	0.977
0001[b]	1.022
0010	0.933
0011	1.108
0100	0.965
0101	1.004
0110	0.898
0111	1.068
1000	0.981
1001	1.049
1010	0.966
1011	1.191
1100	0.969
1101	1.033
1110	0.936
1111	1.102

a. Low variance.
b. High variance.

overall productivity level differences between runs of high and low variance in research outcomes.

A corollary implication is that no simple connection exists between the dispersion of research outcomes and interfirm variability in productivity levels. Hence, our hypothesized causal linkage running from research outcome variability to interfirm productivity differences to interfirm growth rate differences and finally to the growth of concentration is problematic at the first link. Because research outcomes that are inferior to existing technique are disregarded, the effective distribution of next-period productivity levels facing a firm has smaller variance than the research outcome distribution; furthermore, the better the firm's initial position, the more the truncation matters. And, as Table 13.4 confirms, the average "initial position" itself changes when the research outcome variance rises. Through additional calculations that are too detailed to report here, we have confirmed that the interplay of these considerations can be such as to substantially attenuate the effect of the research outcome variance on the final concentration figures. A likely explanation for the ambiguous experimental results has therefore been identified.

Another way we explored our hypotheses was to run least-squares regressions with the Herfindahl equivalent number of firms as the dependent variable and with the various experimental conditions represented as binary-valued dummies. Table 13.5 displays the results of such calculations on a data set where all the sixteen-firm runs were pooled (making thirty-two observations in all). The coefficients on the dummy variables in the first regression are simply the *differences* between the average value of the Herfindahl equivalent number of firms in the relevant binary comparisons of Table 13.2. The interpretation of the coefficients in the second regression, in which interaction terms are included, is somewhat more complex.

The results of the first regression confirm, of course, those of the binary comparisons. The coefficients relating to investment policy, the rate of latent productivity growth, and the ease of imitation all have the right sign. From the binary comparisons, we know something stronger: that in each binary comparison these variables worked in the expected direction. The lack of sensitivity of concentration to the variance of innovative R&D outcomes shows up in the regression. (The "t" statistics should be interpreted as descriptive. The distribution-of-error assumptions required for them to serve as the basis of significance tests are almost certainly violated.)

The regression format has certain advantages over the binary comparison format for probing interaction effects. Regression (2) displays a variety of interaction effects. The strong interaction between

Table 13.5. Regressions of Herfindahl numbers equivalent on dummy variables for experimental factors and interaction terms.

Equation	Constant	X_4^a	X_3^b	X_2^c	X_1^d	X_1X_2	X_1X_3	X_1X_4	X_2X_3	X_2X_4	X_3X_4	R^2
(1)	16.19	−3.85	−2.38	−4.23	−0.79							.86
	(30.07)	(8.00)	(4.94)	(8.78)	(1.65)							
(2)	14.78	−1.39	−1.84	−2.62	0.23	−0.04	−0.94	−1.08	0.27	−3.43	−0.38	.94
	(24.70)	(1.94)	(2.56)	(3.64)	(0.33)	(0.05)	(1.30)	(1.50)	(.037)	(4.76)	(.53)	

a. X_4 = dummy variable for output restraint factor.
b. X_3 = dummy variable for ease of imitation factor.
c. X_2 = dummy variable for rate of latent productivity growth factor.
d. X_1 = dummy variable for variance of innovative R&D draws factor.
Note: In all cases the "1" level of the factor is hypothesized to lead to higher concentration (lower numbers equivalent). Figures in parentheses are absolute values of t-ratios.

rate of latent productivity growth and investment restraint does not come as a surprise. If the rate of latent productivity growth is slow, one firm does not have a significant chance of suddenly getting a major productivity advantage over other firms, which it then could exploit competitively. When the rate of latent productivity growth is high, the chances of this are much greater. But if the firm with a competitive advantage is concerned about growing too much, it exerts less pressure on the lower-productivity firms and gives them a chance to recover. On the other hand, where the productivity leader invests aggressively, the effect of its growth will be to force low-productivity firms to decline. As they decline and cut back their R&D spending, their chances of ever catching up are diminished. This reasoning suggests that the "ease of imitation" variable should also be playing a role in the interactions. However, it is not easy to discern such a role in the regression displayed in Table 13.5.

The above discussion suggests an alternative way of analyzing interaction effects—namely, split the sample in two ways. We separated the runs with aggressive investment policies from those in which there was investment restraint. And we separated the runs in which the rate of latent productivity growth was high from those in which it was low. Table 13.6 presents regressions of the Herfindahl equivalent number of firms against the three remaining independent variables, in the case where firms exercised investment restraint and in the case where they behaved aggressively. The rate of latent productivity growth has a much greater effect on the extent to which concentration develops in the latter case than in the former. And although the evidence is far from sharp, one can faintly discern that the ease of imitation also matters more in the case of aggressive investment than in the case where firms restrain their growth. The same results appeared when separate regressions were run for cases in which the rate of latent productivity growth is high and for cases in which it is low.

It is clear enough from the above analysis that one would expect a positive relationship to develop over time between the size of a firm and its productivity level: firms grow big because they are productive. One also would expect the variance of productivity to be smaller among large firms than among smaller ones. The simulation data confirm these expectations. Figure 13.3 is a good illustration of these relationships. In addition to advantages of higher average productivity, large firms have a higher expectation of discovering a new technique. One would expect, therefore, a positive relationship between expected growth rates and firm size, at least up to some critical size level, beyond which point restraint on further growth might flatten the relationship or make it turn down. This suggests regressing

Table 13.6. Concentration: comparison of regressions results for subsamples with and without output restraint (variables as in Table 13.5).

Equation	Constant	X_3	X_2	X_1	X_1X_2	X_1X_3	X_2X_3	R^2
			Output restraint ($X_4 = 0$)					
(3)	14.97	−2.19	−2.51	−0.25				.77
	(28.77)	(4.20)	(4.83)	(0.48)				
(4)	14.84	−1.40	−2.67	−0.36	1.06	−0.83	−0.74	.82
	(20.65)	(1.47)	(2.84)	(0.39)	(0.98)	(0.76)	(0.68)	
			No output restraint ($X_4 = 1$)					
(5)	13.57	−2.57	−5.95	−1.33				.94
	(28.55)	(5.41)	(1.25)	(2.81)				
(6)	13.34	−2.68	−6.01	−0.73	−1.14	−1.06	1.28	.96
	(23.21)	(3.56)	(7.8)	(0.32)	(1.31)	(1.21)	(1.47)	

a. *Note*: Figures in parentheses are absolute values of *t*-ratios.

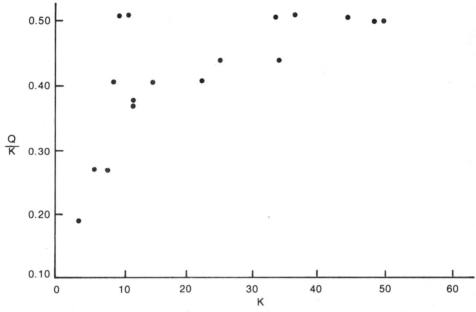

13.3   Plot of productivity level against capital stock in one sixteen-firm run (experimental condition 0110, period 81).

growth rates as a quadratic function of firm size and separating the sample between those runs where firms exercised investment restraint as they grew large and those runs where they did not. The results are displayed in Table 13.7. All expectations are confirmed, including that the curvature of the relationship is much greater in the

Table 13.7.   Regressions relating firm growth rates (periods 81–101) to firm size in period 81.

Equation	Constant	K_{81}	K_{81}^2	R^2
	Output restraint ($X_4 = 0$)			
(7)	−1.957	0.1204	−0.0017	.13
	(3.59)	(2.96)	(2.56)	
	No output restraint ($X_4 = 1$)			
(8)	−3.014	0.0659	−0.0002	.64
	(15.01)	(5.83)	(2.37)	

Note: Dependent variable is percentage rate of firm growth, per quarter, periods 81–101. K_{81} is firm size (capital stock) in period 81. All sixteen firms in runs coded 0011 and 0111, for Equation (7), or 1011 and 1111, for Equation (8). $N = 64$ in each case. Figures in parentheses are absolute values of t-ratios.

runs where firms restrained growth than in those where they did not.

As noted above, the logic of the model also would seem to imply a rather strong serial correlation of growth rates in the short run, with the extent of correlation diminishing as longer time intervals are considered. This expectation also was confirmed.

The model we are exploring was designed to give insight into the nature of Schumpeterian competition, and the experiments reported here were focused on forces generating and limiting the growth of concentration. Unlike many of the stochastic models of firm growth, this one was not developed for the specific purpose of generating a distribution that fits actual data. We should report, however, that the firm-size distributions generated by the model have at least a family resemblance to empirical distributions. In some cases, the simulated distributions closely approximate the log normal. Figure 13.4 shows the cumulative distribution for $\log K_i$ in run 0110, plotted on normal probability paper (so that an actual cumulative normal would trace out a straight line). This particular run produced one of the closer approximations to log normal. When we focused attention on the validity of the Pareto law for the upper tail of the distribution (the large firms), the log size/log rank plot typically displayed concavity for the investment restraint cases.

Qualitatively, the simulation model clearly behaves in ways that correspond for the most part to our hypotheses. The model also illustrates and exemplifies various mechanisms and patterns that empiri-

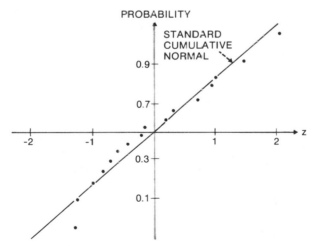

13.4   Plot of standardized cumulative distribution of $\log(K)$ on normal probability paper (experimental condition 1110, final period).

cal studies of industrial concentration have brought to light. It remains to consider, briefly, the *quantitative* import of our simulation results.

It seems clear that the differences between fourteen or fifteen firms and four or five firms would be seen as an "interesting" difference in industrial market structure. This is the difference, by the Herfindahl numbers equivalent measure, between our 0000 and 1111 experimental conditions after twenty-five years of simulated change from essentially identical initial conditions. We are not, of course, in a position to support any bold claims that these simulated effects are of a realistic magnitude. We have stressed that this is essentially a theoretical exercise, and that no serious calibration effort has been made. If we had chosen different parameter settings, the results would have been different.

On the other hand, the model is fairly simple, as simulation models go. Its parameters are not numerous, and most of them can be interpreted and checked against known empirical magnitudes. We chose unity for our elasticity of demand; we had no particular industry in mind, but the value is not bizarre. The capital-output ratio in value terms—which determines how unit cost advantages translate into excess returns and hence into firm growth rates—is 1.6 on an annual basis. Our two conditions for latent productivity growth are 2 percent and 6 percent per year; there are empirical measures of observed productivity growth below our low value and above our high value. And so it goes, through most of the parameter list. To the best of our ability, we have chosen parameter values and levels of experimental factors to be at least "in the ball park." In our view, therefore, the quantitative results do carry some weight. They are at least suggestive of the sorts of effects that might arise in the stochastic processes of economic reality. A critic skeptical of even this rather timid assertion faces the challenge of explaining where we might have left the ball park.

We can offer such a critic a little help. There is one important segment of the model in which the abstractions we employ are a bit hard to interpret, and hence to check, in terms of observable magnitudes. This is the characterization of the form of the results of R&D activity in terms of probability distributions. The indivisibility of a "draw" is an important feature of the model. If parameters are set so that innovation and imitation draws are rare in the industry as a whole, each successful innovation draw will tend to have a large transforming effect on industry structure. Latent productivity will have increased substantially since the last draw, and imitation will be slow. The lucky firm will surely grow rapidly and for an extended period, perhaps to the point where little luck will be needed for it to get the next draw as well. By contrast, a steady, gentle rain of technological advances on the industry will tend to make all firms move forward together; each individual success will matter less, and the larger total number of successes will reduce the variability among firms.

We explored this issue by doing two additional runs under the 1111 experimental condition, except that the rates of both innovation and imitation draws were at least three times the levels of that condition. The resulting Herfindahl numbers equivalents were 5.4 and 8.3; as expected, these values are well above those obtained in the 1111 condition itself. At the higher rates, a firm of average size gets (by innovation or imitation) a new technique to consider more than one quarter in three, on the average. Firms then track latent productivity growth more closely and more smoothly.

With the vision of hindsight, we now believe that we should have interpreted the "Phillips hypothesis" along the lines sketched above, rather than in terms of variance of the outcomes of research draws. It matters whether R&D projects are expensive so that a given R&D budget yields periodic large successes, or whether R&D projects are inexpensive so that that same R&D budget can yield a steady flow of more minor advances. In the former circumstance, concentration is more likely to develop. We think this is a better formulation of the Phillips hypothesis than the one we started with initially.

3. SUMMARY AND CONCLUSIONS

Schumpeterian competition is, like most processes we call competitive, a process that tends to produce winners and losers. Some firms track emerging technological opportunities with greater success than other firms; the former tend to prosper and grow, the latter to suffer losses and decline. Growth confers advantages that make further success more likely, while decline breeds technological obsolescence and further decline. As these processes operate over time, there is a tendency for concentration to develop even in an industry initially composed of many equal-sized firms.

In the logic of our model, we have attempted to reflect the principal causal mechanisms operative in Schumpeterian competition. In choosing parameter values, we have tried to stay "in the ball park," so that the numerical examples we generate have a claim to attention as illustrations of realistic possibilities. Our experimental results indicate that the tendency to increasing concentration, arising from the workings of the competitive process itself, is quite strong—strong enough to be interesting from a policy point of view. They indicate also that there is interesting variation in the strength of this tendency as a function of industry characteristics. We think of our results concerning this variation as a set of propositions that might ultimately provide a basis for empirical test of some descendant of the present model, but there is obviously much work to be done before such testing would be feasible or appropriate.

The results linking the growth of concentration to the investment policies of firms seem particularly deserving of emphasis. They can be summarized succinctly in a proposition that at first appears paradoxical: the actual exercise of market power by the larger firms in an industry may be an important factor tending to limit the growth of concentration in the industry. In spite of the note of paradox, the proposition is quite an obvious consequence of the logic of our model. There is nothing mysterious in the fact that the effect shows up clearly in our experimental contrast between a price-taking model and a Cournot model of investment decisions in the individual firm. It would be incorrect to say that this perspective on concentration is absent from the industrial organization literature; for example, the proposition that a dominant firm tends to decline (Scherer, 1980, pp. 239–240) is a close relative of our proposition. But it does seem that this perspective is seriously underemphasized relative to the proposition that an existing state of high concentration signifies the existence of market power.

Our experiments also yielded striking illustrations of the relationships noted by Phillips. What Phillips proposed, and illustrated in a convincing case study, was that an environment that offers abundant opportunities for technological advance and in which advances are not easily imitated is one of high uncertainty for the individual firm. Hence, by the working of the mechanisms of stochastic firm growth, it is an environment in which concentration tends to rise. Our model offers a specific formalization of Phillips' account of this mechanism, and the experimental results concerning latent productivity growth and imitation corroborate his judgment on the implications for concentration. Our initial attempts to formalize his hypotheses regarding variability of research outcomes turned out to be logically flawed. We think, however, that our subsequent reinterpretation confirms his judgment there, too.[2]

---

2. We have preserved in this chapter both our original specification of this hypothesis and the subsequent modification, together with discussion of the considerations that led us to move from the first to the second, for an important reason. Most published analytic models in economics probably turn out in places to be specified in ways that are significantly different from those that the author initially had in mind. The reason is that the model as originally conceived did not work out as expected, and

Not surprisingly, in view of its antecedents in the stochastic models of Simon and others, our model also does a respectable job of generating firm-size distributions that are at least superficially realistic. We have not emphasized this point in our discussion, and we certainly could not assert it as a distinctive virtue of our model as against other stochastic models. However, we take the point more seriously as a virtue of the class of stochastic models when compared with other contenders. There are strong and reliable regularities in empirical firm-size distributions. To disregard those regularities when modeling firm size or industry structure phenomena is, in our view, to waste one of the rare opportunities to guide theorizing by empirical constraints. Only the models involving random differences in firm growth rates seem, at present, capable of satisfying those empirical constraints in a parsimonious fashion.

To appreciate the empirical strength of the stochastic models is not, of course, to deny the importance of systematic determinants of industry structure. Our own stochastic model illustrates the point—presumably obvious—that the explicit recognition of random elements in a class of phenomena is not antithetical to the causal explanation of regularities in those phenomena. Our model is stochastic, but not to the exclusion of systematic causation; it does not portray industry evolution as "merely random." The model would be improved if it were generalized to reflect more of the systematic influences on industry structure—for example, technological economies of scale, product differentiation, and entry conditions. But there is no reason to think that the model, when thus modified, would somehow become unresponsive to the considerations that we have explored in our experiments—or that the basic empirical strength of the stochastic approach would be forfeited.

The role of entry conditions deserves more than passing mention in this connection, since entry and the barriers thereto figure so importantly in the industrial organization literature on concentration. The degree to which our results might be sensitive to the exclusion of entry depends critically on the model of entry one has in mind. More specifically, it depends on how the model answers questions in three critical areas: (1) the scale at which entry occurs; (2) the technological

---

the model builder was faced with an instructive set of puzzles whose solution led to the modified model. Our point is that the same sort of fruitful rethinking can be stimulated by simulation results—provided that the simulation model is not so opaque that it is impossible to develop expectations as to how it will behave. Further, in this particular case we judge that not only we ourselves, but also the reader, might gain in understanding by entertaining the initial misconception and following the path toward a better formulation.

progressiveness of entrants; and (3) the operative incentives for entry—that is, the nature of the calculation on which an entry decision is presumed to depend. We would expect our results to be little changed if the entry model: (1) restricted entry to relatively small scales (initial firm scales or smaller), and to small percentages of industry capacity in any single period; (2) made the typical entrant merely imitative (at best) of prevailing technology; and (3) allowed entry processes to be triggered only if entry appeared to be profitable on the basis of simple calculations based on industry experience over a short period of time. Under these conditions, the situation of a new entrant would be quite comparable to the situation of a small firm already in existence. Informational economies of scale would still favor the large established firms, and one would expect new entrants to have a hard time of it. However, things would clearly be different if entrants came in at large scale, as technological leaders, and motivated by subtle, long-run strategic calculations.

As this brief discussion of entry illustrates, there are many difficult problems to be wrestled with before we can hope to put forward a coherent general model of the forces generating and limiting concentration. What we have presented in this chapter is only a partial view of the matter, but it is a partial view that is clearly quite distinct from the other partial views that currently dominate discussion in this area. It offers a novel perspective on a wide range of positive and normative issues in industrial organization. For example, our model could be taken as the basis for an alternative interpretation of the sort of empirical data confronted by the "survivor technique" approach to assessing economies of scale. In the antitrust area, it offers a possible basis for formal analysis of the "dominant firm" problems discussed by Williamson (1972), including specifically that of the firm that achieves dominance through its innovative prowess and then stops innovating. And, as our discussion of the Phillips hypothesis illustrates, both the empirical and normative discussions of the relationship between concentration and innovation can usefully be illuminated by an explicit model of the causal forces running from the latter to the former. In the following chapter, we focus on the normative issues relating to Schumpeterian competition and analyze the "Schumpeterian tradeoff" in a context in which industry structure and innovative performance are recognized as interdependent.

14

The Schumpeterian Tradeoff
Revisited

MUCH of the economist's interest in the Schumpeterian controversy derives from the observation that aspects of structure that are conducive to innovation may be detrimental to the achievement of Pareto optimality in the short run. Contemporary economists have tended to identify as the static cost of a progressive (concentrated) industry the welfare losses from output restriction associated with product market power. That this is too simple an appraisal seems quite clear in the context of the model of Schumpeterian competition that we have been exploring. We continue the exploration in this chapter, and the first order of business is to develop a more adequate picture of the performance dimensions and policy problems that Schumpeterian competition presents. We then describe and analyze a third group of simulation experiments with the model that we set forth in Chapter 12. These experiments further illuminate the dynamic interplay of changing concentration with progressiveness and illustrate the influence of the exogenous considerations that shape that dynamic process. Among the results are some that afford novel perspectives on the policy issues.[1]

---

1. For an early review of the discussion, see Nelson, Peck, and Kalachek (1967). For more recent reviews, see Kamien and Schwartz (1975, 1981), Scherer (1980), Dasgupta and Stiglitz (1980b), and Flaherty (1980). We return in Chapter 16 to the discussion of the policy issues related to Schumpeterian competition.

1. Tradeoffs and Policy Tools

Several kinds of social costs are incurred when technological progress is "purchased" through a system of economic organization that pits private business firms against one another in a struggle for competitive advantage.

One of these is the cost associated with less than competitive output levels. The presence of such a cost is signaled by a gap between price and the marginal production costs in the most progressive firms. However, static inefficiencies also reside in the extent to which the "best technology" is monopolized by one firm in the industry, independent of whether that firm is large enough to have market power. Indeed, there are two different kinds of costs associated with limits on the use of technical information imposed by the patent system or simply by industrial secrecy. One is a higher average production cost than given technological knowledge would permit, a cost associated with a gap between best practice and average practice. Another is the presence of duplicative or near-duplicative R&D efforts, resulting in a lower best practice for a given amount of cumulative industry R&D (or more R&D needed to achieve a given best practice). In addition, of course, there is a possible distortion of the level of total R&D effort, which may be greater or less than it would be in a hypothetical second-best optimum in which the other costs are accepted.

Setting aside for the moment the last of these considerations, the other costs can be depicted as in Figure 14.1.[2] Let C equal unit production costs if industry R&D were spent perfectly efficiently and all firms had access to the best known technology. With a demand curve A-B, potential consumer-plus-producer surplus is triangle ABC. Let c equal unit production costs with the actual best-practice technology (given some near-duplicative R&D efforts) and the jagged line c-c' represent an industry production cost schedule, arraying costs by firms from the most efficient (cost c) to the least efficient firm actually producing (cost c'). Let actual output be $\bar{Q}$. Actual surplus then is $AP'c'c$. The difference between actual and potential surplus is accounted for by three areas: (1) $P'de$, a conventional deadweight loss triangle associated with the output shortfall relative to competitive equilibrium at best-practice cost; (2) $cc'e$, or excess production costs due to a gap between best and average practice; (3) $CcdB$ associated with lower best practice due to inefficient industry R&D.

Assume that costs of one or more of these forms are unavoidable if innovation is to occur in a market setting. If there are to be private

---

2. This graphic representation was suggested to us by Richard Levin.

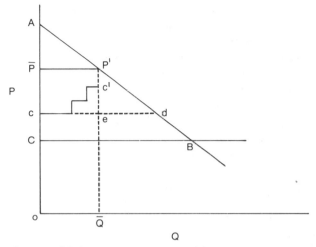

14.1 Social costs of Schumpeterian competition.

incentives for innovative effort, there must be some degree of private property (at least *de facto*) in the fruits of such effort; practically speaking, this means that some social costs of the sorts identified above must be accepted. How should one then approach the problem of assessing the social gains from more industry R&D so as to reach some conclusion regarding the suitability of the total R&D effort that private incentives would produce? In the first place, the discussion in the two preceding chapters points out that some key determinants of the social gains are themselves endogenously determined by, or codetermined with, market structure. For example, it matters whether R&D expenditure is efficiently allocated from a social point of view, and this is partly a function of market structure. But there are also important exogenous considerations. The gains from a higher level of industry R&D spending depend partly on the technological regime that governs R&D outcomes. For example, it matters whether diminishing returns to R&D effort set in early and sharply (the science-based case of the preceding chapters), or whether marginal returns continue to be high at high levels of expenditure. In the former case, but not the latter, low levels of industry R&D expenditure may buy society much of what a significantly higher level would.

Policy Issues

Assume that there is indeed a tradeoff between the industry structure that performs best, given the set of available technologies, and the structure most conducive to advancing technology. And assume that somehow society could agree on the nature of the tradeoff and on the target point for policy. Although the discussion above identifies causal links between innovative opportunities and the market structure that evolves, it offers no reason to expect that the social tradeoff might be optimized by the automatic functioning of those links. It is quite reasonable, therefore, for economists to be interested in policies that can influence structure. But most of the studies that purport to address this issue are not very clear about what policy instruments could influence structure.

There seems to be a notion implicit in many studies that industry structure itself is the policy variable and that structure should be *chosen* so as to optimize the tradeoff. However, it is not clear how far the policy tools presently existing or proposed can go toward affecting structure in a durable way. In particular, even if it could be argued that a lesser degree of concentration than prevails in an industry would promote more innovativeness, and would hence be desirable on both static and dynamic grounds, a deconcentration achieved by policy may be undone over time as firms grow and decline in the now more innovative environment. And repeated structural interventions would certainly lead to behavioral changes that might be costly in themselves.

On occasion, policy can influence structure directly if not durably, as by requiring divestitures or by forbidding or encouraging mergers or entry. But much of policy aimed at influencing industry performance operates by constraining or requiring certain behavior and affects structure indirectly. In terms of the discussion above, government policies—for example, regarding the rights and obligations of patent holders—can influence whether imitation is hard or easy. Or antitrust policy may permit firms with a large market share and a strong technological position to exploit these advantages and take a larger market share; or policy may restrain such tendencies. Policies aimed at controlling behavior influence performance directly—and also indirectly, by influencing the structure that evolves, which in turn determines performance.

Another complication of the policy task arises from the fact that structure is likely to respond rather slowly to feasible policy adjustments. It is at least reasonable to propose that the time patterns of social costs and benefits ought to receive some consideration when policy measures affecting structure are analyzed. And it may be that differences among industries in terms of stage of historical development and dynamic response to policy should be included, along with differences in the technological change regime, in the list of considerations that tend to fragment the grand Schumpeterian question into a diverse set of issues relevant to narrowly defined contexts.

In sum, much of the analysis relating market structure to technological advance and static efficiency does not really connect with the policy instruments that are available. A serious analysis must probe deeper, recognizing that structure is endogenous to a regime of Schumpeterian competition, and attempt to identify the policy variables that can influence structure.

2. THE EXPERIMENTS

The model we shall use to explore these issues has been described in Chapter 12. As in that chapter, the focus here is upon the competitive struggle between firms with different R&D policies.

Again as in Chapter 12, we will explore the effects of initial industry concentration upon the survivability of the innovative firms. But in addition to initial variation in industry structure, we here explore the implications of different assumptions about the difficulty of innovation and imitation and about the aggressiveness of investment policies of large profitable firms for the viability of the innovating firms.

This chapter is especially concerned with the Schumpeterian tradeoffs. The different social costs identified above are all reflected in the model. The fact that imitation is costly and usually takes time means that the use of the best technology is limited. This will show up in a gap between best practice and average practice. Also, when there are many firms in the industry, more innovative R&D (and more R&D successes) may be required to keep the industry as a whole on a given productivity track than would be the case if access to the best technology were free to all. As indicated above, investment restraint on the part of firms who perceive that they have market power may also be reflected in the model. The consequences, as in textbook theory, are a wider gap between price and average cost, a lower level of output, and a higher price than would be the case if firms did not exert market power.

We will examine the benefits of a higher level of R&D spending and a higher rate of innovation in both science-based and cumulative technology cases. There are three parameters in the model that can be interpreted as abstract counterparts of policy variables. They relate to the ease with which technologies can be imitated, the extent to which large firms exert investment restraint, and the initial size distribution.

We undertook three sets of simulation experiments. In each experiment, half of the firms do innovative R&D as well as imitative R&D, while the other half do imitative R&D only. Imitative R&D spending per unit capital is constant across all firms; similarly, spending on innovative R&D per unit capital is the same in all the firms that spend at a positive level. In each case we have established initial conditions in which all firms are the same size and in which the industry is approximately in equilibrium at the prevailing productivity level. We have also ruled out entry. These assumptions give us a clear innovator-imitator struggle and a definite reference point for the degree of concentration that exists in the industry at any stage of the process.

The numbers used to calibrate the model were chosen so that four simulation "periods" correspond to one calendar year. Under this interpretation, the average annual sales-capital ratio in the industry is in rough accord with that in technologically progressive industries. The rate of growth of latent productivity is roughly 2 percent per year in our slow-growth condition and 6 percent per year in the fast-growth condition. The ratio of innovative R&D spending to sales is 6 percent—a more realistic value than was used in the preliminary study reported in Chapter 12. In the difficult-imitation setting, a given probability of imitating best practice required twice as much imitative R&D as in the easy-imitation setting. We ran the simulation for 101 periods, or twenty-five years after initial conditions.

Within this framework, the three sets of experiments described below correspond to more specific contexts. In each set we explored the behavior of the system under different settings of particular parameter values.

Behavior and Performance in a Science-Based Oligopoly

Our first set of experiments was concerned with the behavior of an industry in which concentration is initially high and in which the investment policies imputed to firms produce a regime of relatively restrained competition. The industry involved is science-based, in that latent productivity evolves over time at a rate determined by outside forces. All firms start out with productivity levels close to then-prevailing latent productivity. Of the four firms in the industry, two spend resources on R&D, aiming to keep up with the moving frontier of possibilities. The other two do not spend resources for this purpose, but aim to imitate the R&D leaders (the R&D leaders also look to technologies used by other firms).

In the context of this science-based oligopoly, we wanted to explore the effect on behavior and performance of two variables: rate of growth of latent productivity and ease of imitation. To what extent does the evolution of the industry—in particular, the relative success of the firms that do innovative R&D and of those that aim to imitate—depend on the pace at which new R&D targets evolve over time? How does the ease with which one firm can imitate the technology of another influence the evolution? The runs here are, we think, interesting in their own right. They also are interesting as a base of comparison for simulation experiments in which initially the industry is less concentrated. Understanding the results of the four-firm runs greatly facilitates one's ability to see through the workings of the model more generally and thus to interpret what is going on in other contexts.

Our past experience with running our model industry, starting it out with a quite concentrated structure, led us to make several predictions.[3] First, latent productivity will be tracked relatively well by the innovative firms because their level of innovative R&D spending, given the other parameters of the model, is sufficiently high so that each samples the evolving distribution of new technological possibilities relatively frequently. Second, the imitating firms will track the innovating firms relatively closely because their level of imitative R&D expenditure is sufficiently high that, even in the difficult-imitation setting, it is unlikely that many periods go by without their being able to imitate the best technology in practice. Third, under some circumstances firms that do not bear the costs of innovative R&D may tend to be slightly more profitable than the firms that do, but the innovative firms will nevertheless survive, make money, and even grow relative to the imitators. The investment restraint shown by the large firms in this context limits the extent to which a firm more profitable than its competitors exploits that advantage by trying significantly to increase its market share. In this atmosphere of restrained competition, firms that are not maximally profitable are sheltered. And even if they have a run of bad luck their capacities for recuperation are not quickly eroded.

Regarding the social merit of the industry behavior considered in these runs, certain predictions are relatively obvious. One is that the industry will be characterized by high markups over production cost; thus, there will be significant "triangle losses." A second is that, compared with a more competitive industry, there will be less waste due to the use of inferior technologies (there will be less of a gap between average and best practice). Third, R&D spending will be more efficient in the sense that less total R&D outlay is required to keep average practice moving at a given distance from potential best practice. Whether price will be higher or lower is an open question.

---

3. Of course, the relevance of our experience is partly attributable to the fact that we are here working with roughly the same values of most of the model's parameters as we did in the previous chapters.

A More Competitive Science-Based Industry

In the second simulation experiment we started the industry initially with sixteen equal-sized firms, eight of these doing both innovative and imitative R&D and eight doing only imitative R&D. As in the four-firm case, in some of our runs latent productivity advanced at a rapid rate and in others latent productivity grew more slowly; we set imitation as easy in half of our runs and "hard" in the other half. One important difference between the range of experimental variation in the sixteen-firm runs and the four-firm runs is this: in some of the sixteen-firm runs we preserved the assumption, contained in the four-firm runs, that a firm's desired net investment rate falls as its market share increases; in other words, we explored what would happen if a firm, as its market share grew in relation to that of its competitors, continued to expand rapidly even if it had only a moderate gap between price and cost. We did not experiment with this variant in the four-firm case both because we wanted to employ that case as a benchmark interpretable as restrained oligopoly and because the experiments of Chapter 13 suggest a tendency for relative shares to be relatively well preserved in the four-firm case even if investment behavior is not restrained. In the sixteen-firm case, in contrast, it seemed worthwhile to experiment with this variant for two reasons. First, because the focus here is on the effect of a more competitive structure than is presumed under the four-firm case and because the extent to which firms as they grow large exploit their advantage or hold back seems to be an important dimension of competitive behavior. Second, as suggested earlier, a central question to be explored is the extent to which a certain degree of restraint in pushing one's advantage is a requirement if firms that do innovative R&D are not to be destroyed by those that pursue the strategy of a "fast second."

There are several things that can be predicted with some confidence about the industry performance in the sixteen-firm case as contrasted with the four-firm case. Above we discussed the expected differences in average price-cost margins, the gap between average practice and best practice, and R&D efficiency for regimes with the same rate of growth of latent productivity. Another expected difference between the four-firm and sixteen-firm runs is that in the latter the initial industry structure will not prove to be stable. In general, concentration can be expected to increase under the force of Schumpeterian competition. There is one particular competitive struggle that we will want to watch attentively and to consider as a function of the various parameter settings: the performance and survival of the firms that do innovative R&D, compared with those that do imitative R&D. A straightforward conjecture is that the ability of innovative firms to prosper and survive depends positively on the rate of latent productivity growth (which determines the average advance achieved through innovative R&D) and negatively on the ease of imitation.

A Competitive Industry with a Cumulative Technology

In this third set of simulation experiments we preserved the basic assumptions of the second set, with the following exceptions. Instead of assuming that innovative R&D yielded random draws on a moving distribution of technological possibilities, we assumed that innovative R&D involved the incremental improvement of prevailing techniques. The probability distribution of innovative R&D successes for a firm was centered on its existing technique. Thus, the firms doing innovative R&D incrementally grope their way upward through the set of technological possibilities.

The alternative assumptions about the rate of growth of latent productivity that were built into the earlier two experiments were replaced in this experiment by the following. Under one assumption the distribution of innovative R&D finds is packed close around the prevailing technique and a major advance in productivity is unlikely. Under the alternative assumption the distribution is more spread out, and the firm has a greater chance of coming up with a significant increase in productivity from a single innovation.

We varied the parameter settings regarding ease or difficulty of imitation in the same way in these runs as in the science-based case. We also explored the difference that it would make if firms as they grew large did or did not exert investment restraint.

The most important contrast between this set of runs and the earlier set of sixteen-firm runs is that in the earlier cases there is an exogenous force pushing forward the frontiers of knowledge. If only a little innovative R&D is done in the industry, the average success from that effort will be a relatively spectacular advance, reflecting the movement forward of latent productivity since the prior R&D success. In the present experimental context there is no such outside force. If innovative R&D in the industry is squeezed down by the dynamics of Schumpeterian competition, the rate of progress of best practice and average practice can be predicted to decline also.

3. THE RESULTS OF THE SIMULATION EXPERIMENTS

The data from our simulations are set out in Tables 14.1–14.6. The abbreviations used in these tables should be interpreted as follows. The first row displays for period 101 the share of industry capital held by firms that do innovative R&D. In general, a share less than 0.50 indicates that firms that did innovative R&D were less profitable than those that did not; a share slightly over 0.50 is, however, also compatible with inferior profitability. The second row shows the average rate of excess return (profit) in the industry as a whole, as a percentage rate *per quarter*. Rows 3 and 4 show, respectively, the percentage margin between price and average production costs, $(P - C)/C$, in the industry as a whole, and the percentage margin for the firm with best-practice technology.

The next five rows display statistics of industry concentration in period 101: rows 5–8 the share of industry output accounted for by the largest and second-largest innovators and imitators, and row 9 the inverse of the Herfindahl-Hirschman index of (capital) concentration—that is, the numbers equivalent of the value of the concentration index.

The next five rows outline productivity statistics: row 10 shows average industry productivity, rows 11 and 12 average productivity of innovators and imitators, row 13 best practice (all for the final period of the run) and row 14 a measure of the average gap over 101 periods between average productivity and latent productivity.

Rows 15 and 16 show total industry innovative R&D over the 101 periods and the number of innovation draws. The bottom line shows price in period 101.

The symbols S, F, E, and H in the column headings refer, respectively, to slow and fast growth of latent productivity and easy and hard imitation. The two columns under each heading show the results of two different runs with the same parameter settings.

Tight Oligopoly

Table 14.1 displays data from our simulation experiment with an industry structure consisting of four firms, initially of equal size, two of which spend only on imitative R&D. The striking characteristic of all the runs shown was that the four firms tended to stay close together both in productivity and in size. Under these circumstances, it is not surprising that the rate of growth of best-practice productivity and the rate of growth of average productivity (or their levels at the end of the run) tended to be functions only of the rate of growth of latent productivity. These variables were insensitive to the ease or difficulty of imitation.

Table 14.2 presents comparable data for runs that started out with sixteen firms of equal size. We shall scrutinize differences among the sixteen-firm runs shortly. Here, we make some rough comparisons of what happened in the four-firm runs as contrasted to the sixteen-firm

Table 14.1. Four-firm runs.

	SE		FE		SH		FH	
	1	2	1	2	1	2	1	2
1. CAP SHR: IN	0.51	0.49	0.50	0.50	0.52	0.50	0.50	0.51
2. EX RET (%/QTR)	4.8	4.8	4.7	4.7	4.8	4.8	4.8	4.8
3. MARGIN AV COST (%)	33.7	33.3	33.0	31.3	33.2	33.2	32.4	31.4
4. MARGIN BEST PRAC (%)	33.7	33.3	33.0	31.3	33.2	33.2	47.8	38.0
5. Q SHR: IN1	0.26	0.25	0.25	0.26	0.27	0.25	0.27	0.28
6. Q SHR: IN2	0.26	0.24	0.25	0.24	0.24	0.25	0.25	0.22
7. Q SHR: IM1	0.26	0.25	0.25	0.26	0.25	0.25	0.25	0.27
8. Q SHR: IM2	0.23	0.25	0.25	0.25	0.23	0.25	0.23	0.22
9. H NUM EQV	4.0	4.0	4.0	4.0	4.0	4.0	4.0	4.0
10. AV A	0.28	0.28	0.82	0.94	0.28	0.29	0.86	0.75
11. AV A: IN	0.28	0.28	0.82	0.94	0.28	0.29	0.89	0.75
12. AV A: IM	0.28	0.28	0.82	0.94	0.28	0.29	0.83	0.75
13. BEST PRAC A	0.28	0.28	0.82	0.94	0.28	0.29	0.96	0.79
14. AV A GAP	0.05	0.04	0.22	0.18	0.03	0.08	0.15	0.17
15. IN R&D SUM	156.	153.	156.	157.	156.	155.	153.	154.
16. IN DRAWS	77	76	79	78	72	88	62	81
17. P	0.75	0.76	0.26	0.22	0.76	0.73	0.25	0.28

Table 14.2.   Sixteen-firm runs, science-based case, with investment restraint.

	SE		FE		SH		FH	
	1	2	1	2	1	2	1	2
1. CAP SHR: IN	0.51	0.55	0.55	0.50	0.60	0.61	0.80	0.70
2. EX RET (%/QTR)	0.77	0.77	0.66	0.77	0.87	0.92	0.69	0.81
3. MARGIN AV COST (%)	7.9	9.8	7.5	8.3	9.6	10.8	11.9	12.5
4. MARGIN BEST PRAC (%)	12.1	13.7	27.4	12.3	13.6	15.1	37.9	35.5
5. Q SHR: IN1	0.09	0.11	0.16	0.11	0.11	0.14	0.19	0.27
6. Q SHR: IN2	0.09	0.11	0.09	0.11	0.10	0.14	0.16	0.17
7. Q SHR: IM1	0.08	0.12	0.15	0.12	0.11	0.12	0.09	0.20
8. Q SHR: IM2	0.08	0.12	0.15	0.11	0.08	0.07	0.02	0.04
9. H NUM EQV	13.7	11.8	11.3	12.2	12.4	11.1	8.0	7.3
10. AV A	0.26	0.28	0.81	0.82	0.27	0.27	0.86	0.83
11. AV A: IN	0.26	0.28	0.81	0.81	0.27	0.28	0.91	0.85
12. AV A: IM	0.26	0.28	0.81	0.82	0.26	0.26	0.65	0.79
13. BEST PRAC A	0.27	0.29	0.96	0.85	0.28	0.28	1.06	1.00
14. AV A GAP	0.06	0.06	0.02	0.12	0.04	0.03	0.09	0.05
15. IN R&D SUM	196.	206.	197.	187.	200.	186.	242.	210.
16. IN DRAWS	87	110	78	97	104	106	137	102
17. P	0.66	0.63	0.21	0.21	0.65	0.65	0.21	0.22

runs. For a given rate of growth of latent productivity, there are not many noticeable differences between the rate of growth of best practice in the four-firm runs as compared with the sixteen-firm runs. However, average practice tended to be higher in the four-firm runs than in the sixteen-firm runs. In the sense of making the most widespread use of the best available technologies, the more concentrated industry structure scored better than the less concentrated one. Also, the more concentrated industry generally achieved this better productivity growth performance with a smaller aggregate volume of innovative R&D expenditure. The concentrated industry structure was more efficient in its use of R&D.

On the other hand, average markups over variable costs were significantly higher in the four-firm runs, and the static triangle losses, therefore, were greater there. And the higher markups more than offset the higher average productivity in the sixteen-firm run, so that price was higher in the concentrated industry case than in the sixteen-firm case, given the rate of growth of latent productivity.

A More Competitive Science-Based Industry

Perhaps the most significant aspect of the sixteen-firm runs was alluded to above when we compared growth of best practice and average productivity in the sixteen- and four-firm runs for a given rate of growth of latent productivity, without finding it necessary to take into account the settings of other parameter values, such as the ease of imitation or the degree of aggressiveness of profitable firms. Note that, in fact, these parameters seem to have only minor effects. At first thought, this might be something of a surprise. While it is plausible that growth of best-practice productivity would be insensitive to these institutional variables, one might have expected that in regimes where imitation of prevailing best practice was difficult, average productivity in the industry would tend to lag behind best practice to a greater extent than in regimes where imitation was easier. In fact, in the cases where latent productivity growth was rapid and imitation of best practice was difficult, a significant productivity gap opened up between the firms that did innovative R&D (particularly the productivity leader) and the firms that only imitated. But it was also true that in these cases the imitating firms tended to shrink in size relative to those that successfully innovated; thus, although there was a greater gap between the leaders and the laggers, a smaller share of industry capital was accounted for toward the end of the run by the laggers.

As suggested above, a striking contrast between the four-firm runs and the sixteen-firm runs was a tendency for industry structure to change significantly in the latter but not in the former. The initial distribution of firm sizes tended to be moderately stable where latent productivity growth was slow (regardless of the ease of imitation) or where latent productivity growth was rapid but imitation easy, so long as profitable firms showed restraint regarding their output expansion as they grew large. In runs with these settings, the firms that did not engage in innovative R&D tended to be more profitable than those that did. In other words, innovative R&D was not profitable to undertake. But given the output restraint showed by the slightly more profitable imitators, competition was orderly enough so that innovators were not driven out of business.

Where latent productivity growth was rapid and imitation hard, the firms that did innovative R&D fared much better and the firms that only imitated did much worse, even though profitable firms showed output growth restraint. In these runs it was apparent that the imitators were gradually being driven out of business, even though the innovators were showing considerable restraint in pushing their advantage.

Table 14.3 displays statistics for runs in which profitable firms continued to expand aggressively even when they grew large in relation to the market. The comparison between Tables 14.2 and 14.3 is quite interesting. If one normalizes for the rate of latent productivity growth and for the imitation regime, in each and every case where profitable firms did not show output restraint the fate of the innovators was less fortunate relative to the imitators than it was when large profitable firms did show output restraint. In every one of the runs of the aggressive competition case, by the end innovators accounted for significantly less than half of the industry capital stock.

The comparison is particularly striking for the case of rapid growth of latent productivity and hard imitation. Under restrained competition, the innovators clearly dominate and have 70 percent or more of industry capital by the end of the run. When firms have aggressive investment policies, the imitators prevail, and by much the same decisive margin. Although it would be easy to understand why the intensity of the struggle might affect the margin of "victory," it is something of a surprise to find that it also affects, quite systematically, the identity of the victor.

The explanation for this phenomenon, and for the asymmetry of results in the investment restraint case, resides in the following. In this model an imitating firm can never achieve a higher productivity level than the best of the innovators. An imitator that matches an innovator's productivity will have higher profits, because it does not incur the innovative R&D costs. But if it stops its output growth at reasonable size, pressures on the innovating firm to contract are re-

Table 14.3. Sixteen-firm runs, science-based case, with aggressive investment.

	SE		FE		SH		FH	
	1	2	1	2	1	2	1	2
1. CAP SHR: IN	0.32	0.31	0.34	0.32	0.38	0.36	0.36	0.32
2. EX RET (%/QTR)	0.19	0.19	0.03	0.09	0.28	0.21	-0.01	-0.15
3. MARGIN AV COST (%)	2.3	2.9	1.1	1.8	4.7	4.9	0.1	-1.1
4. MARGIN BEST PRAC (%)	2.3	9.6	13.0	4.7	12.7	8.9	6.0	4.1
5. Q SHR: IN1	0.06	0.06	0.13	0.10	0.07	0.08	0.11	0.12
6. Q SHR: IN2	0.05	0.05	0.08	0.06	0.06	0.07	0.11	0.05
7. Q SHR: IM1	0.13	0.12	0.22	0.23	0.21	0.18	0.44	0.54
8. Q SHR: IM2	0.12	0.12	0.16	0.18	0.13	0.15	0.15	0.07
9. H NUM EQV	12.1	12.3	8.6	8.5	10.3	10.8	4.4	3.4
10. AV A	0.26	0.27	0.85	0.70	0.26	0.26	0.71	0.97
11. AV A: IN	0.26	0.27	0.80	0.69	0.27	0.26	0.70	0.96
12. AV A: IM	0.26	0.28	0.87	0.70	0.26	0.26	0.72	0.98
13. BEST PRAC A	0.26	0.29	0.95	0.72	0.28	0.27	0.76	1.02
14. AV A GAP	0.02	0.04	0.11	0.10	0.00	-0.05	0.05	0.33
15. IN R&D SUM	162.	165.	174.	176.	174.	161.	175.	188.
16. IN DRAWS	72	76	99	79	85	77	92	104
17. P	0.63	0.60	0.19	0.23	0.63	0.65	0.23	0.16

laxed, the R&D budget is not eroded, and there is a chance of recovery for the innovating firm. (On the other hand a large innovator will stochastically extend its advantage over a small imitator.) But if the large imitating firm continues to grow, it forces the innovating firm to continue to contract. As the innovator's R&D budget contracts, the chances of an innovative success that will spark recovery diminish, and the expected lead time before the big imitator imitates diminishes as well.

We think there is a phenomenon here, albeit in stylized model form, that is well worth pondering. In our model world, an imitative strategy may, if supported by luck early in the industry's evolution, be a runaway winner. And certainly imitators will have good luck at least some of the time. Is it really socially desirable that they should press their advantage? Earlier we argued that the answer might depend on what a lower level of innovative R&D costs society.

In these simulation runs there was little tendency for best practice or average practice in the last period to be lower in the aggressive investment case than in the restrained investment case, for a given rate of growth of latent productivity. To some extent this is because total industry output and capital tended to be greater (although in the former case the innovators' share of total capital tended to be less) and total innovative R&D spending over the simulation run was therefore not radically different in the two cases. The result points in part to the real social advantage of a structure dominated by large imitators: once an innovation exists, it is rapidly applied to a large fraction of industry capacity. (Note the high average productivity of imitators in the FH cases of Table 14.3.)

But the central reason is that relatively sharply diminishing returns on innovative R&D are inherent in the science-based technological regime. A smaller R&D expenditure means that the path of latent productivity is tracked less well and that on average the difference between industry best practice and latent productivity is greater. But even an occasional innovative R&D hit suffices to keep the average distance from being very great. However, the social costs that occur if imitators come to dominate an industry might be significantly greater in a regime where the opportunities for today's technical change are more influenced by the industry's own prior R&D efforts and less influenced by developments outside the industry than has been the case in the runs considered thus far.

Cumulative Technological Advance

In the simulation runs reported here, there is no outside augmentation of the set of possible innovations. Rather, the outcome of any innovation draw is very much influenced by the prevailing technique of the firm making that draw. In particular, technological advance is assumed to be cumulative in the sense defined above.

Tables 14.4 and 14.5 display relevant industry statistics for runs with a structure of different parameter settings that is similar to that in Tables 14.2 and 14.3. Many of the same relationships that held in the earlier cases hold in these as well: the character of innovation and imitation affects industry concentration in the same way; the fast innovation, hard imitation condition tends to lead to concentration; where innovation is slow and imitation easy, such tendencies were far less marked. Regarding the competitive contest between innovators and imitators, innovators do well when the conditions permit fast technical advance and where imitation is difficult, provided large firms show restraint in further expanding output. The imitators do well and the innovators do poorly in the opposite parameter settings. Where firms continued to be aggressive in their output decisions even as they grew large, profits of both innovators and imitators were less than in cases where more restrained behavior obtained. But it was especially the innovators whose fortunes were hurt. The asymmetry in the model continues to have force under these different assumptions regarding the nature of innovation. Imitators cannot have a higher productivity level than that of the best of the innovators. If they restrain their output growth, innovators can recover. But if a profitable imitator grows aggressively, the recuperative powers of the innovators are diminished. These results are similar to those reported above.

What is different about these simulation runs is that aggressive competitive behavior has a clear negative effect on both best-practice productivity and average productivity. Comparing runs with the same setting of other parameters, each of the pair of best-practice statistics almost invariably is larger in the runs where the firms restrained their output growth than in the runs where they did not. As in the earlier runs, aggressive competitive behavior tends to generate a structure in which there is at least one large imitator that is capable of quickly mimicking any new innovation and that operates with lower costs than the innovators. As the profitless innovating firms shrink, so does total industry innovative R&D. In every one of the comparisons, innovative R&D for the industry was less in the aggressive competition case than in the restrained competition case and the number of innovation draws was smaller. And in contrast to the science-based cases, where such a cutback in industry innovative R&D and innovation draws had little effect on the time path of industry best practice (save to make it more jagged and somewhat lower), in these runs reduced industry innovation shows up in a slower growth of best practice.

As one would expect, there is less of an effect on average produc-

Table 14.4. Sixteen-firm runs, with cumulative technical change and investment restraint.

	SE		FE		SH		FH	
	1	2	1	2	1	2	1	2
1. CAP SHR: IN	0.56	0.50	0.64	0.49	0.57	0.50	0.77	0.68
2. EX RET (%/QTR)	0.72	0.74	0.78	0.75	0.84	0.78	0.77	0.83
3. MARGIN AV COST (%)	8.6	8.6	10.0	8.3	9.0	8.5	10.7	12.6
4. MARGIN BEST PRAC (%)	13.1	12.9	32.4	22.3	13.7	13.2	31.1	31.4
5. Q SHR: IN1	0.10	0.11	0.17	0.19	0.10	0.10	0.23	0.20
6. Q SHR: IN2	0.10	0.09	0.14	0.08	0.10	0.09	0.19	0.19
7. Q SHR: IM1	0.08	0.10	0.17	0.18	0.10	0.09	0.07	0.11
8. Q SHR: IM2	0.08	0.10	0.06	0.17	0.09	0.08	0.07	0.08
9. H NUM EQV	14.3	12.6	10.7	9.4	13.1	13.4	7.2	8.1
10. AV A	0.24	0.25	0.59	0.62	0.23	0.23	0.83	0.60
11. AV A: IN	0.24	0.25	0.62	0.61	0.24	0.23	0.89	0.64
12. AV A: IM	0.24	0.25	0.55	0.62	0.23	0.23	0.64	0.52
13. BEST PRAC A	0.25	0.26	0.71	0.70	0.24	0.24	0.98	0.70
14. AV A GAP	n.a.	n.a.	n.a.	n.a.	n.a.	n.a.	n.a.	n.a.
15. IN R&D SUM	197.	190.	210.	182.	206.	188.	235.	208.
16. IN DRAWS	99	104	105	100	102	100	130	107
17. P	0.72	0.69	0.30	0.28	0.74	0.75	0.21	0.30

Table 14.5. Sixteen-firm runs, with cumulative technical change and aggressive investment.

	SE		FE		SH		FH	
	1	2	1	2	1	2	1	2
1. CAP SHR: IN	0.23	0.29	0.26	0.40	0.32	0.35	0.38	0.48
2. EX RET (%/QTR)	0.14	0.17	0.19	0.19	0.17	0.20	0.00	0.02
3. MARGIN AV COST (%)	2.3	2.4	3.0	2.5	4.3	3.3	1.3	2.1
4. MARGIN BEST PRAC (%)	2.3	2.4	9.1	9.3	9.5	7.8	6.2	5.7
5. Q SHR: IN1	0.05	0.06	0.06	0.10	0.05	0.07	0.12	0.14
6. Q SHR: IN2	0.04	0.05	0.05	0.09	0.05	0.06	0.08	0.13
7. Q SHR: IM1	0.13	0.14	0.24	0.16	0.14	0.13	0.20	0.27
8. Q SHR: IM2	0.12	0.14	0.16	0.14	0.12	0.12	0.20	0.14
9. H NUM EQV	11.4	10.9	8.5	11.2	12.1	11.8	7.1	7.0
10. AV A	0.22	0.24	0.51	0.75	0.20	0.23	0.62	0.56
11. AV A: IN	0.21	0.23	0.50	0.73	0.20	0.23	0.61	0.56
12. AV A: IM	0.22	0.24	0.51	0.77	0.20	0.22	0.62	0.55
13. BEST PRAC A	0.22	0.24	0.54	0.80	0.21	0.24	0.65	0.58
14. AV A GAP	n.a.	n.a.	n.a.	n.a.	n.a.	n.a.	n.a.	n.a.
15. IN R&D SUM	148.	158.	146.	189.	156.	161.	192.	209.
16. IN DRAWS	80	84	83	86	64	88	99	115
17. P	0.75	0.69	0.32	0.22	0.83	0.73	0.26	0.29

tivity than on best practice. Where there is one huge imitator comprising a large share of industry capital, average productivity is largely determined by its productivity, and its productivity stays close to best practice. In most of the cases, however, average productivity was lower in the aggressive competition case than in the comparable case of more restrained competition.

The effect of aggressive competition on the price of the industry product is less certain. To some extent, lower markups over costs in the strong competition case offset higher costs in that case. Nonetheless, and in striking contradiction to textbook wisdom, by and large end-period industry price tended to be higher in the aggressive competition case than in the restrained competition case, for similar parameter settings. Furthermore, examination of price trends in the two contrasting settings suggests that, if the simulation run were longer, price under aggressive competition would grow progressively higher than would price under more gentlemanly competition. Our 101-period simulation runs end with some innovators continuing to exist with nontrivial capital stocks, but in retreat. As the retreat continues, industry innovative R&D expenditures should dry up. And ultimately the industry should settle into something quite close to a competitive equilibrium with zero profits and static technology.

Table 14.6 presents data for simulations that we ran for 201 periods. In the science-based technology regime the innovators have indeed shrunk further in the aggressive investment behavior case, but best-practice productivity is not badly affected. On the other hand, in the cumulative technology regime, period 201 best practice is much lower in the aggressive competition case than in the case where competition is more restrained. The hidden hand has throttled the goose that lays the golden eggs.

4. SOME POLICY AND EMPIRICAL IMPLICATIONS

Undoubtedly, the difficulties that beset the literature on the Schumpeterian arguments are in large part a reflection of the complexity and difficulty of the subject matter. But part of the problem has been that economists have not tried to confront those complexities with a model designed for that task.

We have presented an abstract model of Schumpeterian competition that is designed to help economists think through some of the processes involved, sharpen their intuitions regarding the relationships between technical progress and market structure, and see more clearly the public policy issues that are latent in those relations. Some

of the implications of our model are consonant with less formal asser-
tions about the characteristics of Schumpeterian competition. There
are advantages to a firm in being large. In particular, the larger
a firm, the greater the ability to appropriate returns from its own
successful R&D efforts. Also, the larger R&D spending of a larger
firm tends to provide a smoother, more reliable advance of
productivity—and thus a lower vulnerability to declines brought on
by temporary innovative dearth.

Our model helps sharpen certain propositions that when presented informally tend to be rather fuzzy. In particular, its workings
are such that market structure *per se* matters. If the rest of the industry is small in total size or consists largely of very small firms, this
enhances the extent to which a firm of a given size can appropriate
the returns from its own innovation. Also, market structure and
behavior can shelter or lead to the decline of firms that spend on in-

Table 14.6. Sixteen-firm runs, with 201 periods, rapid growth
of latent productivity, and difficult innovation.

	Science-based		Cumulative	
	Aggressive	Restrained	Aggressive	Restrained
1. CAP SHR: IN	0.23	0.87	0.30	0.49
2. EX RET (%/QTR)	−0.13	2.27	0.03	3.68
3. MARGIN AV COST (%)	0.75	16.24	0.13	28.36
4. MARGIN BEST PRAC (%)	12.5	29.1	7.8	31.5
5. Q SHR: IN1	0.20	0.22	0.22	0.26
6. Q SHR: IN2	0.01	0.20	0.02	0.22
7. Q SHR: IM1	0.73	0.08	0.55	0.24
8. Q SHR: IM2	0.02	0.01	0.14	0.23
9. H NUM EQV	1.71	6.25	2.81	4.41
10. AV A	3.48	3.66	2.62	4.77
11. AV A: IN	3.54	3.75	2.48	4.80
12. AV A: IM	3.47	3.00	2.68	4.74
13. BEST PRAC A	3.81	4.05	2.81	4.90
14. AV A GAP	0.16	0.15	n.a.	n.a.
15. IN R&D SUM	339.	484.	383.	389.
16. IN DRAWS	183	254	175	185
17. P	0.04	0.05	0.06	0.04

novative R&D in circumstances in which a strategy of imitating is more profitable.

Some policy conundrums that may well be presented by economic reality are illustrated by the model. It leads us to contemplate the possibility that not only may a relatively concentrated industry provide a better shelter for R&D than a more fragmented industry structure, but that production and technical advance may also be more efficient in such a setting. Thus, some tradeoffs are revealed, but not necessarily the same ones that have been identified previously. In particular, in an industry in which technology is science-based, greater concentration "trades off" higher markups for a smaller gap between average and best practice and for more efficient R&D (in the sense that a given productivity level is tracked more cheaply), but does not buy a faster rate of growth of productivity. Further, the tradeoff may be different in some industries than in others; in our experiments with an industry whose technology is cumulative, a more sheltered competitive environment, with its associated higher markups, does lead to more rapid productivity growth.

The results that show a tendency for firms that do innovative R&D to lose out in a competitive struggle with skillful and aggressive imitators are particularly provocative, and illustrate a possibility not much discussed in the economic literature. Nor has there been much discussion differentiating the kinds of regimes for technical progress under which the social costs are slight (science-based industries) or heavy (cumulative technology industries) when firms that invest in innovative R&D are driven to the wall or out of business.

There are some interesting predicted empirical relationships that derive from the model, but, as with the policy conundrums, they are somewhat more subtle than those that many economists seem to think reside in Schumpeterian competition. Most of the reported empirical "tests" have rested on the supposition that the Schumpeterian arguments imply that large firms tend to spend relatively more on R&D than do small firms. Under the stylized conditions of our experiments, such a correlation can arise only as a result of selection—that is, of differential growth of innovators relative to imitators. In experimental settings in which innovative R&D is profitable, the firms that spend on innovative R&D (and hence that have a higher ratio of total R&D to capital) do tend to grow in relation to the imitators, but in such a setting the small firms tend to be eliminated. Where innovative R&D is not profitable but where market structure permits it to survive, the R&D-intensive firms tend to be small.

On the basis of our model, one can predict that industries with rapid technical progress ought to be marked by high average R&D intensity and, as the industry matures, by a more concentrated industry structure than industries in which technical progress is slower. And, interestingly enough, various studies attempting to explain cross-industry differences in productivity growth rates have identified roughly the above relationship. The model also suggests that concentration is likely to increase over time in a technologically progressive industry—another relationship that seems to hold empirically.

Some other interesting relationships are suggested that present intriguing (though difficult) targets for empirical research. For example, the relationship between R&D expenditure and rate of productivity growth in an industry may depend on the character of technical advance in the industry—in particular, on whether there is an exogenous flow of new innovative opportunities and on whether technical change in the industry is cumulative in the sense that today's advances build on yesterday's. In actuality, these possibilities are not likely to be mutually exclusive, but there may be some situations that approach one or the other of the pure cases. It would be interesting to try to classify industries by regimes of technological change and to test whether there are differences between the regimes in the relations connecting technical progress with internal R&D expenditure. Similarly, it would be interesting to attempt to measure "technological opportunity" and thus to explore *directly* the question of whether industries in which opportunities are rapidly expanding tend to generate both high innovative R&D expenditure and a concentrated industry structure (as contrasted with *inferring* this indirectly from regressions relating industry R&D intensity and concentration to rates of measured technical change). Does the survivability of innovative R&D depend on the difficulty of imitation? Again, an answer to the question depends on being able to measure the ease of imitation.

It should be clear that Schumpeter's appraisal of progressive capitalism continues to present an imposing challenge to theorists, econometricians, policy analysts, and scholars of technological change.[4] We hope that this analysis will prompt researchers to view the Schumpeterian arguments in a new light.

---

4. On the theoretical front, analytical models of Schumpeterian competition that are akin to our simulation model have been analyzed by Horner (1977) and, more recently, by Iwai (1981a, 1981b).

VI

ECONOMIC WELFARE AND POLICY

15

Normative Economics from an Evolutionary Perspective

IN THE EVOLUTIONARY PERSPECTIVE we have presented, the stress thus far has generally been on positive theory rather than normative theory. However, in several places normative issues have been addressed explicitly; our discussion of factors influencing the performance of an industry in a regime of Schumpeterian competition is a case in point. And in many other places—for example, the discussion of the factors influencing the magnitude of the substitution response to changed factor prices—the commentary had obvious normative implications.

It is apparent that an evolutionary view of what *is* going on in the world of firms and industries strongly influences how one looks at the question of what *should be* going on. Our criticisms of orthodox theory extend to its normative branch. Contemporary normative theory regarding allocation and distribution is based on the same assumption of given and known opportunity sets as is employed in contemporary positive theory. The normative economic problem is seen in terms of characterizing the point within the set that maximizes social welfare. The recognized theoretical stumbling point along the analytical path involves the social welfare function, not the choice set.[1] But if the scope of feasible choice is ambiguous, then (problems with the maximand aside) one cannot define, much less identify, a maximal element. If the discovery or invention of new alternatives is an integral aspect of economic activity, then any useful

---

1. The classic statement of course is by Arrow (1951).

attempt to characterize desirable allocation must take into account the effect of particular allocations on alternatives that in the future will be perceived and understood.

Relatedly, if the organizational aspects of the economic problem are viewed in evolutionary perspective, the traditional virtues ascribed to competition no longer seem sufficient for its espousal as an ideal (or even a satisfactory) organizational arrangement. For if the economic world is in continuing flux, as our positive theory suggests is the case, the normative properties associated with competitive equilibrium become meaningless, just as that equilibrium is meaningless as a description of behavior. The Schumpeterian concerns about the relationship of market structure to innovation move from the periphery of normative discussion to the center.

An evolutionary approach to positive economics thus calls for a complementary rethinking of normative economics—a difficult task. A normative theory consistent with an evolutionary approach to positive theory almost certainly will be complex and messy. It is unlikely that one will be able to prove many sweeping normative theorems of the sort that are now contained in our advanced treatises and elementary texts. This, however, should not cause despair. Economists have been commenting on microeconomic policy issues for hundreds of years, and only recently has this commentary been based on the neat theorems of contemporary welfare economics. Moreover, a good portion of the contemporary argument for heavy reliance on markets and competition rests not on the formalism of contemporary theory, but rather on an implicit evolutionary view of what is going on and of the organizational alternatives. Compared with the normative arguments of contemporary orthodoxy, the arguments of Hayek (1945) or of Schumpeter lack rigor but perhaps are more convincing. And there is a subtlety to the analysis that enables the contemporary reader to see the limitations of competitive enterprise as well as its strengths, and thus to begin to appreciate the varieties of organizational forms and the subtleties of interdependence that characterize the actual institutional ecology of modern society.

1. RETRACING A FAMILIAR PATH

Contemporary welfare economics sees the economic problem in two different ways: from one angle the problem is seen as that of choosing an allocation of resources; from the other vantage point the problem is seen as organizational. We propose that much of the organizational argument is implicitly evolutionary.

The allocation problem is formalized in optimization language. A given set of resources, technologies, and preferences is postulated. Resources and technologies together define a set of production possibilities. Efficiency at the level of production requires that the economy be at the frontier of that set. When preferences for commodities are considered as well, the set of allocations that involve the efficient production and distribution of an efficient output mix gives rise to a utility possibility frontier. If one postulates, in addition, a social welfare function that relates social preferences to individual preferences, the economic problem can be posed as that of maximizing that function—subject, ultimately, to the underlying conditions of resource availability, technology, and preference.

From another perspective, welfare economics views the economic problem as choosing an organizational structure rather than as (directly) choosing an allocation and distribution. Onto the economic problem defined in allocational and distributional terms, let us graft such assumptions as convexity of preferences and production sets, that all goods are private, that perfect contracts can be costlessly written and enforced, and that private firms can be expected to correctly maximize profits and private households to maximize utility. Then the *dual organizational* theorems of contemporary welfare economics emerge. Any competitive equilibrium is Pareto optimal, and any Pareto optimal position (including that which maximizes social welfare) can be achieved as a competitive equilibrium with a suitable set of transfer payments (Arrow and Hahn, 1971).

Notice an important difference between the contemporary discussion of the allocation problem and the organization problem. While in analysis of the allocation problem the full set of possible *allocations* is recognized and defined, no such explicit recognition of possible *organizational* alternatives is made in the argument about the optimality (given the ancillary assumptions) of a regime of consumer sovereignty and free-market enterprise. The task of explicit consideration of organizational alternatives is finessed by the proposition that a competitive regime, given the extra assumptions, will do as well as can be done. Note that the argument does *not* hold that competition can outperform central planning or any other organizational alternative; rather, it is that other alternatives can at best tie competitive equilibrium.

Once these facts are noted, it is apparent that contemporary arguments in favor of real free enterprise cannot be rationalized by modern analytical welfare economics alone. Many sophisticated economists have recognized this explicitly, and some even have proposed that the most important achievement of modern normative theory is to demonstrate dramatically the striking implausibility of the proposition that a regime of free enterprise would ever achieve optimality. Yet Western economists tend to advocate free enterprise as a basic organizational solution to the economic problem, even though it is admitted that many of the conditions required for the optimality theorems do not obtain. It is acknowledged that in many technologies there are economies of scale that give rise to nonconvexities (and hence in these industries profit-maximizing firms will not likely act as price takers). Many goods are "public" and externalities are pervasive. Complex contracts are hard to write and enforce. It is acknowledged that firms and households may lack perfect information. And it is certainly recognized that the political economy of reality may not generate an ethically ideal (or even humane) system for redistribution of wealth. These problems with the competitive organizational solution are viewed as partially remediable with ancillary organizational machinery to spur competition as much as possible, make demand effective for public goods, control externalities, and aid the needy. It is this patched-up system, with admitted flaws, that Western economists tend to support and advocate. It should be apparent that such advocacy cannot rest much weight of argument on modern welfare economics.

It also is clear that in advocating the free enterprise solution with patchups, most economists have an alternative (of a stylized variety) in mind. At the economic system level, this alternative is Soviet-style central planning. At the sectoral level, the alternative is public ownership or detailed governmental regulation. Despite the recognized flaws in private enterprise, there is near consensus among Western economists that a regime of central planning will do (and, where it is established, *does* do) a worse job. There is, furthermore, widespread disenchantment with attempts on the part of government to regulate particular sectors in economies that rely primarily on markets for coordination. These negative reactions to planning and regulation do not find any basis in the theorems of welfare economics. Nothing in those theorems says that planning or regulation cannot be made to work (optimally).

Clearly, modern economists have some ideas about the role of organization in guiding economic activity and about the way in which different organizational structures perform that are disjoint from the analysis in Arrow and Debreu. In contemporary discussion it is possible to discern two roughly distinguishable analytic aspects of the problem. One of these involves information and computation. If we accept for the moment the way in which modern welfare economics poses the allocation and distribution problem and the conditions for its optimal solution, it is apparent that to achieve that solution an enormous amount of disparate data need to be somehow acquired, brought to appropriate places for computation, and combined in a computation task of staggering scope. The data involve personal preferences, characteristics of available technologies, and assessments of resource availability. The other analytic aspect involves problems of command and control. Assume that the appropriate information has been gathered, the computations made, and the appropriate allocations and distributions discovered or decided upon. Farms, factories, distribution centers, and consumers are widely scattered. Within any particular factory a large number of people may be involved in activities that must mesh together. A "solution" to the economic problem cannot be effected unless these disparate actors are informed as to what they should do. And once they are informed, they must somehow be motivated or coerced to do the right things.

It is clear that many economists believe that the market competition alternative has attractive characteristics regarding both the information and computation problem and the command and control problem. Decentralized free enterprise operating in a market environment has been touted as superior to government ownership of firms and central planning on the grounds that the latter solution would involve vastly more information sending and would require the computation of much larger problems. It also seems to be believed strongly by most Western economists that free enterprise is much more sensitive to demands, more strongly motivated to cater to preferences of consumers, and more likely to produce efficiently than is government bureaucracy.

This, we argue, is one key to the puzzle of why contemporary economists tend to argue *for* free enterprise and *against* central planning much more strongly than could possibly be justified by the theorems of welfare economics that are often held up as the scientific basis of the argument. Behind the scenes is an implicit theory of the role of organization in solving big allocation problems, and some conjectures about the way in which different organizational structures perform. However, in contrast to the optimal allocation arguments that at least have rigor, the organizational arguments are poorly articulated and often seem more to reflect casual empiricism or prejudice than careful theorizing and empirical study. Also, while there seems to be a belief that the organizational arguments can simply be tacked onto the optimal allocation arguments, there is reason to wonder about this. The problems addressed by the organizational arguments—problems involving information and computation, command and control—have no explicit place within the mainstream of modern welfare economics.[2]

---

2. Some recent works do attempt to deal with these aspects explicitly. Perhaps the most elaborate discussion is in Marschak and Radner (1972).

In particular, although the welfare economics arguments presume an equilibrium context, most of the discussions of organizational problems explicitly or implicitly assume a dynamic context, in which preferences, resources, and technologies are changing over time in a way that is not fully predictable. Thus, allocation must track a moving optimum. Were the context static or predictable, the organizational aspects of the problem might not be overwhelmingly difficult or costly. The information-computation problem could be solved "once and for all" (and this *is* the way the problem is viewed in formal theory). The costs of making this once-and-for-all analysis might not loom large when they are amortized over the time horizon of the economic system; arguably, the differences between organizational structures regarding these costs would not be particularly important. Similarly, the command and control problem does not seem particularly difficult or costly if what everybody is supposed to do can be specified in advance once and for all. Then effective command and monitoring schemes would likely be relatively simple to devise, under a wide range of organizational alternatives.

In reality, the nature and magnitude of the organizational problem is intimately connected with the degree of economic flux.[3] In a world of flux, organizational performance comparisons must be concerned with accuracy and speed of response to changed conditions. This perception is explicit in the writings of the classical economists. From Smith to Marshall, the arguments in favor of free enterprise tended to stress the adaptive and energetic aspects of private enterprise. The problems of command and control and of information computation were both recognized, although the former tended to be better articulated than the latter. And it is clear that, from the beginning, private enterprise was compared with a regime of greater governmental involvement. The classical organizational analysis is both more explicitly dynamic and more explicit about comparison than contemporary formal thinking.

The Mises-Lange-Hayek interchange brings out the relevant issues strikingly.[4] It proceeded without the advantage (or disadvantage) of post–World War II formal welfare economics. Mises proposed that prices arising out of free competitive markets were an *essential* aspect of any decently working information and computation system. Absent these, producers have no economically relevant information to enable them to judge what consumer goods to produce or what input mixes to employ in production. *With* these, the computation problem simplifies to calculations of profit or cost. Lange rec-

---

3. This point of view has been forcefully advocated by Hayek (1945), among others.
4. See Mises (1951), Lange (1938), and Hayek (1945).

ognized the role of prices and responded to Mises with his proposal that in socialism, as in capitalism, consumers should make their own spending decisions, given their incomes and prices, and that producers should choose input mixes to minimize the cost of production and output levels such that marginal cost equals price; excess demands and supplies of final products and inputs should be fed back to a central agency which adjusts prices up or down accordingly—in effect, simulating a market.

Hayek's objection to the Lange proposal involved an interesting blend of propositions about information computation and about command and control. He argued that Lange's information-flow scheme could not handle the enormous amount of detailed data specific to particular times and places. A rise in the demand for apples in local region X ought to be reflected in a rise in the price of apples in local region X. To channel excess-demand information back to the center for processing and to wait for central determination that prices ought to rise would be time-consuming and cumbersome. Farmers and grocers in region X would act to increase prices much more rapidly if they themselves had the authority to do so. A consequence is that internal supply would be stimulated and apples would flow into the region from outside more quickly under real free enterprise than under Langian socialism. Hayek also argued that private profit-seeking farmers and grocers have greater incentive to take the appropriate output actions in response to changed prices than would bureaucrats occupying the same jobs.

This discussion of the comparative merits of market socialism and private enterprise was noteworthy both for the explicitness with which the case for the latter was made in comparative terms and for the scope of the considerations adduced. But from the earliest days of the discipline, the case for markets and competition was always implicitly (and sometimes explicitly) a comparative case. It had in view alternative approaches, recently experienced or proposed, to important issues of economic policy. And it was not a case for a perfect organizational answer to a static and stylized problem, but for a real organizational answer to a real, ambiguous, and ever-changing problem. More than Hayek, but perhaps less than Schumpeter, the classical economists saw the virtues of the system as including an ability to generate a variety of innovations, to screen and select from these, and to assure that in the long run most of the gains would accrue to consumers.

Clearly it is a serious oversimplification to view the discipline's long tradition of concern with the merits of competition as involving little more than a series of primitive attempts to articulate the theorems of modern welfare economics. Contemporary welfare economics sees the allocation problem in terms of picking a best element from a set. When the organizational problem is formalized, it is in terms of getting the signals and incentives right for the control of clerks. The older view of the allocation problem, like our view, sees the allocation problem as involving in an essential way the exploration of new alternatives; the organizational problem is viewed in a similar light. An evolutionary perspective on welfare economics, then, is not a radical departure. Rather, like our evolutionary positive theory, it represents a return to the traditional perspectives of classical economics and makes explicit the views that are implicit in contemporary appreciative reasoning.

While sympathetic with the older tradition and with contemporary informal normative discussion, we diverge from these in at least three respects. First, we think that the advocates of free enterprise have been too facile in arguing the merits of the stylized system in a stylized dynamic environment. The issue here is theoretical. Second, there is inadequate recognition of the extent to which some of the most fundamental problems of economic organization are either dispatched by assumption in those stylized arguments or are subsumed in a "minimal" list of governmental functions—the implication being that they could be easily handled if only the government would mind its own business. Here, the problem involves the dubious linkage between the institutional assumptions of theory and the range of institutions that could conceivably exist in a real system. Third, we note that these advocates often have had a tendency to apply general stylized argument to real policy issues and hence to neglect the fact that the actual economic system is much more complicated than the stylized model. The issue here is that in real policy analysis the details of the situation and of the specific organizational alternatives under consideration often are of central importance.

Regarding the theoretical argument, it ought to be noted that there is little in the way of theoretical justification for the apparently widespread belief that free enterprise is capable of rapidly and accurately tracking changing optimal configurations of inputs and outputs. Not only is there no theoretical support for the proposition that a competitive regime tracks a moving equilibrium closer than other (undefined) organizational regimes, but there is very little understanding about how a competitive regime tracks a moving target at all. Mathematical theorists have yet to work out theoretical proofs of the stability of competitive equilibrium that are based on plausible institutional assumptions and adequately reflect the important elements of irreversibility in economic decisions. Neither have they made a case that the seemingly inevitable departures from intertemporal efficiency in real market systems can be counted on to be "small" in some interesting sense. Similarly, as we have stressed, it is apparent that there is no way that the performance of a competitive regime in generating innovations can be brought within the scope of the standard optimality theorems. It is, of course, an important virtue of modern *formal* theory that it is quite clear about which propositions are established theorems and which are not. The difficulties arise in appreciative discussions of intended practical relevance, when the implications of theorems are handled loosely or abandoned in favor of more primitive promarket intuitions.

Any number of examples could be chosen to illustrate the point that modern advocacy of private enterprise solutions tends to suffer from vagueness or utopianism in its treatment of institutional matters. Three particularly important (and closely interrelated) ones involve the treatment of property rights, contracts, and law enforcement. In almost all formal economic theory, property rights and contractual obligations are assumed to be costlessly delineated in unambiguous terms and enforcement of the civil and criminal law is perfect and costless. By virtue of the combined force of these assumptions of clarity, perfection, and costlessness, the problem of providing the basic institutional underpinnings of a system of voluntary exchange is assumed away. It is then not too surprising that voluntary exchange can be shown to be a largely effective solution to such social problems as are left.

A real legal system that could approach the theoretical standards of clarity and perfection in the delineation and enforcement of entitlements would be an elaborate and expensive system indeed. This is particularly obvious if the system of entitlements is supposed to be so sophisticated as to bring within its scope all of the externality problems that economists sometimes treat as "merely" problems in the definition and enforcement of property rights—for example, the question of whether a chemical plant is entitled to dispose of its hazardous wastes in ways that contaminate the ground water, or whether neighboring property owners are entitled to uncontaminated ground water. Of course, informal advocacy of free-enterprise solutions is rarely encumbered by explicit reliance on the blatantly unrealistic institutional assumptions of formal theory. But it avoids the issue at the price of being vague about crucial parameters of the system advocated. Is it one in which an elaborate state apparatus exists to make sure that social interactions conform to a paradigm of voluntary exchange, assuring protection of an elaborate and sharply defined schedule of entitlements for each member of society? If so, how is the impartiality of this apparatus to be guaranteed? Or is this ideal society one that is much more anarchic, in which the coercive application of various forms of private power is routinely a determinant of important social outcomes? If so, how can the analysis of a stylized system of voluntary exchange be considered indicative of the nature of those outcomes?

Regarding the importance of looking at the details when examining real policy issues, we note first that arguments in the Hayekian vein often seem to have in view an image of private-enterprise institutions that is both narrow and idealized. The image is exemplified by the apple-market example we gave above and seems to share some of the nostalgic rusticity of that example. It is essentially an image of a collection of geographically dispersed spot markets in which atomistic competition prevails. But we know that the private-enterprise "solution" to the problem of economic organization is not always a market solution; for better or for worse, it clearly involves large elements of centralized planning and direction within the boundaries of large private corporations. It is rarely an atomistically competitive solution. And often when competition is keen, it is because it is national or global in scope. Alongside the favorable image of the responsiveness of the local apple market should therefore be placed the darker pictures associated with the shutdown of the local applesauce plant—a decision made in a remote corporate headquarters in response to actual or conjectured developments in even more remote sectors of the globe. And the real private-enterprise solution is often not all that private: it draws on a variety of forms of governmental support. Those apple growers probably belong to a producers' cooperative organized under government auspices.

These considerations do not imply any particular judgment on the merits of the private-enterprise solution as against any specific realistic alternative, nor do they render Hayek's insights irrelevant. They do, however, caution against the ascription of general systemic virtues and faults to particular real organizational arrangements. The "private enterprise" of agriculture is vastly different from the "private enterprise" of aircraft manufacturing. And both of these sectors are substantially and differently shaped by public programs. The unique organizational characteristics of a particular sector ought to come to the fore in the analysis of policy toward that sector.

Institutional diversity and complexity clearly poses a challenge to any theoretical scheme that is intended to illuminate a broad range of specific questions. The response of evolutionary theory to this challenge is set forth in more detail in the following chapter. Here we simply note that evolutionary normative analysis adheres naturally to a principle espoused by many economists before us: the most useful form of normative analysis is the detailed comparison of relatively specific organizational alternatives. It is not helpful to compare the performance of real markets with that of idealized central planners, or to compare the performance of real planners to that of idealized markets. It may be helpful, however, to consider at a relatively abstract level the kinds of policy problems that seem almost inevitably to arise in a political economy that places heavy reliance on profit-seeking firms and markets.

2. REAPPRAISING THE STANDARD PROBLEMS OF WELFARE ECONOMICS

Economic evolutionary dynamics is guided by information flows: information about new scientific developments, information regarding the success or failure of R&D projects to guide the next round of R&D decisions, information regarding the characteristics of new products to guide potential purchasers, information regarding costs of production and purchases to guide producers, information about profits to guide investors. The organizational dilemma posed for a predominantly market-organized economy is that it is efficient to make available information public, but the existence of private incentives for information gathering often requires that the information be private. The dilemma of a socialized system is that the information flow overwhelms a centralized system if it is open to new ideas and data, that closing the system and forcing the plan to work forecloses alternatives and risks unhedged mistakes, and that decentralizing without real markets poses the problems discussed by Hayek.

These information problems permeate virtually all economic processes. Some uncertainties are resolved and some information is generated in R&D, but much of the discovering process is not easily relegated to an isolated learning activity neatly separated from doing. Consumers learn about the new product after R&D is done, and through experience. Producers learn what consumers will buy only after consumers find out themselves. New information and economic change are integral. The information is about change. In turn, the information guides change, which provides new information, which stimulates and molds the next round of change.

Two kinds of things are represented as evolving in the evolutionary theory we have been elaborating: one of these is capabilities and behavior; the other is the mix and character of organizations that possess the capabilities and decision rules. This evolution of institutional structure proceeds in part through the market mechanisms we have considered. Thus, Schumpeterian competition selects both on inventions and on firms, and molds market structure as well as the flow of technology. But it also proceeds in part through conscious social policy. Thus, for example, antitrust laws were put in place to prevent or retard the growth of concentration, and various regulatory regimes have been imposed to moderate the incentive structure associated with concentration.

The following chapter contains detailed discussion of conscious public molding of institutional change. But it is important to recognize here that if the anatomy of market failure is a function of institutional structure, institutional structure itself evolves in part in response to perceived problems with the status quo.

The "anatomy of market failure" discussion in neoclassical economics is focused on equilibrium conditions of stylized market systems. We propose that, from an evolutionary perspective, such a discussion should properly focus on problems of dealing with and adjusting to change. The shift in perspective is important. It involves abandonment of the traditional normative goal of trying to define an "optimum" and the institutional structure that will achieve it, and an acceptance of the more modest objectives of identifying problems and possible improvements. However, the traditional literature of market failure does provide a useful rough categorization. There are real problems in coping with concentrations of power on the supply side, regardless of the theoretical perspective in which the problems are viewed. Externalities and publicness have similar meanings in evolutionary theory and in orthodoxy, and are seen to pose requirements for regulation and collective-choice machinery. A tension between distributional equity and efficiency seems to be a fact of life that any theory must comprehend. But these problems take on somewhat different guises within evolutionary theory and neoclassical orthodoxy.

In the orthodox view, the social cost imposed by private monopoly is describable in terms of a deadweight loss arising from noncompetitive pricing. The policy dilemma in dealing with monopoly is that monopoly may arise out of economies of scale that would make fragmentation of the industry inefficient. These conceptions remain significant in the evolutionary appraisal, but other aspects come into prominent view. The monopoly problem is also the "single-mind problem": in monopoly there is only one source of innovation. An additional tension regarding resolution through fragmentation is that there are major advantages to having a coherent overview of R&D.

Orthodox equilibrium analysis sees monopoly as "there." An evolutionary theory sees structure as evolving. Indeed, the canonical monopoly problem in evolutionary theory is that in which a firm has achieved dominance in an industry because of past skill or luck. This dynamic monopoly problem poses a severe dilemma for social policy. On the one hand, stepping in and breaking up firms that have grown large as a result of past successes certainly will dampen the incentives for other firms to engage in significant innovation. On the other hand, the consequence of inaction may be an industry that is dominated by a company that has lost its innovative prowess. Many economists are tempted to be optimistic about this problem, positing that if the company loses its innovational effectiveness and zeal, new firms or small firms will be able to enter and grow and the monopoly will turn out to be transient. However, our analysis of the situation suggests that if large firms preserve their capacity to imitate, the industry may be effectively barricaded from the entry and growth of small innovators. This problem of entrenched monopoly may be even more severe in circumstances in which experience counts. The only thing that may save the situation is the development elsewhere of significantly different technologies that can evolve along trajectories sharply different from those of the past; it was this prospect, of course, that underlay Schumpeter's rather optimistic view of the monopoly problem. This will give new firms a chance to arise and will wash out some of the advantages that large existing firms derive from their experience and imitative ability.

The concepts of externalities and publicness tend to be linked in the discussion of modern welfare economics. They both are "demand-side" organizational issues, in that they call for regulatory or collective-choice machinery to present incentives to producers that would not be reflected in market prices in the absence of such machinery. In general, but not always, the term "externality" is used to refer to a cost or benefit involving "secondary" effects to which producers would not attend except under regulatory incentives or controls—effects such as pollution, noise, job experience, or safer neighborhoods. In contrast, "publicness" refers to some indivisibility of the *intended* principal output (for example, defense). Although in some contexts this distinction is useful and illuminating, its arbitrariness is signaled by the fact that while pollution would thus be labeled an externality, clean air might well be labeled a public good. Also, in these definitions the number of people influenced is not an essential element of the distinction. Pollution can damage all people or just a few. Your rose garden may be enjoyed by only you and your neighbors or by the whole community. However, the distinction between small numbers and large numbers does seem to correspond to the distinction between issues that can be settled by small-group negotiation or litigation and issues that require larger-scale collective-choice machinery, and the latter distinction is important. Here we will not be particularly concerned with the distinction between externalities and publicness but will focus more generally on situations that call for collective machinery of demand aggregation. Dealing with externalities such as pollution does call for collective-choice machinery when the bargaining option is not realistically available. Somehow this point tends to be overlooked in the maze of arguments about whether effluent charges or other adaptations of the price system can deal with pollution. Perhaps they can. But the prices on pollution must be set publicly, and their setting involves all the problems of choosing the level of a public good.

In the evolutionary perspective, the phenomena to which the "externality" tag is applied seem less susceptible to definitive once-and-for-all categorization and more intimately related to particular historical and institutional contexts. To a large extent, the externality problems that dominate the policy discussions (and to which academic researchers belatedly direct their attention) are aspects of economic change. The processes of change are continually tossing up new "externalities" that must be dealt with in some manner or other. In a regime in which technical advance is occurring and organizational structure is evolving in response to changing patterns of demand and supply, new nonmarket interactions that are not contained adequately by prevailing laws and policies are almost certain to appear, and old ones may disappear. Long-lasting chemical insecticides were not a problem eighty years ago. Horse manure polluted the cities but automotive emissions did not. The canonical "externality" problem of evolutionary theory is the generation by new technologies of benefits and costs that old institutional structures ignore.

There is similarly an evolutionary view on the nature of the activities, and of the goods and bads, that society perceives as being of collective rather than private concern. Publicness is almost always a matter of degree. What is "public" depends in part on certain technological attributes of products and services and in part on what people think is important and valuable. The increasing recognition that the air we breathe and the water we drink are strongly public has stemmed in part from the decreasing separation of individual breathing spaces and drinking places, but there is more to it than that. Conscious collective action also has been stimulated by the fact that people now seem to care about these things more than they used to. Whether I care about how the neighborhood on the other side of town looks and how people there live, and the strength of my feelings, partly determine the extent to which goods associated with those variables are private or public. While modern economics has tended to enshrine the pluralistic notions of Adam Smith, modern societies seem to resonate more with John Donne. There is no reason to believe that the lines between what society wants to leave private and what society wants to make public will remain constant over time. A central part of society's economic problem, then, is the need to continuously draw and redraw the boundary lines. Whereas orthodoxy stresses achieving optimal provision of goods that by their nature are public, the evolutionary approach focuses on the changing circumstances and demands that call for collective-choice machinery.

Economists increasingly are coming to recognize that the income distribution problem is the inverse of the incentive problem. From the orthodox perspective, differences in income stem from differences in endowments; the transfer problem is to compensate for these without damping incentives. The evolutionary view emphasizes that a nontrivial part of the income distribution problem is associated with people who have been hurt, through no fault of their own, in the course of economic progress. The "gales of creative destruction" blow down the incomes not only of capitalists and managers but also of workers whose skills have become obsolete and of people who were unlucky enough to live in places where industry has become obsolete. On the one hand, this implies that compensation and rehabilitation ought to be viewed as routine aspects of social policy in a world of rapid economic change. But on the other hand, efficient economic performance in a dynamic world puts a high premium on job and locational mobility. The income distribution problem ought to be looked at more in terms of income security than in terms of transfers to compensate for initial lack of assets and more in terms of easing transitions than of subsidizing outmoded patterns of activity. The policy dilemma becomes: How "secure" can income (or command over standard of living) become before people become disinterested in learning new skills or picking up old stakes?

Thus, all the traditional "market failure" problems will have to be attended to by evolutionary welfare economics, although they will have to be analyzed somewhat differently. In addition, there will be a central welfare economic problem that needs to be addressed—a problem that is absent from a static world but strikingly present when information is incomplete and in flux and when tastes and values are constantly being reformed. The orthodox theory of consumer behavior posits that consumers have well-established preference orderings over all possible commodity bundles (and, indeed, in all time periods and all possible states of the world). But how do I know whether I will like a new product if I have never tried it? If I try it, will it make me sick? How do I know? Available information is fragmentary and experts disagree. Regarding collective choices, the situation is similar. How do I know how much improvement in air quality I will get under different legislative proposals? Do I know how much the possible improvements might mean to my enjoyment of life or to my life expectancy?

The world seen by evolutionary theory differs from an orthodox world not only in that things always are changing in ways that could not have been fully predicted, and that adjustments always are having to be made to accommodate to or exploit those changes. It differs, as well, in that those adjustments and accommodations, whether private or public, in general do not lead to tightly predictable outcomes. For better or for worse, economic life is an adventure.

16

The Evolution of Public Policies and the Role of Analysis

PUBLIC LAWS, policies, and organizations are an important part of the environment that shapes the evolution of private sector activities. Laws and policies regarding what is patentable and what is not, and about acceptable or required licensing agreements, influence the relative advantages of innovating and imitating. Antitrust law and its administrative and judicial interpretation define acceptable competitive behavior. Regulatory regimes constrain and mandate certain private actions. Public school systems and educational support programs influence the flow of trained personnel into research and development activity. Government R&D support programs have, since World War II, provided approximately half of the total funding for research and development. More generally, a significant portion of economic activity is conducted by public rather than private organizations. The evolution of economic capabilities and behavior must be understood as occurring in a mixed economy.

Although for some purposes it is useful to think of public laws, policies, and organizations as being part of the landscape, these, like private sector activities, undergo continuing evolution. Over the long run the cumulative result of private and public actions and reactions is a gradual modification of the basic structure of society. Karl Marx, of course, was concerned above all with the patterns, and potential discontinuities, of such long-run changes. Much of Schumpeter's *Capitalism, Socialism, and Democracy* was an elaborate prognostication that the natural dynamics of capitalistic competition would lead to the political enactment of some form of socialism.

Our focus in this chapter is less broad, and shorter-range. We consider the evolution of particular public policies, or policies addressing particular phenomena. We shall, first, develop a general view of the processes by which public policies come into being, are modified, and (sometimes) fade away. Then we will turn to a particular aspect of those processes—conscious attempts to marshal knowledge to guide policy. As with our evolutionary theory of capabilities and behavior of business firms, in our analysis of the determinants of government policies we recognize that people and institutions often try to be rational about decision making, but also that human understanding is incapable of what Lindblom has called effective "synoptic" analysis, and hence that even very thoughtful behavior has major elements of "muddling through" (Lindblom, 1972). We also recognize, with Keynes, that human attempts to analyze problems are powerfully influenced by the theoretical perspective from which the problems are viewed.

Indeed, we have stressed at several places in the book that the ability of a theory to illuminate policy issues ought to be a principal criterion by which to judge its merit. We conclude this chapter, therefore, by considering how our evolutionary theory of technical change—a topic we have considered at some length—illuminates the question of the fruitful, and unfruitful, roles for government to play in industrial innovation.

1. MECHANISMS AND ACTORS

Public policies evolve partly in response to changes in perceived demands and opportunities, changes that may result from the evolution of private technologies and market structures or from other identifiable shifts in objective conditions. Public policies may reflect not changes in objective conditions but shifts in values, or understanding. Change over time in the relative power of different interests and groups within society likely will pull changes in policy in their wake. The particular institutions and procedures for arriving at and modifying policies determine the way in which the various forces mentioned above are translated into new policy departures. Sometimes the institutional machinery for making policy seems to take on a life of its own.

The evolution of air quality regulation in the United States displays the workings of all these forces and mechanisms. Air quality in the United States generally declined during the 1950s and 1960s. Although in some communities, like Pittsburgh, air quality was improved as a result of local initiatives to roll back the emission of pollutants (in this case, prohibitions on the burning of soft coal), in

communities like Los Angeles a combination of significantly increased automobile traffic and petroleum refining led to noticeable
deterioration. The sources of the deterioration were not obvious *a
priori*. Assessment of the effects of various pollutants on health has
been, and still is, constrained by the state of biological knowledge
and by limits on measurement techniques. Thus, until recently concern about the emissions from coal-burning electrical generating
plants was focused largely on sulfur dioxide, whereas recent studies
suggest that sulfates may be a more serious problem.

Published studies played a central role in the consciousness-
raising regarding air quality. Some of the studies were narrowly focused; for example, during the 1950s scientists at the California Institute of Technology implicated auto exhaust as a source of the smog
besetting Los Angeles. Some were quite sweeping. Rachael Carson's
Silent Spring (1962) sounded the alarm regarding industrial pollutants
in general. During the 1960s the trickle of studies became a flood.
The Club of Rome forecasted impending disaster (see Meadows et
al., 1972). More focused and cautious studies—for example, that by
Ridker (1967)—provided some of the first estimates of the economic
costs of air pollution.

The policy response developed hesitantly. Several states enacted
laws to protect air quality; California's auto emission control standards of the early 1960s is a prominent example. Federal action was
piecemeal. In 1965 Congress authorized the setting of auto emission
control standards. Generally, however, at the start the federal legislation shied away from imposing particular standards, and a considerable amount of responsibility and freedom of initiative was vested
with the states. The 1970 amendments to the Clean Air Act located
significantly more power in a federal bureau—the Environmental
Protection Agency (EPA)—and wrote into the legislation more detail
about how regulation was to proceed. The 1970 amendments took the
form they did in part because of the political aspirations and strategies of some of the key legislators involved. Jacoby and Steinbruner
(1973) note that Edmund Muskie was chairman of the key Senate
committee and, at the time of the hearings, was considering a run for
the presidency. He and other legislators believed (and they seemed
to think that a good share of the American electorate agreed) that the
states had not been acting forcefully enough—that the private companies who were creating the pollution, or designing the automobiles that polluted, were culpable and ought to be brought to
account. There also was a belief that if particular technological requirements were imposed, the companies would have the incentive
and the ability to achieve these and the costs involved would not be
unduly burdensome.

The particular form of the new legislation, the way the legislation was interpreted by EPA, and the subsequent experience of administrative and legislative amendment, was somewhat different in the several areas of application. However, the stories told by Jacoby and Steinbruner (1973), Sonda (1977), and White (1981) about automobile emissions control, by Lurie (1981) about emissions from copper refineries, and by Ackerman and Hassler (1981) about the regulation of coal-burning electrical generating plants have many elements in common. While the 1970 legislation fenced in the range of action open to the EPA, in the nature of things Congress could not specify all the details, and the constraints were roomy enough so that the EPA still retained considerable discretion. Partly because Congress had so mandated and partly because of the way in which the EPA interpreted the legislative mandate, EPA regulations took the form of particular required standards, often tied to assessments of what would be safe for humans, sometimes keyed to judgments about what the best technologies would be capable of achieving. Environmental protection groups and the industries being regulated both tried to pressure or persuade Congress and the EPA to modify the regulations. A portion of this pressure was exerted through litigation and the courts.

To set and justify the standards and to protect those in litigation, the EPA undertook many studies, attempting to assess the scientific evidence about health effects and the evolving state of the technological arts. These studies generally did not concern themselves with the broader questions of the benefits and costs involved in various strategies of environmental protection, or even with exploring the range of possible instruments; rather, they were focused on a particular regulation to be formulated or one that was under attack, and attempted to justify a particular proposed or extant standard or to examine certain specific changes in that standard. Recognition of a wider range of values at stake in environmental protection legislation was forced upon Congress and the EPA by the pressure and litigation of various interest groups. The automobile companies claimed impossibly high costs and lost jobs as a consequence of prevailing regulation, as did the Eastern coal companies and the coal unions. EPA studies in general did not anticipate these complaints and did not attempt to come to grips seriously with the tradeoffs they implied. Similarly, EPA studies seldom explored seriously different regulatory instruments, such as the use of effluent fees instead of the setting of requirements.

In contrast, at universities and at such research centers as the Brookings Institution these broader questions of values, tradeoffs, and strategies were being explored. Studies such as the one by Kneese and Schultze (1975) were intended for a nonacademic audience, and by the mid 1970s the political climate had changed noticeably. Some of the change surely reflected a new understanding of the tradeoffs involved and of the range of possible regulatory instruments.

By the late 1970s, under the Carter administration, regulatory reform became a byword. Under Charles Schultze's leadership, various checks on the EPA (and other regulatory agencies) were established within the administration—checks that surely forced the EPA to pay more attention to tradeoffs and alternative instruments, which in turn strengthened the hand within the EPA of civil servants who believed in regulatory reform. Despite some move in the direction of balancing benefits and costs, by 1980 the public mood had swung even farther. The presidential candidates of both major parties ran partly on deregulation planks.

This has been a terse account of the history, from 1967 to 1980, of clean air regulation, but enough has been said to suggest the broad outlines. While in some ways very particular to the case, in many ways the pattern is typical.

For example, the study by Crain and colleagues (1969) of the spread and then the halt of fluoridation of public water supplies reveals many similarities with the air pollution case. Initiation of a public program was triggered by perception of a need that could be met by public-sector activity—the desirability and the possibility of reducing tooth decay in children through fluoridation of public water supplies. The workings of public institutions and mechanisms strongly influenced how fluoridation proceeded and how that policy was effectively stopped. In the early stages local administrative agencies—health departments and water supply departments—treated the fluoridation question as within their province and as outside the arena of democratic politics. Eventually, voices were raised questioning the safety of fluoridation and even the legitimacy of governmental decisions to add substances like fluoride to public drinking water regardless of the possible benefits to children. It was proposed that children could drink fluoridated milk. The question of whether or not to add fluoride to the public water supplies became one on which political candidates often had to take sides. In some cases specific referendums were held on the subject.

Again, while there are important elements specific to the case, the history of public policies regarding fluoridation has a pattern that fits the evolution of many other policies. There are many threads in common with the story told by Steiner (1971) about the evolution of welfare policy in the United States, and with Heclo's account (1974) of the evolution of welfare policies in Britain and Sweden. Similar elements are apparent in the analyses by Art (1964) of the TFX decision and by Nelson (1977) of policy toward the supersonic transport.

All of these studies suggest certain similarities in the evolution of public- and private-sector activities. At any time, public policies, like private technologies and policies, are implemented by organizations largely as a matter of "organizational routine." Changes from existing routine usually are local, although there may be an occasional major change. Those changes may survive and take hold, or they may be turned back. Because a good share of the changes proposed are local and because the selection environment is comparatively constant, public policies tend to follow certain trajectories. Thus, a policy change today might fruitfully be understood as evolving from a policy base that was itself the outcome of a sequence of earlier changes, and, in turn, as setting the stage for future evolutionary developments.

The case studies also point to important differences between private and public policy making. The key ones are, first, the multiparty nature of public decision making and, second, the complex machinery that it involves. In orthodox economic theory (if not necessarily in actuality) the goals of a private business firm are treated as those of a single person. Although much political discussion proceeds in terms of a search for the "public interest," political scientists as well as economists understand that such a "public" is more a figure of speech than a concrete entity with identifiable goals. The actual "public" that is interested in policy choices and outcomes has a diverse, divergent makeup and interests that are at least in partial conflict. Further, there are several different ways by which interested parties can influence policy making. The case studies discussed above indicate that in many instances several different types of actors and a variety of mechanisms are involved.[1]

In a democratic society, citizens and citizen interest groups ultimately are sovereign. Occasionally, as was the case with fluoridation, sovereign power may be expressed in a specific referendum on the issue. In other cases there may be no specific referendum, but candidates for electoral office may take particular stands on the issue and the outcome of the election may be interpreted as that of a referendum. More commonly, a particular policy is not advertised as part of electoral politics, but elected officials and interest groups have worked out their own understood accommodation.

---

1. Although the multiplicity of kinds of actors is apparent in most case studies, many theoretical treatments of political decision making focus on one, or maybe two, different actors. Thus, for example, Downs (1957) deals with the electorate and politicians running for office, and Niskanen (1971) with departmental bureaucrats and executive-level budget officers. In both the clean air and fluoridation cases, at one time or another the electorate, officials running for office, civil servants, and the courts all played important roles.

As suggested, specific referenda are rare. Because of this, elected officials—both executives and members of legislatures—generally have considerable freedom of action. The air pollution and fluoridation cases both demonstrate the importance of the values and perceptions of elected officials.

Just as voter sentiment generally provides only loose constraints on the actions of elected officials, so the decisions of elected officials generally leave a considerable amount of discretion for the civil servants and others who carry out a program or policy. Prior to the 1960s the role of "administration" was seen in the political science literature as simply technical, consisting of working out the best way to achieve an objective or to carry out a policy defined by elected officials and mandated by the electorate. Since that time, it has become better recognized that the shape of a policy is to a considerable extent determined by how it is implemented.

In addition to voters, elected officials, and bureaucrats, the courts often play a significant role in determining policy. Many activities are controlled by regulatory authorities. In a federal system there may be several layers of involved governments. Policy making and revising is a complex multiactor game.

The relative importance of the different actors and the way in which they play their roles certainly differ among the various arenas of public-sector activity. Dahl (1961) stressed this diversity in his discussion of pluralistic democracy. The politics and administration of defense clearly differ from those of education, which in turn differ from those of welfare. And, as the cases of air quality regulation and fluoridation both show, the roles of the different political actors can change over time.

These differences and changes are in part determined by and reflected in the particular design of the political machinery. The machinery determines and defines how the various parties interact and how, out of that interaction, policies emerge and change. Students of voting theory long have known that, for given preferences and alternatives, the particular voting rules and the way in which the alternatives are presented strongly influence the outcomes. Wildavsky's (1964) study of the federal budgeting process alerted scholars to the key role played by the administrative machinery of budgeting. It also seems inadequate to view the political and administrative machinery merely as a way that the weights of different interests are determined. The machinery plays a powerful role in its own right. Thus, in the case of air quality regulation it was important that the Senate hearings not only were part of the machinery for determining what to do in that instance but also were a stage for politicians interested in reelection or in other future posts.

Throughout this book, and especially in Chapter 5, we have stressed that knowledge of *how* decisions are arrived at in business firms may tell us something about *what* decisions will be reached. To focus exclusively on the benefits and costs that a firm derives from actions and to ignore how it gathers, processes, and evaluates information and options is to be blind to useful predictive information. This is even more strikingly true regarding governmental decision making.

Political machinery involves actors in posturing, as well as arm-wrestling, bargaining, debating, and deliberating. For a student of political process, or more specifically of the evolution of public policies, all aspects are interesting.

However, for a social scientist the deliberative aspects have a special standing. After all, if our researches are to influence policy, they are most likely to do so by affecting the way in which policy contexts are interpreted. Many public policy issues are complex, the nature of the problems and the options not well understood, and the values at stake far from transparent. Beliefs about the nature of the problem play an important role at several stages: first, in diagnosing a situation and defining it as a particular kind of policy problem in the first place; second, in interpreting experience with a policy and establishing the context within which minor modifications of the initial program are proposed and debated; and, third, in influencing the broader evaluation of whether the program is basically on track, needs to be changed drastically, or should be killed.

Much of the interpretative framework is broadly oriented by a society's cultural heritage, by deep-seated beliefs and ideological predilections which define legitimate and illegitimate roles of government, worthy and unworthy causes, what is attended and not attended about a situation. Within this broad context, particular technical interpretations are lent by the general state of scientific understanding of various topics. Interpretation is influenced only marginally by studies or analyses aimed specifically at the particular policy issue in question and these studies, too, are strongly conditioned by ideology and scientific understanding rather than providing independent interpretations. But such studies do play a role. The history of the Clean Air Act clearly shows that specific policy analyses played a nontrivial role in influencing beliefs at each of the stages mentioned above. In the 1950s and early 1960s policy analysis was recognized as an important part of the administration of programs and policies. But, as with administration more generally, it is more apparent that analysis plays a much broader role in modern government than merely guiding effective choice among known alternatives given prespecified ends. Some commentators, such as Wildavsky (1966), have argued that the role played by analysis has become too large and should be confined. In any case, it seems important to understand that role better.

2. THE ROLE OF ANALYSIS IN POLICY MAKING

We use the term "analysis" here to mean the inquiry of professionals trained in social science or in other disciplines into the policy alternatives, the values at stake, the likely consequences of adopting different policies, and the articulation of the findings of such inquiry with the express aim of illuminating and influencing policy choices. It is useful to examine the ways in which different schools of economic thought view the role of policy analysis.

If one takes seriously the assumption made in some "rational expectations" models—that all individuals know all the public policy options and the consequences (perhaps state-contingent) of the choice of any one—it is hard to discern *any* role for policy analysis. The presence of public goods and other reasons for collective action call for collective-decision-making machinery, but there is no such thing as a "public interest" to be served, only a collection of individual interests. In arriving at collective decisions, conflicts of interest need to be resolved. But, from this perspective, no one interest is "better" than any other. And since everybody knows the structure of the economic (and political) problem as well as anyone else, there are no "experts" and there is no need for "analysis." The policy-making problem is simply one of arriving at a Pareto-optimal agreement. This, of course, may be no simple task, given actual collective-choice machinery. Many simple voting schemes do not achieve it. One possible role of policy analysis, within a rational expectations framework, might be to constrain the set over which voting or bargaining proceeds to alternatives that are "efficient" or at least for which "benefits exceed costs." But such "analysis" would simply define the constraints on the choice set, and would not provide any new "information."

In contrast, economists who during the early 1960s expressed a strong faith in "policy analysis" adopted a position that stresses the limitations of existing knowledge and the importance of particular studies to marshal knowledge. Analysis is needed to illuminate the current policy problem, and to educate elected officials, bureaucrats, and the electorate about the right way to look at it. From this point of view, lack of knowledge is highlighted and conflict of interest played down. There is a "public interest" to be found and analysis can help to find it.[2]

It should be apparent that actual policy making involves both wrestling and bargaining among different interests and an attempt to identify a public interest. There is some truth in the Downsian view of politics in which elected officials, interested only in reelection, cater to equally self-interested voters, but there is more to it than that.[3] As a special case, relevant to analysis of the Clean Air Act, we concede the limited power but reject the completeness of revisionist theories of regulation.[4] A striking feature of both the clean air and fluoridation cases is that for many parties there was no strong private interest. Yet they were interested in the policy issue, felt it important, and took stands. It is reasonable to say that they were attempting to identify a public interest, and to support it.

We think it useful to view the role of analysis in public decision making as part of the process by which a public interest gets defined. By that we do not mean that studies *identify* a true public interest in any strictly objective sense. We mean that studies help to *define* a public interest. This is not just a quibble over the meaning of words. We, as do other scholars, have trouble with the concept of an objective public interest. We observe, however, that political actors often behave as if they were searching for one. In recent years studies seem to play a large role in that search. And we do not deny that studies can be and often are put forth to further a particular private interest. Rather, our point is that, unlike the testing of strength and bargaining that also are part of the political process, studies are expected to present arguments that rationally persuade people that one policy is better than another, in terms of values that are widely accepted and that are viewed as applying to the society as a whole rather than to a particular group.

Our position here is similar to that taken by some philosophers regarding science. It may be doubted that an objective truth really exists or, if one does, that science can find it. Nonetheless, science can be perceived as a quest for truth, and that quest may be fruitful even if the ultimate objective is not attainable.

This perspective certainly is consistent with portions of the articulated faith of the policy analysts, particularly the more recent state-

---

2. A classic early statement is by Hitch and McKean (1960). A contemporary theoretical exploration of the role of policy analysis is contained in Mishan (1971) and Stokey and Zeckhauser (1978). See Lindblom and Cohen (1979) for a view similar to ours in many ways.

3. See Downs (1957).

4. See Stigler (1971) and Peltzman (1976). For a critique, see Levine (1981).

ments. Thus, Schultze (1968) stresses the role of policy analysis, in an interactive process, as that of holding forth an "efficiency goal." Efficiency may not be the only public interest, but it certainly is widely regarded as one general characteristic of good policy. We diverge from modern policy analysts, however, in treating the public interest as something that is created in political dialogue rather than as being something objective, as something around which widespread political support clusters, given a particular interpretation of the problem, rather than an objective that reflects definitive understanding of the problem and the values at stake, and durable agreement on goals.

We likewise have trouble with the idea that analysis helps to identify a "best" policy, and with the style of analysis associated with this view. According to this view, the right way to do analysis is to construct a model of the situation and find the best policy within this model. The model may be rich and complex, or it may involve simply a listing of a finite set of alternatives and the calculation of benefits and costs for each. In either case, there is an implicit belief that the choice that is best within the model is an optimum, or at least a good, policy within the real context, or that in any event going through the optimizing exercise is the most useful way to focus intellectual attention.

There is a large leap of faith here. In his presidential address to the Operations Research Society, Hitch (1955) recognized this leap explicitly. He stressed that models are highly simplified and often misleading characterizations of the real context, but proposed nonetheless that going through the exercise of building a model and searching for an optimum within that model is a useful heuristic for finding or designing good policies for the actual context. Perhaps so, but this is far from obvious. The work of Newell and Simon (1972) on human problem solving in a context as "simple" as a game of chess suggests that there are better heuristics than building a simple model of chess and optimizing within that model. These better heuristics involve the recognition of patterns, the use of pattern recognition to focus quickly on one or a small number of alternatives, exploring only these in any depth, and the consideration of the merits of various moves in terms of their positioning advantages and disadvantages. The values, of course, of different positions are "proximate." Given limits on computational power, they cannot be calculated by dynamic programming. They have to be formed and reformed on the basis of experience and general understanding of the game. Proximate values are an important part of problem-solving heuristics.

Posing the task as the identification of (Pareto) optimum policies serves to distance analysis from the tug-of-war of competing goals and values in ways that sometimes reduce the ability of analysis to contribute to the political dialogue. Economists, of course, differ in the extent to which they take seriously the warning of Arrow's impossibility theorem against the posing of policy problems as if there were a technically correct way to brush aside differences in interests among individuals and groups. Those who have learned the lesson have a greater tendency to recognize that social decision mechanisms, beyond analysis, are needed to decide what is to be done. But in most cases they still view good analysis as laying out the alternatives and tracing their consequences, while remaining neutral regarding which or whose values should be weighted most heavily. However, from the perspective being developed here, even this position is simplistic. One little-recognized consequence of our bounded rationality is that we lack the capability to sharply separate our values from our knowledge. Indeed our (proximate) values form a large part of our knowledge. Analysis of proximate values is an important part of good policy analysis.

We are not endorsing here a Panglossian view that what appear at first thought to be conflicting interests can be discerned, after more careful analysis, to be truly not conflicting, or that analysis can always identify the more salient interest. In some cases study and persuasion can result in the emergence of a recognized public interest; in other cases it may be impossible to gain any agreement upon this among informed interested parties. Even when it is so possible, the process by which a recognized public interest is defined in a pluralistic democracy involves a complex interchange of views, and often bargaining, among different interests. Studies should be seen as handmaiden to that political process, not as having political legitimacy in themselves. In some cases studies may play a dominant role, and in others a minor role. Were that not so, democracies could dispense with all the complicated and expensive apparatus we have for making political decisions, and simply establish an analytic office that would decide things for us. Some writers who puff the role of analysis seem disturbed that we do not do just that.

Is it possible to draw some guidelines for good policy analysis, recognizing explicitly that our rationality is bounded, and that in most instances there really are conflicting values and interests and that a public interest, if one be defined, is a matter of (perhaps temporary) social agreement rather than an objective fact? We think it is.

First, the role of analysis is to enhance understanding of the problem. The objective is not to find an optimum. The tactical objective is to identify reasonable next moves in the chess game of policy development. Articulation of the higher-order objectives (winning) may provide some guidance as to what not to do next, but often is not very helpful in discriminating among plausible (not clearly losing) next moves. In order to make that evaluation, it is necessary to have a good strategic understanding of the sort of chess game being played. And it is here, we believe, that policy analysis can and does have its greatest impact. Analysis helps people think about the problem—what they see as a reasonable range of options, the consequences of choosing one or another, the proximate values at stake. Like tactical analysis, strategic analysis should not be thought of in optimizing terms. People simply cannot know the best way to get from here to some unfamiliar and distant place, and cannot even know exactly what it will be like when they get there. However, a good road map, and some thoughtful consideration of the purpose of the trip, certainly can help. As the air quality regulation story and many others signal too clearly, a real danger is that policy making can get so bogged down in argumentation about which turn to take next that the purpose of the trip and the map are forgotten.

Second, analysis should be understood as influencing the discourse and bargaining of democratic politics. Analysis cannot make a "public interest" out of a set of divergent private interests. But it can unmask proposals, put forth as equitable, that in fact sharply benefit one interest at the expense of others. It can help to identify policies that have promise of achieving a broad public purpose (such as reducing hazardous air pollution at reasonable cost) where that purpose has been obscured or lost in a tangle of specific piecemeal policies and narrow vested interests. Discussion of the objective and the trip plan does influence the bargaining about which turn to take next.

Often discussions of policy analysis implicitly assume that the most important studies are produced in government itself or by hired consultants. Analyses done in or close to government clearly are important. However, as indicated by the clean air case and others, it is often the scholar outside government who calls attention to the problem, who provides the most illuminating and scathing criticism of existing policies, who opens thinking to new ones. Perhaps it is characteristic of democratic politics that governments in power are incapable of fresh strategic thinking, or even of keeping the existing strategy in mind when making tactical decisions, unless forced by outside criticism or new blood to back off and think. In such a context, analysis (done outside government) is an important component of the system by which society keeps its government under control and tolerably alert.

Third, the flexibility of an action today in terms of the range of choice kept open for tomorrow, and the information about alternative future paths that action will create, are important desiderata. At best, strategic road maps are grossly drawn. While they provide direction and broad guidance, they may not tell you that a certain road is in an unexpectedly bad state of repair. They are sure to omit certain newly built roads which become visible when one comes to a branch point and looks about with open eyes. Policy making is a continuing evolutionary process. Analysis should not proceed as if pragmatic social learning could take an easy short cut.

Fourth, if one views policy making as a continuing process, the organizational and institutional structures involved become critical. Public policies and programs, like private activities, are embedded in and carried out by organizations. And, in a basic sense, it is the organizations that learn, and adapt. The design of a good policy is, to a considerable extent, the design of an organizational structure capable of learning and of adjusting behavior in response to what is learned. The legislative mandate should provide broad guidance to the values to be pursued, but should not tie the hands of the administrating agency regarding choice of means. If the value tradeoffs or the nature of the most appropriate instruments is uncertain, exploration ought to be an explicit part of the legislative mandate and of the administrative strategy.

These propositions are, of course, old saws in the field of public administration, but their intellectual basis there is almost exclusively experiential. Economists instinctively find them attractive, and seem to think that they are deducible from standard microeconomic theory. But they are not, unless perhaps one introduces to that theory considerable *ex ante* uncertainty, and costs of information transmission as well as acquisition. These factors, of course, are central to our evolutionary perspective.

In a recent article Majone and Wildavsky (1978) took a point of view similar to that sketched above. Their article is titled, interestingly, "Implementation as Evolution." They, too, see policies as institutionally embedded. Policies are articulated often at a relatively high level of government, but are carried out by lower levels of government in interaction with private parties. The way in which a broadly articulated policy is implemented depends on the administrative structure. The implementation of a policy both generates new information about what works and doesn't work, and involves the working out of conflicts of interest among the potential benefiters and losers. As a result of experience, the way a broadly articulated policy actually proceeds is modified. The articulation may change as well.

Fifth, just as many analyses of the workings of the market economy tend to abstract the private economy from public policies, programs, and institutions, too many analyses of public policies and programs do not recognize adequately that their effects will be determined, to a considerable degree, by private and not governmental actors. Indeed a wide range of public policies can be viewed as defining a mix of market and nonmarket activity, or a mode of government-private interaction, in a particular area. The problem of regulating air pollution certainly can be regarded in this way. The fluoridation policy dialogues turned increasingly on the appropriate limits on governmental action.

Certainly there are some issues in which the choice of private-public mix is not central. The question of which defense system to procure is to only a very limited extent an issue about public and private responsibility. In recent years the discussion about policy in primary and secondary education may have excessively centered on the question of the private-public mix (vouchers, tax deductibility of tuition payments, and so forth). But there is certainly an interesting area of policy discussion where the mix and fit questions are crucial.

Serious policy analysis of any such arena requires detailed understanding of the institutions, mechanisms, interests, and values at stake. For all the reasons discussed in the preceding chapter, simple (and simple-minded) arguments about the optimality of private enterprise, or simple pointing to market failures, does not carry the analysis very far. Serious analysis of a particular policy problem inevitably means immersion in a set of relatively unique attributes of that context. It is beyond the scope of this book, which is about theory, to actually engage in such a detailed analysis of a policy problem. Nonetheless, we have stressed the importance of a theoretical perspective in the interpretation of particular phenomena and situations. In view of our argument that a principal criterion by which a theory ought to be judged is its ability to illuminate policy issues, it is incumbent upon us to indicate at least roughly how our evolutionary theory frames certain policy questions.

Much of this book has been concerned with developing theory about technological change in industry. It seems appropriate, therefore, to consider how our evolutionary theoretical ideas illuminate policy issues relating to that topic. Earlier we have considered, in a piecemeal manner, some of the policy implications, for example conundrums regarding antitrust policy. We conclude this chapter by considering more systematically the question of appropriate government policy toward industrial R&D.

3. Government Policy toward Industrial R&D

From the perspective sketched above, a wide range of policy analyses are potentially relevant to a particular policy discussion. At one end of the spectrum, there are studies focused on the particular policy options under immediate consideration and on plausible alternatives to these. These kinds of studies are very dependent on the particular context and are designed to explore the qeustion: What should be the next move? At the other end of the spectrum are studies that broadly survey the terrain. They aim to help improve strategic planning. Because the narrower studies are so particularized, unless they involve a methodological breakthrough they seldom are of durable interest. The focus of discussion here, therefore, is not on a particular present policy issue, such as whether the federal government should now aid the aircraft industry in developing the next generation of commercial aircraft or whether it should join with the American automobile industry in the support of automotive R&D. Rather we offer here a background analysis of the general issue of the appropriate and fruitful roles that active governmental support of industrial R&D can play. Any particular policy study, after all, assumes such an analysis.

Such an analysis depends, of course, on assumptions made about industrial R&D. Here we will make basic assumptions about R&D that are reminiscent of the discussion in Chapter 11, but somewhat different from those employed in the more stylized models. R&D is an activity separate from production. It is a highly uncertain activity, and reasonable people will disagree on the rankings of R&D projects. The outcome of an R&D project may include a technology ready for implementation, or nothing may be found or invented. In either case, the outcome of a project also includes revised knowledge about technological alternatives. In particular, a successful R&D project reveals that similar but not identical R&D projects may yield similar but not identical technologies. An unsuccessful project provides general information about the location of "dry holes." As a consequence, if the topography of innovation is sufficiently regular, technical advance will be cumulative in the following sense. The outcome of one round of research and development projects (which includes some successes and some failures) defines a set of "neighborhoods" where it is a good bet that further R&D will locate technologies similar to and better than the technologies developed previously. These neighborhoods may not be in close proximity to each other; rather, the promising lines of search branch into an exploration of distinguishable subclasses of technology. Research and development projects within one class provide knowledge relevant to the next round of research and development projects within that same class. However, they do not contribute much understanding that is relevant to research and development activity aimed at another class of technology.

It also is important to be explicit about where the information relevant to industrial R&D decision making resides. In general, it resides with the organizations that are engaged in producing and marketing the product. These are the organizations that know about the strengths and weaknesses of prevailing technologies and of the targets and opportunities for improvement. They know how customers react to different product designs. At best it is time-consuming and costly to relay the bulk of this information to an R&D organization that stands significantly apart from the producing and marketing organizations. And without the cooperation of the firms in question, it is impossible. Thus, in an economy that relies basically on profit-seeking private enterprise to provide goods and services, it is virtually inevitable that much R&D decision making will be decentralized to private business firms, with returns to R&D internalized through secrecy, patent protection, or market domination.

The questions under consideration are these. First, what will be the strengths and weaknesses of leaving industrial R&D totally in the private domain? Second, what are the opportunities and limitations for governmental involvement in industrial R&D? We will argue that both the anatomy of market failure and the opportunities and constraints on governmental action depend on the character of market structure and competition in the industry, as well as on such institutional variables as the strength and scope of patents and the extent of industrial secrecy.[5]

Consider an industry consisting of a large number of competing firms, each doing its own R&D. There are several different kinds of "market failure" that need to be recognized. First, if firms have less than perfect ability to exclude other firms from using their technology, there is the well-known "template externality," which stems from the chances that a technology that is found (created) by one firm will be imitated by others. If patents prevent direct mimicking, but there is a "neighborhood" illuminated by the innovation that is not foreclosed to other firms by patents, the externality problem remains, though in modified form. Second, and more recently emphasized in the literature, there are problems akin to those of multiple independent tappers of an oil pool or of fishermen working the same fishing ground. Incentives to be the first to invent, to get the patent, may induce many firms to try to invent early. Barzel (1968) and others have pointed out that, under certain assumptions, in such a competitive race too many resources are applied too early. Given a set of established patents and imperfect license markets, individual companies can make money from projects that would not be worthwhile had

---

5. The analysis that follows is drawn from Nelson (1981).

they access to the best technologies developed by others—projects that yield little social value. The stronger the patent rights, the greater the importance of the oil pool problem relative to the template problem. The template problem tends to hold total R&D spending to a level below a social optimum. The oil pool effect may spur R&D spending, but toward an allocation of effort that is socially inefficient.

Still another allocational problem emerges if technological advance is cumulative. In the competitive situation there would appear to be a problem regarding R&D that is similar to the one described by Hotelling in the case of location decisions. Where the returns to a firm from a technical advance must be assessed against the technology it currently is using rather than against the best technology in the industry, and where the rough location of the best available technology is known and the neighborhood looks both promising and unprotected by patents, there are incentives in the system for everybody to cluster around the same broad opportunity. In the development of technology over an extended period, too much attention is focused on particular parts of the technological landscape and not enough real diversification of effort is achieved. If a firm explores new terrain, it is less likely to come up with something. And if it does, it knows that other firms will soon cluster around.

Consider now a monopolized industry, noting first the differences in its incentive structure relative to that of the competitive case. In a monopolized industry, neither template externality nor the oil pool externality exists. And the knowledge externalities that come from successful exploration of uncharted regions of the set are internalized. There may be cost-side advantages as well. For many kinds of R&D there are economies of scale, at least up to a point, arising from several different sources. Certain kinds of R&D inputs and outputs are lumpy: a significant quantity of R&D effort must be directed to a project if there is to be any hope of success. A small-scale R&D effort may not be able to achieve success at all, and, if it does, will achieve it significantly later than an effort that is funded at a higher rate. There also are diversification advantages of a large-scale research and development effort. Multiple attacks on particular objectives can be mounted. A large and diversified range of projects can help guard a company from the economic disadvantages of a long dry spell between R&D successes. And to the extent that the rate of growth of capital or sales of a firm is limited, there is an economy of scale associated with the fact that a big firm can quickly apply a new technological development to a larger quantity of output and capital than can a small firm.

What are the debits of monopoly to be charged against these credits? Traditional theory would argue that the size of output in the industry would be lower. This causes the traditional triangle loss. It also feeds back to R&D incentives by reducing the size of the output to which R&D applies. It is hard to say whether there would be more or less R&D undertaken in the monopolized case than in the competitive case. The greater degree of internalization and the smaller scale of output pull in different directions. In the monopolized case there will be less incentive to do the kind of R&D that is profitable in a competitive case only because someone else has a patent. While this is another factor that acts to lower the R&D level in the monopolized case relative to the competitive case, it suggests that the most important difference in the two regimes is the efficiency of R&D allocation. If the monopolist can be assumed to be a profit maximizer and if the consequences of choosing any particular R&D project are more or less obvious, there are strong arguments that monopoly would generate a better portfolio of R&D projects than would a regime of competition.

However, this tentative conclusion looks less compelling if we note that different people see alternatives in different ways and that organizations have tendencies to adopt parochial viewpoints and simplified decision-making styles. Then a centralized regime looks less attractive in terms of the portfolio of projects it would be likely to carry, and a competitive regime looks more attractive. The argument here against monopoly and for competition is not the standard one of textbook economic theory. It does not derive from the logic of maximizing choice or from arguments akin to the proposition that it is socially desirable to set the level of output at the point where marginal cost equals price. Rather, the argument is in part that differences in perception as to what are the best bets will in a competitive regime have a greater chance to surface and be expressed in a diversified portfolio of R&D projects than they would in a monopolized regime. The argument also is that large, sheltered organizations tend to be stodgy and uncreative or narrowly messianic in the R&D they do, rather than ingeniously and flexibly creative. It is not just that monopoly limits the sources of new ideas, but that an industry dominated by a large, secure firm is not a setting that spurs the generating and sensitive screening of good ideas. Any regime of competitive R&D is bound to involve some waste and duplication. The costs and dangers of monopoly are principally those of reliance on a single mind—unlikely to be an agile one—for the exploration of technological alternatives.

One is tempted to look to a regime of oligopoly—involving neither the R&D incentive problems of a multitude of small producers, nor the pricing and single-source reliance problem of a true monopoly—as the most desirable institutional structure. Many prominent economists, from Schumpeter to Galbraith, are associated with this position. And, interestingly, oligopoly tends to be the market structure that naturally seems to evolve in industries where the funding or inventing of new technologies has proceeded relatively rapidly. An oligopolistic structure has the potential of combining the best aspects of competition and pluralism and of R&D benefit internalization.

But such a structure also has the potential for combining the worst features of monopoly and competition. In many oligopolistic industries, a considerable amount of R&D done by firms seems to be "defensive" and aims to assure that a firm has available a product similar to that developed by a competitor, rather than aiming to come up with something significantly different. Small numbers may yield considerable duplicative R&D without any real R&D diversity.

And economists who tout oligopoly as progressive should be more alert to the possibility that, where oligopolistic rivalry in R&D does involve firms exploring significantly different parts of the range of technological alternatives, oligopoly may be unstable. A monopolized structure may gradually evolve. A central feature of Schumpeterian competition is that the profits that are the reward of successful innovation provide both motivation and the funds for firm growth. And there are social economic advantages of having the firm with a better technology (the lower cost or the better product) supply a growing share of the market. However, to the extent that firm research and development expenditures are keyed to size and to the extent that there are advantages of scale of any of the sorts discussed above, a successful innovator may reduce its rivals to a point where they can be effective competitors no longer. Where oligopolistic Schumpeterian competition has the merits that some observers assign to it, our simulation studies suggest that the structure may tend to self-destruct.

The "failures" of market-induced R&D may well be serious, at least if performance is judged against the standards of an ideal planning model. There is indeed a fundamental dilemma in using profit-seeking firms and competitive markets as the organizational device for stimulating and guiding R&D. If the problem were simply "externality," as some economists seem to believe, it could be resolved through tightening patents or providing simple R&D subsidies. But the problem is much more complex than that, involving overspending on certain types of R&D as well as underspending on others, the warping of R&D strategies, and constraints on the use of what is essentially a public good: knowledge. Market failure regarding R&D is not neatly resolved by giving a small adjusting twist to conventional policy instruments or by introducing a few new ones.

Of course, it is possible to take R&D or some component of R&D largely out of the market system. This is what has happened regarding basic research, which is conducted mostly at universities rather than at profit-seeking firms and is funded largely by the government. This strategy has been relatively successful for two reasons (if the analysis above is accepted). First, the information needed to guide basic research decision making is not located in the operating parts of organizations that produce goods and services, but rather in the minds and experience of basic research scientists. Relatedly, the opportunities and problems guiding allocation are signaled by the logic and values associated with advancing scientific understanding, rather than by the profit objectives of enterprises. Indeed, these distinctions form a basis for defining basic research. Second, basic research decision making has been largely decentralized and pluralistic; the proposals come mostly from research scientists and institutions and are subject to a peer review system or something equivalent.

Society in effect has a *choice* regarding what arenas of research it will define as basic research, to be funded publicly and guided by the tenets of a scientific discipline, and what arenas it will regard as applied and to be guided (if not necessarily funded) by criteria close to the values of the organizations using particular technologies. The lesson of history is that the former approach has large long-run practical payoffs, when a field thus defined as a science can advance progressively and when the scientific understanding illuminates technological options and their connections with economic values. It should be recognized that many of the same kind of inefficiencies of market decentralized R&D-allocating mechanisms reside in this decentralized "Republic of Science," which allocates basic research resources.[6] No hidden-hand theorems obtain for either system. But so long as it pays to have some bodies of research guided by the logic inherent in the natural unfolding of certain bodies of understanding, it is viable to have scientific criteria (as contrasted with profitability criteria) guide R&D allocation in those areas. So long as good decision making needs detailed access to the particulars of ongoing research and so long as there are dangers of a single central mind anyhow, decentralization seems far preferable to a more centrally planned system.

But for the bulk of R&D that bears on advancing industrial technology, much of the relevant information is located in the production

---

6. The idea of a Republic of Science originated with Polanyi (1967).

enterprises, and good R&D decision making involves attending directly to economic benefits and costs. The Republic of Science is not an appropriate system for governing the problem-oriented R&D work aimed at advancing production technology. Let us ignore here the cases in which government itself is a heavy purchaser of the product in question or is its provider (where special considerations obtain) and focus on private industry selling products largely to other private parties. In these circumstances, government is severely constrained in terms of what it can do to guide and support R&D. There are, first, informational constraints; second, constraints imposed by the requirement for "fairness"; and, third, constraints arising from bureaucratic politics.

The first two constraints turn out to be closely connected. Where the suppliers of goods and services are not rivalrous, the governmental information access problem can be resolved. Agriculture and medical practice are good examples. In these cases governmental information gathering and R&D support are not viewed as helping one part of the industry at the expense of another, but as helping the whole industry. (Whether this conception is justified or not is another matter.) Not only governmental R&D support but public institutions to allocate these funds, and even public R&D undertakings, generally are welcomed in these arenas.

The difficult problem of information access arises, along with real problems of "fairness," where private suppliers are rivalrous. This is the situation that characterizes much of American industry. In such a regime, the kind of information that enables good R&D decisions to be made is the kind of information that gives one firm a competitive advantage over another. Since R&D often is an important instrument of competitive policy, firms are not likely to be cooperative when governmental programs are proposed that might upset the competitive balance. Governmental or other outside interests may conjecture that the risks and limited capturability of certain technological ventures are deterring private investment, but they are likely to have great difficulty in finding out exactly how much private firms are spending on these endeavors. Proposals that companies share their technological knowledge are likely to unify the companies and the antitrust division in resistance. It is hard for public policy to fill in the holes in the portfolio when there is no solid information as to what that portfolio actually is.

Governmental policies not only are limited by information access constraints, but are limited to those actions that industry considers as generally supportive, neutral, and unthreatening to the status quo. Thus, industry has long advocated even-handed tax credits. Support of cooperative research institutions run by industry and guided to keep out of fields of proprietary interest has been employed widely in Europe, less widely in the United States. Not surprisingly, cooperative R&D tends to concentrate on techniques of common interest not likely to give any firm a competitive advantage.

Support of industry-specific basic research and pilot development of certain technologies at universities, nonprofit institutions, and governmental laboratories has been used occasionally by the United States. This seems to be viable politically, so long as governmental funds go into projects far enough away from actual practice so that there are no obvious likely gainers and losers among private companies. Support of atomic energy and civil aircraft technology are good examples. The experience in these fields has been quite mixed. A good part of the difficulty certainly has been that, unless the government completely takes over industry research on the frontiers of technology, the informational and fairness constraints in a sense force the government to explore alternatives that no private firms think are worthwhile funding themselves. In some cases, there may be a real "market failure" problem that governmental funding is resolving. But all too often, what industry was not funding was not worthwhile funding (even by broad social criteria), at least not at that particular time.

The aircraft and atomic energy cases also signal the "bureaucratic politics" problem. While governmental support of R&D activities in these fields initially was justified in terms of the "public knowledge" nature of frontier-probing R&D, over time there developed within government a constituency for particular technological options and R&D projects. As suggested above, this does not seem inevitable regarding governmental R&D programs, but avoidance seems to require building in pluralism either through geographic and political decentralization (agriculture) or the use of outside peer reviews (National Institutes of Health, National Science Foundation). This is difficult to do if the relevant long-run criteria are commercial, if much relevant knowledge is industrial rather than open and scientific, and if the relevant industries are rivalrous.

So, although the "market failure" may be serious if the basis of comparison is R&D allocation under an idealized optimized plan, surely this is the wrong basis for comparison.[7] In economies where the production of goods and services is largely conducted through profit-seeking business firms selling their goods and services on reasonably competitive markets, it is inevitable that these organizations be the locus of the bulk of R&D activity. Certain kinds of R&D can be established in other institutional regimes guided by other informa-

---

7. Again, we return to the proposition espoused by Coase (1960).

tion and incentive systems. Perhaps the regime of academic basic research is the best example. But a good share of industrial R&D must be guided by information available in and criteria relevant to the firms who eventually use the technology. Government is quite limited in the extent to which it can effectively supplant the market. And government-business cooperation is severely constrained by business rivalry.

The point of view on market failure, and limits on government action, in industrial R&D lent by evolutionary theory is not totally divergent from that which would be lent by positive orthodox theory. But the emphasis is different. In the first place, the current state of uncertainty regarding the range of things that can be done, and the consequences of doing various things, is stressed. Second, no attempt is made to define an optimum policy; rather, the style of analysis is to try to identify policies that should be avoided and others that appear more promising, and to focus attention on the latter. In part this represents carrying over to the arena of policy analysis our explicit recognition of bounded rationality. In part it represents a more general acknowledgment that notions like "market failure" cannot carry policy analysis very far, because market failure is ubiquitous. Finally, it involves an explicit recognition that governments are quite limited in the things they can do well, and that therefore policy analysis should be concerned with these constraints as well as with the inefficiencies of private action. Third, flexibility, experimentation, and ability to change direction as a result of what is learned are placed high on the list of desiderata for proposed institutional regimes.

Frankly, we do not know of any "orthodox" economic analysis of the fruitful and unfruitful roles of government in industrial R&D to contrast with our own. This is largely because those economists who are seriously interested in the question, while they often use orthodox language and concepts, tend to adopt a point of view that is implicitly, if not explicitly, evolutionary. See, for example, Marschak, Glennan, and Summers (1967) or Noll (1975). Our point is that analysis of the problem is hindered, not advanced, by the assumption that firms literally maximize profit and industries are in equilibrium, and is advanced when bounded rationality and slow-moving selection are recognized explicitly.

As scholars who have drawn so much from Schumpeter, we find it interesting that our policy perspective on industrial innovation apparently differs significantly from his in at least one important respect. As part of his prognostication of socialism arising out of capitalism, he spoke of the pending routinization of innovation and the decline of the entrepreneur. He seemed to argue that these developments would tame technological advance, or the economic adjustments required by it, but not hobble or badly distort innovation. Our analysis, perhaps influenced by our knowledge of the fate of such efforts to plan and optimize technological advance as the supersonic transport and the breeder reactor, leads us to a different position. The attempt to optimize and accordingly to control technological advance will, according to the evolutionary theory we espouse, lead not to efficiency but to inefficiency.

VII

Conclusion

17

Retrospect and Prospect

THIS VOLUME has been concerned with developing a general
way of theorizing about economic change and with exploring particular models and arguments, consistent with that broad approach, focused on particular features or issues about economic change. Of the
two parts of the endeavor, we view the development of the general
theoretical approach as by far the more important. The particular
models are interesting in their own right, but we regard them primarily as examples of the class of models consistent with our proposed way of theorizing. As believers in the veracity of Polanyi's
point about the limitations of explicit knowledge and exposition, we
took the position that the best way of communicating what we had in
mind generally was to produce a few specific examples.

1. RETROSPECT

We would not have been drawn to try to develop the evolutionary
approach had we not come to believe that the canonical ideas of
orthodox microeconomic theory obscure essential features of the processes of economic change. The insistence on strict "maximization"
in orthodox models makes it awkward to deal with the fact that, in
coping with exogenous change and in trying out new techniques and
policies, firms have but limited bases for judging what will work
best; they may even have difficulty establishing the range of plausible alternatives to be considered. It is an essential feature of such

situations that firms do different things, and some of those things turn out to be more successful than others. Over time the least satisfactory of the responses (from the point of view of the organizations making them) may tend to be eliminated and the better of the responses may tend to be used more widely, but it is another essential feature of such situations that these selection forces take time to work through. Since orthodox microeconomic theory is based on the ideas that firms maximize and that the industry (or, more generally, the system of firms involved) is in equilibrium, we think it inevitable that models built according to the orthodox blueprints miss completely or deal awkwardly with these features of economic change. We do not deny the enormous flexibility of the ideas of maximization and equilibrium, and readily concede and admire the ingenuity that theorists have employed in turning these ideas so that models based on them can cope with aspects of the economic change process. But we contend that the analytic task would be much easier, and the intellectual endeavor would proceed more smoothly and fruitfully, in a different conceptual framework.

We have expounded three basic concepts for an evolutionary theory of economic change. The first is the idea of organizational routine. At any time, organizations have built into them a set of ways of doing things and ways of determining what to do. Our concept of routine cuts across the more orthodox notions of capabilities (the techniques that a firm can use) and of choice (the maximization part of the orthodox theory of the firm) and treats these as similar features of a firm. To view firm behavior as governed by routine is not to say that it is unchanging, or that it is ineffective, or that it is "irrational" in the everyday sense of the term. It is to say, however, that the class of things a firm is actually doing or has recently done deserves a very different conceptual status than a hypothetical set of abstract possibilities that an external observer might conceive to be available to that firm. Most important, it is to recognize that the flexibility of routinized behavior is of limited scope and that a changing environment can force firms to risk their very survival on attempts to modify their routines.

Second, we have used the term "search" to denote all those organizational activities which are associated with the evaluation of current routines and which may lead to their modification, to more drastic change, or to their replacement. We have stressed that these kinds of activities are themselves partly routinized and predictable, but that they also have a stochastic character both from the point of view of the modeler and the point of view of the organization that undertakes them. Routines in general play the role of genes in our evolutionary theory. Search routines stochastically generate mutations.

Third, the "selection environment" of an organization is the ensemble of considerations which affects its well-being and hence the extent to which it expands or contracts. The selection environment is determined partly by conditions outside the firms in the industry or sector being considered—product demand and factor supply conditions, for example—but also by the characteristics and behavior of the other firms in the sector. Differential growth plays much the same role in our theory as in biological theory; in particular, it is important to remember that it is ultimately the fates of populations or genotypes (routines) that are the focus of concern, not the fates of individuals (firms).

These concepts provide the foundations for a variety of models of considerable scope and power. The first set of models we considered were focused on questions of the nature of a competitive industry equilibrium and on the response of firm and industry behavior to changed market conditions. These are the kinds of questions with which orthodox models have coped with considerable success. Even here, on the home grounds of orthodox theory, models based on the ideas of firm routines, search, and selection can perform adequately and interestingly. Evolutionary models are consistent with, and can "predict" the same sorts of characteristics of equilibrium and the same kinds of qualitative responses to changed market conditions, as can models built out of more orthodox components. However, the explanations for these patterns are different, and so are the assumptions that delimit the circumstances under which these patterns might be expected to obtain. Further, the focus of analytic interest should realistically be on the character of the path to a new equilibrium, and evolutionary models provide insight about adjustment mechanisms that orthodox theory's *ad hoc* treatment of disequilibrium adjustment processes does not.

With regard to processes of long-term economic change fueled by industrial innovation, orthodox modeling approaches have had moderate (but not outstanding) success in explaining time paths of aggregate variables. This success, however, has been at the expense of confining the analysis within a framework that is inconsistent with known empirical aspects of the processes of technological advance. Our models, based on the canonical ideas of evolutionary theory, have been shown capable of the same kind of qualitative consistency with the aggregative data as are orthodox models. But ours also are consistent with at least the broad features of the processes of technological advance, and can generate predictions that are qualitatively consistent with such microeconomic phenomena as the size distribution of business firms and the qualitative shape of "diffusion curves"—topics on which orthodox models are mute.

Similarly, it seems clear that orthodox conceptions of maximization and equilibrium must be stretched severely if they are to encompass much of the Schumpeterian formulation of the competitive process. Although some recent orthodox work has responded to this challenge, the models put forward do not contain a serious dynamic disequilibrium analysis. Such an analysis seems essential to a fully Schumpeterian model, especially if one concedes the importance to the story of Phillips' proposal that concentration arises as a consequence of innovation. Our models contain such a dynamic analysis. And they point clearly to some key determinants of industry structure and performance under Schumpeterian competition: ease of imitation, the degree to which large firms restrain investment, the character of the technological change regime.

Finally, our qualitative examination of the problems of normative economic analysis, albeit a preliminary one, makes it clear that an evolutionary perspective can provide insight into what the economic system "ought" to be doing. In our analysis, the concept of a social optimum disappears. Occupying a central place are the notions that society ought to be engaging in experimentation and that the information and feedback from that experimentation are of central concern in guiding the evolution of the economic system. Hidden-hand theorems disappear, or at least recede to their proper status as parables. In their place, however, one can discern the basis for arguments in favor of diversity and pluralism. More important, when one views normative economic questions from an evolutionary perspective one begins to get a better appreciation not only of why our current economic system is so mixed in institutional form, but why it is appropriate that this is so.

Most generally, evolutionary theory identifies a more complex "economic problem" than does orthodox theory, and we think this is an advantage. Evolutionary models tend to be more complicated than orthodox ones, if the examples presented in this volume are indicative. In part this is due to the natural affinity of evolutionary theorizing and simulation techniques that permits models to encompass greater complexity than is acceptable in models constrained to be analytically tractable. But the basic reason is that evolutionary theory is intrinsically dynamic theory, in which the diversity of firms is a key feature.

Of course, willingness to recognize complexity is not an unmitigated virtue. Models in economics must be greatly simplified abstractions of the situation they are intended to illuminate; they must be understandable and the logic must have a certain transparency. Artful simplification is the hallmark of skillful modeling. In spite of their somewhat greater complexity, several of our evolutionary models are significantly more "transparent" than some models we might cite that are of orthodox descent. And the greater flexibility built into evolutionary theory gives model builders more choice regarding where to make their simplifications and where to recognize the complexities.

The advantages show up even when we explore within evolutionary theory the hoary question of the effect of changes in prices on the behavior of key economic actors. Does it not seem correct that the response of firms to the increase in energy prices should involve their trying to do things that they had not thought of seriously before? Is it not highly likely that firms differ in the extent to which they find ways they can cope? The ability to see those features, which is lent by an evolutionary perspective, seems to us to be well worth the increase in the complexity of the analysis. Indeed, it is hard to see how it could be possible to make real contact with the policy issues of energy pricing, and to make responsible recommendations concerning them, without taking these features into account. They are, after all, prominent realities for the actors that policy seeks to influence. As we have noted, economists *do* seem to become a great deal more flexible and openminded about the way things work when they enter the policy arena in a serious way. But orthodox theory provides them with very little support.

To return to the point that launched this discussion of complexity, it seems to us that one of the central present tasks of normative microeconomics is to begin to recognize and try to understand the great institutional complexity of Western market-based economies. For several reasons, evolutionary theory provides an appropriate framework for this undertaking.

First of all, its view of business firms as complex organizations invites extension to other sorts of organizations and subsequent examination of the important distinctions. The notion of an organizational memory embedded in routines is as relevant to organizations with highly ambiguous objectives, such as universities, as it is to organizations with the modestly ambiguous objective of making money. Issues relating to the control and replicability of routines are of at least as much interest in connection with teaching first-graders to read as they are in providing the population with ready access to fast-food hamburger stands.

Second, evolutionary models break out of the trap of regarding prices and markets as the only social mechanisms that actively transmit information—a trap that still restrains virtually all orthodox theorizing, including the most advanced. Our simple models of imitation, and of industrial R&D that seeks to realize a "latent productivity" level determined elsewhere in the system, are only the beginning of a formalized treatment of other mechanisms. But the general framework is readily adaptable to the task, and the task is an important one. If anything is clear about contemporary institutions, it is that they pass a lot of information around.

Third, as we stressed in Chapter 16, the process of institutional development *is* an evolutionary process, both linked and akin to the process of evolution of firms and industries. It is a groping, incremental process, in which the conditions of each day arise from the actual circumstances of the preceding day and in which uncertainty abounds. Thus, at the level of the larger social system it is clear— even clearer than at the level of the firm or industry—that the evolutionary perspective is the appropriate one.[1] In the face of the enormous complexity of that system, our main hope for understanding and predicting it rests on the fact that there is substantial temporal continuity. Accordingly, our task is to understand the structure and sources of that continuity.

Fourth, the evolutionary perspective is fully and necessarily consistent with a view of normative analysis that a number of economists have taken before us: the proper task is the analysis and comparison of existing institutional structures and the design of alternatives that show promise of superior performance in the actual situation as it exists. It is also, we would emphasize, a task best approached in a practical and undogmatic spirit, with considerable wariness regarding the possibility that institutional change will produce important unanticipated effects. Abstract analysis of institutional arrangements that would be "optimal" in idealized situations is at best only one useful heuristic for the main work, and at worst a diversion from it.

Finally, it seems likely that, in comparison to orthodox analysis, normative analysis guided by evolutionary theory would sound more sensible and be more accessible to other participants in the policy discussion. This is really a point of broader significance, for in positive economics, too, the language of contemporary economic theory is a factor that tends to inhibit constructive dialogue and exacerbates other tendencies to intellectual autarky that also derive from the character of orthodox thought.

---

1. On questions of evolution in the larger system, we converge substantially with the older tradition of evolutionary thinking in economics that has had institutional evolution as its principal concern—a tradition maintained today by the Association for Evolutionary Economics and its journal, *The Journal of Economic Issues*. There is similar kinship in this area between our work and that of Edgar Dunn (1971) and Mancur Olson (1976).

2. A Digression on the Intellectual Autarky of Economics

Any sort of technical jargon tends to isolate its users intellectually, but the effect in economics seems exceptionally and unnecessarily severe. Then, too, it is well known that all specialists tend to overestimate the fraction of the proverbial elephant that their own gropings have discerned—but economists seem on the average to be unusually oblivious to the existence of this sort of bias, and they respond rather weakly to the intellectual ideal of "seeing the problem whole." We have no doubt that this defiantly autarkic stance is largely a consequence of the extreme inflexibility of the abstractions employed in orthodox theory, and of undue reliance on the "as if" principle of methodology—reliance that sometimes comes down to saying, "Don't bother me with facts." The discipline seems to have an obsessive affection for its first-approximation answers to a number of questions, and proposals to make room for subsequent approximations are often treated as dire threats to these cherished insights. This attitude certainly keeps many economists from engaging in useful dialogue about what those subsequent approximations should be, even with those who are quite prepared to concede that the first approximations of economic analysis have great explanatory power. In our view, the key problem is that formal orthodoxy's first-approximation commitments to unbounded rationality and optimization are inherently inflexible. Thus, whatever their common sense may lead them to concede in appreciative discussion, most economists simply do not know how to do formal theory in a more flexible style.

One consequence of this linguistic and conceptual isolation is that economics today is quite cut off from its sister social sciences. A number of research findings relevant to economics have accumulated over the years in psychology, sociology, and political science. But most economists do not pay attention, for example, to psychologists' findings that individual choice under uncertainty follows principles quite different from those adduced in Bayes' theorem and the von Neumann-Morgenstern utility axioms.[2] Similarly, they have shown no interest in the findings of students of organizational behavior that have demonstrated that what is done within organizations is only loosely circumscribed by "technology." Nor have they made use of

---

2. We have particularly in mind the work of Tversky and Kahneman (1974, and references cited therein). A few economists have paid attention—for example, Grether and Plott (1979) and Thaler (1980).

the abundant evidence on organizational decision-making processes that conflicts with the notion of maximization.[3]

In analyzing the sources of governmental intervention in the economy, economists tend to wobble back and forth between two models. Sometimes economists try to rationalize governmental programs as compensating for some market failure. At other times they see governmental policy as the outcome of a political game among self-interested players. Both of these perspectives were discussed in Chapter 16 and were found wanting. Given the apparent importance of actual political machinery in determining policy outcomes, it would seem that study of the works of political scientists ought to be a central part of the education or self-education of economists who try to understand governmental action.[4] For their part, scholars in the other social sciences tend to take a relatively hostile view of economic theory because they find it simply an unbelievable characterization of what is going on, inconsistent with what they themselves know. An alternative theory that is *prima facie* more consistent with what has been learned in the other social sciences, and that is plainly more open to elaborations and corrections from them, would greatly expand the range of knowledge that economists could tap. And rendering the substance of economic models more believable would help make the case that social science knowledge in general, not merely knowledge relevant to traditional economic questions, can be enhanced by the building and exploration of formal models.

Although there are important exceptions, dismal intellectual relations are also the general rule along most of the frontiers that separate economics from research and practice in the natural sciences and the professions. Obviously, for example, nothing could more effectively isolate economists from what is going on in the study and practice of management than their conviction that, whatever it is, it is all ("as if") optimizing—and they already know all about optimizing. Equilibrium, similarly, is a concept that leads economists to dismiss the significance of other areas of inquiry. The problems of business policy, for example, hold little interest for investigators who are con-

---

3. Recognition of the loose controls on human action in a firm that are afforded by technology, or by management monitoring for that matter, go back to Roethlisberger and Dickson (1939). Recently Perrow (1979) has surveyed this literature. Winter (1975) addresses the problem of providing an operational version of the claim that the firm decision *process* is one of maximization, and cites illustrative empirical evidence that it is not.

4. Our own education on this topic has been enriched greatly by study of Allison (1971), Wildavsky (1964), Wohlstetter (1962), Pressman and Wildavsky (1973), Dahl (1961), and Mayhew (1974), to name just a few.

vinced from the start that properly calculated profits are always zero. In the directions of engineering and the natural sciences, the disciplinary boundary is well defined by the production set concept: whatever is on the far side of the production set concept belongs to disciplines; everything on the near side belongs to economics. In the absence of that wall, the opportunities for cultural interchange would be obvious. The situation is somewhat less oppressive on the frontier with law. In exchange for some help with the economic analysis of liability rules and other matters, economists have had the opportunity to deal with, for example, the fact that contracts are not always clear, not always costlessly enforced, not always written down. But there are still many areas in which cultural exchange has barely begun—for example, in areas of limited liability, bankruptcy, and corporate taxation.

It is noteworthy that, in every one of these areas, the evolutionary viewpoint supplies an immediate argument as to why the area should be one of concern to economists. A significant advantage of adopting an evolutionary theory, we suggest, is that it would be a step toward freer trade in ideas.

3. Prospect

In this volume we have only begun to explore the range of topics to which an evolutionary theory might be applied. A number of general theoretical problems have been left untouched. Although several empirical issues have received some attention in the course of our theoretical discussion, we have not mapped out a general program of empirical research relevant to the testing and further development of evolutionary theory—let alone begun to carry out such a program. We have argued for but have not illustrated in detail the fruitfulness of the evolutionary perspective when applied to questions of economic policy. Under each heading—theoretical, empirical, and policy—there remains a range of concerns that includes strengthening the foundations of the evolutionary approach, defining its areas of compatibility and conflict with orthodoxy, further exploring the areas of application that we have considered in this volume, and developing entirely new areas of application.

Theoretical Problems

In Chapter 1 we describe a class of Markov models of industry behavior that is vastly larger than the set of particular models explored in this book. More significantly, there are considerations of obvious and general importance that are neglected in the models we have analyzed and that must be incorporated in formal models if evolutionary theory is to address a broad range of phenomena and contend with orthodoxy on a wide front. There is, for example, a need for analytical insight into the conditions for survival in an evolutionary struggle in a changing environment—a struggle in which firms' routines are responsive to environmental variables. Included in this general question are such specific problems as the analysis of evolutionary contests in which firms differ not in production techniques or R&D policies, but, for example, in markup pricing rules or desired debt-equity ratios. Our analysis in Chapter 7 of the effects of input price changes needs to be extended to better illuminate the conditions under which "standard" results will be realized in dynamic systems involving selection and search effects as well as routinized response. Finally, it is noteworthy that none of our formal models recognize any causal role for the firm's balance sheet beyond the simple determination of the scale of the firm by its capital stock. The fact that past events influence a firm's current behavior through its balance sheet, and in more subtle ways than as a simple scale determination, may be a deep and important complication in the basic story of how the market functions as a selection mechanism.[5]

With regard to Schumpeterian competition, our models represent initial steps down a trail that branches in several important directions. They provide the basis for a "life cycle" approach to the structure of industries or of specific product markets—that is, an account of the way in which new industries are born, mature, and ultimately stagnate or decline. To construct a theory of this type, we obviously need to give explicit attention to phenomena such as entry, exit, "learning curves," vintage effects in productive capital, merger, and strategy change. It seems particularly important to develop and explore evolutionary models in which firm strategies include routine responses to the actions of rivals, and are occasionally subject to innovative change on the basis of more comprehensive analysis of rivals' behavior. Product differentiation plays an important role in the histories of many industries; to understand this fully, we need to admit more complexity to the demand side of the markets in which our evolving firms operate. We are persuaded that detailed modeling of many capital and consumer goods industries requires recognition of both strategic interdependence and product differentiation.

---

5. The dissertation of Herbert Schuette (1980) constitutes the first attack on this problem. He examines an evolutionary model in which competing firms with differing cost conditions apply to a simple capital market for funds to finance expansion, and in which the capital market response relies on standard routines of financial analysis.

Although we believe that, in this area as in others, the evolutionary approach surpasses orthodoxy in long-run promise, there is no denying that fruitful modeling of oligopolistic industries remains a challenging task.

Although our discussion of alternative search strategies and of the topography over which search proceeds was quite rich, our treatment of these topics in the formal models was quite simplistic. We discussed technological regimes and natural trajectories, but in the models firms either drew from an exogenously given population or they searched locally. Aside from the cumulative technology models, we did not treat any "natural" evolution of a technology. Aside from our models in which we permitted firms to differ in their emphasis on innovation and imitation, we did not treat alternative search strategies. Future work on Schumpeterian competition should include explicit modeling of technological regimes and firm strategies. More generally, there are important questions to explore involving change in regime—for example, a breakout from an old regime to a new one in which opportunities for innovation are significantly enriched, or perhaps one that requires a significantly different R&D "strategy" for successful exploration.

All of these inquiries would, in addition to being useful in themselves, contribute to the development of an evolutionary view of the "product cycle" phenomenon in international trade in manufactured goods. Verbal accounts of product cycle theory suggest that what is going on is international Schumpeterian competition in which different countries have different factor prices, different capabilities for innovating, and perhaps different circumstances affecting the growth of latent productivity. When technological advance in an industry is rapid, the countries that are more effective in achieving technical advance have a competitive advantage, even though they may have higher factor prices. As the pace of technical advance slows, technological prowess counts for less and high factor costs impose a greater penalty. The parallels between this and the Schumpeterian dynamics we explored in Part V are obvious—but so is the fact that a full evolutionary model of the product cycle would require a great deal more work.

Empirical Issues

An important virtue of orthodox theory is that it offers a relatively definite idea of what it is that firms do: they maximize profits, subject to constraints. In practice, of course, the great diversity of the problems that can be cast into this framework, as well as the conflicting predictions that the resulting models yield about the same observables, largely undercuts any claim that orthodox theory has specific empirical content regarding firm behavior. Nevertheless, orthodox theory does impose a definite discipline on the character of formal models. It may well be impossible for a real firm to behave in ways that cannot be represented by some suitably elaborated orthodox model, but it is certainly possible for a paper submitted to a journal to be judged unsound by orthodox referees because it does not model firm behavior "properly." And this modeling discipline is a valuable one, at least in the sense that it perpetuates the intellectual routines of the orthodox theoretical enterprise.

In evolutionary theory, the ultimate discipline on the representation of firm behavior is considered to be empirical. Notions that firms pursue profits, that they satisfice, that they follow relatively simple rules, that they expand when profitable, and so on are all appropriate grist for the evolutionary theorist's mill, but only because (and to the extent that) they are plausible as empirical generalizations. This viewpoint gives the study of firm behavior *per se* a very different status in evolutionary theory from the one that it has in orthodoxy. The more we can learn about the way in which firms actually behave, the more we will be able to understand the laws of evolutionary development governing larger systems that involve many interacting firms in particular selection environments.

In particular, the routines actually employed by business firms present a broad field of inquiry from which, ideally, evolutionary theorizing would draw the needed empirical discipline. The issues involved are as diverse as our use of the term "routine" is flexible, and the viable approaches to the topic are correspondingly numerous. The markup pricing study of Cyert, March, and Moore (Cyert and March, 1963, Ch. 7) is a classic of one sort of work: the detailed examination and simulation by a computer program of a particular decision rule in a particular firm. Pricing behavior has been examined with a variety of other methodologies; in fact, research on pricing accounts for a major segment of the empirical critique of the orthodox representation of firm behavior.[6] Unfortunately, the absence of an appropriate theoretical structure to guide the research and build upon its results has limited its usefulness. Evolutionary theory provides the needed structure, and the earlier work on pricing deserves reexamination and extension.

One area of firm behavior that plainly is governed by a highly structured set of routines is accounting. Like other routines of real

---

6. The *locus classicus* for that sort of work on pricing is Hall and Hitch (1939). Silberston (1970) provides a survey and discussion of much of the evidence.

organizations, accounting procedures have the important characteristic that they can be applied on the basis of information actually available in real situations. For orthodoxy, accounting procedures (along with all other aspects of actual decision processes) are a veil over the true phenomena of firm decision making, which are always rationally oriented to the data of the unknowable future. Thanks to orthodoxy's almost unqualified disdain for what it views as the epiphenomena of accounting practice, it may well be possible in this area to make great advances in the theoretical representation of firm behavior without any direct empirical research at all—all one needs is an elementary accounting book. There are, however, some very interesting and important empirical questions concerning the extent to which accounting conventions systematically "distort" real decisions, whether by promoting what economists would regard as fundamental misunderstanding of decision problems, or for reasons having to do with cosmetic concerns about measured performance. We expect that such effects will be found to be commonplace and in many cases quite important; this view is a facet of our general belief that there is no unobservable process that somehow overrides the decision mechanisms that appear to be operative in real firms and replaces their results with the conclusions of orthodox theory. Orthodoxy's indifference to accounting presumably is premised on the opposite view of the matter. This is one arena in which the clash between the two theoretical perspectives seems to be quite direct, and in which, therefore, some significant empirical tests might be possible.

The "routine as target" discussion in Chapter 5 constitutes a guide to other areas of empirical research relevant to evolutionary theory. Organizations that operate many very similar establishments—for example, retailing and fast-food chains—provide a natural laboratory for studying the problems of control and replication. There have been a multitude of studies of the diffusion of new technologies and considerable work on the problems of technology transfer. In these areas, as in that of pricing behavior, we believe that the interpretive framework of evolutionary theory would provide useful structure and guidance for future work.

For a final example of a class of empirical issues relevant to the theory, we chose one that is well suited for examination with the sorts of econometric techniques that dominate empirical work in the discipline today. It is remarkable that there is a large empirical literature on investment and a significant empirical literature on firm growth, but that the two literatures are virtually disjoint. One would think that the investment and growth of an individual firm would be intimately related; certainly they are so in our models. But for a variety of reasons having mostly to do with the relations of available data sets to differing foci of theoretical concern, this relationship is not apparent in the econometric literature. In the simplest evolutionary models, profit-seeking firms invest because they can cheaply replicate their distinctive routinized ways of doing things and because the prevailing market signals indicate that it is profitable to do so; investment produces growth in capacity if not in sales revenue, and growth differences among firms are a mechanism of adaptive change in the mix of routines displayed in the industry. Of course, this picture is oversimplified, and conceptual and data availability problems would in any case stand in the way of estimating the relations involved. For example, capacity is not sharply defined in many industries, particularly those in which firms are multiproduct, and there may be complex and variable lags linking profitability to investment decisions to capacity growth. Nevertheless, it seems clear that a concern with the quantitative appraisal of the selection mechanism has not been a major factor in guiding empirical research in this general area in the past, and that there are many feasible and theoretically significant projects waiting to be done.

Policy Questions

What public policy questions might appropriately be explored with the aid of evolutionary theory? The term "policy research" does not identify a category parallel to "theoretical research" and "empirical research"; rather, every policy-oriented study has its theoretical and empirical components. On the other hand, one hopes that all research is ultimately relevant, by whatever roundabout path, to some real question that needs an answer; in the light of that hope, all research can be seen as policy research. The distinction that, in our view, warrants separate consideration of a narrower domain of policy research is one of motive and structure: policy research is undertaken for the purpose of answering policy questions and is visibly structured by that purpose.

In the broadest terms, evolutionary theory is concerned with the fates of "ways of doing things." It views functioning organizations as the repositories of an important part of society's know-how, and also as the creators of new types of know-how. These core concerns suggest the sorts of policy questions to which the theory is most directly applicable and reveal the nature of the perspective it offers. Our studies of Schumpeterian competition in Part V, for example, provide the essential background for a more directly policy-oriented exploration of structure and progressiveness. What is required for such an inquiry is, first of all, an abstract representation of an array of alternative policy regimes that is more realistic than the one offered in our model. We intend in particular to assess the consequences of stylized antitrust policies, such as placing an absolute upper limit on permissible market share. The consequences of this policy will be assessed in terms of its expected implications for the entire course of industry evolution; in effect, the policy is part of the characterization of the selection environment. Only such an assessment fully allows for all the indirect effects of the policy intervention on structure and progressiveness.

Our discussion of government policy toward R&D is similarly a starting point for further inquiry. It reveals some of the subtlety of the problems involved in using policy tools to amplify and modify the private incentives to create new technologies. The importance of the stakes, the diversity of industrial situations, and the complexity of the technical issues all combine to suggest that, in the future as in the past, policy interventions relating to R&D will be numerous, diverse, and situation-specific. As in the past, general principles and propositions about the appropriate roles and relative merits of governmental and private activity will neither describe the experience accurately nor provide much normative guidance. Aside from their inevitable rhetorical uses, such propositions are useful mainly as warnings posted on the various forks of the policy road. Unfortunately, in our imperfect world the warnings voiced in the policy debates seem to have more substance than the promises.

To recommend reasonable policy for a particular case, it is necessary to assess the existing institutional framework in detail, to make tentative judgments about an uncertain future, to draw on the fund of experience with related problems, and—above all—to recognize that new information will be coming in as the future unfolds. In these policy-development activities, expert knowledge of the array of options and speculations that define the technological situation should be teamed with sophisticated economic analysis and institutional understanding. Orthodox theory cannot adequately provide that analysis and understanding because, fundamentally, it is about an ahistorical world in which genuine novelties do not arise. The evolutionary approach, though in need of further elaboration to deal with specific cases, has at least the merit of placing the problems of change at center stage.

Finally, there are areas somewhat remote from the concerns of this book that are of great importance and in which we believe an evolutionary viewpoint would ultimately prove fruitful. The quest for the "microeconomic foundations of macroeconomics" has had limited success because the appropriate microeconomics has not existed. In the areas of pricing, employment and output determination, and investment, economists have displayed great reluctance to make contact with the available evidence on microbehavior, probably because that evidence seems riddled with "arbitrary" features that square imperfectly with maximization-in-equilibrium—and should therefore, according to orthodoxy, be disregarded. It might be useful to take the behavioral data more at face value—to ask whether they are compatible with an approximate evolutionary equilibrium, and, if not, what the pace and direction of evolutionary change would be. Perhaps it would turn out that the orthodox economists' difficulties in understanding the macro economy arise in large part from their insistence on imposing their notions of unbounded rationality on the behavior of the individual actors in their models—whereas real actors behave in highly patterned ways, often skillfully or according to complex routines, but with a rationality that is definitely bounded.[7]

In summary, the analytic vantage point of an evolutionary theory reveals things from a different angle. After one gets used to that viewpoint, it turns out that much of what is seen is familiar. However, previously unnoticed features of the familiar objects become apparent, and some objects once visible from the orthodox angle have mysteriously vanished. Were they real or only an illusion? Things hitherto overlooked come into view—not merely different facets of familiar objects, but also entirely new objects. In all, the view seems clearer, as if the different angle had provided relief from distorting shadows. One hopes that others will come to appreciate the view.

---

7. In his last work, Arthur Okun (1981) gives an extended account of the economic mechanisms that are the source of the poor macroeconomic performance of the past decade. His account reveals both his unparalleled grasp of the institutional realities of the contemporary economy and the seriousness of his quest for sound microeconomic foundations for his macroeconomic analysis. That quest was heavily focused, however, on the recent literature of orthodox microeconomics. In our view, it likely would have been more successful if the bounded rationality that is so plainly involved in the institutions and practices he describes had been allowed a more explicit and central place in his theoretical explanations. A contrasting approach is that of George Akerlof (1979), who is explicit in acknowledging that social custom or "standard business practice" is frequently an effective constraint on individual optimizing behavior. In its emphasis on the importance of giving theoretical attention to the equilibrium or disequilibrium properties of the sets of actions that are actually tried, his work parallels our own.

REFERENCES
INDEX

References

Ackerman, B., and W. Hassler. 1981. *Clean Coal, Dirty Air*. New Haven: Yale University Press.

Akerlof, G. 1979. "The Case against Conservative Macro-Economics: An Inaugural Lecture." *Economica* 46: 219–238.

Alchian, A. A. 1950. "Uncertainty, Evolution and Economic Theory." *Journal of Political Economy* 58: 211–222. Reprinted in *American Economic Association Readings in Industrial Organization and Public Policy*, ed. R. B. Heflebower and G. W. Stocking. Homewood, Ill.: Irwin.

———— and H. Demsetz. 1972. "Production, Information Costs, and Economic Organization." *American Economic Review* 62: 777–795.

Allison, G. 1971. *Essence of Decision: Explaining the Cuban Missile Crisis*. Boston: Little, Brown.

Arrow, K. J. 1951. *Social Choice and Individual Values*. New York: Wiley.

———— 1962a. "The Economic Implications of Learning by Doing." *Review of Economic Studies* 29: 155–173.

———— 1962b. "Economic Welfare and the Allocation of Resources for Invention." In *The Rate and Direction of Inventive Activity*, ed. R. Nelson. Princeton: Princeton University Press.

———— 1974. *The Limits of Organization*. New York: Norton.

————, H. B. Chenery, B. S. Minhas, and R. M. Solow. 1961. "Capital Labor Substitution and Economic Efficiency." *Review of Economics and Statistics* 43: 225–250.

Arrow, K. J., and F. H. Hahn. 1971. *General Competitive Analysis*. San Francisco: Holden-Day.

Art, R. 1968. *The TFX Decision, McNamara and the Military*. Boston: Little, Brown.

Asher, H. 1956. "Cost Quantity Relations in the Airframe Industry." Report no. R-291. Santa Monica: RAND Corporation.

Atkinson, A., and J. Stiglitz. 1969. "A New View of Technical Change." *Economic Journal* 79: 573–578.

Barzel, Y. 1968. "Optimal Timing of Innovation." *Review of Economics and Statistics* 50: 348–355.

Baumol, W. J. 1959. *Business Behavior, Value and Growth*. New York: Macmillan.

——— 1962. "On the Theory of Expansion of the Firm." *American Economic Review* 52: 1078–87.

——— 1967. "The Macro Economics of Unbalanced Growth." *American Economic Review* 57: 415–426.

——— 1968. "Entrepreneurship in Economic Theory." *American Economic Review* 58: 64–71.

——— and R. E. Quandt. 1964. "Rules of Thumb and Optimally Imperfect Decisions." *American Economic Review* 54: 23–46.

Baumol, W. J., and M. Stewart. 1971. "On the Behavioral Theory of the Firm." In *The Corporate Economy: Growth, Competition and Innovation Potential*, ed. R. Marris and A. Wood. Cambridge, Mass.: Harvard University Press.

Becker, G. S. 1962a. "Irrational Behavior and Economic Theory." *Journal of Political Economy* 70: 1–13.

——— 1962b. "Investment in Human Capital: A Theoretical Analysis." *Journal of Political Economy* 70: 9–44.

——— 1976. "Altruism, Egoism and Genetic Fitness." *Journal of Economic Literature* 14: 817–826.

——— 1977. "Reply to Hirshleifer and Tullock." *Journal of Economic Literature* 15: 506–507.

Berle, A. A., Jr., and G. C. Means. 1933. *The Modern Corporation and Private Property*. New York: Macmillan.

Binswanger, H. D., and V. N. Ruttan. 1976. *The Theory of Induced Innovation and Agricultural Development*. Baltimore: Johns Hopkins Press.

Boorman, S., and P. Levitt. 1980. *The Genetics of Altruism*. New York: Academic Press.

Box, G. E. P., and N. R. Draper. 1969. *Evolutionary Operation: A Method for Increasing Industrial Productivity*. New York: Wiley.

Campbell, D. 1969. "Variation and Selective Retention in Socio-Cultural Evolution." *General Systems* 16: 69–85.

Carson, R. 1962. *Silent Spring*. Boston: Houghton Mifflin.

Caves, R. 1980. "Corporate Strategy and Structure." *Journal of Economic Literature* 18: 64–92.

——— and M. E. Porter. 1977. "From Entry Barriers to Mobility Barriers." *Quarterly Journal of Economics* 91: 241–261.

Chandler, A. 1962. *Strategy and Structure*. Cambridge, Mass.: MIT Press.

——— 1977. *The Visible Hand: The Managerial Revolution in American Business*. Cambridge, Mass.: Harvard University Press.

Clark, J. M. 1955. "Competition: Static Models and Dynamic Aspects." *American Economic Review* 45: 450–462.

Coase, R. 1937. "The Nature of the Firm." *Econometrica* 4: 386–405.

——— 1960. "The Problem of Social Cost." *Journal of Law and Economics* 3: 1–44.

Coleman, J., E. Katz, and H. Menzel. 1957. "The Diffusion of an Innovation among Physicians." *Sociometry* 20: 253–270.

Cooter, R., and L. Kornhauser. 1980. "Can Litigation Improve the Law without the Help of Judges?" *Journal of Legal Studies* 9: 139–163.

Crain, R. 1966. "Fluoridation: The Diffusion of an Innovation among American Cities." *Social Forces* 44: 467–484.

———, E. Katz, and D. Rosenthal. 1969. *The Politics of Community Conflict.* New York: Bobbs-Merrill.

Cyert, R. M., and J. G. March. 1963. *A Behavioral Theory of the Firm.* Englewood Cliffs, N.J.: Prentice-Hall.

Cyert, R. M., and C. Hedrick. 1972. "Theory of the Firm: Past, Present, and Future: An Interpretation." *Journal of Economic Literature* 10: 398–412.

Dahl, R. 1961. *Who Governs?* New Haven: Yale University Press.

Dansby, R. E., and R. D. Willig. 1979. "Industry Performance Gradient Indices." *American Economic Review* 69: 249–260.

Dasgupta, P., and J. Stiglitz. 1980a. "Uncertainty: Industrial Structure and the Speed of R&D." *Bell Journal of Economics* 11: 1–28.

——— 1980b. "Industrial Structure and the Nature of Innovative Activity." *Economic Journal* 90: 266–293.

David, P. A. 1974. *Technical Change, Innovation and Economic Growth.* London: Cambridge University Press.

Day, R. H., and T. Groves, eds. 1975. *Adaptive Economic Models.* New York: Academic Press.

Day, R. H., and E. H. Tinney. 1968. "How to Cooperate in Business without Really Trying: A Learning Model of Decentralized Decision Making." *Journal of Political Economy* 76: 583–600.

Day, R. H., S. Morley, and K. R. Smith. 1974. "Myopic Optimizing and Rules of Thumb in a Micro-Model of Industrial Growth." *American Economic Review* 64: 11–23.

Debreu, G. 1959. *Theory of Value.* New York: Wiley.

Doeringer, P., and M. Piore. 1971. *Internal Labor Markets and Manpower Analysis.* Boston: D. C. Heath.

Downs, A. 1957. *An Economic Theory of Democracy.* New York: Harper and Row.

Dunn, E. S. 1971. *Economic and Social Development.* Baltimore: Johns Hopkins Press.

Early, J. S. 1956. "Marginal Policies of 'Excellently Managed' Companies." *American Economic Review* 46: 44–70.

——— 1957. "The Impact of Some New Developments in Economic Theory: Discussion." *American Economic Review* 47: 330–335.

Eliasson, G. 1974. *Corporate Planning—Theory, Practice, Comparison.* Stockholm: Federation of Swedish Industries.

——— 1977. "Competition and Market Processes in a Simulation Model of the Swedish Economy." *American Economic Review* 67: 227–231.

Enos, J. L. 1962. *Petroleum Progress and Profits.* Cambridge, Mass.: MIT Press.

Evenson, R., and Y. Kislev. 1976. "A Stochastic Model of Applied R and D." *Journal of Political Economy* 84: 265–281.

Farrell, M. J. 1970. "Some Elementary Selection Processes in Economics." *Review of Economic Studies* 37: 305–319.

Feller, W. 1957. *An Introduction to Probability Theory and Its Applications*. Vol. 1. New York: Wiley.

Fellner, W. J. 1949. *Competition among the Few*. New York: Knopf.

―――― 1951. "The Influence of Market Structure on Technological Progress." *Quarterly Journal of Economics* 65: 556–577.

Fisher, F. M. "Aggregate Production Functions and the Explanation of Wages: A Simulation Experiment." *Review of Economics and Statistics* 53: 305–325.

―――― and P. Temin. 1973. "What Does the Schumpeterian Hypothesis Imply?" *Journal of Political Economy* 81: 56–70.

Fisher, R. A. 1958. *The Genetical Theory of Natural Selection*. New York: Dover, (originally published 1929).

Flaherty, T. H. 1980. "Industry Structure and Cost Reducing Innovation." *Econometrica* 48: 1187–1210.

Freeman, C. 1974. *The Economics of Industrial Innovation*. Harmondsworth, England: Penguin.

Friedman, L. 1973. "Innovation and Diffusion in Non-Markets: Case Studies in Criminal Justice." Dissertation. New Haven: Yale University.

Friedman, M. 1953. "The Methodology of Positive Economics." In *Essays in Positive Economics*. Chicago: University of Chicago Press.

Futia, C. 1977. "The Complexity of Economic Decision Rules." *Journal of Mathematical Economics* 4: 289–299.

―――― 1980. "Schumpeterian Competition." *Quarterly Journal of Economics* 94: 675–696.

Galbraith, J. K. 1952. *American Capitalism: The Concept of Countervailing Power*. Boston: Houghton Mifflin.

―――― 1967. *The New Industrial State*. New York: New American Library.

Gordon, R. A. 1945. *Business Leadership in the Large Corporation*. Washington, D.C.: Brookings Institution.

Graaf, J. de V. 1957. *Theoretical Welfare Economics*. Cambridge: Cambridge University Press.

Grabowski, H. G., and D. C. Mueller. 1972. "Managerial and Stockholder Welfare Models of Firms' Expenditures." *Review of Economics and Statistics* 54: 9–24.

Grether, D. M. dand C. R. Plott. 1979. "Economic Theory of Choice and the Preference Reversal Phenomenon." *American Economic Review* 69: 623–638.

Griliches, Z. 1957. "Hybrid Corn: An Exploration in the Economics of Technological Change." *Econometrica* 25: 501–522.

―――― 1967. "Distributed Lags: A Survey." *Econometrica* 35: 16–49.

―――― 1973. "Research Expenditures and Growth Accounting." In *Science and Technology in Economic Growth*, ed. B. R. Williams. New York: Wiley.

Grossman, S., and O. Hart. 1980. "Takeover Bids, the Free Rider Problem, and the Theory of the Corporation." *Bell Journal of Economics* 11: 42–64.

Habakkuk, H. J. 1962. *American and British Technology in the Nineteenth Century*. Cambridge: Cambridge University Press.

Hadar, J., and W. R. Russell. 1969. "Rules for Ordering Uncertain Prospects." *American Economic Review* 59: 25–34.

Hahn, F. H. 1949. "Proportionality, Divisibility and Economies of Scale: Comment." *Quarterly Journal of Economics* 63: 131–137.

——— 1970. "Some Adjustment Problems." *Econometrica* 38: 1–17.

Hall, G. R., and R. E. Johnson. 1967. *Aircraft Co-Production and Procurement Strategy*. Santa Monica: RAND Corporation.

Hall, R. L., and C. J. Hitch. 1939. "Price Theory and Business Behavior." *Oxford Economic Papers* 2: 12–45.

Hannan, M. T., and J. Freeman. 1977. "The Population Ecology of Organizations." *American Journal of Sociology* 82: 929–964.

Hart, O. A. 1977. "Take-Over Bids and Stock Market Equilibrium." *Journal of Economic Theory* 16: 53–83.

Hause, J. 1977. "The Measurement of Concentrated Industrial Structure and the Size Distribution of Firms." *Annals of Economic and Social Measurement* 6: 73–108.

Hayami, Y., and V. Ruttan. 1971. *Agricultural Development: An International Perspective*. Baltimore: Johns Hopkins Press.

von Hayek, F. A. 1945. "The Use of Knowledge in Society." *American Economic Review* 35: 519–530.

Heal, G. M., and A. Silberston. 1972. "Alternative Managerial Objectives: An Exploratory Note." *Oxford Economic Papers* 24: 137–150.

Heclo, H. 1974. *Modern Social Politics in Britain and Sweden*. New Haven: Yale University Press.

Henderson, J., and R. Quandt. 1980. *Microeconomic Theory: A Mathematical Approach*. New York: McGraw-Hill.

Hicks, J. R. 1932. *The Theory of Wages*. New York: Macmillan.

Hirsch, W. Z. 1952. "Manufacturing Progress Functions." *Review of Economics and Statistics* 34: 143–155.

Hirshleifer, J. 1977a. "Economics from a Biological Viewpoint." *Journal of Law and Economics* 20: 1–52.

——— 1977b. "Shakespeare vs. Becker on Altruism: The Importance of Having the Last Word." *Journal of Economic Literature* 15: 500–502.

Hitch, C. J. 1955. "An Appreciation of Systems Analysis." *Journal of the Operations Research Society of America* 6: 466–481.

——— and R. McKean. 1960. *The Economics of Defense in the Nuclear Age*. Cambridge, Mass.: Harvard University Press.

Hogan, W. P. 1958. "Technical Progress and Production Functions." *Review of Economics and Statistics* 40: 305–325.

Hollander, S. 1965. *The Sources of Increased Efficiency: A Study of Dupont Rayon Plants*. Cambridge, Mass.: MIT Press.

Horner, S. 1977. "Stochastic Models of Technology Diffusion." Dissertation. Ann Arbor: University of Michigan.

Houthakker, H. S. 1956. "The Pareto Distribution and the Cobb-Douglas Production Function in Activity Analysis." *Review of Economic Studies* 23: 27–31.

Hufbauer, G. C. 1966. *Synthetic Materials and the Theory of International Trade*. London: Duckworth.

Hughes, W. 1971. "Scale Economies and Electric Power." In *Technical Change in Regulated Industries,* ed. W. Capron. Washington, D.C.: Brookings Institution.

Ijiri, Y., and H. A. Simon. 1964. "Business Firm Growth and Size." *American Economic Review* 54: 77–89.

—— 1974. "Interpretations of Departures from the Pareto Curve Firm-Size Distributions." *Journal of Political Economy* 82: 315–331.

Iwai, K. 1981a. "Schumpeterian Dynamics I: An Evolutionary Model of Innovation and Imitation." Mimeo. New Haven: Cowles Foundation.

—— 1981b. "Schumpeterian Dynamics II: An Evolutionary Model of Innovation and Imitation." Mimeo, New Haven: Cowles Foundation.

Jacoby, H., and J. D. Steinbruner. 1973. *Clearing the Air: Federal Policy on Automobile Emission Control.* Cambridge, Mass.: Ballinger.

Jensen, M. C., and W. H. Meckling. 1976. "Theory of the Firm: Managerial Behavior, Agency Costs and Ownership Structure." *Journal of Financial Economics* 3: 305–360.

Jewkes, J., D. Sawers, and R. Stillerman. 1961. *The Sources of Invention.* New York: Norton.

Johansen, L. 1972. *Production Functions.* Amsterdam: North-Holland.

Joskow, P. L. 1973. "Pricing Decisions of Regulated Firms: A Behavioral Approach." *Bell Journal of Economics* 4: 118–140.

Kamien, M. I., and N. L. Schwartz. 1975. "Market Structure and Innovation: A Survey." *Journal of Economic Literature* 13: 1–37.

—— 1981. "Market Structure and Innovation." Cambridge: Cambridge University Press.

Katona, G. 1963. "The Relationship between Psychology and Economics." In *Psychology: A Study of a Science,* vol. 6, ed. S. Koch. New York: McGraw-Hill.

Kaufman, H. 1975. "The Natural History of Human Organizations." *Administration and Society* 7: 131–149.

Kennedy, C. 1964. "Induced Bias in Innovation and the Theory of Distribution." *Economic Journal* 74: 541–547.

—— and A. P. Thirlwall. 1972. "Technical Progress." *Economic Journal* 82: 11–72.

Keynes, J. M. 1936. *The General Theory of Employment, Interest and Money.* New York: Harcourt Brace.

Kirzner, I. M. 1979. *Perception, Opportunity, and Profit.* Chicago: University of Chicago Press.

Klein, B. 1967. "The Decision-Making Problem in Development." In *The Rate and Direction of Inventive Activity,* ed. R. Nelson. Princeton: Princeton University Press.

—— 1977. *Dynamic Economics.* Cambridge, Mass.: Harvard University Press.

Kneese, A., and C. Schultze. 1975. *Pollution, Prices, and Public Policy.* Washington, D.C.: Brookings Institution.

Knight, F. 1921. *Risk, Uncertainty, and Profit.* Boston: Houghton Mifflin.

Kohn, M., and S. Shavell. 1974. "The Theory of Search." *Journal of Economic Theory* 9: 95–123.

Koopmans, T. C. 1957. *Three Essays on the State of Economic Science.* New York: McGraw-Hill.

Kuhn, T. S. 1970. *The Structure of Scientific Revolutions,* 2nd ed. Chicago: University of Chicago Press.

Kunreuther, H., with R. Ginsberg et al. 1978. *Disaster Insurance Protection: Public Policy Lessons.* New York: Wiley-Interscience.

Landes, D. 1970. *The Unbound Prometheus.* London: Cambridge University Press.

Lange, O. 1938. "On the Economic Theory of Socialism." In *On the Economic Theory of Socialism,* ed. O. Lange and F. M. Taylor. Minneapolis: University of Minnesota Press.

Leibenstein, H. 1966. "Allocative Efficiency vs. X-Efficiency." *American Economic Review* 56: 392–415.

——— 1976. *Beyond Economic Man.* Cambridge, Mass.: Harvard University Press.

——— 1979. "A Branch of Economics is Missing: Micro-Micro Theory." *Journal of Economic Literature* 17: 477–502.

Leontief, W. 1971. "Theoretical Assumptions and Nonobserved Facts." *American Economic Review* 61: 1–7.

Levin, R. 1974. "Technical Change, Economies of Scale, and Market Structure." Dissertation. New Haven: Yale University.

Levine, M. 1981. "Revisionism Revised? Airline Deregulation and the Public Interest." *Law and Contemporary Problems* 44: 179–195.

Lindblom, C. E. 1959. "The Science of Muddling Through." *Public Administration Review* 19: 79–88.

——— 1965. *The Intelligence of Democracy.* New York: Macmillan.

——— and D. Cohen. 1979. *Usable Knowledge.* New Haven: Yale University Press.

Lippman, S., and J. McCall. 1976. "The Economics of Job Search: A Survey." *Economic Inquiry* 14: 155–189.

Littlechild, S. C., and G. Owen. 1980. "An Austrian Model of the Entrepreneurial Market Process." *Journal of Economic Theory* 23: 361–379.

Loury, G. C. 1979. "Market Structure and Innovation." *Quarterly Journal of Economics* 93: 395–410.

Lowi, T. 1969. *The End of Liberalism.* New York: Norton.

Lucas, R. E., Jr. 1967a. "Tests of a Capital Theoretic Model of Technological Change." *Review of Economic Studies* 34: 175–189.

——— 1967b. "Adjustment Costs and the Theory of Supply." *Journal of Political Economy* 75: 321–334.

Lurie, R. S. 1981. "The Diversion of Investment Due to Environmental Regulation." Dissertation. New Haven: Yale University.

Machlup, F. 1946. "Marginal Analysis and Empirical Research." *American Economic Review* 36: 519–554.

——— 1967. "Theories of the Firm: Marginalist, Behavioral, Managerial." *American Economic Review* 57: 1–33.

Majone, G., and A. Wildavsky. 1978. "Implementation as Evolution." In *Policy Studies Annual Review,* vol. 2, ed. H. Freeman. Beverly Hills: Sage Publications.

Mansfield, E. 1962. "Entry, Gibrat's Law, Innovation and the Growth of Firms." *American Economic Review* 52: 1023–51.

—— 1968. *Industrial Research and Technological Innovation.* New York: Norton.

—— 1971. *Research and Innovation in the Modern Corporation.* New York: Norton.

—— 1972. "The Contribution of R&D to Economic Growth in the U.S." *Science* 175: 477–486.

—— 1973. "Determinants of the Speed of Application of New Technology." In *Science and Technology in Economic Growth,* ed. B. R. Williams. New York: Wiley.

——, J. Rapoport, A. Romeo, E. Villani, S. Wagner, and F. Husic. 1977. *The Production and Application of New Industrial Technology.* New York: Norton.

March, J. G. 1962. "The Business Firm as a Political Coalition." *Journal of Politics* 24: 662–678.

—— 1978. "Bounded Rationality, Ambiguity and the Engineering of Choice." *Bell Journal of Economics* 9: 587–608.

—— and J. P. Olsen. 1976. *Ambiguity and Choice in Organizations.* Bergen: Universitetsforlaget.

March, J. G., and H. Simon. 1958. *Organizations.* New York: Wiley.

Marris, R. 1964. *The Economic Theory of "Managerial" Capitalism.* New York: Macmillan.

—— and D. Mueller. 1980. "The Corporation, Competition, and the Invisible Hand." *Journal of Economic Literature* 18: 32–63.

Marschak, J. 1953. "Economic Measurements for Policy and Prediction." In *Studies in Econometric Method,* ed. W. C. Hood and T. C. Koopmans. New York: Wiley.

—— and R. Radner. 1972. *Economic Theory of Teams.* New Haven: Yale University Press.

Marschak, T. A., T. K. Glennan, and R. Summers. 1967. *Strategy for R and D.* New York: Springer-Verlag.

Marshall, A. 1948. *Principles of Economics,* 8th ed. New York: Macmillan.

Mayhew, D. 1974. *Congress: The Electoral Connection.* New Haven: Yale University Press.

Maynard-Smith, J. 1976. "Evolution and the Theory of Games." *American Scientist* 64: 41–45.

McFadden, D. 1969. "A Simple Remark on the Second Best Pareto Optimality of Market Equilibria." *Journal of Economic Theory* 1: 26–38.

McNulty, P. J. 1968. "Economic Theory and the Meaning of Competition." *Quarterly Journal of Economics* 82: 639–656.

Meadows, D. H., D. L. Meadows, J. Randers, and W. Behrens. 1972. *The Limits to Growth.* New York: Signet.

Meyer, J. R., and E. Kuh. 1957. *The Investment Decision: An Empirical Study.* Cambridge, Mass.: Harvard University Press.

Meyerson, M., and E. Banfield. 1955. *Politics, Planning, and the Public Interest.* New York: Free Press.

Miller, G. A., E. Galanter, and K. H. Pribam. 1960. *Plans and the Structure of Behavior.* New York: Holt, Rinehart and Winston.

Miller, R. E., and D. Sawers. 1968. *The Technical Development of Modern Aviation.* London: Routledge and Kegan Paul.

von Mises, L. 1951. *Socialism: An Economic and Social Analysis.* New Haven: Yale University Press.

Mishan, E. J. 1971. *Cost Benefit Analysis.* London: Allen and Unwin.

Mohr, L. B. 1969. "The Determinants of Innovation in Organizations." *American Political Science Review* 63: 111–126.

Morgenstern, O. 1972. "Thirteen Critical Points in Contemporary Economic Theory: An Interpretation." *Journal of Economic Literature* 10: 1163–1189.

Mueller, D. C. 1967. "The Firm's Decision Process: An Econometric Investigation." *Quarterly Journal of Economics* 81: 58–87.

Nadiri, M. I. 1970. "Some Approaches to the Theory and Measurement of Total Factor Productivity: A Survey." *Journal of Economic Literature* 8: 1137–77.

——— and S. Rosen. 1973. *A Disequilibrium Model of the Demand for Factors of Production.* New York: Columbia University Press for the National Bureau of Economic Research.

Nasbeth, L., and G. Ray. 1974. *The Diffusion of New Industrial Processes.* Cambridge: Cambridge University Press.

Nelson, P. B. 1981. *Corporations in Crisis: Behavioral Observations for Bankruptcy Policy.* New York: Praeger.

Nelson, R. R. 1961. "Uncertainty, Learning and the Economics of Parallel R and D." *Review of Economics and Statistics* 43: 351–364.

——— 1968. "A 'Diffusion' Model of International Productivity Differences in Manufacturing Industry." *American Economic Review* 58: 1219–48.

——— 1972. "Issues and Suggestions for the Study of Industrial Organization in a Regime of Rapid Technical Change." In *Policy, Issues and Research Opportunities in Industrial Organization,* ed. V. R. Fuchs. New York: National Bureau of Economic Research.

——— 1973. "Recent Exercises in Growth Accounting: New Understanding or Dead End?" *American Economic Review* 63: 462–468.

——— 1977. *The Moon and the Ghetto.* New York: Norton.

——— 1978. "R and D, Knowledge, and Externalities." Mimeo. New Haven: Yale University.

——— 1979. "The Resource Allocation Problem When Innovation Is Possible." Mimeo. New Haven: Yale University.

——— 1980. "Production Sets, Technological Knowledge and R and D: Fragile and Overworked Constructions for Analysis of Productivity Growth?" *American Economic Review* 70: 62–67.

——— 1981. "Balancing Market Failure and Governmental Inadequacy: The Case of Policy Towards Industrial R&D." Mimeo. New Haven: Yale University.

———, M. J. Peck, and E. D. Kalachek. 1967. *Technology, Economic Growth and Public Policy.* Washington, D.C.: Brookings Institution.

Nelson, R. R., and S. G. Winter. 1973. "Toward an Evolutionary Theory of Economic Capabilities." *American Economic Review* 63: 440–449.

——— 1974. "Neoclassical vs. Evolutionary Theories of Economic Growth: Critique and Prospectus." *Economic Journal* 84: 886–905.

────── 1975. "Factor Price Changes and Factor Substitution in an Evolutionary Model." *Bell Journal of Economics* 6: 466–486.

────── 1977a. "Simulation of Schumpeterian Competition." *American Economic Review* 67: 271–276.

────── 1977b. "In Search of Useful Theory of Innovation." *Research Policy* 5: 36–76.

────── 1977c. "Dynamic Competition and Technical Progress." In *Economic Progress, Private Values and Public Policy: Essays in Honor of William Fellner*, ed. B. Balassa and R. Nelson. Amsterdam: North-Holland.

────── 1978. "Forces Generating and Limiting Concentration under Schumpeterian Competition." *Bell Journal of Economics* 9: 524–548.

────── 1980. "Firm and Industry Response to Changed Market Conditions: An Evolutionary Approach." *Economic Inquiry* 18: 179–202.

Nelson, R. R., S. G. Winter, and H. L. Schuette. 1976. "Technical Change in an Evolutionary Model." *Quarterly Journal of Economics* 90: 90–118.

Nerlove, N. 1972. "Lags in Economic Behavior." *Econometrica* 40: 221–251.

Newell, A., and H. A. Simon. 1972. *Human Problem Solving*. Englewood Cliffs, N.J.: Prentice-Hall.

Newell, A., J. C. Shaw, and H. A. Simon. 1962. "The Processes of Creative Thinking." In *Contemporary Approaches to Creative Thinking*, ed. H. E. Gruber, G. Terrell, and M. Wertheimer. New York: Atherton Press.

Niskanen, W. 1971. *Bureaucracy and Representative Government*. Chicago: Aldine Publishing.

Noll, R. 1975. "Government Policy and Technological Innovation: Where Do We Stand and Where Should We Go?" Social Science Working Paper. Pasadena: California Institute of Technology.

Nordhaus, W., and J. Tobin. 1972. "Is Growth Obsolete?" In *Economic Research: Retrospect and Prospect, Economic Growth*, ed. R. A. Gordon. New York: National Bureau of Economic Research.

O'Brien, G. L. 1975. "The Comparison Method for Stochastic Processes." *Annals of Probability* 3: 80–88.

Okun, A. 1981. *Prices and Quantities: A Macro-Economic Approach*. Washington, D.C.: Brookings Institution.

Olson, M. 1976. "The Political Economy of Comparative Growth Rates." In *U.S. Economic Growth from 1976 to 1986*, vol. 2, Joint Economic Committee. Washington, D.C.: U.S. Government Printing Office.

Pavitt, K. 1971. *The Conditions for Success in Technological Innovation*. Paris: Organization for Economic Cooperation and Development.

Peck, M. J. 1962. "Inventions in the Postwar American Aluminum Industry." In *The Rate and Direction of Inventive Activity*. Princeton: Princeton University Press for the National Bureau of Economic Research.

Peltzman, S. 1976. "Towards a More General Theory of Regulation." *Journal of Law and Economics* 19: 211–240.

Penrose, E. T. 1952. "Biological Analogies in the Theory of the Firm." *American Economic Review* 42: 804–819.

────── 1959. *The Theory of the Growth of the Firm*. New York: Wiley.

Perrow, C. 1979. *Complex Organizations: A Critical Essay*. Glenview, Ill.: Scott, Foresman.

Phelps Brown, E. H. 1972. "The Underdevelopment of Economics." *Economic Journal* 82: 1–10.

Phelps, E. S., et al. 1970. *Microeconomic Foundations of Employment and Inflation Theory*. New York: Norton.

Phillips, A. 1971. *Technology and Market Structure: A Study of the Aircraft Industry*. Lexington, Mass.: D. C. Heath.

Pigou, A. C. 1957. *Economics of Welfare*. London: Macmillan.

Piore, M. J. 1968. "The Impact of the Labor Market upon the Design and Selection of Productive Techniques within the Manufacturing Plant." *Quarterly Journal of Economics* 82: 602–620.

Polanyi, M. 1962. *Personal Knowledge: Towards a Post-Critical Philosophy*. New York: Harper Torchbooks.

————— 1967. *The Tacit Dimension*. Garden City, N.Y.: Doubleday Anchor.

————— 1969. "The Republic of Science." *Minerva* 1: 54–73.

Porter, M. E., and A. M. Spence. 1982. The Capacity Expansion Process in a Growing Oligopoly: The Case of Corn Wet Milling." Forthcoming in *The Economics of Information and Uncertainty*. Chicago: University of Chicago Press.

Pressman, J., and A. Wildavsky. 1973. *Implementation*. Berkeley: University of California Press.

Preston, L. 1975. "Corporation and Society: The Search for a Paradigm." *Journal of Economic Literature* 13: 434–453.

Quine, W. V. 1961. "Two Dogmas of Empiricism." In *From a Logical Point of View*, 2nd ed. New York: Harper Torchbooks.

Quirk, J. P., and R. Saposnik. 1962. "Admissibility and Measurability of Utility Functions." Review of Economic Studies 29: 140–146.

Radner, R. 1975a. "A Behavioral Model of Cost Reduction." *Bell Journal of Economics* 8: 196–215.

————— 1975b. "Satisficing." *Journal of Mathematical Economics* 2: 253–262.

————— and M. Rothschild. 1975. "On the Allocation of Effort." *Journal of Economic Theory* 10: 358–376.

Ridker, R. 1967. *Economic Costs of Air Pollution*. New York: Praeger.

Roberts, K., and M. Weitzman. 1981. "Funding Criteria for Research Development and Exploration Projects." *Econometrica* 49: 1261–88.

Roethlisberger, F., and W. Dickson. 1939. *Management and the Worker*. Cambridge, Mass.: Harvard University Press.

Rogers, E., and F. F. Shoemaker. 1971. *Communication of Innovations*. New York: Free Press.

Rosenberg, N. 1969. "The Direction of Technological Change: Inducement Mechanisms and Focusing Devices." *Economic Development and Cultural Change* 18: 1–24.

————— 1972. *Technology and American Economic Growth*. White Plains, N.Y.: Sharpe.

————— 1974. "Science, Invention, and Economic Growth." *Economic Journal* 84: 90–108.

————— 1976. *Perspectives on Technology*. Cambridge: Cambridge University Press.

Ross, S. 1973. "The Economic Theory of Agency: The Principal's Problem." *American Economic Review* 63: 134–139.

Salter, W. E. G. 1966. *Productivity and Technical Change,* 2nd ed. Cambridge: Cambridge University Press.

Samuelson, P. A. 1947. *Foundations of Economic Analysis.* Cambridge, Mass.: Harvard University Press.

―――― 1967. "The Monopolistic Competition Revolution." In *Monopolistic Competition Theory: Studies in Impact. Essays in Honor of Edward H. Chamberlin.* New York: Wiley.

―――― 1972. "Maximum Principles in Analytical Economics." *American Economic Review* 62: 249–262.

Schank, R., and R. Abelson. 1977. *Scripts, Plans, Goals and Understanding.* Hillsdale, N. J.: Lawrence Erlbaum Associates.

Schelling, T. C. "The Ecology of Micromotives." *Public Interest* 24: 61–98.

Scherer, F. M. 1980. *Industrial Market Structure and Economic Performance,* 2nd ed. Chicago: Rand McNally.

Schmookler, J. 1966. *Invention and Economic Growth.* Cambridge, Mass.: Harvard University Press.

Schuette, H. 1980. "The Role of Firm Financial Rules and a Simple Capital Market in an Evolutionary Model." Dissertation. Ann Arbor: University of Michigan.

―――― and S. G. Winter. 1975. "SSIR2: A Computer Simulation Model Based on 'Satisficing, Selection, and the Innovating Remnant.'" Discussion Paper No. 51. Ann Arbor: University of Michigan Institute of Public Policy Studies.

Schultze, C. 1968. *The Politics and Economics of Public Spending.* Washington, D.C.: Brookings Institution.

Schumpeter, J. A. 1934. *The Theory of Economic Development.* Cambridge, Mass.: Harvard University Press.

―――― 1950. *Capitalism, Socialism, and Democracy,* 3rd ed. New York: Harper.

Setzer, F. 1974. "Technical Change over the Life of a Product: Changes in Skilled Inputs and Production Processes." Dissertation. New Haven: Yale University.

Shubik, M. 1970. "A Curmudgeon's Guide to Microeconomics." *Journal of Economic Literature* 8: 405–434.

Silberston, A. 1970. "Surveys in Applied Economics: Price Behaviour of Firms." *Economic Journal* 80: 511–582.

Simon, H. A. 1951. "A Formal Theory of the Employment Relation." *Econometrica* 19: 293–305. Reprinted in *Models of Man.* 1957. New York: Wiley.

―――― 1955a. "A Behavioral Model of Rational Choice." *Quarterly Journal of Economics* 69: 99–118. Reprinted in *Models of Man.* 1957. New York: Wiley.

―――― 1955b. "On a Class of Skew Distribution Functions." *Biometrika* 42: 425–440.

―――― 1959. "Theories of Decision Making in Economics." *American Economic Review* 49: 253–283.

―――― 1965. *Administrative Behavior,* 2nd ed. New York: Free Press.

―――― and C. P. Bonini. 1958. "The Size Distribution of Business Firms." *American Economic Review* 48: 607–617.

Singh, A., and G. Whittington. 1975. "The Size and Growth of Firms." *Review of Economic Studies* 42: 15–26.

Solow, R. M. 1957. "Technical Change and the Aggregate Production Function." *Review of Economics and Statistics* 39: 312–320.

—— 1970. *Growth Theory: An Exposition.* New York: Oxford University Press.

—— 1980. "On Theories of Unemployment." *American Economic Review* 70: 1–12.

——, J. Tobin, C. E. VonWeizacker, and M. E. Yaari. 1966. "Neoclassical Growth with Fixed Factor Proportions." *Review of Economic Studies* 33: 79–116.

Sonda, J. 1977. *Technology Forcing and Auto Emissions Control.* Dissertation. Ann Arbor: University of Michigan.

Spence, A. M. 1979. "Investment Strategy and Growth in a New Market." *Bell Journal of Economics* 10: 1–19.

—— 1981. "The Learning Curve and Competition." *Bell Journal of Economics* 12: 49–70.

Steinbruner, J. D. 1974. *The Cybernetic Theory of Decision.* Princeton: Princeton University Press.

Steindl, J. 1965. *Random Processes and the Growth of Firms.* New York: Hafner.

Steiner, G. 1971. *The State of Welfare.* Washington, D.C.: Brookings Institution.

Stigler, G. J. 1957. "Perfect Competition, Historically Contemplated." *Journal of Political Economy* 65: 1–17.

—— 1971. "The Theory of Economic Regulation." *Bell Journal of Economics and Management Science* 2: 3–21.

Stokey, E., and R. Zeckhauser. 1978. *A Primer for Policy Analysis.* New York: Norton.

Teece, D. J. 1977. "Technology Transfer by Multinational Firms: The Resource Cost of Transferring Technological Know-How." *Economic Journal* 87: 242–261.

—— 1980. "Economies of Scope and the Scope of the Enterprise: The Diversification of Petroleum Companies." *Journal of Economic Behavior and Organization* 1: 223–247.

Thaler, R. 1980. "Toward a Positive Theory of Consumer Choice." *Journal of Economic Behavior and Organization* 1: 39–60.

Tobin, J. 1972. "Inflation and Unemployment " *The American Economic Review* 62: 1–18.

Treadway, A. B. 1970. "Adjustment Costs and Variable Inputs in the Theory of the Competitive Firm." *Journal of Economic Theory* 2: 329–347.

Tullock, G. 1977. "Economics and Sociobiology: A Comment." *Journal of Economic Literature* 15: 502–506.

Tversky, A., and D. Kahneman. 1974. "Judgment under Uncertainty: Heuristics and Biases." *Science* 185: 1124–31.

Vernon, R. 1966. "International Investment and International Trade in the Product Cycle." *Quarterly Journal of Economics* 80: 190–207.

Vining, D. R., Jr. 1976. "Autocorrelated Growth Rates and the Pareto Law: A Further Analysis." *Journal of Political Economy* 84: 369–380.

Walker, J. L. 1969. "The Diffusion of Innovation among American States." *American Political Science Review* 63: 880–899.

Warner, K. E. 1974. "Diffusion of Leukemia Chemotherapy." Dissertation. New Haven: Yale University.

Weitzman, M. 1979. "Optimal Search for a Best Alternative." *Econometrica* 47: 641–654.

White, L. 1982. "Industrial Innovation and Public Policy: The Motor Vehicle Industry." In *Government Policies that Promote Industrial Innovation: The Diverse U.S. Experience*, ed. R. Nelson. Forthcoming.

Whitehead, A. N. 1938. *Science and the Modern World*. Harmondsworth, England: Penguin.

Wildavsky, A. 1964. *The Politics of the Budgetary Process*. Boston: Little, Brown.

—— 1966. "The Political Economy of Efficiency." *Public Administration Review* 26: 298–302.

Williamson, O. E. 1963. "Managerial Discretion and Business Behavior." *American Economic Review* 53: 1032–57.

—— 1964. *The Economics of Discretionary Behavior: Managerial Objectives in a Theory of the Firm*. Englewood Cliffs, N.J.: Prentice-Hall.

—— 1970. *Corporate Control and Business Behavior*. Englewood Cliffs, N.J.: Prentice-Hall.

—— 1972. "Dominant Firms and the Monopoly Problem: Market Failure Considerations." *Harvard Law Review* 85: 1512–31.

—— 1975. *Markets and Hierarchies: Analysis and Antitrust Implications*. New York: Free Press.

—— 1979. "Transaction-Cost Economics: The Governance of Contractual Relations." *Journal of Law and Economics* 22: 233–261.

—— 1982. "The Modern Corporation: Origins, Evolution, Attributes." *Journal of Economic Literature*, forthcoming.

Wilson, E. O. 1975. *Sociobiology: The New Synthesis*. Cambridge, Mass.: Harvard University Press.

—— and W. H. Bossert. 1971. *A Primer of Population Biology*. Stamford, Conn.: Sinauer Associates.

Winter, S. G. 1964. "Economic 'Natural Selection' and the Theory of the Firm." *Yale Economic Essays* 4: 225–272.

—— 1971. "Satisficing, Selection and the Innovating Remnant." *Quarterly Journal of Economics* 85: 237–261.

—— 1975. "Optimization and Evolution in the Theory of the Firm." In *Adaptive Economic Models*, ed. R. H. Day and T. Groves. New York: Academic Press.

—— 1981. "Attention Allocation and Input Proportions." *Journal of Economic Behavior and Organization* 2: 31–46.

Wohlstetter, R. 1962. *Pearl Harbor, Warning and Decision*. Stanford: Stanford University Press.

Worswick, G. D. N. 1972. "Is Progress in Economic Science Possible?" *Economic Journal* 82: 73–86.

Wright, B. 1980. "The Economics of Invention Incentives: Patents, Prizes, and Research Contracts." Mimeo. New Haven: Yale University.

Index